ALL MEN FREE AND BRETHREN

ALL MEN FREE AND BRETHREN

ESSAYS ON THE HISTORY
OF AFRICAN AMERICAN FREEMASONRY

EDITED BY PETER P. HINKS AND
STEPHEN KANTROWITZ

FOREWORD BY LESLIE A. LEWIS,
PAST MOST WORSHIPFUL GRAND MASTER,
PRINCE HALL GRAND LODGE, F. & A.M.,
JURISDICTION OF MASSACHUSETTS

CORNELL UNIVERSITY PRESS
Ithaca and London

First published 2013 by Cornell University Press

Printed in the United States of America

An earlier version of chapter 7 was published as "The Prince Hall Masons and the African American Church: The Labors of Grand Master and Bishop James Walker Hood, 1831–1918," in *Church History* 69, no. 4 (2000): 770–802. Copyright © 2000 The American Society of Church History. Reprinted with the permission of Cambridge University Press.

Library of Congress Cataloging-in-Publication Data

All men free and brethren: essays on the history of African American freemasonry / edited by Peter P. Hinks and Stephen Kantrowitz; foreword by Leslie A. Lewis.
    p. cm.
  Includes bibliographical references and index.
  ISBN 978-0-8014-5030-3 (alk. paper)
  1. African American freemasonry–History. 2. African American freemasons–History. I. Hinks, Peter P. II. Kantrowitz, Stephen David, 1965–
  HS883.A44 2013
  366′.108996073–dc23   2012033412

Cloth printing   10 9 8 7 6 5 4 3 2 1

Contents

FOREWORD

> Live and act as Masons, that you may die as Masons;
> let those despisers see, although many of us cannot
> read, yet by our searches and researches into men and
> things, we have supplied that defect; and if they will
> let us call ourselves a Chartered Lodge of just and
> lawful Masons; be always ready to give an answer to
> those that ask you a question; give the right hand of
> affection and fellowship to those it justly belongs; let
> their colour and complexion be what it will, let their
> Nation be what it may. For they are your Brethren
> and it is your indispensable duty so to do.
>
> —Prince Hall, 1797

On December 7, 1807, a large procession of black Bostonians followed Prince Hall to his grave in their town's Copps Hill Burial Grounds. In his seventies, he concluded his ceaseless labors of the previous thirty years to build a firm foundation for a vital Freemasonry among men of African descent. The long train of grieving African Americans accompanying him honored that labor and dedicated themselves to its continuation. Yet many also feared for the future of that Masonry without Hall at its helm. Could they possibly make this passage without him? While Hall had also extended the hand of fraternal fellowship to his white brethren and several of them joined the procession, his black brethren knew they would have to navigate their Freemasonry separate from white Masons.

Nearly two centuries later, I had a singular opportunity to uphold the dramatic success of that first passage and the many following it over the ensuing generations. On May 3, 2003, along with my fellow Prince Hall Masons, I returned as Senior Grand Warden of the Prince Hall Grand Lodge, Free and Accepted Masons of Massachusetts, to renew our pledge to Hall at the cenotaph memorializing him at Copps Hill. Our Grand Lodge now stood at the center of a vast network of Prince Hall Lodges in every state of the nation and numerous countries beyond it. As we quietly reflected, we acknowledged that our Masonry had more than overcome all the uncertainty and adversity that had so long confronted it. Attesting to the depth of that accomplishment were all the leaders of Massachusetts's white Freemasons who stood alongside us that day as we celebrated this fruit of American Freemasonry in full fraternal fellowship. As I prepared over the subsequent months to assume the seat Hall had first occupied, I could not have been more proud to have supported the universal fellowship that had always guided him as a first principle.

Now, as Past Most Worshipful Grand Master, I am delighted to oversee the publication of this volume, which casts such refreshing light on a history so often obscured and misunderstood. Along with numerous colleagues fraternal and otherwise, we have been working since 2003 to support this detailed chronicle of Prince Hall Freemasonry. At last it is here and I could not applaud its arrival more enthusiastically.

Most Worshipful Leslie A. Lewis
Past Most Worshipful Grand Master
Prince Hall Grand Lodge, F. & A.M.
Jurisdiction of Massachusetts

PREFACE

       The key concern of the editors of this volume is to highlight recent exemplary work that illustrates and explicates the history of African American Freemasonry and its significance. Yet the following chapters actually only inaugurate an inquiry into this history; much about it still remains to be examined, and we are equally concerned to encourage scholars to launch their own investigations into the many rich lacunae in its historiography. One of the key impediments for historians to exploring this history has been gaining access to its documents, which have often been assumed unavailable to those not members of the select fraternity. In fact, an abundance of documentation is available to the public, even for the earliest decades of black Freemasonry. However, awareness of where to locate this material has been very limited, perhaps even obscured. Thus, throughout this volume, the authors have carefully identified the repositories housing their sources. The excellent catalog of relevant Masonic libraries compiled by Mark A. Tabbert in appendix C provides invaluable further information.

    Regarding the earliest history of Prince Hall Freemasonry, the single most important repository is the Samuel Crocker Lawrence Library at the white Grand Lodge of Masons in Boston, Massachusetts. Its unrivaled collection includes microfilm of seminal documents from the earliest years of the first black lodge, African Lodge No. 459, as well as remarkably revealing minutes into the 1830s from the lodge's monthly meetings. Important records from Philadelphia's first black lodge are also contained here. Moreover, well organized in several filing cabinets are an abundance of pamphlets from the nineteenth and twentieth centuries published by black and white Masons about the history of African American Freemasonry and their numerous controversies over its legitimacy and their interracial fellowship. Some of these files also contain correspondence about these matters. The three men most responsible for gathering this extraordinary collection in the mid-twentieth century at the Massachusetts Grand Lodge were Harold Van Buren Voorhis, Henry Wilson Coil, and John MacDuffie Sherman. In 1982, Coil and Sherman published *A Documentary Account of Prince Hall and Other Black Fraternal Orders*. It contains a rich array of documents, along with the authors' interpretation of their significance. This volume, however, must be supplemented by the authors' original transcription in typescript and manuscript of all these documents. This original transcription can be seen only at the Lawrence Library. It is an invaluable resource for understanding the complicated early history of African Lodge No. 459. It includes both important documents and editorial commentary omitted from the published volume.

The editors thank Peter Potter and Donald Yacovone for the important contributions they made to launching this project. They also thank the Masonic brethren, archivists, and historians who gave so much of their time and energy to helping us see the work through. Their passions and labors reflect the best our shared profession—and their fraternal bonds—have to offer. Michael McGandy's editorial acumen shepherded us throughout the project.

A Chronology of Major Events in Prince Hall Freemasonry

This chronology was compiled by Mark A. Tabbert, Director of Collections at the George Washington Masonic National Memorial Association. Principal sources were Alton G. Roundtree's *The National Grand Lodge and Prince Hall Freemasonry: The Untold Truth* (Camp Springs, MD: KLR Publishing, 2010), and Alton Roundtree and Paul M. Bessel's *Out of the Shadows: The Emergence of Prince Hall Freemasonry in America* (Camp Springs, MD: KLR Publishing, 2006). All Masonic bodies mentioned below from 1784 on, except where noted otherwise, were composed exclusively (or nearly so) of men of African descent. Dates for some events that took place in the eighteenth and early nineteenth century are in dispute; in these cases, we provide the most commonly accepted dates.

1717   Creation of the first Grand Lodge of Freemasons in London, later known as the Modern Grand Lodge

1733   First duly constituted lodge in North America, later known as St. John's Lodge, Boston, by the Modern Grand Lodge of England

1735   Birth of Prince Hall, possibly in Barbados

1751   Formation of the Second Grand Lodge of England. Later known as the Ancient Grand Lodge of England

1775   Prince Hall and fourteen other Africans initiated in a British Army regimental lodge stationed in Boston

1784   African Lodge No. 459 chartered by Modern Grand Lodge of England

1791   African Lodge renumbered from 459 to 370 by the Grand Lodge of England

1797   First lodge in Pennsylvania (Philadelphia) chartered through Massachusetts

       First lodge in Rhode Island (Providence) chartered through Massachusetts

1807   Prince Hall dies, buried in Copps Hill Cemetery, Boston

1808   African Grand Lodge of North America constituted in Massachusetts

1812   First lodge in New York chartered through Massachusetts

1815   First Independent African Grand Lodge of Pennsylvania

1820   First Grand Chapter Royal Arch Masons, Philadelphia

1825   First lodge in the District of Columbia, chartered through Pennsylvania

1827   Masonic "Declaration of Independence" printed in Boston

1832   First Masonic Knight Templar Commandery, Philadelphia

1845   Grand Lodge of New York
        Independent Grand Lodge of Maryland
        First lodge in New Jersey (Trenton) chartered through Pennsylvania

1847   First Independent Grand Lodge of Pennsylvania
        Hiram Grand Lodge of Pennsylvania
        Second Grand Lodge of Maryland
        National Grand Lodge (NGL) formed by Massachusetts, New York, Pennsylvania and other grand lodges. State grand lodges assenting to union with the NGL become "Compact Grand Lodges"; others designated "Independent Grand Lodges."

1848   Compact Grand Lodge of the District of Columbia
        Compact Grand Lodge of Maryland
        Compact Grand Lodge of New Jersey
        Independent Grand Lodge of New York
        First lodge in Indiana (Indianapolis) chartered through NGL

1849   Independent Grand Lodge of Delaware
        Compact Grand Lodge of New York
        Independent Grand Lodge of Ohio
        First lodge in Louisiana (New Orleans) chartered through Pennsylvania

1850   Independent Grand Lodge of New Jersey
        Independent Grand Lodge of Ohio joins NGL
        First lodge in Kentucky (Louisville) chartered through Ohio
        Ancient and Accepted Scottish Rite Supreme Council, 33° in New York City

1851   First lodge in Illinois (Chicago) chartered through Ohio

1852   First lodge in Ontario (Hamilton) chartered through New Jersey

1853   First lodge in California (San Francisco) chartered through NGL

1855   Compact Grand Lodge of California
        Compact Grand Lodge of Delaware

1856   Compact Grand Lodge of Indiana
        Compact Grand Lodge of Ontario

1857   First lodge in Connecticut (New Haven) chartered through New York

1858	Compact Grand Lodge of Rhode Island
1863	Independent Grand Lodge of Louisiana
	First lodge in Michigan (Niles) chartered through Indiana
1865	Compact Grand Lodge of Michigan
	Compact Grand Lodge of Missouri
	Compact Grand Lodge of Virginia
	First lodge in Kansas (Lawrence) chartered through Ohio
1866	Independent Grand Lodge of Kentucky
	First lodge in Alabama (Selma) chartered through Missouri
	First lodge in Arkansas (Helena) from Missouri
	First Lodge in Georgia (Savannah) chartered through Massachusetts
	First lodge in North Carolina (New Bern) chartered through New York
1867	Compact Grand Lodge of Illinois
	Compact Grand Lodge of Kansas
	Compact Grand Lodge of Kentucky
	Independent Grand Lodge of Liberia
	Compact Grand Lodge of Louisiana
	Independent Grand Lodge of Virginia
	First lodge in Colorado chartered through Kansas
1868	Grand Lodge of Ohio declares independence from NGL
1869	Compact Grand Lodge of North Carolina
	Compact Grand Lodge of South Carolina
1870	Independent Grand Lodge of Alabama
	Compact Grand Lodge of Florida and Belize
	Compact Grand Lodge of Georgia
	Independent Grand Lodge of Tennessee
1871	Independent Grand Lodge of California
	Grand Lodge of the District of Columbia declares independence from NGL
	Independent Grand Lodge of Michigan
1872	Grand Lodge of Ontario declares independence from NGL
	Grand Lodge of South Carolina
	Compact Grand Lodge of Tennessee
	First lodge in Texas (San Antonio) chartered through Kansas
1873	Independent Grand Lodge of Arkansas
	Grand Lodge of Massachusetts declares independence from NGL
	Independent Grand Lodge of Connecticut
1874	Compact Grand Lodge of Alabama
	Grand Lodge of Arkansas

Merger of Independent and Compact Grand Lodges of California
Independent Grand Lodge of Georgia
Grand Lodge of Indiana declares independence from NGL
United Grand Lodge of Maryland
Grand Lodge of North Carolina declares independence from NGL
Independent Grand Lodge of Rhode Island
First Order of the Eastern Star chapter, Washington, D.C.

1875   Grand Lodge of Kansas
Grand Lodge of Kentucky declares independence from NGL
Compact Grand Lodge of Mississippi
Grand Lodge of Missouri declares independence from NGL
Merger of Independent and Compact Grand Lodges of New Jersey
Independent Grand Lodge of Texas
Merger of Independent and Compact Grand Lodges of Virginia

1876   Independent Grand Lodge of Colorado
Independent Grand Lodge of Kansas
Merger of Independent and Compact Grand Lodges of Maryland
Grand Lodge of Mississippi

1877   Grand Lodge of Florida declares independence from NGL
Merger of Independent and Compact Grand Lodges of New York
First lodge in West Virginia (Charlestown) chartered through Maryland

1878   Merger of Compact and Independent Grand Lodges of Alabama
Compact Grand Lodge of Colorado
Grand Lodge of Illinois declares independence from NGL
Merger of Independent and Compact Grand Lodges of Louisiana
Compact Grand Lodge of Nebraska

1880   First Order of the Eastern Star grand chapter, North Carolina

1881   First Independent Grand Lodge of Iowa
Independent Grand Lodge of West Virginia
Creation of Supreme Council, 33° for the Northern Jurisdiction
and the Supreme Council, 33° for the Southern Jurisdiction
Creation of the United Grand Knights Templar Commandery of
the United States

1882   Grand Lodge of Pennsylvania declares independence from NGL
Compact Grand Lodge of Indian Territory/Oklahoma
First partial merger of Independent and Compact Grand Lodges of
Tennessee
Compact Grand Lodge of Texas

1883	Compact Grand Lodge of Arkansas
	Grand Lodge of Mississippi declares independence from NGL
	Grand Lodge of South Carolina declares independence from NGL
1884	Second Independent Grand Lodge of Iowa
1885	Merger of Compact and Independent Grand Lodges of Alabama
1887	Merger of First and Second Independent Grand Lodges of Iowa
	Merger of Compact and Independent Grand Lodges of Michigan
1888	Merger of Compact and Independent Grand Lodges of Georgia
1890	First lodge in Washington State (Roslyn) chartered through Iowa
1893	Independent Grand Lodge of Oklahoma
	The Ancient Egyptian Arabic Order of the Nobles of the Mystic Shrine (Shriners)
1894	Independent Grand Lodge of Minnesota
	Second partial merger of Independent and Compact Grand Lodges of Tennessee
1903	Independent Grand Lodge of Washington
1910	Imperial Court Daughters of Isis (female auxiliary of the Shrine)
1919	Independent Grand Lodge of Nebraska
1920	Independent Grand Lodge of Arizona
1921	Independent Grand Lodge of New Mexico
1925	Independent Grand Lodge of Wisconsin
1951	Independent Grand Lodge of the Bahamas
1936	First Order of Pythagorans chapter (for young men) organized in Boston
1960	Independent Grand Lodge of Oregon
	Prince Hall Grand Council Order of Knights of Pythagorans
1969	Grand Lodge of Alaska
1980	Grand Lodge of Nevada
1989	Prince Hall Grand Lodge of Connecticut and the Grand Lodge of Connecticut (Mainstream) recognize each other. First grand lodges to do so.
1993	Grand Lodge of the Caribbean (Barbados)
1994	The United Grand Lodge of England and the Prince Hall Grand Lodge of Massachusetts recognize each other. This opens the way for other Mainstream and Prince Hall grand lodges in the United States and around the world to recognize each other.
1997	Grand Lodge of Alberta

ALL MEN FREE AND BRETHREN

Introduction

The Revolution in Freemasonry

PETER P. HINKS AND STEPHEN KANTROWITZ

In March 1775, something special happened in
Boston. Quarantined and punished under the harsh political and commercial
restrictions of the previous year's Coercive Acts, a humiliated and restive Boston had witnessed British troops cascade into its homes and public spaces: by
that spring, more than 3,500 troops occupied a town of 17,000 inhabitants.
Tension and uncertainty simmered everywhere: the man-of-war *Somerset* off
Boston Neck, the domineering General Gage, and constantly parading and
drilling troops arrayed against the vocal orchestrations of the Sons of Liberty
and their vast army of the discontented, many of whom had lost their jobs
when the port closed. Lines were drawn; one had to choose sides. In early
March, fifteen or so of Boston's black men—probably most of them free but
perhaps some enslaved—did just that: they interacted with a small cluster of
these British troops, perhaps because they determined that the British might
serve the enslaved and marginalized free blacks of Boston better than had
the white Bostonians, who, after all, had subjugated them. Indeed, in June
1775, General Gage considered raising a regiment of freed slaves to assist his
troops.[1] If this conjecture informed the black men's actions, then they were
spot on. Over the course of their conversations and minglings, something
extraordinary and unprecedented happened on March 6: John Batts, a soldier in an Irish military regiment and also a member of a mobile military

lodge of Freemasons, initiated all these black men as apprentices or more elevated members into the military lodge, making them likely the first people of African descent formally admitted into Freemasonry in the Atlantic world.[2]

Over the preceding half century, Freemasonry had emerged as an important arena for men of the Anglo-American world to imagine themselves as brothers, citizens, and cosmopolitans. Freemasons were meant to be comrades. The order aspired to be "the Means of conciliating true Friendship among Persons that must else have remain'd at a perpetual Distance," and Masonic intellectuals envisioned the lodge as a place of "innocent mirth" as well as high drama through its scripted rituals and secret signs. But Anglo-American Freemasonry's appeal reached beyond sociability or secrecy. It fused an ecumenical Christianity with values of universalism, brotherhood, and mutual support. It challenged brethren to see themselves as the inheritors of a millennia-old legacy of universal truths that were destined to help perfect the world. Freemasonry declared itself a cosmopolitan project that welcomed men "of all nations, tongues, kindreds, and languages."[3]

We may never know what precipitated the fateful March 1775 meeting. Perhaps it required the uncertainty and tumult of revolutionary times, as well as their novelty and opportunity, to bring together these black and white men. It is possible that the fellowship among the black American and British Freemasons may even have deepened over the following months, with the fifteen continuing to gather with the members of Batts's lodge as lesser Masonic brothers. We can only speculate, as no records or recollections of any further meetings exist. Yet as Concord and Lexington exploded the next month, soon followed by Bunker Hill and a wholesale British evacuation in March 1776, dislocations, dangers, and departure must also have disrupted shared fellowship and eventually ended it. Yet what is clear is that this moment of interracial fellowship and love—at a time when its absence was pervasive—baptized African American Masonry in a commitment to universal brotherhood so vivid and fierce that the order never failed to steer toward it over the ensuing two hundred years of continuing proscription, persecution, and grace.

In the months and years that followed, Prince Hall, a formerly enslaved leatherworker, would emerge as a leader among the fifteen as they worked together, largely disregarded by white American Masons, who by the time of the Revolution had several well-established lodges in Boston. Apparently Hall and a few of the others approached them on a few occasions seeking Masonic fellowship and the further warranting required to admit new members and expand their lodge. Some claim that the martyr of Bunker Hill, Dr. Joseph Warren, endorsed their inclusion. By about 1779, John Rowe, the grand master of St. John's Provincial Grand Lodge, granted a permit to the fifteen to meet and to march on key Masonic dates but not to initiate any new members. He also conferred the title African Lodge No. 1 upon them. But most white Masons rebuffed black Masons' fraternal overtures.

The black Masons of Boston turned again to the British by 1784. Denominating themselves "Poor yet Sincere Bretheren of the Craft," they beseeched the Grand Lodge of England, perhaps the most powerful lodge in the Atlantic world, to grant them a fully empowering charter. Again, the British did not disappoint: by 1787, Prince Hall and his fellow Masons had received a charter, a "Warrant of African Lodge, No. 459." Possessed now of this powerful document, the newly enumerated lodge required no certification from any other lodge in Boston. Yet the African Lodge did seek the official recognition of white Masons in Boston. Unlike its chartering from England, this pursuit would prove much more troubled.

Meanwhile, the black Masons labored among themselves and their broader fledgling community with even greater vigor. Joanna Brooks has argued that Hall and the African Lodge forged a "counterpublic," a space or niche where they could constitute the apparatus of their own self-governance parallel to the much larger civic machinery of Massachusetts and the federal government from which they were largely excluded.[4] The lodge unquestionably fulfilled this constructive enterprise. Yet it was one always oriented toward expanding access to that larger polis. They early set this compass: in January 1777, Prince Hall with at least three fellow Masons submitted a petition to the Massachusetts House of Representatives decrying the "great number of blacks detained in a state of slavery" here who "have in common with all other men a natural and unalienable right to that freedom which the Great Parent of the Universe hath bestowed equally on all mankind." As Chernoh Sesay reveals, Boston's black Masons strove to maintain the selectivity and insular integrity of their lodge while living actively amid a broader community of people of color just emerging into freedom.[5] The travails of that community summoned Hall and his brothers to extend to them as well the charity, benevolence, and fellowship they shared among themselves. Indeed, the black Masons shared intimately in the material privations and insecurities and social marginality and proscriptions common to the community as a whole. The forging of an early class of respectable leaders through the black Masons—especially Hall—enabled them to approach influential whites and state institutions to address the manifold grievances of a stigmatized people just beginning to assume freedom. Establishing schools, protecting the numerous black seamen from kidnapping, opposing the slave trade, indicting white violence against blacks (and especially black women) in the streets and common of the town, even seeking support to assist those who sought to resettle in Africa—Hall and his brothers petitioned and pronounced publicly on all these matters through the 1790s. Through the lodge's intricate intermingling of Masonic universalism, benevolence, and fellowship with revolutionary ideals of equality, fraternity, and expanding freedom, opportunity, and mobility, African Lodge No. 459 became the first institutional rock of Boston's fledgling free black community.

Indeed, the early African lodges attached themselves to the virtues of charity and benevolence with an unusual intensity. While revolutionary ideals helped bolster their Masonic universalism, so also did an unusually intense evangelicalism that they nurtured. Its seed was planted by the Reverend John Marrant. Marrant, like many early black Freemasons, had itinerated widely in the Atlantic world. Born in 1755, he moved in his youth from New York to Georgia and then to South Carolina. During the Revolution, he was impressed onto a British vessel, where he remained for the balance of the war. Evacuated to London at the war's end, Marrant received religious training there from the Huntingdon Connection, a sect of arch-Calvinist evangelicals who dissented from Anglicanism. Inspired earlier by the Reverend George Whitfield, this sect, underwritten and led by Selina, Countess of Huntingdon, particularly intended to train a cadre of black ministers to carry their Calvinist, neo-Edwardsian message throughout the Atlantic world.[6] Upon his ordination in 1785, Marrant sailed to Nova Scotia to minister to the many blacks who had relocated there from America after the war. Yet, desperately short of funds by early 1789, he traveled to Boston, where he soon befriended Prince Hall, who promptly initiated him into the African Lodge and installed him as its chaplain. The most learned of all the lodge's members, Marrant introduced Hall and the members to the theology of Jonathan Edwards and his later adherents, who emphasized the centrality of selfless charity to the true loving of God. In the first formal oration presented before the lodge after its chartering, Marrant summarized how this grace must inform all true Masons:

Let us then beware of such a selfishness as pursues pleasure at the expense of our neighbour's happiness, and renders us indifferent to his peace and welfare; and such a self-love is the parent of disorder and the source of all those evils that divide the world and destroy the peace of mankind, whereas Christian charity—universal love and friendship— benevolent affections and social feelings, unite and knit men together, render them happy in themselves and useful to one another, and rec- ommend them to the esteem of a gracious God, through our Lord Jesus Christ. . . . Every one may see the propriety of a discourse on brotherly love before a society of free Masons.[7]

Hall himself had belonged since 1762 to the Congregational church of the Reverend Andrew Croswell, an early enthusiastic supporter of the Great Awakening's most intense revivalism who shared fellowship with blacks in his church, not only in the pews but in the pulpit as well. Not surpris- ingly, then, Hall would echo Marrant's admonitions in his own addresses—or charges—to the lodge in 1792 and 1797, deeply imprinting benevolence, charity, and Evangelicalism as the virtues and grace that particularly distin- guished black Masons.[8] Marrant deposited manuscripts on Edwards and early church fathers with Hall, which may have sustained the influence of the min- ister's religious instruction even after his departure in late 1789. Furthering their impact, Hall's and Marrant's orations were printed, constituting not only the first publications of any black Masons but among the first of any persons of African descent in the Atlantic world.

Charity, benevolence, and universal love were all graces of particular value to African Americans of the late eighteenth century, a diasporic people struggling for freedom and community. While evidently applicable to build- ing settled lodges and communities, these values also transferred well to a people in motion who were often distant from their homes and lodges. Marrant's itinerancy was not unique among early black Masons; the earliest black lodges in Boston, Philadelphia, and Providence were all rooted in the labors of black seamen on the Atlantic. Chernoh Sesay suggests that some of the original black initiates of 1775 in Boston may have been mariners.[9] Prince Hall initially deputed a seaman from the lodge, William Gregory, to secure the charter in London in 1785, though he failed in his mission. Hall's petition of 1788 eventually won the release of three lodge members who had been kidnapped from the Boston wharves and enslaved in the French West Indies. And black seafarers became Masons abroad before joining American lodges: as Julie Winch illuminates, when black Masons in

Philadelphia approached Hall to charter a lodge there in 1797 after white Masons rejected them, no fewer than eleven potential members had already been initiated into Masonry at Golden Lodge No. 222 in London.[10] The rootedness of the early black Masons in a diasporic communitarianism, a peregrination from bondage into freedom, was vividly encapsulated in the Philadelphia lodge's early name for itself—approved but never adopted—Moses African Lodge of Philadelphia.[11] In 1789 and the early 1790s, Hall discussed the possibility of emigrating to Africa for the purpose of evangelizing it with members of the Free African Union Society in Providence, a number of whom may also have been Masons and would become members of a lodge Hall chartered there later in the decade. After the turn of the century, black seafaring men who had become Masons elsewhere may have been responsible for seeking to establish the first black lodge in New York City.[12] Early African American Freemasonry was inextricably interwoven with Atlantic itinerating. As some shared Masonic fellowship with British soldiers in 1775, the fraternizing would continue in England's towns, wharves, and colonies and even on board ships, cementing hopes for an ever-broadening interracial fraternity of love and charity.

The very inception of black Masonry was grounded in the receptivity of some white Masons to share Masonic fellowship with black men. That awareness should always inform our explorations of the halting communications of black and white Masons in the Northeast in the late eighteenth century and beyond: hopes for interracial Masonic communion lived on as a vital reality for numerous African American Masons into the nineteenth century. A 1787 poem entitled "Masonry" included the following lines:

No more shall COLOURS disagree;
But hearts with hands unite;
For in the wond'rous mystery,
There's neither BLACK nor WHITE.[13]

Despite the evident shortcomings of early interracial interactions of American Masons, the inception in 1775 of what would become African American Freemasonry, renewed and expanded by white English Masons in 1787, probably led the black Masons to understand those shortcomings as merely transient and contingent. Out of a whirlwind of slavery, anticolonial revolution, mercantile imperialism, radical evangelicalism, roving Atlantic mariners, emancipation, and cosmopolitan universalism, black Freemasonry was born and nurtured. Its emergence was in fact a singular illumination, an incandescence that would only grow over the next two hundred years as black Freemasonry and fraternalism illumined, on the one hand, paths for vigorous racial identity and advance while, on the other, continuing to uphold the prospect of greater union with white Masons.

"We Will Not Be Tributary"

By late 1807 and the death of Prince Hall, African Lodge No. 459 was well established—meeting regularly, initiating new members, electing officers, collecting dues, resolving disputes, and chartering a handful of new lodges. Its orientation was largely insular, focused on reinforcing the coherency of the existing lodges, 459's supervision of them, and their settlement in their respective communities. By the early 1820s, perhaps as many as six or seven lodges existed in Boston, Philadelphia, Providence, and New York City, with a second grand lodge chartered in Philadelphia in 1815 by the original one in Boston.

The interest in emigration from America evident among black Masons in the late eighteenth century persisted with some vitality into the 1820s. Though previously focused on Africa, their attention now moved much more specifically to the new black republic of Haiti. Leading Masons through-out the Northeast—the Reverends Thomas Paul, Richard Allen, and Ben-jamin Hughes and influential laymen including John T. Hilton and Prince Saunders—enthusiastically endorsed African American emigration to Haiti by the early 1820s as an antidote to the grim restrictions placed in America upon black economic and political initiative. In Haiti, they proclaimed, black men might finally realize the fullness of their manhood in a young nation black Masons had always upheld as the exemplar of black independence and agency. In a decade when the structures of white supremacy were becoming more systematized and aggressive, such arguments carried weight. By 1826, as many as six thousand emigrants had moved to Haiti. Yet by the end of the same year, most had returned, deeply disappointed and bearing stories of exploitation, disease, penury, and popery.

For African American Masons, however, emigration had yielded a new fraternity with the Freemasonry blossoming among Haitian men, especially in the area around Port-au-Prince. Freemasonry had expanded rapidly in Haiti (or Saint-Domingue, as it was then known) in the latter decades of the eighteenth century when it was a French sugar colony with four hundred thousand slaves. But that Masonry had excluded free people of color almost completely. When the colony broke decisively with France in 1804 after a decade-long revolution and the victorious black general, Jean-Jacques Dessalines, declared the republic of Haiti, a Freemasonry for people of color slowly began to take root in the nation. Dispensing with the colonial allegiance to the Grand Orient in Paris, Haitian Masons turned to the Grand Lodge of England, which afforded some sanction for their Grand Provincial Lodge in the south. King Henri-Christophe, who ruled the north of a divided Haiti in the 1810s, suspected the Masons of conspiracy against him and apparently routed the fraternity from his realm. Yet once Jean-Pierre Boyer reunited the nation in 1820, he renewed the centrality of Freemasonry to Haiti's elite by designating himself the grand master of the Grand Provincial Lodge and eliminating any further ties with the English Grand Lodge. By 1826, Haitian Freemasonry was wholly self-sustaining and independent. Hundreds of returning emigrants carried knowledge of this dramatic development back to the United States.[14]

Although the Haitian reception of the black American emigrants in the 1820s had been troubled, Haiti as exemplar never lost luster for African American Masons. Repeatedly in their celebrations and ceremonies, they lauded the nation's roots in a black insurgency that destroyed the world's most profitable slave colony and transformed it into their own republic premised on emancipation. John Telemachus Hilton, grand master of African Lodge No. 459 and America's foremost black Mason by the late 1820s, could not have helped but have Haiti in mind when, assuming a bold new stridency for black Masons in 1828, he decried that

> there are in this boasted land of liberty, christianity, and civilization, over twenty hundred thousand of our race kept in perpetual slavery, without one ray of hope, of their ever being released from their state of bondage, but by death.... Americans, does not this picture of human depravity...move you so to implore the aid of your God to assist in removing this foul spot from thy fair country's name?[15]

This had not been the rhetorical strategy of Prince Hall or of Philadelphia's first grand master, the Reverend Absalom Jones. The 1820s were not the 1790s. A new generation of black Masonic leaders had arisen to challenge more frankly and publicly the accumulating dross of a vigorously expansive southern slavery, gross civic and economic discrimination against free blacks, and pervasive racial violence and invective. As antislavery societies and black political associations of wide configuration effloresced in the 1830s and beyond, black Masons were at the forefront of all of them. With the ascendance of John Hilton and the coterie of young black activists about him, including David Walker, black Freemasonry came to engage much more immediately with the crisis of being black—free or enslaved—in America. The universal fellowship and love they passionately embraced as Masons and as Christians now necessitated radical action to preserve and extend them.

For the balance of the antebellum era, Hilton and his associates throughout the North harnessed their common struggle to a "triple cord of Masonry, Church fellowship, and Anti-Slavery association."[16]

Their radical new action included reconfiguring their relationship with the wider Masonic world. Likely following the lead of Boyer and the Haitian Masons, Hilton and the African Lodge announced in 1827,

> [W]ith what knowledge we possess of Masonry, and as people of Color by ourselves, we are, and ought by rights, to be free and independent of other Lodges. We do therefore, with this belief, publicly declare ourselves free and independent of any Lodge from this day, and that we will not be tributary, or be governed by any other lodge than that of our own.

With a single bold gesture, Hilton asserted the inherent legitimacy of Masonry as organized under African Americans and disavowed any further understood requirement to certify the regularity of black lodges and Masonry definitively through the imprimatur of the states' white grand lodges. Despite the stirring tone of Hilton's pronouncement, the measure in fact was not a thoroughgoing innovation. Since its chartering in 1787, the members of African Lodge No. 459 had understood the extraordinary endowment with which a charter from the Grand Lodge of England—a "mother lodge"—had invested them: not only had it entitled them to make new Masons, but it had empowered 459 as a grand lodge to make new lodges. It was not now seizing some new power. Rather, after the African Lodge had renewed efforts unsuccessfully in the mid-1820s to unite in deeper fellowship with white Masons in Massachusetts and England, Hilton issued a declaration publicly clarifying what black Masons had always known as fact—that their Masonry was not "tributary," not dependent upon any other Masonry for its legitimacy. This measure was neither isolationist nor hostile. It in no way renounced black Masons' abiding dedication to fellowship with white Masons.

The National Grand Lodge and Late Antebellum Growth of Black Freemasonry

Hilton's declaration did, however, newly assert a more explicit black Masonic independence, one that could be confidently applied over the ensuing years to an unprecedented expansion of African American Freemasonry. Despite the damage done to white Freemasonry by the disappearance of William Morgan in upstate New York in 1826 and the ensuing emergence of the anti-Masonic movement, black Freemasonry suffered little from popular opprobrium and grew dramatically. The results of the invigoration of the movement in the second half of the 1820s soon became apparent. Up to 1825, seven black lodges had existed in the North—one in Massachusetts, four in Pennsylvania, one in Rhode Island, and one in New York, which may not have been duly chartered originally by African Lodge No. 459. By 1847, no fewer than seventeen lodges had been added to a black Masonic movement that now included Maryland, the District of Columbia, New Jersey, and Ohio. With the opening of St. Cyprian in Pittsburgh in 1846 and Corinthian soon after in Cincinnati, African American Freemasonry had passed into the trans-Allegheny West, where its expansion would accelerate in the 1850s into Indiana and Illinois. Indeed, black lodges apparently emerged in Canada at Hamilton and possibly Saint Catharines by the 1850s. By 1847, there were also four grand lodges—one in Massachusetts, one in New York, and two in Pennsylvania. Black Freemasonry had broken from its northeastern enclave to permeate the North; it would soon establish beachheads even in the South, preliminary to its much deeper movement into that region after 1865.

But relatively rapid growth also precipitated internal conflicts over jurisdiction and legitimacy—African American Masonry was outgrowing an organization centered around the indisputable dominance of one grand lodge. But how was the seed of Masonry to be carried into states where no black lodges existed, especially in those states rapidly cohering after the 1820s whose ties with the original black Masonry were thin? How were credible lodges to be organized in them and under whose auspices? How was the regularity of their grand lodges to be verified when it came time for each of these states to form one? While the growth was applauded and encouraged, the fraud and bloody intrastate conflicts that emerged by the forties were not. They threatened the very premises of the Freemasonry Hall and Hilton had labored over the decades to erect: an ever-broadening encompassment of black men united in Masonic regularity, fellowship, and harmony. And as the nation moved deeper into the crises of the 1850s, black Masons did not want their association besmirched as the struggle against slavery and racial injustice intensified.

Once again Hilton offered a solution. He proposed assembling all African grand lodges during the Festival of St. John the Baptist in Boston in late June 1847. The convocation would resolve the various extant jurisdictional disputes and create a new overarching authority—the National Grand Lodge (NGL)—which would immediately move to "heal" any improperly certified lodges or grand lodges and restore Masonic harmony in previously troubled states. This was particularly important for Pennsylvania, where for a number of years two competing grand lodges had chartered rival lodges as well as in other states. More broadly, the NGL would now serve to verify the legitimacy of all grand lodges, to regularize further growth among all affiliated lodges, and to adjudicate any future jurisdictional disputes that might arise among them "so that every colored Mason in the United States could enjoy the same privileges and protection and not be divided." By July 1847, the new national structure had passed the council of grand masters, and Hilton had been appointed as the NGL's first grand master. Acclaim for it was swift and culminated in a grand parade in New York City in late June 1848 in which Masons from throughout the Northeast celebrated the NGL. As Samuel Van Brakle, a key participant in the 1847 meeting, wrote a few years later, "the several Grand Lodges working under the jurisdiction of the National Grand Lodge of Color of these United States . . . will sweep down, and carry into oblivion all spurious and pretended aspirants that infest our country."[17]

Nevertheless, some soon began to complain that the NGL was operating imperiously. In 1849, the New York Grand Lodge bitterly withdrew from the NGL, which responded by heaping opprobrium on it. Many of the newly spawned lodges in Ohio and other western states refused to affiliate with the NGL—often because of fears that the NGL was improperly infringing on the jurisdiction of the state grand lodges. In the 1860s, Lewis Hayden, by then one of the nation's most eminent black Masons, attempted to alleviate their fears by emphasizing that the NGL could not create grand lodges—that only lodges within a state could do so, and that the NGL in no way threatened their authority. As he stated, the NGL did not exist to rule over the grand lodges, but rather just the reverse—it existed to reinforce their legitimate rule. Yet a number of lodges remained outside the web of the NGL. Indeed, some leading African Americans condemned Freemasonry altogether. Frederick Douglass scoffed at it as "swallowing up the best energies of many of our best men, contenting them with the glittering follies of artificial display, and indisposing them to seek for solid and important realities. . . . We desire to see these noble men expending their time, talents and strength for higher and nobler objects."[18]

But, in fact, most black leaders in the antebellum North did not agree with him at all on the character of black Freemasonry. Although they would not have all been of one mind on the NGL, that fact should not obscure what the NGL achieved—an energetic cadre of northern blacks created one of the most extensive wholly black organizations in antebellum America, one that would not only oversee expansion and help to resolve some controversies in the antebellum North but also contribute enormously to black Freemasonry as it rapidly expanded among black men in the postbellum South. In 1853, Martin Delany— a member of Pittsburgh's Cyprian Lodge and an eminent black intellectual and activist of the ante-and postbellum years—designated the creation and work of the NGL "the most important period in the history of colored Masons in the United States." And their ceaseless labors against slavery and racial injustice revealed just how far removed black Masons actually were from "the glittering follies of artificial display."[19]

Black Freemasonry in the Era of Universal Emancipation

Wartime emancipation unshackled the order itself. As thousands of young black men enlisted in the Union army by 1863, Freemasonry accompanied them. While encamped on Morris Island in Charleston Harbor, not far from Fort Wagner, First Sergeant W. H. Gray of the Fifty-Fourth Regiment of the Massachusetts Volunteer Infantry organized a military lodge among some of the troops. Chartered by the African Grand Lodge in Boston, the group continued to meet in the center of Charleston after the regiment's forces had seized the city.[20] When the Twenty-Ninth United States Colored Troops "prayed for a Charter" in early 1864, David Gorden, the grand master of the New York Grand Lodge, chartered them as the Phoenix Lodge No.1, empowering them to meet as a lodge.[21] For some black troops, Freemasonry provided a lifeline of meaning during the war's tribulations.

Throughout the Civil War Freemasons remained a small, select band, despite the growth of lodges. At war's end black Masons numbered no more than seven thousand. But by that time the initiation of men in the slave states of 1861 was already under way, a process that quickly accelerated.[22] The liberation of nearly four million slaves and the emancipation of hundreds of thousands of freeborn black southerners from the strictures of slave-state life opened a vast new field for Freemasonry. Four decades later, the order was vastly larger, at least forty-six thousand men (and perhaps many more), well over half of them residents of Civil War-era slave states.[23]

The liberation of nearly four million southern slaves during and after the Civil War, which left no aspect of national life untouched, dramatically transformed the scale, geography, and impact of the black Masonic world. In the years after the war, the recruitment of freed and freeborn southerners in unprecedented numbers moved black Freemasonry's geographical center of gravity southward. Formerly a small, mainly northern enterprise, Freemasonry rapidly became a much larger and South-leaning body, a transformation leading black Masons found both heady and daunting. Prominent antebellum Masons such as Chicago's John Jones and Boston's Lewis Hayden—leaders in the defense of fugitive slaves and the recruitment of black troops for the Union—understood Freemasonry as a crucial means by which people born in slavery might throw off the mental shackles of slaveholders' white supremacy.

"[S]laveholders and those under the influence of slavery have endeavored and almost succeeded in making us believe that we were born their slaves," Jones explained at war's end, but Masonry could "eras[e] this idea from the mind of the colored man, and teach him that he was born as free as the other types of the human family."[24] Hayden similarly told his Boston brethren that Masonry was essential to the emergence of former slaves from the "state of oppression." Taking up its "sacred" obligations, men would find that "confidence is restored, and each can trust the other with safety."[25]

Antebellum principals clearly imagined that black Freemasonry would serve the liberated states as a school for leadership and a network linking the antebellum black political world of the North with newly emerging communities in the South. Lewis Hayden emphasized just how deeply the Freemasonry of African Americans steered the moral compass of America:

> Who among us are ready to say that God had not a great purpose in the organization of the National Grand Lodge? This question is answered in the affirmative to all reflecting minds who have studied our condition as a people in the light of Masonic history.... [I]n accordance with the fixed laws of that Supreme Intelligence, slavery is no more; and in its abolition new elements are developed, and they impose new duties.... [We must] be now in readiness for the mission assigned to us as a Masonic body, to labor in these United States.[26]

Hayden was not the only one to assert that black Freemasonry, newly national, would play a critical—even providential—role in the battles to come.

Making good on the promise of the brotherhood's antebellum training ground, Masons played crucial roles in the politics of Reconstruction. Black Freemasonry seemed poised to play a shaping role in the emancipated nation. But Jones's and Hayden's words reveal anxieties as well as hopes—concern that the freed people might need a great deal of help becoming the self-confident and open-hearted men Masonry idealized. Lewis Hayden envisioned Freemasonry's march southward as a careful mobilization of those already capable of "united and harmonious" action, and he offered some unflinchingly negative assessments of the character of the men that the order had recruited in the South during the Civil War. As David Hackett's discussion in chapter 7 shows, the Masonic and AME Zion organizer Bishop James W. Hood similarly recognized the need for some exclusivity: it was understandable that new southern Masons might lack "polish," but they nevertheless must be "men of active minds" and good repute.[27]

Black Freemasons and Freemasonry played central roles in the political development of the postwar South. A host of the leading black elected officials and political organizers in the region, from 1867 to the end of the century, were deeply involved in Freemasonry. These included such key figures as Hiram Revels (U.S. senator from Mississippi and the first African American member of Congress), Richard Howell Gleaves (lieutenant governor of South Carolina), and John Mercer Langston (congressman from Virginia). Notably, all these men had deep roots in the antebellum North, where they had been born or educated, and they carried the values and perspectives of pre–Civil War black Freemasonry with them to the postemancipation South. The correlation between Masonic membership and political prominence, in the North and West as well as in the South, is unmistakable.[28]

Yet the sheer number of southern freed people, a population vastly larger than the antebellum free black population, presented serious challenges to the model of Masonic recruitment and activity these men brought with them from their northern lodges of origin. Black southerners did not wait to be organized: as soon as emancipation permitted, they established mutual benefit and secret ritual associations that formed an important part of freed people's reconstitution of their lives and communities.[29] At the same time, the politics of Reconstruction reshaped the meaning of Freemasonry's "school for leadership," encouraging closer connections between Masonry and electoral politics than the order had previously imagined possible. Freedom unleashed the aspirations for private fellowship and public power that slavery had so long denied, and Freemasonry became an important conduit for both desires.

How many men should become Masons, and how quickly, soon divided the fraternity, particularly as these questions converged with the ongoing struggle over the National Grand Lodge. The NGL's postbellum national grand master, Richard Howell Gleaves, vowed "to cement the craft in every State of the Union…into one common band of Masonic workmen."[30] As Stephen Kantrowitz shows in chapter 5, his methods quickly drew sharp criticism. The speed both of Gleaves's Masonic recruitment and of his forging of new lodges into grand lodges loyal to the NGL struck many antebellum Masons as ill conceived at best. Soon, as the NGL's grand lodges absorbed lodges established by non-NGL grand lodges, supporters and foes of the NGL traded charges of bad faith and malfeasance. Lewis Hayden, once a leading figure in the NGL, denounced Gleaves and his followers as "these new despoilers who are of our own race and people…fraudulently obtaining the fruits of our toil by taking fees and receiving dues under the pretence" that they were practicing actual Masonry.[31] National Grand Lodge officials fired back, claiming that Hayden's home lodge seemed "to have regarded the *pecuniary interest,* much more than the harmony, prosperity, general interest, and welfare of the lodges which it had erected."[32] Much remains to be learned about the struggle over the NGL and about Gleaves, its longtime champion.[33]

The question of women's place in the order—a question emerging from at least the 1850s but apparently tabled during the war—also resurfaced in the postwar era.[34] From the 1870s on, the Order of the Eastern Star (OES) became the primary gender-integrated auxiliary of black Freemasonry. But it was far from the only place where women continued to take part in Masonry and other black "fraternal" groups. Earlier gender-integrated orders such as the Brothers and Sisters of Love and Charity persisted in some areas, and new ones emerged in the organizational boom years of the early twentieth century.[35] Nor was the OES the only form of female Masonic belonging: an earlier form, the Heroines of Jericho, continued to form its courts well into the twentieth century.[36] But what did it mean to be an "auxiliary"? Brittney C. Cooper's pioneering discussion in chapter 6 explores early twentieth-century struggles over women's leadership in the larger black Masonic world. As with the case of the NGL, struggles emerging from the "ambiguous position of women within the Masonic universe" led to charges and countercharges.[37] OES leaders such as Mrs. S. Joe Brown rejected Masonic men's assertions of authority; the male leadership role within the OES, such women argued, was not one of "superior dictator."[38] But when the OES leadership moved to bar those holding leadership positions in other bodies from serving in it—a provision that would have effectively prevented Masonry's male leaders from exercising oversight over Eastern Star—leading Masons denounced this as "flagrant effrontery."[39] In the era of women's political enfranchisement, the question of women's role—or women's subordination—within the larger world of Freemasonry remained a potent source of conflict and debate.

Black Freemasonry also of course envisioned itself as a force for unity and even universalism, and members cherished its secret rituals. These "secret and inviolable signs, carefully preserved among the fraternity throughout the world," constituted "a universal language" that served to "unite men of the most opposite tenets, of the most distant countries, of the most contradictory opinions, in one indissoluble bond of affection."[40] Yet beyond such expression it is not easy to plumb the meanings Freemasons attached to their ritual lives.[41] Leading Masons often spoke of Masonry's "mysteries" as the essence of the craft, and some historians have argued that ritual was the very center of fraternal life, to the exclusion of almost all else; others have suggested that the fraternal orders' provision of social welfare services was far more important to their popularity than any cultural forces (although such an argument has less bearing on Freemasonry, which was rarely configured primarily as a mutual benefit association).[42] Brittney C. Cooper shows in chapter 6 how biblical stories allowed women as well as men to claim ancient heritages, and the work of other scholars shows Masonic and religious bodies continuing to twine around one another in the decades after Reconstruction.[43] In each case, Masonry claimed to embody timeless wisdom and ethical teachings, mirroring those expressed in the Gospels but explicitly not limited to Christianity. As Richard Greener told the brethren of Savannah, Georgia, in 1876, "In that state where true Masonic light is shed there will be no longer, 'Barbarian, Scythian, bond nor free,' but Israelite and Gentile, black and white, Turk and Christian, king and peasant, shall sit as equals and brothers."[44]

In keeping with this universalist vision, postbellum black Masons continued and even intensified their campaign for recognition by white Freemasons in the United States. and overseas. As Stephen Kantrowitz details in chapter 5, these efforts sometimes seemed on the verge of success, as in Massachusetts in the late 1860s and Ohio in the mid-1870s. The form recognition would take always mattered to black Masons, and they do not seem to have sought absorption within white Freemasonry so much as white Masons' acknowledgment of their legitimacy and right of visitation; some form of institutional integration appears to have been discussed.[45] But these efforts in northern states came to naught, blocked by white northerners, with the loud encouragement of their southern brethren. The last of these efforts came in Washington State at the turn of the century. Meanwhile, black Masonic bodies across the nation continued a century-old tradition of seeking recognition from the United Grand Lodge of England. In 1869, the Massachusetts Masonic official A. W. A. DeLeon wrote to the English mother lodge of his eagerness for "the auspicious era when the genius of universal Masonry shall trample in the dust the foul incubus of caste" and replace it with the "indissoluble ties of common interest and common brotherhood."[46]

Even as they reached out to white Freemasons, black Freemasons cultivated ties with black brethren around the world. The antebellum importance of Haiti in black Masonic lives and imaginations was the beginning, not the end, of black American Masonry's connections to other parts of the African diaspora and to Africa itself. Some ties were figurative: John Jones claimed that Pythagoras became a Mason in Africa; Martin Delany argued that it was "[i]n the earliest period of the Egyptian and Ethiopian dynasties [that] the institution of Masonry was first established."[47] But men as well as ideas continued to circumnavigate the globe. By the late nineteenth century, African American Masons had personal or institutional ties to brethren in Liberia, South Africa, and the Gold Coast, as well as Jamaica, Barbados, the Bahamas, and other parts of the Caribbean.[48] These linkages might have been primarily symbolic, or they might have been unambiguously human and real. Reflecting on the significant fraction of Brooklyn Masons who were of Caribbean or other non–United States birth, Martin Summers astutely conjectures that such a Mason might think of himself as "joining an institution that had a history and a presence throughout the diaspora rather than as an African Caribbean who was joining an African American institution."[49]

Prince Hall in the Era of Jim Crow

The order's growth during the early twentieth century dwarfed even the post–Civil War boom. The number of black Freemasons—about fifty thousand at the turn of the century—grew dramatically through the late 1920s, dipped slightly during the Great Depression, and by 1955 was over three hundred thousand.[50] Despite considerable anecdotal and local evidence, the social composition of the order is not fully understood. Some scholars assert that black Freemasons constituted an elite "only in terms of the black community," remaining by overall national standards mostly "either poor or at least lower income."[51] Yet the Prince Hall leadership included many of the wealthiest and most influential African Americans of the Jim Crow era, from Booker T. Washington to Arthur Schomburg to Thurgood Marshall. There is no question as to Masons' continuing collective sense of themselves as a special class of men. Most black Masons did not regard the order as a missionizing body: it should seek out worthy men but not try to create them. In 1893, the grand master of Alabama told an audience of leading Masons from around the country that "Masonry is not a reformatory society" and ought not to accept men until they were ready for it. John T. Hilton had said much the same thing sixty-five years before.[52] Yet more than any particular degree of wealth or attainment, the values and expressions of middle-class identity defined eligibility for the brotherhood.

Prince Hall Freemasonry remained as it had been: a place where men simultaneously declared their commitments to dignified, bourgeois respectability and to a militant tradition of protest and resistance. But to say that black Freemasons aspired to lives of comfort and security is not to say that the order was conservative rather than insurgent; the early twentieth century made such a stance unthinkable for many African Americans. Black Freemasonry remained a school for leadership and a vehicle for collective expression outside the channels of formal politics.

Particularly in the early twentieth-century North, some African American Freemasons gave voice to the enduring argument that blacks would bring prejudice to an end by setting a good example. Proving by their conduct that the libels against them were untrue, they would "force" whites to acknowledge their claims to equal rights as men and Masons. This century-old vision of racial progress had in the past provided little protection against storms of racial antipathy. Yet it retained sufficient force that the grand master of

New York could tell a Brooklyn lodge in 1926 that building a grand temple for the order would "contradict the white man's saying that Masonry is too big for the colored man."[53]

Such expressions notwithstanding, white supremacy's nationwide reach in the era of Jim Crow presented stark challenges to black Americans who sought to live and work with dignity. In the bleak years just after World War I, when white mobs rampaged against blacks from the Arkansas Delta to Tulsa to Chicago, the grand master of Texas's Prince Hall Masons offered a quite different vision from that of his New York compatriot of how "respectability" would be achieved: the "proud, arrogant, intolerant white race," he explained, would "see and acknowledge the Brotherhood of Man" only when the "darker races of the world" united to stop their depredations.[54] Some went further than this, abandoning anything that might conceivably be called conservative in favor of "radical social change." The grand master of Georgia in these years foresaw a coming class war, and he understood his people to stand clearly on one side of it—among the "toilers," not the rich.[55]

Black southern activists in this era had to rely on one another for self-defense, and here Masons and other ritual associations played important roles. In a study of black organization in early twentieth-century Florida, Paul Ortiz argues that the struggle survived amid conditions of great hardship and violence because "African Americans drew upon the secular and sacred ties they had forged with one another in their organizations and used these ties as a starting point for creating new political insurgencies."[56] Lodges were prized for their secrecy and solidarity—pearls beyond price in the vicious labor market of the Jim Crow South—as well as for their capacity to mobilize people and resources to defend victims of white supremacy, advocate for education, and engage in a host of other activities.[57] No wonder the Masons and other orders grew so rapidly in the early twentieth century during the period that historian Rayford Logan dubbed the "nadir" of American race relations.

No wonder either that white fraternal organizations across the South sought to shut down black associations. State legislation aimed squarely at the black fraternals enabled white groups to sue, claiming that the existence of black orders bearing the same name violated their copyrights or trademarks. Prince Hall Masons' origins under English authority spared them the heated challenges that faced organizations such as the Elks and the Knights of Pythias, but the Shriners—a Masonic order of U.S. origin—took part in the wave of litigation during the first three decades of the twentieth century in which black fraternals sought to move these claims from state to federal court, where they hoped for better results.[58]

Despite differences of experience and perspective, interregional ties and common struggles brought black northern and southern Masons together. Arthur Schomburg, a leading New York Mason, protested to the Justice Department about the assaults on southern Masons.[59] Even the most "bourgeois" of black Freemasons could discover the white supremacist wolf at their door, as when in the 1920s New York's grand lodge received a plea for financial aid from a brother in neighboring Staten Island, where the Ku Klux Klan sought to run him out.[60] And as the Great Migration brought black southerners north in increasing numbers from the 1910s onward, they even reversed the direction of Prince Hall's nineteenth-century growth, establishing lodges among themselves in their new northern homes—including the northeastern cities that had nurtured the order in its earliest days.[61]

Prince Hall in the Second Reconstruction

African American Masonic orders played important roles in the twentieth-century movements for educational, political, and civil rights. At the state level, grand lodges organized to demand better educational opportunities and worked together with other orders to demand access to the ballot in southern states.[62] From the 1920s on, leading Masons publicly demanded federal antilynching legislation.[63] Despite the strictures against party politics within the lodge, Masons sometimes even ventured directly into those waters, as in Illinois in the 1920s. Given the tight connections between Freemasonry and politics going back to Reconstruction, it is not surprising that the first African American congressman from the north—Oscar De Priest, elected in 1928—was an Illinois Mason.[64]

The nature and extent of the fraternity made it a powerful vehicle for the post–World War II freedom movement. As Theda Skocpol and her collaborators conclude, "Because black fraternal groups included members across class and occupational lines, and because they operated on local, state, and national levels, they were important operators and allies in the modern Civil Rights movement...bringing together people and resources from various realms of black business, religious, and associational life."[65] This was nowhere more evident than in black Masons' 1951 endowment of the Prince Hall Masons Legal Research Fund, overseen by the NAACP, to which Masonic bodies continued to contribute large sums.[66] Thurgood Marshall himself declared this aid essential to the NAACP's legal victories: "Whenever and wherever I needed money and did not know of any other place to get it," he said in 1958, "Prince Hall Masons never let me down."[67] Just as tellingly, the Southern Christian Leadership Conference established its headquarters in the offices of the Prince Hall Grand Lodge of Georgia.[68] Despite the pioneering work of Alferdteen Harrison on Mississippi's Stringer Grand Lodge, the study of black Freemasonry's organic connection to the postwar freedom movement remains in its infancy.[69]

By the late twentieth century, the civil rights campaigns black Freemasonry had ardently supported bore long-sought fruit: mutual recognition with many state-level white Masonic bodies. By 2010, in most states (including several in the former Confederacy), white and black Masonic bodies had recognized one another. Some of the ceremonies marking these occasions recalled the order's long history of racial division as a way of beginning to heal those ruptures. On the morning of May 10, 2003, officers of the (white) Grand Lodge of Massachusetts assembled with the state's Prince Hall Grand Lodge, marking their formal reconciliation with a pair of shared graveside observances—first at the tomb of the eighteenth-century Mason Paul Revere in the Old Granary Burial Ground just off the Boston Common and immediately afterward at the Copp's Hill monument to Prince Hall himself. During the morning's events the black and white brethren initially stood in segregated groups, but soon they began to mingle with one another. After the last ceremony was completed, at the graveside of Prince Hall, they enthusiastically exchanged ritual handshakes across the color line that had so often set them at odds.[70]

CHAPTER 1

Emancipation and the Social Origins of Black Freemasonry, 1775–1800

CHERNOH M. SESAY JR.

On August 19, 1786, the *Massachusetts Centinel* described the August 14 funeral of the late African American Freemason Luke Belcher. The ceremony for Belcher, "aged 42, by birth an African," and "formerly of the family of his late Excellency Governour Belcher," attracted "a lengthy procession of friends and respectable characters, preceded by a band of brothers, in union, denominated the African Lodge of Free and Accepted Masons, in the garb and ornaments of the craft, led by the Tyler and Stewards of the order, bearing the insignias of their respective offices, preserving that due decorum and becoming respect requisite on so serious an occasion, and characteristick of the honourable fraternity."[1] Eulogizing Belcher, the notice explained that "[t]hough our departed friend could not boast of any very elevated distinctions in life, he has left behind the 'pearl of great price'—a character many of his apparent superiors need not be ashamed to imitate, but without which even the sons of affluence are poor indeed."[2] This Masonic funeral constituted an event around which blacks—Freemason or not, with property or without, resident or itinerant—could coalesce in celebration not only of Luke Belcher but of the values and coherence of their community.[3]

A later obituary also emphasized Belcher's status in a slightly different way, one that reveals an important transformation in eighteenth-century free black life. The entire notice read, "Died, his excellency Luke Belcher, late governour of the Africans in this town. He was universally respected by every rank of citizens."[4] That Belcher was native to Africa and an African governor during Election Days, suggests continuity and change. The public funeral for Belcher signified the gradual disappearance of the eighteenth-century slave holiday celebrations known as Negro Election Day in Connecticut, Rhode Island, and Massachusetts; Pinkster in New York and New Jersey; and General Training, or Training Day, in various other northern locales.[5] These uniquely African American festivals symbolized public realms wherein slaves worked out complex figurations of identity and community. Belcher's changing status and leadership, from African governor to Freemason, reflected the transition from slavery to freedom and marked an important evolution in the practice of African American leadership. Furthermore, Belcher's dual roles reveal the significance of black Freemasonry as a pivot on which turned a changing black politics of public presentation and abolition.

While scholars have examined in detail the writings of Prince Hall, the leading black Mason of the late eighteenth century, they have not fully reckoned with the significance of Luke Belcher and the other initiates of the first black Masonic lodge. Hall was a founder of northern free black institutions and political initiatives.[6] A former slave, literate and property-owning, Hall launched African Lodge No. 1 in 1775, setting black Freemasonry's history in motion.[7] Scholars recognize the importance of black Freemasonry insofar as they agree on the importance of Hall's leadership; however, interpretations of black Freemasonry as both institution and ideology reveal interpretive controversy. Recent work describes black Freemasonry as either exclusionary and elitist or representative and activist.[8] Scholars have largely depicted the black lodge as either a manifestation of class difference within the community or as a pillar of that community's infrastructure. The elitist interpretation has discussed black Masons as a new and distinct social group who stood distant from a broader black populace grounded in folk traditions that paid little attention to the ideals and learning of the eighteenth-century Enlightenment. The pillar thesis has described African American Freemasons as part of the urban lower orders because of racial caste.[9] The surviving record of Luke Belcher's life suggests that these interpretations of black Freemasonry may be more complementary than contradictory: the order's social roots were planted firmly in inclusive communal traditions that also established social distinction through popular slave festivals. The origins of the African Lodge itself, the demography of the earliest membership, and the leadership of Hall relative to both were always complex matters and cannot be reduced to straightforward elite versus nonelite interpretations.

Black Freemasonry is described in such divergent ways because it emerged at a peculiar moment in American history—the era of the steady expansion of northern abolition.[10] Massachusetts ended slavery with relative ease and speed; however, it failed to acknowledge African Americans as fully capable political and social actors. With freedom suddenly gained, blacks in Massachusetts were granted the unprecedented opportunity to make claims, as a group and not just as individuals, for citizenship in the creation of the nation. Yet their highly uncertain relationship to citizenship complicated their mobilization to end slavery. This conundrum informs this chapter's investigation of the social origins of African American Freemasonry.

Approaching the origins of black Masonry as a form of either class distinction or community leadership limits our capacity to examine its more nuanced and multifaceted dimensions. A reconsideration of basic questions concerning the order's earliest days can help us move toward a richer understanding of its meaning and configuration within its community. How did the emancipation process of Massachusetts affect the origins of the African Lodge, and what were the backgrounds of the first members? Given the complexities of forming their own lodge, what explains the attraction of African American men to Freemasonry? Answering these questions affords us new understandings of the relationship between the development of the black lodge, black leadership, and new forms of social distinction.

By analyzing church records, newspaper accounts, previously unused African Lodge records, individual manuscripts, and the complete Boston tax list—the Taking Books—recorded from 1780 to 1801, this chapter provides an original prosopography of the black Masonic founders.[11] It also resituates current understandings of the origins and meanings of African American Freemasonry and of Hall's leadership relative to the formation of the African Lodge. Charting the earliest development of black Freemasonry in Boston by investigating the lives of its first generation illustrates how the African Lodge represented a complicated form of northern urban leadership arising from the tensions produced by gaining release from bondage but not achieving equal citizenship.

The Problem of Emancipation

For numerous political, economic, and religious reasons, states in the North and upper South had begun to question the legal sanction of slavery by the era of the Revolution. By 1804, all the northern states had committed to abolishing lifetime servitude. Public opinion, judicial decree, legislation, the rhetoric of political and religious rights, a diversifying economy, and increasing slave agitation all fused to alloy the idea of freedom as an inherent right and refute the long-standing doctrine that one human could own another.

Differing historical perspectives and trajectories yield different arguments about the degree to which late eighteenth-century emancipation in the northern former colonies constituted a gradual process. However, when considered in the context of centuries of New World slavery, northern abolition emerged suddenly and rather unexpectedly.

Despite broad abolitionist momentum, the process of emancipation differed in each state. Vermont was the first state to expressly outlaw slavery, and it did so in its state constitution of 1777. As in Vermont, slavery ended in Connecticut, Rhode Island, Pennsylvania, New York, and New Jersey by legislative action; however, by contrast with Vermont, the process in the other states occurred slowly. In 1777, Connecticut considered the enlistment of slaves in exchange for their freedom. The next year, Rhode Island executed the policy, which ultimately freed no more than a hundred slaves. Because of broad disapproval, the state repealed the bill before war's end. In 1780, Pennsylvania was the first state to enact full-scale gradual emancipation. This law prohibited the importation of slaves into Pennsylvania, but it did not immediately outlaw human bondage. Slaves born before the act became law retained their status, and the offspring of enslaved mothers could be held as indentured servants until the age of twenty-eight, at which time they had to be released. By the mid-nineteenth century, most blacks in Pennsylvania had gained their freedom; however, it was not until 1847 that Pennsylvania law formally freed all slaves.

A similar process occurred in Connecticut and Rhode Island. In 1784, both states put forth laws stating that owners could release adult slaves without having to bond them and that children born to enslaved parents after March 1, 1784, had to provide service to the owners of the mother until they attained a designated age of maturity. Connecticut stipulated that slaves born after March 1, 1784, owed twenty-five years of service. Rhode Island set limits of twenty-one years and eighteen years for males and females, respectively. Connecticut passed the Slave Prohibition Act in 1788 and amended it in 1792 to more effectively guard against the illegal movement of slaves into and out of the state. In 1797, the Connecticut assembly lowered the mandated age of majority from twenty-five to twenty-one. Rhode Island and Connecticut expressly banned bondage in 1843 and 1848, respectively. New York and New Jersey passed gradual emancipation laws in 1799 and 1804, but did not fully abolish slavery until 1827 and 1863, respectively.

Freedom arrived differently in Massachusetts. Instead of enacting gradual emancipation statutes, the Bay State ended human bondage through black activism and judicial decree. Declaring "all men are born free and equal," the Massachusetts state constitution of 1780 set the foundation for Chief Justice

William Cushing to rule slavery unconstitutional in 1783 in the criminal case of the slave Quok Walker against his owner, Nathaniel Jennison.[12] This decision signaled the end of slavery in the Bay State. Litigation by African Americans and legislation by colonial leaders framed abolition in Massachusetts. Thomas Pemberton, an esteemed historian of the Revolution and Boston remembered a Massachusetts suit brought in 1770, by a slave, Dolton Stockbridge, "as the first instance I have heard of a negro requesting his freedom as his right."[13]

As African Americans throughout the North pushed for their freedom, they developed varied abolitionist strategies that reflected different social and political environments. During the 1770s, blacks in Massachusetts wrote more abolitionist petitions to their state government than did blacks in any other state. In January of 1773, Felix, an African American servant, petitioned the Massachusetts colonial legislature.[14] This petition began an unprecedented wave of published antislavery critiques in Massachusetts, mostly written by black men, that numbered no fewer than ten published articles and addresses by 1777.[15] In contrast, blacks in Pennsylvania worked with white abolitionists and only began petitioning by the late 1770s.[16]

Black Masons led the petition writing. Before his death on June 20, 1778, Peter Bestes signed the 1773 petition and then helped to form African Lodge No. 1, in 1775. Three of the first fifteen initiates—Peter Bestes, Brister Slenser, and Prince Hall—soon authored a January 13, 1777, petition.[17] Another signer of this statement, Lancaster Hill, though not one of the original members, did join the African Lodge soon thereafter, for he attained the degree of master and became lodge treasurer by June 1779.[18] In the 1777 petition, Hall and others wrote to the Massachusetts legislature demanding the end of slavery. The language of the letter reflected deepening frustration and growing confidence.

Slavery ended with relative speed in Massachusetts; however, it did not end quickly enough for blacks. These authors criticized legislative inaction by explaining that they had "Long and Patiently waited the Evnt of petition after petition By them presented to the Legislative Body of this state." Moreover, they could not understand "that It have Never Bin Consirdered that Every Principle from which America has Acted in the Cours of their unhappy Difficultes with Great Briton Pleads Stronger than A thousand arguments in favours of your petitioners." Yet they also outlined a process of measured liberation, suggesting that "their Children who wher Born in this Land of Liberty may not be held as Slaves after they arive at the age of twenty one years."[19] Even as they grew more publicly dissatisfied with governmental hesitation, blacks did not abandon respectful action through established channels. Abolition steeled black Masonic leadership, and Masonry provided an institutional frame for antislavery organizing.

The ending of slavery signified paradox. Many whites believed blacks deserved freedom; however, they also thought that blacks had to prove worthy of it. Ironically, the same forces that framed the issue of abolition in terms of inherent rights also defined freedom as an earned status.[20] In consequence, the sources that acknowledged the importance of black Freemasons could be both complimentary and critical. The learned Boston minister and historian Jeremy Belknap interviewed Hall as a representative voice of former bondsmen and bondswomen. The prominent Salem minister and Freemason William Bentley also acknowledged Hall's status. During the summer of 1801, only six years before his death, Hall catered "A Turtle Feast of the Marine Society at Osgood's in South Fields."[21] Bentley attended the event and remarked that "Our chief cook was Prince Hall, an African, & a person of great influence upon his Colour in Boston, being Master of the African Lodge, & a person to whom they refer with confidence their principal affairs." "The Clergy was introduced" to Hall, continued Bentley, and "the principal gentlemen took notice of him." Bentley remembered that during the dinner, "Brother Freeman of Boston [the Reverend James Freeman of the Episcopal Stone Chapel in Boston] pronounced [Hall] a very useful man." Freeman further remarked that "the Masonic Negroes are evidently many grades above the common blacks of Boston."[22] This praise of a few blacks implicitly denigrated all the others.

The Warranting of the African Lodge

It was important for black Masons to cultivate the kind of approval given by Freeman; however, their efforts to gain repute also buttressed their confidence to make uncompromising critiques of American society. Hence, the successful warranting of the African Lodge constituted part of a broad strategy to prove black civic capabilities but also to demand access for African American political participation. On November 26, 1786, Hall wrote to the governor of Massachusetts, James Bowdoin, pledging the support of the black Masons to any state-supported efforts against Shays's Rebellion, an insurrection of poor farmers in western Massachusetts led by Daniel Shays, a veteran who had fought at the Battle of Bunker Hill.[23] Seventeen eighty-seven was also the year in which Hall and approximately seventy-two others applied to the Massachusetts General Court with a plan to emigrate to Africa.[24] Nevertheless, later that year, Hall and thirty-two other men wrote to the Boston selectmen requesting funding for a black school.[25] The following year, Hall successfully complained in New England newspapers about the kidnapping of three blacks from Boston, one of them being a Masonic brother.[26] The efforts of black Freemasons to build repute arose from their desire to prove worthy of compliment and fueled their insistence that they deserved protection and citizenship.

Questions of reputation related to discussions about freedom and citizenship, and they also shaped debates arising from the broadening of Masonic membership just after the Revolution. Issues of legitimacy were always central to the spread of Freemasonry and particularly so in the late eighteenth century. Beginning at midcentury, a group of London Freemasons, mostly of Irish origin, convened a grand lodge in London in opposition to the English grand lodge in London. This Irish cohort called themselves Ancients, laying claim to an earlier and hence supposedly more legitimate Masonic heritage. Ancients derisively labeled the English grand lodge a Modern grand lodge. African American Masonry arose from this rivalry.[27] The man who initiated the group with Prince Hall, Sergeant John Batt, was probably an officer in the Irish Thirty-Eighth Regiment of Foote and a member of Freemasonic Lodge No. 441.[28] The mobility of military lodges made correspondence with them more difficult, and hence they were more difficult to track and regulate. Lodge No. 441 was a traveling lodge warranted by an Ancient lodge, and it illustrated how Ancient grand lodges, actively innovating methods of expansion, were more patient with the problems of regulating military lodges.

The African Lodge in Boston gained its official charter from the Modern grand lodge in London just as new lodges proliferated and American Freemasonry as a whole was reestablishing official procedures for maintaining the sanctity and homogeneity of Masonic rule and ritual after the separation from England. Freemasonry first arrived in colonial North America in the 1730s with the formation of St. John Lodge in Philadelphia. The first American Masons, men of high social rank, emphasized the tenets of love and honor to buttress solidarity among the colonial elite.[29] After the Revolutionary War, the expansion of American Freemasonry involved the establishment of new patterns of sociability and leadership. Younger and less established men climbed, but also widened, the social ladder on the top rungs of which had previously sat an older and wealthier group of men. Ancients extended and diversified North American membership while continuing to demonstrate the conflict within Freemasonry between universality and exclusivity.

By the 1790s, Ancients had overtaken Moderns in numbers and influence. The historian Stephen Bullock noted that Ancient Masons, even as they branded Moderns inauthentic, outdated, and elitist, also "sought to keep social distinctions meaningful."[30] In 1763, when a group of white Bostonians approached the Lodge of St. Andrews, an Ancient assembly, the members scorned the petition, saying that the applicants were "very improper Persons" who "will inevitably bring the Craft into the greatest Disgrace imaginable."[31] White applicants for Masonic membership could confront significant hurdles; the realities of race and reputation only heightened those obstacles for black candidates.

About 1795, the Reverend John Eliot commented on divisions between white and black Masons in Boston.[32] Eliot became pastor of the New North Church in 1779 after the death of its former minister, his father, Andrew. Eliot found it "remarkable" that "White and Black Masons do not sit together in their lodges." "The African Lodge in Boston tho professing a charter from England, signed by the Earl of Effingham and countersigned by the Duke of Cumberland, meet by themselves" and, continued Eliot, "Masons not more skilled in Geometry than their black brethren will not acknowledge them." "The reason given," explained Eliot, "is that the Blacks were made clandestinely in the first place which being known would have prevented them from receiving a Charter."[33] "But this inquiry," continued Eliot, "would not have been made about White Lodges many of which have not conformed to the rules of Masons."[34] Although not a Mason himself, Eliot stated that the "truth is [whites] are ashamed of being on an equality with Blacks." Further complicating the matter of legitimacy, Eliot added that blacks "on the other hand valuing themselves upon their knowledge of the Crafts, think themselves better Masons in other regards than the Whites, because Masonry considers all men equal who are free; and Massachusetts Laws admit of no kind of slavery."[35]

Similar conditions existed in Philadelphia. In 1797, black Masons in that city, writing to Hall to gain recognition as a lodge, remarked on how intolerance limited their numbers. These subscribers commented that "the White Masons here say that they are afraid to grant us a warrant for feare the Blackmen living in Virginia would get to be free masons too."[36] Regardless, Philadelphians of color stated that "we had rether be under our Dear Brethren in Boston then the Pennsylvania Lodge."[37] On March 6, Israel Israel and several other white Freemasons visited a black lodge in Philadelphia. Israel described the black Freemasons as ignorant of the proper ritual and ceremony, and he caused the white grand lodge of the city to threaten the expulsion of any of its members who subsequently visited the lodge of color. Yet other white Masons in Philadelphia continued to visit the lodge.[38] The situations in Boston and Philadelphia demonstrate the contest over legitimacy between black and white Masons. White Masons' efforts to establish their own legitimacy by delegitimizing black Masons actually only highlighted the unsettled state of postrevolutionary American Masonry as a whole.

Before 1787, the new black lodge, although active in Boston and able to accept as members men already initiated, did not have the authority to make new members. For this reason, prior to 1787, the number of black Masons in African Lodge No. 1 remained low. Hall followed Masonic rule by not making new brothers before receiving the warrant from the Modern grand lodge. He explained in a letter of June 30, 1784, to William M. Moody, a master Mason in the Modern grand lodge, that our lodge "hath Bin Founded almoust this Eaght yeears and had no Worrent yet But only a Premete from Grand Master Row to Walk on St Johns Dayes and to Burey our Dead in forme; which we now Injoy."[39] The provisional permit given by "Grand Master Row" allowed Hall and his cohort to meet together in public only to observe Masonic anniversaries, like St. John's Day, and perform particular rituals, like Masonic funerals. John Rowe was the grand master of the Grand Lodge of Massachusetts.[40]

The 1787 warrant from England, by contrast, certified that African Lodge No. 1 had gained complete recognition from one of the highest Masonic authorities, the English Modern grand lodge in London, seemingly overriding the authority of the Massachusetts Grand Lodge—yet at a time when the authority of the English grand lodge to create new lodges in America itself was increasingly denied. The warrant also allowed the African Lodge to initiate members. Gaining the charter represented a victory for its autonomy and integrity, yet the advance fell far from securing black Masons full political representation in the new nation.

Property, Wealth, Mobility, and Status

Recognition of African Lodge No. 1 as Lodge No. 459 fully launched the public presence of African American Masons. The lodge members now became more prominent for other reasons as well. Though its membership constituted a very tiny fraction of the total black population in Boston, it included some of the most esteemed black leaders in Boston and the North.[41] Some lodge members, like Prince Hall, owned property, and some labored in jobs occupied by few other African Americans. Black Freemasons clearly constituted a black elite, yet the dimensions and significance of that stature require examination. Although the outlines of new economic divisions were becoming visible, the appearance of the African Lodge should not be seen simply as the consequence—or even necessarily as an indication—of nascent class differentiation.

By 1800, only a minute fraction of Boston's blacks and black Masons had acquired personal and real estate.[42] Between 1783 and 1798, Boston tax assessors recorded an annual average of 8 property-owning blacks, with a high of 20 in 1798. From 1798 to 1801, 22, 34, 49, and 116 blacks possessed valued real estate.[43] In 1801 the proportion of property-owning black

Masons reached its eighteenth-century height, 14. In this period, only one man, Bristol Morandy, had his real estate taxed while sitting as a member of both the African Lodge and the African Society.[44] Most Freemasons, like most Bostonians of color, did not own property.[45] Among black Freemasons Prince Hall stands out. He owned taxable assets for longer than most of the general black populace and black Freemasons, and hence he appeared in tax records more than any other resident of color.[46] Between 1780 and 1800, only 13 other black men had their property taxed for two or more years, including 3 who had entered the craft—Juba/Jube Hill, George Middleton, and Boston Faddy/Fadey.[47] Hill owned a house on "so called Hills Wharf."[48]

Ties of occupation, property ownership, and social prominence connected Middleton, Faddy, and Louis Glapion. By 1808 Middleton had become Senior Warden of the lodge and, over the next two years, would serve as the worshipful master of African Lodge No. 459.[49] He also helped found the African Society.[50] Like most blacks in Boston, Middleton, a coachman for Dr. James Lloyd, provided personal services to whites.[51] Faddy, an apprentice in African Lodge No. 1 by 1778 and one of only two black sextons named in eighteenth-century Boston, served as a witness to the baptism of Middleton's third child, James.[52]

Both Middleton and Louis Glapion owned land and property.[53] A 1782 description of a black Masonic celebration noted that the "aprons and jesels" worn by the African Lodge for their celebration of St. John the Evangelist came from "Brother G[lap]ions."[54] In 1778, Glapion advertised himself as a French "Barber and Hairdresser" who had "just opened a Shop in Congress Street near the State-House where he dresses in the nicest fashions." "[C]onstant attendance will be given on Ladies and Gentlemen who choose to favor him with their custom."[55] Perhaps Glapion was the source to whom Hall referred in his 1784 letter to the London grand lodge explaining his decision not to apply to a French lodge for a warrant.[56] Glapion, like Middleton and Hall—whose work as a leather-dresser depended upon an interracial clientele—interacted closely with both whites and blacks.[57]

These individuals achieved levels of success and self-sufficiency attained by few other people of color. Yet their relative security remained uncertain and did not pass to later generations.[58] As an elderly man, even Prince Hall, literate and propertied, did not avoid poverty. From 1794 to 1797, assessors abated his taxes, apparently because he was unable to pay.[59] The meager estate left by Hall reflected how poverty especially threatened blacks regardless of whether or not they were of the elite.

The challenges of emancipation were revealed not only in the difficulty of obtaining wealth but even more fundamentally in the insecurity of employment. Abolition ended lifetime servitude, but it released former bondspeople into new worlds of uncertainty and stress. Slaves had gained a wide array of skills useful in a diverse New England economy; however, most of the newly free lacked literacy, competed for work with wary whites, and often had to prove residency when simply establishing a domicile was difficult.[60] For black Bostonians, and many northern African Americans, transience and the search for work underlined the ending of slavery. Seafaring afforded important employment for black men, yet even it was plagued with peril for them.[61] In a 1788 newspaper article, Prince Hall highlighted how free black seamen feared being kidnapped into slavery. "Hence it is," explained Hall, "that many of us, who are good seamen, are obliged to stay at home through fear, and the one half of our time loiter about the streets, for want of employ."[62] Although black seamen feared being captured into bondage, the records of the African Society reveal that they nevertheless put out to sea. The 1798 laws of the African Society, updating those first written two years earlier, explained that any "members" who were "traveling, at a distance by sea or land" could appoint someone to pay their subscription while they were absent and "still be considered as brothers."[63] Six of the sixteen laws addressed the problems associated with members who had to travel by sea or land or who might not come back after leaving.[64] African Lodge No. 459 and the African Society shared members and, while both institutions represented settlement and regularity, they did so amid a mobile population.

Emancipation prompted itinerancy, and the men who became Freemasons were no exception. The Boston tax records indicate that the first black Masons in Boston, like many new freemen, traveled frequently. On average, 13.5 percent of taxable African American males per year were listed as being away from Boston.[65] Of the first fifteen black Freemasons initiated in 1775, only four appeared in Boston tax records—Prince Hall, Boston Smith, Cuff/Duff Buffom/Buform, and Fortune Howard. Although other original members, like John Carter, Boston Smith, and Brister Slenzer, appear in the account books and meeting minutes of the African Lodge, they do not show up in Boston poll records.[66] From the vantage of their brotherhood, these men are part of a self-selected group; yet when examined according to their occupations, they are very representative of the mass of ordinary, local African Americans. Scipio Dalton, a Freemason, was exceptional for his shared ownership of a house in Ward seven with Cromwell Barnes, a black barber. Yet even though he owned property, authorities described Dalton as a laborer and servant and as having "gone to sea." Cuff Buffom, another Freemason, worked as a servant and sailor and resided in a house owned by Boston Faddy, a Mason since 1778. Faddy presumably gave personal aid to

the Buffom family when, in 1798, Buffom's wife fell "very sick" and assessors noted that Buffom was both an "invalid" and a "cripple," That Faddy
probably supported Buffom further highlights the insecurity confronting all
black Bostonians, Masons or otherwise.[67]

Some of the men who formed African Lodge No. 1 might have been
new arrivals to the city. One reading of the 1775 receipt verifying the
initiation of Hall and his cohort suggests that one or more of this group
became Freemasons before March 6, 1775, and perhaps in a place other than
Boston.[68] On the bottom of the membership note was scribbled, "making
those marsters at 15 guineas, Crafts 7 genes and Marsters 3 gineas."[69] Prince
Hall and his peers had to pay as part of their initiation. If these blacks paid
different amounts to receive different degrees, one or more of them might
have already been a Freemason at the level of apprentice or craft.[70] Degrees
reflected accumulated knowledge about the history and rites of Masonry and
the successful execution of increasingly intricate rites of performance and
recitation. Within Masonic ritual, craft, apprentice, and master comprised the
first three degrees, or levels of Masonic knowledge and ritual expertise. Some
of the initial members might have gained degrees at an earlier time and in
a different place. If the pricing of degrees is read simply as a cost listing for
a corresponding level of expertise, then the document shows that all fifteen
black men did in fact first enter into Freemasonry together. Yet the possibility that the receipt reveals the persistent mobility of these African Americans
even on the eve of the Revolution cannot be dismissed outright.[71]

Several black Masons in Philadelphia had in fact been initiated in places
other than America. Writing to Prince Hall in 1797 for recognition and
a warrant, black Masons in Philadelphia noted that they numbered eleven,
"five of which are all M[asters]." Peter Manto[n]e, "is at present Master of
the whole," and had "withstood the amazing triel and after a strect examination." They named the others and their lodges of origination. Four men,
"Peter Rechmon. Johnthen Harding, John [Dow], [and] Rebred Wendbel[or
Yendbel or Yardbel]," were "all Masters," among the "Ancient York Masons."
Ancient York Masonry referred to one of two primary Masonic ritual systems, the Scottish Rite being the other, and to the split between Ancients
and Moderns. It is probable that this group became master masons across the
Atlantic. Another six men, "[Q] Butler[,] C. Brown[,] T[or J or S] Peterson[,]
T Tucker[,] [To Perkins][, and [Jo Keney]," entered explicitly into the
fraternity "in London in the Grand Lodge No. 444."[72]

African American Masons in Boston and Philadelphia moved in transatlantic realms of religion and politics. The noted itinerant Methodist preacher
John Marrant joined African Lodge No. 459 upon his arrival in Boston
after having traveled throughout the North Atlantic. Adam Row, William

Gregory, and Prince Spooner traveled as mariners between Boston and England. John Rowe chronicled the taking of his servant, Adam, by the British as the Crown's soldiers retreated from the city in 1776.[73] Adam had returned to the city four years later, but authorities understood that he had "gone Priv[ateerin]g." Adam became a Freemason as early as 1789; however, records do not indicate where he joined the fraternity. The next year, he had "gone," and in 1792 authorities found him "sick." After 1793 he disappeared from Boston tax lists.[74] Gregory became a member in 1778 and paid dues for a Masonic burial in the 1780s. He appeared only once in the tax records. Assessors, in the only year that they entered Gregory, knew of his traveling "at sea" and that he had "gone to England."[75] In 1785, Prince Spooner, a brother in African Lodge No. 1, wrote from the London grand lodge of England notifying Prince Hall that "Brother Gregory hath been for the charter of our Lodge." Gregory had visited the Modern grand lodge but had failed to procure the proof that African Lodge No. 1 had been placed into the grand lodge register as African Lodge No. 459. Boston black Masons eventually received the certificate in 1787, and Spooner appeared back in Boston at least as early as 1791. The African Lodge received its warrant amid these patterns of transiency and migration.[76]

African Lodge No. 459 obtained the charter because of black sailors, and it in turn bestowed upon those men the benefits of reputation. Although John Marrant did not arrive a Mason, his status provided him immediate access to Prince Hall. Prior to his Boston arrival, Marrant had already written himself into the Anglo-Atlantic world of print. He first arrived in England as a wounded sailor after having been impressed into the British navy during the American Revolution. While in England, he was ordained a minister within the Huntingdonian Connexion, a Methodist society sponsored by Selina Hastings, Countess of Huntingdon, which included George White-field. With the encouragement of the countess and at the request of his brother in Nova Scotia, Marrant sailed from England in August of 1785 and landed at Birchtown, later that year.[77]

After preaching among whites and blacks in Nova Scotia for three years, Marrant sailed to Boston in January 1789, where Hall quickly befriended him. He stayed in Boston just long enough to be made a member of the African Lodge and deliver the public sermon on the anniversary of the Masonic patron, St. John the Baptist.[78] Shortly after Marrant departed Boston that fall, Hall wrote to the Countess of Huntingdon thanking her for supporting Marrant, whom she "under God, hath raised up to be a faithful labourer." Although Hall never traveled far from Boston, he always understood that Freemasonry facilitated transatlantic political and religious bonds. Explaining Marrant's initiation, Hall wrote that "the members of the African Lodge" had made him "a member of that honourable society, and chaplain of the same, which will be a great help to him in his travels, and may do a great deal of good to society."[79] Hall hoped that the endorsement of Marrant would also serve to promote African Lodge No. 459 and black Masonic respectability.

Hall and his brethren distinguished themselves not only by endorsing respectable behavior but also in the way that they reconciled local and Atlantic worlds. Both the members of the African Lodge and the broader black population lived mobile lives. Transience and poverty challenged stable residency and left blacks struggling to consolidate their resources within black Boston. The African Lodge fostered a vocal and concerned African American leadership among an unsettled population. Infused with the virtues of mutualism and universal fellowship, this new black fraternity grew from the local community while creating transatlantic networks dedicated to connecting African descendants whom a paradoxical freedom had increasingly dispersed throughout the North Atlantic basin.

Distinction, Death, and Public Presentation

Although black Freemasonry symbolized certain divisions, it also represented the emergence of a black identity that was understood by people of color to be shared by all African descendants in the Americas. This geographically specific understanding of black identity drew coherence from the common material circumstances experienced by African Americans in the northern states and particularly in Boston. The material and political environment of Boston contrasted subtly with the social situations of blacks throughout the diaspora. In the Bay State, slavery arose from diversified markets, not plantation economies, and slaves always made up less than 10 percent of the population, regardless of locale. Low proportions of slaves resulted in low rates of interracial conception. Hence a light-skinned black elite, the offspring of female slaves and white slave owners, never developed in Boston or in New England more broadly. The reverse was true throughout the rest of the African diaspora. In plantation societies, where slaves greatly outnumbered masters, categories of race and class reflected varying shades of skin color, from light to dark. In contrast, racial categories in New England evolved along a stark binary distinction of black versus white, and most blacks experienced similar material circumstances.[80] By 1800, most African Americans in New England, including Masons of color, owned little if any property. The racial line allowed for blacks, including Masons, to fashion various identities rooted in the belief that people of color were ultimately more alike than different and largely shared a common experience.

The funeral procession for Luke Belcher illustrated that Freemasons of color understood themselves to occupy the top tier of a social hierarchy within which all blacks nevertheless shared a common identity. Therefore, these public gatherings revealed a tension between distinction and representation. African Lodge brothers believed that their status as Masons dignified them and justified their public presentation of black respectability. Yet Masons of color also derived their sense of leadership and representation from experiences prior to initiation. For example, that Belcher had presided as an African governor during slavery illustrated that blacks and whites had, albeit for different reasons, already looked to him as a principal figure. Even in slavery, he acted as a leader among African Americans. Many of the chosen governors and kings were African, and they were apparently chosen for reasons relating to some combination of physical prowess, African aristocratic background, and authority derived from the reputation of their masters.[81] These magistrates mediated disagreements and administered punishments among bondspeople. That an African governor became a Freemason demonstrated continuity in leadership.

Records do not reveal how Belcher, originally from Africa, arrived in the Americas and settled in Boston, nor whether he was ever a slave. At the time of Luke's 1765 marriage in Boston to a black servant named Diana, he worked as the servant of Louisa Belcher of Milton.[82] It is possible that he was a slave for some period; however, he was certainly free at the time of his death. Luke appears never to have owned property or to have been taxed for personal possessions. As of March 6, 1778, he had attained the first two Masonic degrees, and on June 23, 1779, he became a "Marster." He might have had his first encounter with the fraternity while he served the Belcher family. He might also have lived long enough in West Africa to have participated in secret societies, such as the Poro, which might have predisposed him to Freemasonry as an approximation of them.[83]

Within the lodge, Belcher advanced. He may not have lived a life much different from that of other blacks in Boston; however, he could afford to become a Mason and to pay for a proper Masonic burial. He had attained a rank that merited public mourning of his death. Thus black Masons purposefully connected Luke with the esteemed Jonathan Belcher, a Freemason and colonial governor of Massachusetts from 1730 to 1741 and of New Jersey from 1747 until his death in 1757.[84] This connection reinforced the representation of Luke's respectability, that "'pearl of great price,'" that his "apparent superiors," whites, "need not be ashamed to imitate."[85] Distinguishing a lodge brother highlighted the exclusiveness of black Masonry and created a separation between those people of color who could have a Masonic burial and those who could not. Membership in the African Lodge No. 459 required financial commitment. With the promise of aid or of a ceremonial funeral came the price of endowment. The minutes of the African Lodge constantly record payments from brothers for degrees received, for the "Poul and...Right to Bruey there Dead," for the renting of lodge space, and for disbursements from the lodge for a variety of miscellaneous needs and services.[86]

Belcher's personal transition from African governor to honored Freemason marked the shift from slave festivals to more official public processions of free blacks. By mourning Belcher and publicizing his respectability, during both slavery and freedom, the African Lodge highlighted how African Americans had successfully transitioned from bondage to emancipation and how the lodge had played an important role in this process. Yet the representational position of the lodge, combined with racism and the various legacies of slavery, forced the broader African American community to consider whether and how the Belcher procession symbolized their experiences and outlooks. The funerary march introduced these questions because it simultaneously revealed emerging patterns of symbolic status and social differentiation and of racial cohesion and community formation.

The march for Belcher conferred upon him and all Masons a mark of distinction while also implying that the passing of any African American required the same care and attention as that of any white person.[87] From this latter implicit claim arose the need and demand for publicly authorized black sextons. Yet the practice of blacks controlling their own public funeral ceremonies, as black Masons did, was recent and controversial given that law and civic custom mandated that blacks, slave or free, be buried in separate segregated spaces and that whites do the digging.[88] City records first mention an African American sexton, Thomas, who tolled the bell of the Old South Church before 1785.[89] Either the Boston selectman or the Old South Church itself appointed Thomas. Sources reveal nothing about whether Thomas, in addition to bell ringing, had a license to dig and bury black or white bodies.

However, only four years after the mention of Thomas, the selectmen noted the "application of the Blacks for a Person among them to have the burying of the Dead" but stated that the request was "not granted."[90] The role of black undertakers was contentious, thereby further revealing issues of respectability, representation, and Masonic leadership. The selectmen mentioned the eligibility of Boston Faddy and Stephenson, both Freemasons, for the position.[91] In 1791, African American Bostonians again asked "that one of their colour may be permitted as an Undertaker at the Funerals of the Blacks, with permission to break ground in the several burial places." The "request would not be granted," responded the selectmen, "as it would interfere with the present regulations & the duty of those Sextons, to whom are committed the care of the several burial places."[92] The following year, authorities cautiously licensed Stephenson "to take care of the Funerals of Blacks in all respects except breaking Ground."[93] Later records show that authorities also allowed Faddy to do the same.

The roles of Freemason and sexton conferred upon Stephenson and Faddy a unique social standing. They stood apart from but also represented black Boston. For blacks, the two provided the expertise and the access for treating the dead, especially their Masonic brothers, with grace and respect. For whites, Stephenson and Faddy demonstrated trustworthiness by their assent and deference to racial proscriptions. Their respectability did not go unquestioned: on April 25, 1798, a Mr. Blaney inquired into the behavior of "Stephenson & Boston Faddy, who have been employd in burying Negroes attended." After Blaney had investigated Stephenson's actions, he found "that Stephenson had behaved" and could be "permitted to proceed agreable to the former directions untill further Orders." However, for unstated reasons, the selectmen forbade Faddy to "bury any Corps without particular direction obtain therefor of the Selectmen."[94] Perhaps Faddy had performed as a sexton for a black funeral, even a Masonic funeral, without the consent of town leaders, or perhaps his past—he had served time in jail in 1789—had caught up with him.[95]

Secrecy, Private Politesse, and Respectability

The funeral procession for Belcher and the funerary authority of Stephenson and Faddy provided opportunities for black Masons to publicly display modes of respectability they had cultivated within the lodge. For the members, the lodge was both a physical space and a symbolic realm that, by virtue of secrecy, operated as a haven for the fashioning of self-affirming black identities. Joanna Brooks argues that the African Lodge, "like independent black churches[,] . . . provided a precious venue for the development of fellow feeling, the exercise of black political authority, and the discussion of spiritual principles" and also that "members enjoyed the pleasures of ritual, the pride of corporate distinction, and the powers of secrecy."[96] Moreover, Brooks further argues that secrecy afforded the African Lodge "a rare degree of freedom from white oversight and interference."[97]

Although the surviving lodge administrative records reveal nothing of the sublime effects that must have been experienced during the practice and actual performance of initiation rituals and degree examinations, they do illustrate the bureaucratic and institutional effects of lodge membership. Records also do not describe the settings of lodge meetings, but given that religious meetings and early black schools were first organized in homes, administrative lodge meetings probably also occurred in personal residences.

Meeting minutes demonstrate a kind of bureaucratic training. Masonic rituals of initiation, degree examination, burial, and celebration required that masters, apprentices, and crafts perform specific institutional roles defined by protocols of hierarchy and deference. In addition to the degrees of Entered Apprentice, Fellow Craft, and Master Mason, the African Lodge consisted of officers, including the grand master, senior warden, junior warden, senior deacon, junior deacon, chief steward, second steward, outside tiler, inside tiler, and secretary.[98] The performance of Masonic ritual represented more than the enactment of a corporate identity. Instead, the synchronicity required for successful ritual execution reinforced the belief that lodge brothers were inhabiting a living and timeless tradition. Hence Masonry conferred on its black members a sacred and an institutional identity. As Masons, lodge brothers were invested with the responsibility of organizing and representing the African American community.

Black identity was made corporate through participation in Masonic ritual and payment. Many of the lodge minutes merely record payments and fines to the lodge; however, these records also suggest that black Freemasons took the craft seriously rather than approaching it as a means to other ends. Bullock found that among whites, "higher-degree membership tended to be defined largely by Masonic interest rather than occupational or cultural standing."[99] If the same pattern held true for African Americans, then it is worth noting the relatively high percentage of master Masons in the African Lodge. By 1801, from the approximately forty-one members of the African Lodge, at least twelve of them had attained the degree of master.[100]

Seen through a lens focused on issues of status and wealth, the rise of black Freemasonry might improperly be understood as a story of class trumping race. In fact, however, emancipation in Massachusetts always complicated the relationship between race and class. The unfolding of abolition was comparatively short and straightforward, but it left African Americans fighting for the essential dimensions of equal citizenship—enfranchisement, inclusion, and employment. Responding to this paradox, African American Masonry produced its own internal conflict. The ideology of the African Lodge defined all people of African descent as victims of racial prejudice and of the Atlantic slave trade while simultaneously developing an exclusive and masculine definition of leadership.

Members of the African Lodge used ceremony to distinguish themselves even though they entered the same occupations and traveled the same paths as most blacks. African American Masons included the illiterate and those who worked in domestic and maritime trades. Their associational activity and leadership distinguished them from the mass of Boston's blacks much more than did their relative prosperity. No early black Mason amassed a fortune large enough to pass on to progeny. The proximity of Hall's generation to slavery, Boston's depressed postrevolutionary economy, and racial antagonism kept most blacks, including black Masons, on a similar social and economic footing. Hall and the members of the African Lodge derived their authority from this rootstock of black identity while simultaneously distinguishing themselves as leaders. Hence African American Freemasonry should be understood as emerging from a complex intersection of abolitionist activism, community formation, and the exercise of newly gained autonomy.

In 1820, the authority of Prince Hall was remembered in a derisive newspaper piece that nonetheless illustrated the significant linkage between his leadership and evolving forms of public black expression made possible by emancipation. Thirteen years after Hall's death, the *New England Galaxy & Masonic Magazine,* in an article titled "African Independence," criticized the "Selectmen of Boston" for permitting "the town to be annually disturbed by a mob of negroes, whose parade and pageantry are as useless, unmeaning, and ridiculous, as their persons and the atmosphere . . . are offensive and disgusting." This Abolition Day Parade took place annually in Boston on July 14 for the first two decades of the nineteenth century. In New York and Philadelphia, the same holiday was celebrated on the first of January.[101] Apparently this procession included "five or six hundred negroes, with a band of music, pikes, swords, epaulettes, sashes, cocked hats, and standards." The author wrote further that the parade culminated in a clergyman sermonizing "on the blessings of independence" and presenting "for admiration the characters of 'Masser Wilberforce and Prince Hall.'" Even amid sarcastic derision, white critics paired Prince Hall with the prominent abolitionist William Wilberforce and acknowledged his lasting impact and the continued African American reverence for him.[102]

The appearance of black Freemasonry arose from and compelled significant democratic change. Yet the ambiguities of emancipation did not present freedom as a condition easily defined or achieved, and in response, black Freemasons asserted themselves as an exclusive stratum that spoke on behalf of all African Americans. It was because of a problematic freedom, and not in spite of it, that black Freemasonry expressed both racial solidarity and symbolic black exclusivity.

CHAPTER 2

"To Commence a New Era in the Moral World"

John Telemachus Hilton, Abolitionism, and the Expansion of Black Freemasonry, 1784–1860

PETER P. HINKS

In an 1828 address to his black Masonic brethren, John Telemachus Hilton posed an important question to the fraternity's select constituency: "[I]f the secrets of Masonry be of such great advantage to the general improvement of Society, why not reveal it [*sic*] to the world?" He answered directly: the mass of men were not yet prepared to receive its mysteries for they are "more attracted by novelty, than [by] things of more value." Revealing them to those not ready would mean only that the jewels of Masonic enlightenment would be misunderstood, abused, and "sink into disrepute." "Ambition, pride, and selfishness" still drove the vast mass of men and corrupted their understanding; there was "no better proof of this assertion than to see mankind neglect the words of the eternal God, though they are sensible that upon it, rests their future destiny." The fact of America's obdurate commitment to that "neglect" was subsumed in the nation's dedication to slavery, to nurturing the "ambition, pride, and selfishness" of white men while "in this boasted land of liberty, christianity and civilization, over twenty hundred thousand of our race [are] kept in perpetual slavery, ... groping in mental darkness." These men did not afford the stuff of Freemasons; yet black Masons neglected them at the peril of renouncing their professed ideals of universal fellowship and benevolence. Dynamic tension between universality and exclusivity always existed within Freemasonry. But for African American Masons who would develop their fraternity separate from white American Masons, the relationship of the two principles could be particularly complicated. "While we are here assembled under our own vine and fig tree, enjoying these blessings which true liberty imparts, it is... our duty to advert to the causes which oppress our brethren, and endeavour to find out some means of redress for their grievances." To black Freemasons in particular fell the commission to challenge and dispel this hateful oppression, discord, and darkness that engulfed white and black alike. "Let us strive... by combining Masonry and Christianity together, and by living a holy and religious life."

This holy amalgam of the Christian and Masonic must in America of necessity publicly embrace as well an active opposition to slavery and racial injustice as integral to pursuing the grace and ideals of that amalgam. For Hilton and his brethren, the expansion of black Freemasonry was an essential instrument in dismantling the "human depravity" of bondage that America and its white Masonic acolytes embraced. It would move them toward a moral and spiritual regeneration that would herald a broader extension of Masonic principles in the world. Hilton continued:

> The principles of Masonry... are intended to do away all the bad qualities of man; advance the general good, and bring about universal peace among mankind... When the knowledge of Masonry shall have become universal, and her noble principles diffused and practically enforced, then will commence a new era in the moral world; Locks and Keys, Swords and Spears will then become useless; .... virtue and Religion will shield the human race.[1]

An activist and expansive black Freemasonry would be critical to instigating this transformation. Its central role among those advancing organized abolitionism in the antebellum era has been overlooked by scholars.[2] African American Masons reared in the slavery and racial opprobrium of America in the decades after 1783 cherished the core Masonic ideals of universal brotherhood and love with a zeal that eluded white Masons who found little to indict in a nation built on racial subjugation. Antebellum black Freemasonry was not a conservative movement intent on preserving a fraternal enclave of cautious and self-regarding black men isolated from the mass of black northerners. Rather, it was a highly progressive, even radical, order of select black men whose devotion to the principles of Freemasonry energized not only their commitment to mobilize people of color to secure their full freedom and inclusion in America, but to transform the hearts of white America as well by summoning white Masons to the purer Masonry their black brothers embodied. None among that fraternity pursued all these ends with greater dedication than did John Telemachus Hilton. This project for a black Masonic abolitionism coalesced over the decades from the late eighteenth century. This chapter details the process of this coalescence and explains its unrecognized significance. Without understanding the nature and growth of black Freemasonry in the North through the Civil War, we simply cannot appreciate the full spectrum of social forces prompting the dramatic effloresence of antebellum black activism for abolition, equality, and racial integrity.

As the states of the postrevolutionary North steadily dismantled slavery within their borders, some black and white Masons experimented with the possibility of forging closer fraternal ties in the spirit of Freemasonry's commitment to advancing universal fellowship. While the nation's first black lodge, African Lodge No. 459 in Boston, had duly received its charter from the Grand Lodge of England in 1784 and did not require certification from any white Massachusetts grand lodge, the black Masons had earlier unsuccessfully sought chartering from the local St. John's Lodge and after 1784 eagerly sought fellowship with white Masons in Boston and beyond.[3] As Prince Hall, the grand master of the African Lodge emphasized in his charge of 1797 to his brothers, "Live and act as Masons, that you may die as Masons.... Give the right hand of affection and fellowship to whom it justly belongs; let their color and complexion be what it will, let their nation be what it may, for they are your brethren, and it is your indispensable duty so to do."[4]

Some white Masons were ready to accept that extended hand. In Boston, several from St. Andrew's, a rival lodge to St. John's, interacted with the African Lodge, visiting its meetings and assisting at some ceremonies. In turn, Hall visited some white lodges and even reported on the character of some to the Grand Lodge of England. Interactions between black and white lodges and their ceremonies were not uncommon in the late 1790s in Philadelphia, where 459 had recently chartered a new black lodge.[5] A Mason in New Hampshire declared in 1798 that all Masons are "citizens of the world" and are good and true "whether Europe, Asia, or Afric gave him existence."[6] In an imagined oration set to verse before the African Lodge "in a certain metropolis"—evidently Boston—a contributor to the genteel *Columbian Magazine* in August 1788 claimed to translate from "the *Mandingo*... that ancient, musical, and sonorous language" an elegant expostulation on the legitimacy of black Freemasonry *delivered before the* Grand Master, Wardens, and Brethren *of the* most Ancient *and* venerable Lodge *of* African Masons." Inverting the apparent opprobrium of being "the seed of Cain," the orator declaimed "that brother Cain was the first Mason" and Africa and enslaved Hebrews the very source of its knowledge. Indeed, in

America, the African Lodge, "tho' bitterly be-curst / Is justly reckon'd *lodge the first*." The contributor concluded with a proclamation for the legitimacy of all Masons properly made from whatever condition:

> Besides it must not be forgot
> That free or slave, it matters not;
> For Mason's labor has been wrought
> By those who buy and those who're bought;
> We then conclude for weighty reasons
> That Slaves may be ACCEPTED MASONS.[7]

Amid disputes ensuing from the official emergence of African American Freemasonry in public space, this work unqualifiedly hailed the arrival of the charter for African Lodge No. 459 in Boston.

Yet the fact remained that hostile racial preconceptions informed the actions and attitudes of the mass of white American Masons and undergirded their unwillingness to convene in their lodges alongside black men as equal Masonic brothers. The Reverend John Eliot of Boston observed in a 1795 letter to the Reverend Jeremy Belknap, an eminent antislavery Congregational minister in the same town, that local white Masons, "not more skilled in geometry," raised a host of procedural reasons for why they could not recognize the black Masons, but these inquiries "would not have been made about white lodges, many of which have not conformed to the rules of Masonry. The truth is," he wrote," they are ashamed of being on an equality with blacks."[8] This barrier to interracial Masonic fellowship remained far more vigorous than the tentative openness to fraternity. As slavery prospered and expanded in the nation over the following decades, white Masonry's ready acceptance of it only reinforced the barriers. Thus, from its beginning, conundrums unknown to white American Masonry were forced upon the African Lodge and the broader black Freemasonry it would spawn. What was to be their relationship in America to a dominant white Masonry that excluded them? What was to be their relationship to an America that so fundamentally nurtured barriers that seemed to preclude the universal fellowship to which Masonic precepts were dedicated? What was to be their relationship to a white Masonry that fully embraced and extolled this America? How were they to address the slavery and racial injustice in the nation that was the foundation of these barriers? And what relationship was this selective cadre of black Masons to have to the mass of aggrieved non-Masonic blacks in the North and South, a mass from which white Masons refused to distinguish them?

From the late eighteenth century through the Civil War, black Freemasons would respond to these seeming paradoxes with a resolve for themselves as Masons and as Americans: they envisioned themselves as the vanguard of Masonry in America, summoned to regenerate the nation and its white Masons by returning them to the noble ideals of the fraternity from which they had both fallen so far. Over the course of these decades, black Freemasons would strive to sustain their impeccable devotion to internal Masonic regularity and selectivity in order to establish their exemplary fidelity to the operations and protocols of the Craft. This extended as much to the proprieties of the systems under which black Freemasonry expanded the number of its lodges in antebellum America as it did to the consistency of Masonic practices within individual lodges. At the core of their confidence in themselves as a paradigm of Masonic propriety was their chartering in 1784 through the most important lodge in the late eighteenth-century Atlantic—the Grand Lodge of England. Simultaneously, however, this same growing body of black Freemasons would help to mobilize and lead the mass of blacks to fight against slavery and racial injustice. Because of the unique intensity in America of their dedication to universal Masonic ideals—an intensity only finally they could yield because of their singular experience with all African Americans of racial injustice and proscription—their enlightenment and zeal could not rightly be confined exclusively within Masonic space when the scale of the assault on those ideals was as grievous as it was outside that space. They would thus be as fastidious to engage politically with the non-Masonic mass of African Americans in the North as they would be to preserve their select fraternity within which they constantly refreshed and deepened their special Masonic devotion to fellowship and enlightenment. Masonic work outside the lodge among both blacks and whites was the moral equivalent of work within it. In 1795, John Eliot observed that the members of African Lodge No. 459 "think themselves better Masons...than the whites, because Masonry considers all men equal who are free, and our laws admit no kind of slavery."[9] Only through the instrumentality of an expansive and activist black Freemasonry would America gain "the knowledge of Masonry" sufficient "to commence a new era in the moral world." A true black Mason in America of this time could not choose otherwise than to be antislavery and prepare the seedbed for the broader extension of Masonic principles in a renovated America.

The aggrieved members of postrevolutionary northern black communities required the support and voice the few African lodges provided, especially in Boston, which lacked the budding religious and educational institutions such as those in black New York City and Philadelphia, as well as the support and legal assistance afforded by the New York Manumission Society and the Pennsylvania Abolition Society. Number 459 did not hesitate to assume this responsibility: Prince Hall and its members as early as 1777 petitioned the Massachusetts General Court for the abolition of slavery while in the 1780s and 1790s they successfully pursued the return of kidnapped blacks, petitioned for a public school for black children, sought aid for those desiring to return to Africa, and condemned routine acts of violence against black men and women in public spaces. Remarkably, in 1786, they even offered to assist the state as soldiers against the uprising of the Shaysites in western Massachusetts.

Nevertheless, still in its infancy in membership and scale and only beginning to test the boundaries of freedom and justice in postrevolutionary Massachusetts, the fraternity set as its primary concerns the regularity of the organization, its grounding in Masonic and Christian virtues—which for these original black Masons were essentially identical—and its members' capacity to work benevolently among themselves and the broader community of blacks. Especially in these first decades, black Masonry did function as a parallel government of sorts for a people largely deprived of access to the mainstream machinery of social and political power. The Masons elected their own officers within a duly constituted institution to which they assented; they invested these offices with meaning and power through a complex and dignified ritual; they determined jointly a political agenda to which they would adhere locally and beyond; they administered relief and support to their afflicted members and their widows and children; they invested and allied with an expanding body of lodges elsewhere in the North to forge an interregional network of governance and authority. By 1800, these were accomplishments of note for African Americans in the North.[10]

Prince Hall and his brethren sustained their fidelity to regularity and organization with an unusual confidence because they knew their Masonry was grounded in an unmovable cornerstone—a charter granted them by the Grand Lodge of England. It had known full well that it was investing a lodge of black men—thus the designation "African Lodge." Indeed, Prince Hall and others viewed this charter as so empowering that it enabled them to overcome a core problem in their early years: how to create new lodges in a fashion that adhered strictly to Masonic protocol. Because the charter with which they had been invested was deemed an "unlimited" one, they were endowed with the right to create new lodges, which could then spawn their own grand lodges.[11] Thus in 1797, after having earlier in the decade apparently declared itself a grand lodge, African Lodge No. 459 chartered one new lodge each in Philadelphia and Providence.[12]

But finally Hall and his fraternal descendants did not understand their lodges as fundamentally insular parallel governments occupying a niche within free black communities and with little significance beyond them. Prince Hall believed that through this fidelity to right Masonic organization and the steady expansion of black Freemasonry, the broader regenerative capacity of black Freemasonry could act upon white Masons and the nation as a whole. In his charges of 1792 and 1797, Hall emphasized to his gathered fraternity the never-flagging requirement to be faithful to the duties and ceremonies of Masons. In 1792, he highlighted four forefathers "for our imitation": Tertullian, Augustine, Cyprian, and Fulgentius, all of whom did "nothing but to accomplish the precepts of Christ." Moreover, they were all from North Africa, which Hall equated with the continent of Africa as a whole. By emulating these African forefathers, black Masons enriched their Masonry, just as would those white Masons who followed them as well. Hall recounted again the story of Christ among the proscribed Samaritans, summoning all to follow Christ and embrace those who only appeared irretrievably alien.[13]

Yet in 1797 when black Bostonians were only beginning to emerge into an uncertain freedom he prompted his brethren to look not only to the great for exemplars but even more to the lowly and marginal—people who actually looked more like themselves. This recognition was particularly important for Hall's understanding of the regenerative purpose of black Freemasonry in the new nation. He cited first the unnamed enslaved girl from Israel who instructed her master, Naaman, to cure his leprosy by bathing in the Jordan River. Only after he had followed her guidance was he enabled to recognize "that there is no God in all the earth, except in Israel" (2 Kings 5:1–15). Then Hall upheld the hounded prophet Elijah, whom King Ahab had condemned as the "disturber of Israel." Despite the great fear of the king's vizier, Obadiah, of commanding Ahab to meet with Elijah, the presence of God in Elijah summoned Obadiah to obedience and to causing the ultimate meeting of Ahab and Elijah that returned the king to Yahweh and the renunciation of Baal (1 Kings 18). Finally he cited the encounter of the lowly apostle Philip with the powerful steward of the Ethiopian queen while he was riding in his sumptuous chariot. Obedient only to the Lord's commands, Philip approached the steward and ultimately led him to baptism, conversion, and the great gift of "rejoicing" (Acts 8: 26–40). Hall exhorted contemporary black Freemasons to recognize that these humble people of God held a spiritual potency equal to, if not finally greater than, that of Augustine and his eminent cadre: "Thus we see, my brethren, what a miserable condition it is to be under the slavish fear of men." Black Freemasons in particular needed to be free of that slavery. These three individuals delivered those invested in the things and values and rankings of the world to God for regeneration and fellowship. This duty to summon to God those so mired in the world would fall with particular weight upon black Freemasons. Hall charged them all to this faithful obedience to "heal"—as Masonic protocol had it—those who had turned from true Masonic precepts and rituals. "Worship God, this much is your duty as christians and as Masons."[14]

African Lodge No. 459 successfully underwent its first critical transition when Prince Hall died in December 1807: the lodge would continue to hold its requisite monthly meetings over the ensuing years, although its membership appears to have contracted somewhat. While dispute among authorities exists about the date of the creation of the first African grand lodge, some significant agreement exists that Prince Hall had apparently designated African Lodge No. 459 a grand lodge as early as 1791. William Grimshaw, a controversial early twentieth-century chronicler of the first century of black Freemasonry, is the principal proponent of this date.[15] Through this first grand lodge, the first lodges in Philadelphia and Providence were created. Soon after the death of Prince Hall in December 1807, a meeting of the lodge was held in which Nero Prince was appointed grand master, thus reaffirming that African Lodge No. 459 was also a grand lodge.[16] Then, in 1815, the original lodge in Philadelphia—assisted by members from three other lodges chartered by Number 459 in 1810, 1811, and 1814—declared itself a grand lodge, with the Reverend Absalom Jones as its first grand master.[17] According to Grimshaw and other sources, the African Grand Lodge also created a lodge in New York City, Boyer Lodge No. 1, in February 1812. Yet, save for a significant reference in 1814, documentation for a relationship between the two does not exist until the mid-1820s, when the lodge's negotiations for certification with Number 459 were recorded. Moreover, more general records for the New York Lodge are scarce until the lodge was named Boyer, which took place in the mid-1820s (not in 1812, as Grimshaw indicates).[18] These issues of designation and certification are not mere antiquarian concerns; the fidelity of black Masons' adherence—especially that of the first and greatest of their lodges, Number 459—to the precise Masonic protocol for creating new lodges had everything to do with the black brethren's enduring understanding of themselves as the "better Masons" who propagated duly scrutinized new lodges in the North as seedbeds for regeneration of the Craft as a whole in the nation. Although some lapse in administrative coherence may have occurred occasionally in the 1810s, a regular institutional infrastructure oversaw this important but slow expansion of black Masonry through the 1810s.[19]

By the 1820s, however, a renewal and extension of black Masonry in the Northeast and Middle Atlantic states accelerated this moderate growth. Although Reverend Thomas Paul initially spearheaded this drive, John

Telemachus Hilton soon became its principal mover. Hilton was born in Pennsylvania about 1801 and in his youth migrated to Boston, where he became a protégé of the town's eminent black pastor and Freemason Thomas Paul. Hilton was admitted to African Lodge No. 459 late in 1822 and then quickly secured advanced degrees within it.[20] By the 1820s, the minutes of the African Lodge had become lengthier and more detailed, especially regarding the spectrum of matters discussed and the identity of all officers present. By 1825, Hilton and Paul were aggressively expanding the membership of 459 and negotiating with black Masons in other cities about chartering and expanding their lodges. Though precise numbers are not readily available, it is known that quorums of members for monthly meetings were sometimes difficult to achieve even in the late 1810s; by 1825, no such problems existed—membership was overspilling the lodge hall. As numbers grew, so also did funds in the coffer, and on August 31, 1826, the African Lodge dedicated a new lodge hall on the corner of Cambridge and Belknap Streets at the foot of the northern slope of Beacon Hill.[21]

This expansion coincided with the African Lodge's seeking further accreditation for itself. Early in 1824, it had forwarded a request to the Grand Lodge of England to empower it to award the fourth through seventh degrees of Royal Arch Masons, an investiture only such an eminent grand lodge could make: "We therefore humbly solicit the Renewal of our Charter to authorize us legally to confer the same, as we are now getting in a flourishing condition."[22] Without this capacity, the lodge could not continue to grow and offer the most advanced degrees to its members. The Grand Lodge of England never responded. In early 1826, the Boston brethren petitioned the Massachusetts General Court for a charter of incorporation and were denied. Such a charter would have endowed the lodge with valuable state accreditation.[23] Disparagement by whites of the legitimacy of black Freemasonry mounted: a correspondent criticized the selectmen of Boston in 1820 for permitting "the town to be annually disturbed by a mob of negroes, whose parade and pageantry are as useless, unmeaning, and ridiculous, as their persons and the atmosphere... are offensive and disgusting."[24] Adding to the pressure to resolve these matters were requests from the New York lodge for chartering and from Providence for assistance.[25]

The above failures, as well as the urgent need to invest the lodge further with the requisite authority to expand black Freemasonry legitimately, inspired Grand Master Hilton, Paul, and other members of 459 to abandon any further efforts to accredit themselves through the state or any established Masonic organizations. Instead they determined to invest themselves alone with a Masonic authority they had never previously assumed in full. Perhaps they also wished to isolate themselves from the controversies swirling around white Masonry after the abduction and murder of William Morgan, a Mason in upstate New York who threatened to divulge Masonic secrets.

On June 26, 1827, they published in a Boston newspaper their "Declaration of Independence."[26] The declaration asserted that the existing grand lodge on its own possessed the legitimate authority to control the expansion of black Freemasonry. This action differed fundamentally from those taken in 1791 and 1808 to denominate African Lodge No. 459 a grand lodge, for it was vastly more public and decisive in breaking organizationally with white Masonry than the earlier measures. The compact and momentous statement first of all asserted that we "hold in our possession a certain unlimited Charter," their 1784 charter from the Grand Lodge of England. This chartering, proclaimed Hilton, "was to us, as Masons, as great an event as the Declaration of Independence was to the people of the United States."[27] Over the ensuing years, the declaration observed, the lodge had functioned regularly, but "for the want of one" with the requisite Masonic knowledge, it had not been able to move to the higher levels to which a "well-educated Lodge of Masons" would aspire. Nevertheless, the past several years in particular had brought its members to such a "degree of proficiency in the art" that they could now state "that we can at any time select from among us many whose capacity to govern enables them to preside with as much good order, dignity, and propriety as any other Lodge within our knowledge." Gentlemen "whose knowledge of Masonry would not be questioned by anyone" were ready to attest to this "proficiency." The lodge, it continued, had written the Grand Lodge of England to apprise it of 459's recent "rise and progress" so "we might be placed on a different and better standing than we had theretofore." Unfortunately, "we have never received a single line or reply from that Hon. Society," despite waiting a very long time. The lack of a reply, the African Lodge's "remote situation" from England, and the pressing need to advance black Freemasonry had led Hilton and others to conclude that "with what knowledge we possess of Masonry, and as people of Color by ourselves, we are, and ought by rights, to be free and independent of other Lodges. We do therefore, with this belief, publicly declare ourselves free and independent of any Lodge from this day, and that we will not be tributary, or be governed by any other lodge than that of our own." With this brilliantly incisive statement, which asserted the indubitable Masonic regularity of this independence along with the special imperatives placed upon the members "as people of Color by ourselves," African Lodge No. 459 decisively launched itself and the African American Freemasonry it led as an organization that was not "tributary" to any other lodge in the world.

Hilton and the other members did not take this pronouncement lightly. Yet they recognized it was absolutely necessary if black Masonry was to expand and prosper, to sustain the distinctive orientation it had against slavery and racial inequality, and to continue as an institution avowedly consistent with Masonic laws. As Martin Delany would later aver, what else could African American Masons have done "but establish an independent jurisdiction? If they desired to be Masons, they must do this; indeed, not to have done it, would have been to relinquish their rights as men, and certainly be less than Masons."[28] Simultaneous with the declaration's announcement, African Lodge No. 459 was negotiating with New York's Boyer Lodge No. 1 to charter it. Only after the lodge had declared its independence and Boyer recognized that independence did the members agree, as they recorded, to extend "the Independent Charter" to Boyer.[29] Never again would these black Masons seek a charter or renewal from a white Masonic organization. Yet this declaration in no way indicated a turning away from the ideal of fellowship with white Americans, Masonic or otherwise. Only a few months earlier, in January, Hilton and the African Lodge had publicly lauded both the efforts of a congressman from New York City to secure the release of a free black man from illegal detention and Daniel Webster's "indefatigable exertion...to put an end to the horrid, unnatural, and inhuman traffic in blood." "It is the prayer of the Lodge, that the choicest blessings of heaven may be showered down on the heads of the above named friends of...the rights of man,...that they may be made more fit recipients of that Crown of Glory, which await the righteous and merciful."[30]

The declaration of independence and the expansion of black Masonry in the latter 1820s and beyond cannot be understood properly without acknowledging the contemporary emergence of a broader black political and antislavery activism with which they were both integrally intertwined. The declaration simultaneously addressed an insular Masonic issue and a broader civic one. The dramatic abolition of slavery in New York in July 1827 brought renewed attention to both the vanquishing and the persistence of slavery. The launching of the nation's first black newspaper, *Freedom's Journal,* in March 1827 and its undergirding network of agents stretching from Massachusetts to North Carolina strengthened the bonds connecting the nation's free black communities. Hilton and several other Boston blacks were key supporters of the newspaper.[31] The journal was also the primary voice in a rising chorus of black opposition after 1825 to the American Colonization Society (ACS), a popular organization promoting the removal of free blacks to Liberia in West Africa. Innovative and explicitly political groups such as the Massachusetts General Colored Association—an organization that included numerous Masons—added their voice to this protest. It was precisely such favorable soil that allowed for the unprecedented pronouncements of another member of 459, David Walker, to emerge in 1829 and electrify blacks throughout the North and even in the South with his vehement appeal against slavery, colonization, and racial injustice.[32] Of course, this interregional mobilization among blacks would become even more extensive in the 1830s. Among other forces, the growth of black Masonry in the latter1820s was critical to these later leaps.

Indeed, as the African Lodge participated in this swelling African American struggle against slavery and racial inequality, its expansion encompassed those racial struggles and accomplishments beyond its own shore as well. The new lodge hall in 1826 would be a focal point of several large parades in the latter 1820s that heralded the increasing vigor of the lodge. In August 1828, for example, the African Lodge hosted a large parade and dinner to honor Prince Abduhl Rahahman, a West African prince of Footah Jalloh recently manumitted from forty years of slavery in Natchez, Mississippi. Rahahman had become a cause célèbre of the ACS, which underwrote his tour of the northeastern seaboard to raise money for the purchase of his family in Natchez and their joint return to Liberia. The ACS hoped that once repatriated, he would launch commercial ventures linking the society's new colony with Timbuktu and the surrounding interior of Africa. However, the Masons' numerous encomiums to him referred not at all to the colonization enterprise, praising him instead as an emblem "[t]hat Africa's children of right should be free," that all in the South should share in this liberation. Of the eighteen men offering toasts to Rahahman following the dinner for him at the new African Lodge, sixteen were Masons, among them John T. Hilton.[33]

The connection of black Freemasonry in the 1820s to the struggles of people of color elsewhere in the Atlantic world was made explicit with Haiti. At the celebration of Prince Rahahman, Haiti particularly commanded the attention of the orators. Oliver Nash, a Mason, extolled "[t]he Island of Hayti, the only country on earth where the man of color walks in all the plenitude of his rights." Cato Freeman, another Mason, echoed this acclaim: "Haytien Independence, founded on the basis of true republican principles; may that government be as happy as its institutions are permanent."[34] Boston's black Masons had long upheld Haiti: in his 1797 charge to the lodge, Prince Hall recounted the horrors of slavery and racial debasement in the French West Indies but then exclaimed, "[B]lessed be God, the scene is changed...from a sink of slavery to freedom and equality," referring to the black insurgency launched in Saint-Domingue (Haiti's name when it was a French colony) and elsewhere in the French West Indies by 1791.[35]

By the 1820s, the island nation had acquired an even greater significance for the lodge, revealing vital new ways in which black Freemasonry would herald the extension of Masonic ideals into America and beyond. Encouraged in the early 1820s by their colleague and fellow Mason Prince Saunders, both the Reverend Paul and Hilton by 1824 had become principal proponents in Boston of African American emigration to Haiti. Indeed, Paul and Saunders, who both went to England in 1815, had visited Haiti together in 1817.[36] Paul returned to Haiti in 1823 as a representative of the Massachusetts Baptist Home Missionary Society.[37] Haitian emigration had long been promoted by Saunders's friends, the British abolitionists William Wilberforce and Thomas Clarkson, and embraced by the Haitian King, Henri-Christophe in 1818 before his death. Once Jean-Pierre Boyer became president of the newly reunited Haiti in 1823, he envisioned emigration as a means for both increasing and improving the cultivation of Haiti's lands while possibly currying favor with a United States whose recognition he sought. By 1824, Loring Dewey, a disaffected member of the ACS who found little support among African Americans for emigration to Liberia, and Jonathas Granville, Boyer's emissary in America, successfully solicited support for the emigration plan from a number of leading African Americans in the Northeast—especially in Philadelphia, where the eminent Mason the Reverend Richard Allen spearheaded the movement. In New York the prominent teacher and Mason Benjamin Hughes identified himself as "one of the principal promoters" of the plan; he sailed enthusiastically for the island in early 1825. He soon concluded that any emigrant so far with "moderate and reasonable expectations...has realized what he anticipated" in Haiti. "The time, I trust is not far distant," he wrote in 1824, "when all wise and good men will use their influence to place the Free Coloured People of the United States upon the delightful Island of Hayti." Despite all this passionate dedication and hope, many of the roughly six thousand emigrants returned to America by early 1826, discouraged by disease, poverty, linguistic difficulties, and limited land grants that fueled suspicion that the Haitian government really wanted to funnel the mass of the emigrants into rough labor on the distressed sugar plantations.[38]

Nevertheless, the experience of key African American Masons in Haiti likely had something to do with innovating black Masonry in Boston and beyond. Freemasonry had been present in colonial Saint-Domingue since 1738, when the first lodge was established in the town of Les Cayes in the southern province. Though open only to white colonials, Freemasonry there grew slowly through the mid-eighteenth century. In the 1780s, the growth of lodges exploded, numbering about forty with a thousand members or more by 1790. Although Freemasonry in Saint-Domingue declined over the years following the outbreak of the tumultuous slave insurrection in August 1791, it sustained a presence in the south around Port-au-Prince and Les Cayes. In those areas, John Garrigus argues, not only progressive white Masons predisposed "to create a more integrated society" belonged to lodges, but likely several free people of color as well. Elsewhere black military leaders of the insurgency—including, it is speculated, the leading black general, Toussaint L'Ouverture—joined Masonic lodges.[39] The peripatetic movements of blacks and whites between the French West Indies and the eastern seaboard of the United States may have fertilized fledgling Masonic connections among people of color. African American mariners sailed often to Saint-Domingue during the commercially lively 1790s and the early part of the new century. Harry Davis has speculated that some became Masons there. In January 1785, a "Mr. Toussain Courtmanche" was made a "master" at the African Lodge in Boston. Throughout the 1780s and beyond, Jean-Louis Glapion, a mulatto hairdresser from France or, possibly, from the French West Indies, was a key Masonic associate of Hall's who apparently was initiated into Masonry elsewhere. In the early 1780s, he had encouraged Hall to apply to France for a charter, the source at that time of all charters in the French West Indies.[40]

Apparently Freemasonry spread steadily among Haitians over the years after their declaration of independence from France on January 1, 1804. Though it was no longer formally linked with the Grand Orient of France, which had chartered the colonial lodges, Haiti's Provincial Grand Lodge secured some sanction from the Grand Lodge of England in 1809. That endorsement led to the creation of four lodges in the south at Jacmel, Port-au-Prince, Les Cayes, and Jeremie under the authority of Alexandre Petion, the leader in 1812 of the southern half of the then-divided Haiti. After Petion died in 1818, Boyer became not only the president of Haiti but also the "grand protecteur," or grand master, of the Provincial Grand Lodge. On May 25, 1823, the Provincial Grand Lodge, perhaps frustrated over limits placed upon the control it could exercise over lodges in the country, declared its independence from any other grand lodge and founded the Grand Orient of Haiti, which by 1826 comprised at least seven lodges. Thus when the numerous African American leaders of the Haitian emigration movement—many of whom were Masons—arrived in Port-au-Prince in 1823 through 1825, they encountered a Freemasonry on the island centered in Port-au-Prince that was vigorous and independent—and perhaps already connected in one way or another with their own.

The direct relationship of the Haitian 1823 declaration to the virtually identical one by African Lodge No. 459 in June 1827 is quite likely. Knowledge of the 1823 action could also have been promoted by Granville, who also was a deeply dedicated Mason. Indeed, a committee of the Massachusetts state assembly was appointed to investigate Freemasonry in the state amid the anti-Masonic furor and determined, among many other findings, that "an African Grand Lodge now exists, in Boston, deriving its charter from a Masonic body in Hayti." While certainly incorrect, the finding nevertheless illustrates that some local source(s) understood, however roughly, the degree to which exchanges between Haiti and black Freemasonry in Boston had occurred and that, at the very least, the grand lodges of both had officially recognized each other. Although the emigration project eventually collapsed, this encounter extended Masonic connections between black Americans in the North and Haitians in ways that remain almost wholly unexplored by historians. The renaming of the lodge in New York City as Boyer African Lodge No. 1, likely in 1825 or soon thereafter, further testified to the strength of these interconnections. Yet most significantly for our purposes, Haitian Freemasonry likely revealed to African American Masons how they might advance their organization with due regularity to promote their "flourish-ing" in a society freighted with racial barriers.[41]

Fraternal bonds with Haiti deepened in other ways as well in the 1820s. In the 1810s, Number 459 had at least three members with French names—Thomas Revalion, Victor Vilmore, and C. A. De Randamie—the latter of whom was almost certainly Haitian. In 1823, the lodge elevated "Brother Donatien Le Marois to the Sublime Degree of Master Mason." Other men with French-sounding names—Davalent and Orage—were present at meet-ings in the mid-1820s. In April 1825, "Mr. Thomas J. Ramsay of Cape Haytien" received the first three degrees at the lodge. A few months later, "Mr. George K. Barry of (Jacmel) Hayti" was initiated into the lodge. In October 1827, a petition for the first degree of Masonry from "Mr John Cornel of Vermont Hait[i]" was presented to the lodge. Other long-standing members—including Louis Blancard, John Courreaux, and John Pero—had French names. Some of these men apparently had direct familial relations to Haiti; it is not as clear for the others, although connections may be surmised given the great influx of migrants from the French West Indies into eastern seaboard towns from 1790 into the early decades of the nineteenth century. The records also reveal that in 1829, C. A. De Randamie and his family as well as Louis Blancard had relocated to Cape Haytien, where they planned to establish a mercantile house that would market goods sent to them by their Masonic brethren in Boston. The seed of such enterprise was planted during the emigration movement of 1824 and 1825, which President Boyer—in the final stages of concluding negotiations with France for recognition of the island's independence—hoped would help more broadly to renew commer-cial relations with the United States: "The United States will find their com-merce with Hayti enlarged by the frequent intercourse which these new

Haytiens [i.e., African American immigrants] will naturally hold with the country they have left." Because fraternal ties likely facilitated exchange, commercial prospects for black Masons in particular were probably expedited. Perhaps the presence in Port-au-Prince of two agents—W. R. Gardiner and William B. Bowler—for *Freedom's Journal* benefitted De Randamie and Blancard as well. In the 1820s, the multifarious example of Haiti—"the basis of true republican principles" and "the only country on earth where the man of color walks in all the plenitude of his rights"—would prove integral in the expansion of African American Masonry.[42]

By lauding Haiti and its roots in a vast insurgency of black slaves, African American Masons sharply distinguished their understanding of the proper implementation of Masonic principles in the world from that of their white brethren. Unlike white Freemasons who exclusively affirmed the creation and accomplishment of the American nation, African American Freemasons directly challenged the inequalities and stark deficiencies of the nation while simultaneously embracing an identity with it and whatever virtuous ideals it upheld. They were certain the challenges they directed were fundamentally grounded in the precepts of Masonry. No one deployed these complicated twin objectives of opposition and identity more adroitly than John T. Hilton.

On June 24, 1828, the Festival of St. John the Baptist—the most important day in the annual calendar of Freemasonry—Hilton addressed a large convocation of Masons at what was now designated African *Grand* Lodge No. 459. This oration was the first formal recorded statement before the lodge since the declaration of independence issued just a year earlier—it was in fact an *inauguration* of a newly renovated black Freemasonry. It well summarized Hilton's understanding of the meaning of that independence, how it enhanced the mighty confluence of Masonry, Christianity, and republicanism in the black lodges' ongoing endeavor to extend Freemasonry and uplift America to racial justice and equality. Hilton commenced by praising Hall and other founders of African Masonry for introducing the blessings of the Craft into America, which enabled the lodge members "to unite the hearts of many of our colour together." He continued, "[T]he firm attachment to the principles of the Order, and the brotherly affection which cements us into one body of friends and brothers, all declare the sincerity of our intentions, and proves the Institution to be productive of the greatest good." Though Masonry lacked the saving grace with which only God might bless them, its extolling of benevolence, love, peace, and charity made it an essential handmaiden of Christian faith. Hilton admonished his audience to strive, like their virtuous predecessors, "to enter in at the straight gate, by combining Masonry and Christianity together, and by living a holy and religious life." The young nation afforded further paradigms of this virtuousness in its revered patriots, especially Washington, Clinton, Lafayette, and Warren of Bunker Hill, all of whom were Masons. Hilton's call to the African Lodge to participate in this reverence significantly summoned black Masons to attach to an American identity, an idea that had not characterized their earlier charges and orations.[43]

But Hilton upheld that which was Masonic, Christian, and republican in the nation in order to excoriate it all the more vividly for its racial barbarity.

> But brethren, it is a source of pain to me to state, that while we are here, partially enjoying the fruits of liberty…there are in this boasted land of liberty, christianity, and civilization, over twenty hundred thousand of our race kept in perpetual slavery, without one ray of hope, of their ever being released from their state of bondage, but by death.…Americans, does not this picture of human depravity…curdle the blood in thy veins, and move you so to implore the aid of your God to assist in removing this foul spot from thy fair country's name?

While America's virtue was to be embraced and lauded, its shocking corruption was to be condemned and fought vehemently, especially as its victims were one's racial fellows. Hilton's rhetoric embedded blacks within the traditions and virtues of the young nation—not only would they remain in America, but they were an inextricable part of its meaning and promise. Yet that identification also bound them more closely with the nation's sins and the mandate to eliminate them. Immediately after his denunciation of America's racial crimes, Hilton returned the audience to a moral poise: "It is not my intention to awaken any feelings but those which will be consistent with the services of the day. But while we are here assembled under our own vine and fig-tree, enjoying those blessings which true liberty imparts, it is natural, yes, and our duty to advert to the causes which oppress our brethren, and endeavour to find out some means of redress for their grievances; and to offer our sincere prayers for their speedy deliverance from their bondage." In a brilliant deployment of images simultaneously Christian, Masonic, and American, Hilton fused the tenets and imperatives of all three to envision a prompt and determined excising of the scourge of slavery.[44]

Paramount to achieving this cleansing was the fact of the African Lodge's own recent independence: "Brethren let me admonish you not to forget that you have declared yourselves independent.…Let us endeavor to support and maintain it, with credit to ourselves and honour to our Fraternity; that, by our examples, mankind may see, we know how to appreciate the true value of free and liberal institutions." Black Masonic independence and expansion were inextricably allied with black freedom and moral improvement; neither could prosper without the other. "Moved by its pure principles, and animated by its benign influence, we have been attracted to this place as to a common centre; and on this foundation have we been enabled to establish our Masonic Independence." Hilton communicated a lustrous vision of Masonry's promise to vanquish human discord, violence, and hatred. Vigorously yoking black Masonry with an American identity, he imbued the Craft with a singular significance in the struggle for racial justice and universal fellowship never before stated so explicitly. He had successfully transformed it into "this foundation," "a common centre" whose "refulgent rays" would soon render "Locks and Keys, Swords and Spears... useless."[45]

On this primary day of the lodge's rededication of itself to the principles of Masonry, as Hilton affirmed the coherence of this select clustering of men, he reached beyond this insularity by extending the meaning of Masonry to include antislavery specifically and to require his brothers to project their renewed understanding and influence into the communities and nation beyond the lodge walls. Antislavery was not partisan politics that the members were to eschew within the Lodge—Masonry and the fellowship, fraternity, and love at its core were fundamentally antislavery. The life of the brothers within the lodge was critical to enlarging their understanding of these principles. But they must now strive to foster more lodges among men of color, extend this knowledge, and provide enlightened leadership for the destruction of slavery, racial injustice, and racial hatred.[46] On June 24, 1828, Hilton summoned his brothers to an unprecedented mission—we must use our organization and wisdom to destroy this "human depravity" and regenerate the nation stained by it. Called out of their insularity, on the one hand, through a much fuller identification with America, they were, on the other, summoned from it by the Masonic imperative to vanquish human bondage and exploitation. Through the agency of an expansive black Freemasonry with a quickened understanding of its antislavery mission, Hilton hoped to help launch America toward "a new era in the moral world."

After Hilton's passing in March 1864, a eulogist wrote of him that

> His mental and moral excellencies won for him a prominence among those identified with him by complexion and condition; and in the Conventions of colored people, held in those early days throughout the States, his presence and influence were signally potent.... Attached to his fellow men by the triple cord of Masonry, Church fellowship and Anti-Slavery association, he was conspicuous in each.[47]

No phrase was more aptly applied to Hilton than that of "the triple cord." A likely founding member of the pioneering Massachusetts General Colored Association in 1826 with other fellow Masons, including David Walker and

Thomas Paul, Hilton also was a key early supporter of *Freedom's Journal*.[48] Throughout the 1830s, he was an active leader of the Adelphic Society, a literary and oratorical society dedicated to moral improvement among blacks. In 1833, he was elected the vice president of a temperance society for people of color.[49] Throughout the antebellum era, Hilton was zealously dedicated to the African Baptist Church in Boston, whose original minister, Thomas Paul, had nurtured and promoted him when he first arrived in the city. He long served as the clerk for the church. He was an original and enthusiastic supporter of William Lloyd Garrison and his newspaper, the *Liberator*. In February 1831, a month after Garrison began publication, Hilton allied with numerous other local African Americans—many of whom were also Masons—to denounce the ACS and to help author a local indictment of the movement that soon appeared in Garrison's famous *Thoughts on African Colonization*. The committee discerned "with lively interest, the rapid progress of the sentiments of liberty among our degraded brethren, and that we will legally oppose every operation that may have a tendency to perpetuate our present political condition."[50]

Throughout the antebellum years, Hilton was closely allied with the Garrisonian wing of the American abolitionist movement, and he personally came to the defense of the controversial Garrison on numerous occasions.[51] He was a long-serving member of the board of managers of the Massachusetts Anti-Slavery Society. He was the president of a committee including numerous other white and black Garrisonians that fought successfully from 1844 to 1855 to dismantle the racially segregated Smith School in Boston and integrate the city's public schools.[52] Hilton was a principal organizer of British West Indian Emancipation celebrations in Boston from their inception.[53] Moreover, in 1833 he eulogized William Wilberforce, one of the progenitors of that emancipation.[54] Hilton presided over the meeting in Boston in August 1843 to support the upcoming National Negro Convention in Buffalo, to which he was also sent as a representative.[55] However, when an effort was made in 1848 by several local blacks to create a separate all-black antislavery society, Hilton opposed it.[56] In October 1850, he was one of the principal authors of "The Declaration of Sentiments of the Colored Citizens of Boston on the Fugitive Slave Bill," which vehemently condemned the bill and encouraged the continued flight of the enslaved from the South. In an "eloquent and earnest speech" he gave at the mass meeting to endorse the declaration, he challenged all people of color whose liberty was threatened to "not be taken alive, but upon the slave-catcher's head be the consequence."[57] As the clerk for the African Baptist Church, Hilton called for a Fast Day for "all colored churches throughout the United States" on September 28, 1831 to express sympathy for our "afflicted brethren groaning so sadly under every species of cruel barbarity" in Virginia where Nat Turner had only recently rebelled. Perhaps such boldness caused one nervous commentator later that year to aver that black Masons "of all others are most forward in promoting the spirit of revolt among slaves.... [To them] I attribute the late melancholy occurrences in Southampton and other places." Though not possessing the stature of Hilton, numerous other black Masons and their lodges in the North nevertheless replicated this active engagement with abolition and community improvement.[58]

Despite the damage done to white Freemasonry during the anti-Masonic movement of the late 1820s and early 1830s, black Freemasonry suffered little from the popular opprobrium. Indeed, it experienced dramatic growth into the 1840s. Up to 1825, seven black lodges existed in the North—one in Massachusetts, four in Pennsylvania, one in Rhode Island, and one in New York. Between 1825 and 1847, however, no fewer than seventeen lodges were added to a black Masonic movement that now included lodges in Maryland, the District of Columbia, New Jersey, and Ohio.[59] With the opening of St. Cyprian in Pittsburgh in 1846 and Corinthian in Cincinnati in early 1847, African American Freemasonry had passed into the trans-Allegheny West, from where its expansion would accelerate in the 1850s into Indiana and Illinois. By 1847, there were also four grand lodges—one in Massachusetts, one in New York, and two in Pennsylvania.

Growth had indeed been so extensive that conflicts and misrepresentation arose commensurately with it. Fraudulent agents circulated widely and bilked the gullible with fake documents: Richard H. Gleaves, the indefatigable builder of black Masonry in the late antebellum Ohio and Mississippi River valleys, found Cincinnati rife with them in the late 1840s. In 1847, it had been necessary for him to "cleanse" and charter an illegitimate lodge in that city.[60] A leading Massachusetts Mason of the Civil War and Reconstruction era, Lewis Hayden, was apparently lured into another spurious one in Boston in 1846 called the United Brethren, contrived by a white man who cheated them of their money.[61] In 1847, two competing grand lodges in Pennsylvania—Hiram and Independent African—fostered pitched crises over the chartering of lodges there. All of these frauds and embarrassing duels sullied the movement and its stature as the fraternity of the "better Masons."[62]

Into this diverse fray, John T. Hilton would step once again. Hilton immediately proposed convening an assembly of all African grand lodges during the Festival of St. John the Baptist in Boston in late June 1847. The convocation would resolve their jurisdictional disputes and create a new overarching authority—the National Grand Lodge (NGL). Probably the earlier step to proclaim black Masonic independence laid the foundation for this new step to distinguish black Freemasonry organizationally even more decisively from white Masonry. One of the first accomplishments of the NGL was to "heal" the improperly certified grand lodge, Hiram, and resolve the dispute between the two grand lodges of Pennsylvania. More broadly, the NGL would now serve to verify the legitimacy of all grand lodges, to regularize further growth among all affiliated lodges, and to adjudicate any future jurisdictional disputes that might arise among them "so that every colored Mason in the United States could enjoy the same privileges and protection and not be divided."[63] By July 1847, Hilton had been appointed as the NGL's first grand master. The swift acclaim for this organizational advance was illustrated by the mounting of one of the largest exclusively black antebellum parades in New York City on June 26, 1848 during the convention of the NGL in that city. It included many of the members of thirty or more black lodges from throughout the Northeast who marched at length in lower Manhattan and was probably second in scale only to the grand procession celebrating abolition in the state on July 4, 1827.[64] As Samuel Van Brakle, a key participant in the 1847 meeting, wrote a few years later, "[T]he several Grand Lodges working under the jurisdiction of the National Grand Lodge of Color of these United States . . . will sweep down, and carry into oblivion all spurious and pretended aspirants that infest our country."[65]

The NGL by no means ended conflict among antebellum black Masons. In fact, the New York Grand Lodge soon bitterly withdrew from the NGL, which in turn freighted it with all sorts of opprobrium.[66] Many of the newly spawned lodges in Ohio and other western states refused to affiliate with the NGL—in large part because of fears that it improperly infringe the jurisdiction of the state grand lodges. In the 1860s, Lewis Hayden attempted to alleviate their fears by emphasizing that only lodges within a state, not the NGL, could create grand lodges and that the NGL in no way threatened their authority. As he stated, the NGL did not exist to rule over the grand lodges but just the reverse—it existed to reinforce their legitimate rule. Nevertheless, a number of lodges chose to remain outside the web of the NGL.[67] But these difficulties should not obscure the fact that most late antebellum black Masons enthusiastically ascribed to the NGL and that through it an energetic cadre of northern blacks created one of the most extensive wholly black organizations in antebellum America, one that would not only oversee expansion and help to resolve some controversies in the antebellum North but also contribute enormously to black Freemasonry as it rapidly expanded among black men in the early postbellum South.

Yet the significance of the NGL and the black Masonry it helped strengthen and renovate went beyond these structural dimensions, important as they were. Two of the most important black leaders of the nineteenth century who were also ardent Prince Hall Masons—Martin Delany and Lewis Hayden—recognized this greater significance. In 1853, Delany—a member of Pittsburgh's Cyprian Lodge and an eminent black intellectual and activist from the 1840s through the 1870s—designated the creation of the NGL "the most important period in the history of colored Masons in the United States." In 1867, imbued with a poignant knowledge of what a united national government had recently accomplished through the smashing of southern slavery, Lewis Hayden—a former slave from Kentucky who was a leading abolitionist, Mason, and orator in the 1850s and beyond and also served a term as grand master of the NGL—linked the future prospects of black America with its capacity to remain dedicated to the virtues of national unity. A key component of that dedication would be the preservation of the NGL. Indeed, for Hayden, black men laboring through Masonry and the NGL were essential to advancing God's millennial mission for America by purging it of slavery and founding it wholly on freedom and right. The following passage particularly invokes the awesome *national* responsibilities leading African Americans such as Hayden believed black Masons and their racial brethren alone shouldered in the godly transformation of America.

Who among us are ready to say that God had not a great purpose in the organization of the National Grand Lodge? This question is answered in the affirmative to all reflecting minds who have studied our condition as a people in the light of Masonic history.... [I]n accordance with the fixed laws of that Supreme Intelligence, slavery is no more; and in its abolition new elements are developed, and they impose new duties. And are we to learn nothing from the fact that twenty years ago the National Grand Lodge was formed? O ye of little faith! shall we doubt that He who foresees all things did approve and cause that organization to take place at that time, allowing us the intervening space between that time and the present to perfect, complete, and to be now in readiness for the mission assigned to us as a Masonic body?...And now what are the elements most needed in this country, and who are they that are most concerned in maintaining them?...Behold four millions crying, Give us light to guide us!... [I]f our Heavenly Father intends to preserve these United States as one government, he will use the colored men of the country, above all other men, for the purpose of its preservation....And now the Government of the country being national, so should we be national also; and it is well for us that we are so organized as a National Grand Lodge, that the lessons we impart are and must be of a national character, to the end that the unity of the Government may be ever maintained; for all our hopes as a people are involved in the issue, extending even to that of life and liberty. Let us pray, "O God! speed the right!"[68]

Hayden believed that without the NGL, the righteous extension of black Masonry might well collapse. Without black Masonry and the regenerated black race it promised to lead, North and South, the regeneration and enlightenment of America itself would fail. Yet by 1876, the NGL was all but abandoned by the various grand lodges, including that of Massachusetts, as having failed to achieve its moral mission of unity among black Masons. Painful disappointment abounded for African Americans in 1875 that could not have seemed more distant in the first postbellum years. And the salience of this regenerative mission would fade within African American Freemasonry over the years after 1865, perhaps because the religious—and even more specifically, evangelical—imperatives of original black Freemasonry declined as well. Moreover, the hoped-for reformation of white Masonry showed few signs of advance, although the new grounding of the nation on black freedom did create opportunities for some black and white Masons and lodges to experiment with fellowship in the years immediately following the war's end.[69]

But in the year of Jubilee itself, the divine mission of liberation and light unfolded through the Civil War and the NGL's role in it seemed almost self-evident to the leaders of the black fraternity. John Telemachus Hilton was midwife to this illumination. His primacy in establishing a secure foundation for the nationalizing of black Freemasonry through the Civil War was irrefragable. Even a hostile white chronicler of black Masonry regarded Hilton's impact on the movement as so profound that "he probably did more for the lodge than did Prince Hall." When Hilton died in March 1864, a lengthy obituary in the *Liberator* eulogized him and observed how black Masons in full regalia at the grave "performed their mystic ceremonies in honor of one who had been most distinguished in their order." Hilton's "triple cord of Masonry, Church fellowship, and Anti-Slavery association" convened his compatriots on that day, as it had over the past many decades.[70] As they were all now about to witness an allied Masonry and black Christianity advancing in a South over which they had struggled so fiercely to secure a fragile freedom, Hayden's assignment of divine mission to black Masonry only resonated more deeply. Without Hilton, this vital triple cord might never have been entwined to birth a new South and, in Hilton's prophetic words of 1828, "commence a new era in the moral world."[71]

CHAPTER 3

"A Late Thing I Guess"

The Early Years of Philadelphia's African Masonic Lodge

JULIE WINCH

"There was to day a procession of white, and another of black Free-Masons—Absalom Jones, the black Bishop, walked before his brethren to the African Church—the others to St. Pauls—tis the first I have heard of negro masons—a late thing I guess."[1] What the white Quaker diarist Elizabeth Drinker witnessed on June 24, 1797, *was* in one sense "a late thing." For the first time the members of Philadelphia's African Lodge were publicly observing a solemn day in the Masonic calendar, the Feast of St. John the Baptist. Drinker had no way of knowing that the lodge, at least in embryonic form, had been in existence for some time. However, her brief journal entry does capture some of the vital elements in its early history. The black Masons were marching on the same day as the white Masons, but the two bodies of men were not marching *together*, even if they had set out from the same point, nor were they bound for the same destination. Despite their shared devotion to the craft, racial distinctions kept them apart. Then there was the question of leadership. At the head of the procession of black Masons walked the man Drinker described as "the black Bishop," the Episcopal priest Absalom Jones. His presence as master was of the utmost importance. From its earliest days, African American Free-masonry in Philadelphia was closely linked to the nascent black church, and Absalom Jones was a guiding light, real and symbolic, in both institutions.

Drinker's observation actually precedes the point at which the minute book of the Philadelphia African Lodge begins. The minute book commences six months after the march with the entry for the Feast of St. John the Apostle (December 27). On that day the lodge seated its officers for the coming year and listened to Worshipful Master Absalom Jones as he "Deliver'd a fine Prayer and an Excellent Sermon Alluding to the Foundation of Masonry and the advantages thereof."[2] The book ends just over two years later as the lodge was preparing to join in Masonic rites to mark the passing of the former president and Mason George Washington. Within that relatively short span of time, though, the lodge truly came into being, and a great many things happened that speak not simply to the institutional history of the African Lodge but to the role of the lodge and its members in the life of the free community of color in Philadelphia and beyond.

This chapter focuses on the activities of the Philadelphia African Lodge during that formative period, but it seeks to do more than simply recount the doings of the brothers at their weekly meetings. The minute book provides us with the names of that first cohort of Masons, but we need to put faces to those names to understand what the lodge really represented. Who were these early Masons? How many had known what it was to be the property of another human being? Did the specter of slavery continue to haunt them once they had secured their freedom? Were they and the lodge involved in any way in advancing freedom among African Americans during this turbulent decade? How did they grapple with the day-to-day realities of life in Philadelphia? How did they support themselves and their families? Where did they live? Where and with whom did they worship? What did they know of the world around them? What drew them to the craft and what set them apart from other men of color for whom Freemasonry had no real attraction, or for whom, despite an interest, the lodge doors were closed?

The lives of the individual brothers only begin to take on real meaning, though, when they are compared with the broader collective experience of local African Americans. Whites described the black- and brown-skinned people who lived among them as "Africans," ignoring the reality that by the 1790s only a sprinkling of Philadelphia's "Africans" had ever set foot on the African continent. The vast majority had been born in America or the Caribbean. And yet "African" was the term Absalom Jones and his brothers applied to themselves and their institutions, including their lodge. Regardless of where they had been born, they identified themselves as children of the diaspora. Africa mattered to them, albeit in a different and far more subtle way than it did to whites.

The Philadelphia that the members of the African Lodge knew in the late 1790s was small by our reckoning, but by contemporary American standards, it was a metropolis. The Delaware River was the city's lifeline. Warehouses, shipyards, sail lofts, and ropewalks provided employment for many hundreds of men, black and white, skilled and unskilled. A block or two from the river were all manner of markets and stores where everything from eggs and butter to fine Chinese porcelain and Indian muslins were to be had, depending on one's taste and means. Trade had improved dramatically after Britain and France had gone to war in 1793, and it continued to improve as much of the rest of Europe was drawn into the conflict. The demand for American foodstuffs and other commodities soared. Philadelphia witnessed a building boom, fueled at least in part by the upsurge in commerce. The ravages of the British military occupation of 1777–78 had left their mark, as had the devastating outbreaks of yellow fever in the 1790s, especially 1793. By 1797, when the African Lodge was formed, yellow fever showed ominous signs of becoming a regular summer visitor. Nevertheless, despite the periodic crises that Philadelphia endured, the city was growing rapidly. Buildings were going up as far west as Sixth Street, although admittedly anywhere west of that was considered to be in the countryside. Beyond the jurisdictional boundaries of the city proper were the unincorporated suburbs of Southwark and Moyamensing to the south and in the opposite direction the Northern Liberties. City officials tended to regard these outlying areas with suspicion because their writs literally did not run there, but those same neighborhoods were home to hundreds of families, black and white.

The city's status as the nation's capital brought in people from all sections of the United States and from overseas. Politicians rubbed shoulders with diplomats. Government clerks and various functionaries mixed with men who called themselves many things but whom we would recognize today as lobbyists. A bustling administrative center and a hub of national and international trade, Philadelphia offered unrivaled economic opportunities to those perceptive enough, skilled enough, and fortunate enough to be able to exploit them. Dire poverty marched hand in hand with "opportunity," especially for the most marginalized of city dwellers among whom "Africans" were overrepresented. Nevertheless, they were a deeply rooted and vital presence in Philadelphia, and, to the annoyance of at least some white Philadelphians, they had no intention of remaining on the bottom rung of society. Among those determined to build much more on what they had already achieved were the men who united to form the African Lodge.

To the consternation of many of Philadelphia's white residents, the "African" population of the city proper and its still unincorporated suburbs grew quickly in the last decade of the eighteenth century. The official tally leaped from almost 2,500 in 1790 to nearly 7,000 in 1800. The number of slaves dropped precipitously, from 387 to 85 in the course of the decade. On paper, roughly 1 in 10 Philadelphians was a free person of color.[3] However, constant complaints charged that the census count fell woefully short and that many hundreds of black people had escaped the notice of the enumerators. Critics from all classes of the white community, from the city fathers worried about law and order to workingmen who feared job competition, declared that Philadelphia was being swamped by hordes of black newcomers, some free but others still legally enslaved in one or other of the states of the Union. Those same critics did grudgingly concede that some of the growth was due to natural increase as longtime black residents formed stable families and produced children.[4] Freedom from bondage meant freedom to spend one's life with the partner of one's choice and freedom from the dreadful prospect of seeing one's children sold away at the whim of an owner. Despite the heavy toll that disease, malnutrition and privation took on the laboring poor of all races, black Philadelphians released from slavery struggled to establish strong family units, and the resulting progeny born into freedom alarmed many in the white community by the mere fact of their presence.[5]

Of course, black people were hardly a novelty in the City of Brotherly Love. Since its founding, Philadelphia had had a substantial African presence. Indeed, from the days of William Penn, slavery had been a crucial element in the city's prosperity. However, by the time of the birth of the African Lodge, the institution of slavery was dying in the city, thanks to the combined impact of the upheavals of the Revolutionary War, changing economic patterns, and the actions of conscience-stricken (or thrifty) white slaveholders. Slave ownership simply did not pay for itself in the Philadelphia of the 1790s. Bondmen and bondwomen could be expensive to maintain. Liberating them to fend for themselves and hiring them as domestics or day laborers when needed proved far more economical than being always obligated for their full maintenance. Those turned loose by masters or mistresses eager to save their money or their souls were joined by others who had managed to buy themselves out of bondage and by a small group of black men and women who had been born free.[6]

While Elizabeth Drinker and many of her white neighbors may have assumed the African Masons parading on St. John's Day were the direct consequence of Pennsylvania's landmark Gradual Abolition Act of 1780, they in fact were not. However enthusiastically they applauded the passage of the law, Absalom Jones and his brethren knew that its true beneficiaries were not they themselves but rather the members of the younger generation. The law declared that children born to enslaved women in Pennsylvania after March 1, 1780, would become fully free only at the age of twenty-eight, serving a lengthy indenture until then. Not until 1808, more than two decades after that memorable St. John's Day procession, would the first cohort be liberated.[7] The Gradual Abolition Act had not freed the men in the lodge: they were free already. Nevertheless, by their very presence and their unmistakable assertion that they had the same rights as white people to assemble in the city's public spaces and march through its streets, they *did* symbolize the change that was taking place in the racial dynamic of Pennsylvania. The prevailing condition of black people in the Keystone State was destined to be freedom, not bondage.

If white Philadelphians could grudgingly accept the presence of Pennsylvania-born free black people and their children, they were far less resigned to the growing numbers of out-of-state "Africans" who were converging on *their* city. Fugitive slaves, so they claimed, were surging in from all points of the compass. These women and men saw in Pennsylvania, and especially in its great metropolis of Philadelphia, the hope of freedom. They also saw in the city's growing free community of color a chance to lose themselves in the crowd and avoid recapture. Added to the fugitives were many hundreds of free people of color from the Upper South, from New York and New Jersey, and from as far afield as New England, who hoped to improve their prospects by starting anew where, they imagined, white people were more tolerant and employment opportunities more plentiful than in the communities they had left. They were joined by another group of newcomers, the so-called French Negroes. The upheavals on Saint-Domingue in the 1790s displaced people of African descent as well as white plantation owners. The refugees flooded into American cities, including Philadelphia. Some of the new arrivals were free and fairly well-to-do *gens de couleur,* while others were the sullen and bitterly resentful slaves of white refugees. As far as most white Philadelphians were concerned, none of them were welcome. Collectively they constituted a discordant element. They didn't look like the local "Africans." They spoke and dressed differently, and some of the mixed-race *gens de couleur* affronted local whites by insisting on equality with them.[8]

Philadelphia's free people of color were not without white friends. The reconstituted Pennsylvania Abolition Society (PAS) was doing its best to plug loopholes in the Gradual Abolition Act and pressure individual slaveholders to free slaves not covered by its provisions. The PAS also sponsored schools, set up what amounted to an employment office for displaced black workers, and generally did whatever the PAS leadership believed would speed the eradication of slavery as an institution and improve the lot of the black community.[9] In addition to the PAS, there were a handful of white charitable and religious groups that were reaching out to the city's African American residents. By and large, though, Philadelphia's free people of color recognized that they must rely on their own efforts.

The formation of the Philadelphia African Lodge was one manifestation of that self-determination in the burgeoning black communal life of the city. It merits being studied in its own right, but to see it in isolation from developments elsewhere in the African American community is to fail to appreciate its full significance. The lodge evolved out of other initiatives, it enriched them, and it paved the way for yet more endeavors. Black Philadelphians built with unprecedented vigor in the 1790s. They founded two churches, St. Thomas's African Episcopal Church (referred to by Drinker and others simply as the "African Church") and the Methodist congregation that would eventually become Mother Bethel, the original seat of worship for the African Methodist Episcopal Church. Both churches sponsored schools. Both organized mutual benefit societies, with members paying into a common fund from which they could draw in time of need. In 1787, as the Founding Fathers were assembling in Philadelphia to craft the federal constitution, Absalom Jones and his brother preacher, Richard Allen, embarked on their own institution building. Although they intended the Free African Society (FAS) to function as a mutual aid society, it soon became much more: out of it grew St. Thomas's Church.[10] The church in turn developed more beneficial societies. And what St. Thomas's did, Richard Allen's congregation at Bethel would also do. One initiative gave birth to another.

Beyond the religious, the educational, and the charitable—or as an extension of them all—people in the African American community began devising strategies to protect their hard-won freedom and expand it into full citizenship. Through the 1790s and beyond, they petitioned the federal, state, and city authorities for everything from a decent place to bury their dead to legislation to punish those intent on reenslaving them. In 1793, the white printer Mathew Carey insulted black relief workers in the aftermath of the yellow fever epidemic by accusing them of apparently plundering the homes of white people they claimed to have helped. Instead of deferring to his defamations, they published a defense.[11] Over the ensuing years they learned to deploy print culture with ever greater effectiveness to serve their many causes. Again and again they insisted on their rights—to be free, to be heard, and above all to be treated as citizens of the new republic. With "African" churches emerging, adults and children thronging to "African" schools, and a crop of "African" benevolent societies combining to provide an economic safety net for black women and men eager to live as free people, white Philadelphians could not miss that a transformation was under way.

Thus when a notice appeared in the *Gazette of the United States* in June 1797 announcing that the "Ancient York Masons, African Lodge No. 44" intended to march on St. John's Day, it amounted to yet another declaration of black self-determination.[12] "[A] late thing I guess," remarked Elizabeth Drinker as she watched Absalom Jones and his brothers pass by her home. Drinker was a perceptive woman, who took a keen interest in everything that went on around her. Likely she appreciated what the procession meant in terms of the city's racial landscape, for black freedom and black independence were in themselves late things in the Philadelphia of the 1790s.

How African Masonry actually developed in Philadelphia is a complex story that varies in the telling depending on whose account one believes. On one point, however, there is general agreement: black Philadelphians were in correspondence with Prince Hall and the members of Boston's original African Lodge No. 459 well before 1797. In 1789, the FAS sent one of its members, nail maker Henry Stuart (his name also appears as Stewart), on a mission to New England to forge connections with other free black organizations there. In Rhode Island Stuart met with the Newport African Union and then traveled to Boston to talk with Prince Hall and the brothers of the lodge. Stuart told the Bostonians about the FAS, and he returned carrying a letter from Prince Hall expressing the lodge's pleasure to learn that the Philadelphians had a "society...built on so laudable a foundation."[13]

In his *Official History of Freemasonry among the Colored People in North America* (1903), William Henry Grimshaw played fast and loose with the text of Hall's letter to the Philadelphians, most likely in an effort to push back the date when the African Lodge in Boston actually came into existence and Hall, as master, began exercising the authority to establish lodges among men of color in other cities. According to Grimshaw, Hall wrote, "Your brother Stewart will inform you by word of mouth of some Masonic proposals we made to him, which I do not care to write at this time." However, when William Douglass, the minister of St. Thomas's African Episcopal Church, transcribed the records of the Free African Society in 1862, he copied Hall's letter in its entirety and found no mention of "Masonic proposals." More recently, historian Charles H. Wesley meticulously worked through Prince Hall's letter book in the archives of the Massachusetts Grand Lodge in Boston, and he found nothing in Hall's correspondence with the FAS in 1789 about Masonry.[14] Grimshaw's version of the exchange of letters between

Hall and the Philadelphians in 1789 simply is not supported by the records themselves. But although they may not have been mulling over Masonic proposals in 1789, men of color in Philadelphia and Boston obviously were moving in that same direction. When all was said and done, the Free African Society and African Lodge No. 459 were committed to the same goal: while both bodies of men labored for "the benefit of mankind," they also worked specifically to advance men of color.

Between 1789, when Henry Stuart visited Boston, and 1797, when they asked Prince Hall to help them formally organize a lodge, at least some individuals in Philadelphia's free community of color apprised themselves of the progress of Boston's Lodge No. 459. They had learned of the charter the Bostonians had received from the Grand Lodge of England, and they hoped it might benefit *them* as well. In a letter to Hall on March 2, 1797, the men constituting the embryonic Philadelphia African Lodge explained who they were and what their standing was within the craft. There were eleven of them all together. Five were masters and Ancient York Masons. One of their number, Peter Mantore, was "a Super-excellent ... Arch and Royal Arch Knight Templar of Ireland, Carricfergus Lodge, True Blues, No. 253." Half a dozen of them had been admitted to the brotherhood in the Golden Lodge, No. 22 in London.[15] They were eager to have a lodge of their own. Five white Royal Arch Masons had "tried" them and declared them worthy. However, when they had approached the white lodges in Pennsylvania for the necessary authorization to function as a lodge, their request had been rejected outright. Apparently the white Masons "fear[ed] that black men, living in Virginia would get to be Masons, too." In any case, so the black committee members told Hall, they were not sure they wanted to be beholden to the white lodges. "We would rather be under you, and associated with our Brethren in Boston...for, if we are under you, we shall always be ready to assist in the furtherance of Masonry among us."[16]

Hall wrote back within days of receiving their letter to give them his qualified approval. He was pleased to learn that they had "received the light of Masonry," as long as they had "got it in a just and lawful manner." Although he was willing to give them "license to assemble and work" under his charter from England, he injected a note of caution. "I would advise you not to take any in at present till your officers and your Masters be installed in the Grand Lodge." At that point he promised to furnish them with "a full warrant instead of a permit."[17]

Did Prince Hall actually travel down to Philadelphia to install the officers of the lodge, as Grimshaw maintains in his *Official History*? Probably not. That episode owes more to Grimshaw's lively imagination than to historical fact. Indeed, the names of four of the eight men he identifies as the officers Hall supposedly installed do not even appear in the minute book. Jones's brother minister, Richard Allen, was not active in the lodge at this point, and neither was Richard Parker or Thomas Depee.[18] It is not so easy, though, to dispute Grimshaw's claim that Peter Mantore became senior warden and that he held that office at least for a short time. Mantore is a singularly elusive individual. Obviously he was a moving force behind the establishment of the African Lodge, but at some point between March 1797, when he helped write the letter to Prince Hall, and December of that year, when the formal records of the lodge begin, he simply vanished. Did he leave Philadelphia? Perhaps, although a more likely explanation is that death removed Brother Mantore from the scene. He left no will, but then, like so many Philadelphians, irrespective of race, he may have had little to leave. As for a burial record, there is a good reason why his passing might not have been noted. The dreaded yellow fever had returned in the summer of 1797. The dead were hastily buried, scores of them in mass graves, and officials gave more thought to addressing the needs of the living than to recording the names of all the dead. Ironically, the epidemic began just around the time of the St. John's Day parade, as the heat and humidity brought out swarms of disease-bearing mosquitoes. Before it had run its course, it had claimed thirteen hundred victims. Among them may have been Peter Mantore and possibly more of the brothers who had marched with him.[19]

In March 1797, eleven men had asked Prince Hall to help them form a lodge. Individual tragedies notwithstanding, by December the lodge was up and running with more than twenty members. Over the next two years there were more deaths and several disownments, but the overall number of brothers doubled.[20] What kinds of men were attracted to the craft? The roster in the minute book is the starting point, but to begin truly to "people" the lodge we need to draw upon a wide range of sources. Inevitably they have gaps. Compiling a record of their lives for future generations of historians to pore over was hardly a major concern of these late eighteenth-century residents. Census takers were a nuisance. Worse, white strangers prying into one's home life could be dangerous. Who knew what their real intent was? And the census takers themselves did not always bother to write down the names of those they questioned. "Blacks" was all they scribbled down for one African American family after another as they crisscrossed Philadelphia. However, even with all their limitations, the censuses of 1790 and 1800 are not without their usefulness. City directories might register a man with a trade while a day laborer or a sailor, regardless of race, might easily be overlooked. Nevertheless, directories add details about occupations and street

addresses that the census takers were not required to include in their enu-
meration. Probate records and deeds? As sources they are weighted against
those with little to leave and no money to buy real estate. However, some of
the brothers did write wills and buy land. Newspapers? With a few notable
exceptions, the members of the African Lodge did not attract the attention of
the press. They were not lawbreakers and hence did not feature in the more
sensational news items, but neither were they among the rich and powerful whose doings were chronicled by the *Pennsylvania Gazette* and its sister
publications. On the rare occasions when the press did take note of someone
in the lodge, editors hardly ever alluded to that individual's Masonic affiliation. Had Peter Richmond, for instance, not lived to such a ripe old age
and not numbered so many prominent whites among his acquaintances, his
Masonic funeral would have passed unnoticed.[21] One would like to know so
much more, but, with all their shortcomings, enough records have survived to
enable us to recover the lives of a significant number of the men who paraded
past Elizabeth Drinker's front door in the summer heat of 1797 or trudged
through the snow and ice in the winter of 1800 to pay their respects to their
departed brother, George Washington. From that body of data the brothers
emerge as a remarkable group of men whose collective experience says so
much about the complexity of Philadelphia's free community of color.

In terms of their origins, Philadelphia's African Masons were a diverse
group. A good number were Philadelphians but not all. Alexander Logan
and Daniel Sampson were New Yorkers. Absalom Jones was from Delaware.
Jeffrey Meade and Jacob Brown came from Maryland.[22] Samuel Saviel had
arrived in Philadelphia from the island of Antigua when he was in his teens
or early twenties. He had married, and he and his wife, Susanna, had raised
two children together, but he kept in touch with his kinfolk back in Antigua
and he remembered them in his will.[23] Saviel was a West Indian, and there
may well have been other brothers from the islands of the British Empire,
but apparently there were hardly any Masons from the French West Indies.
Despite the influx of *gens de couleur* from Saint-Domingue after the fall of
Cap François in the summer of 1793, there is only one French-sounding
name on the lodge roster, that of James Lavade, and no hard evidence regarding Lavade's background. While Masonry would eventually attract some of
the new arrivals from Saint-Domingue, in the 1790s they were probably
preoccupied with adjusting to their new environment and only slowly awakening to the realization that their exile was a permanent one. Incorporation
into Philadelphia's free community of color would happen but not for at least
a decade or two.

Regardless of the individual Masons' origins, some, at least, were decidedly well traveled. New Yorker Daniel Sampson was a mariner, as was the much younger Pennsylvania-born William Harding Jr. Brothers Logan, Meade, and Brown were sailors as well: all five had their "seaman's papers" on file with the collector of customs for the port of Philadelphia.[24] The probate records further reveal the extent of seafaring among the members of the lodge. When he drew up his will, Brother David Duncan (also Dunkin) explained that he was wisely settling his affairs in case he did not return from the lengthy voyage on which he was about to embark. He did return safe and sound, although he died a few years later.[25] Checking crew lists against the directories yields yet more names. In the directories the "official" occupation of various lodge members might be "laborer" or "grocer," but the crew lists indicate that those same men shipped out on merchant vessels when they had the chance of a good berth and they needed the cash.

With all its dangers, seafaring held many attractions for men of color. It was one of the few occupations in which they could expect to be paid the same as white men for facing risks common to all sailors, irrespective of race.[26] Black mariners helped man the ships then taking the produce of Philadelphia's rich agricultural hinterland to ports throughout the Atlantic world. African American sailors from Philadelphia were likely to turn up in London and Liverpool, in ports throughout the Caribbean and South America, and, with the opening of the China trade, in Canton and the East Indies.

That so many brothers were mariners illuminates the complexity of the early African Lodge. Its members were a cosmopolitan group. The initial letter to Prince Hall alluded to the fact that more than half of the lodge's founders had been introduced to the craft in London, one of the world's great sailor towns. Presumably that was also true of some of those who joined the lodge over the next couple of years. At least some had been initiated overseas. We do not know how many of the seafaring black Masons encountered white brothers, either in a distant port or in the cramped forecastle of a merchant vessel, and shared with them their devotion to the principles of Freemasonry. But the likelihood that it occurred is not unreasonable in the turbulent Atlantic of the late eighteenth century and suggests another unexpected way in which white and black may then have allied sympathetically.

Unquestionably there was a downside to having so many seafarers for members. Many of the brothers could be absent for months at a time. However, when the lodge needed to send emissaries to Boston to negotiate its long-awaited warrant with Prince Hall, it was readily able to find a brother willing to ship to New England and arrange for a berth for another brother to accompany him.[27] If seafaring was disruptive in terms of the growth of the African Lodge, it did help the lodge forge links with the wider world of Masonry.

A Freemason was, by definition and by title, "free." However, freedom for a number of the men in the African Lodge was a very new reality. Absalom Jones had worked for years to scrape together the money to buy his and his wife's way out of bondage, while Samuel Saviel had been emancipated by his master. In contrast, James Forten had been born free, as had his father before him.[28] Like Forten, some of the brothers had probably grown up in Philadelphia with their legal freedom assured, but many had not. The available records indicate that most of the members of the lodge were in their late twenties or early thirties in the 1790s. They had spent their formative years in a city where the vast majority of black people were held in bondage.[29] Even the freeborn witnessed on a daily basis what it meant to be a slave, and for most in the lodge slavery was a reality they had experienced first-hand. As for those who had been born outside Pennsylvania, slavery had of course been woven into the fabric of every one of Britain's thirteen mainland colonies. Like their Philadelphia-born brethren, these men had either been enslaved or seen how slavery impacted those around them.

Not surprisingly, family structure reflected the tangled relationships wrought by enslavement. In 1800, Henry Stuart, the man whom the FAS had dispatched to New England back in 1789, lay on his deathbed. He had his will drawn up and summoned several of his closest friends, among them his minister, Absalom Jones, to witness it. In his will Stuart acknowledged his two young children by his wife, Elizabeth. He also recognized as his "natural" child David Carty, the son another woman, Margaret Carty, had borne him. Stuart could, of course, have been confessing to an adulterous relationship, but the situation seems to have been more complicated than that. The FAS, of which Stuart was a highly regarded member, routinely expelled members for violating their marriage vows, and the minute book indicates the African Lodge was not prepared to overlook what the secretary termed "vicious conduct." Although David Carty might have been the offspring of an extramarital affair, he was apparently older than the children Stuart had fathered with his wife. Just possibly the elusive Margaret had been a slave whom Henry Stuart could not marry. If he had secured his freedom and she had not, force of circumstances could well have separated them. Elizabeth was a free woman, and she and Henry were husband and wife in the eyes of the law. Whatever the tangled web that bound Henry Stuart to Elizabeth and to Margaret, clearly, with his minister's blessing, he was trying to do right by *all* his children.[30]

For the men in the African Lodge, Henry Stuart among them, marriage was the norm. Almost all the brothers were married, had been married, or would marry at some point. Samuel Saviel was a widower, as was Absalom Jones. David Dunkin, Alexander Logan, Nicholas Marks, Thomas Mount, Peter Richmond, Henry Stuart, and Henry Wilshire were more fortunate— they all had wives still living in 1800. Although he was thirty-one and still single when he joined the lodge, James Forten wished to marry. What detained him was his determination to establish himself in business and provide well for his widowed mother. Eventually he would marry, and Absalom Jones would officiate at his wedding.[31]

Concern for the welfare of family members was something that mattered to every one of the brothers. Besides its spiritual and intellectual dimensions, membership in the lodge had material advantages: it assured a man that his wife and children would not find themselves destitute if he died. His brothers would see to it that he was given a decent funeral and that his family was supported. The lodge did lose members. By 1800, no fewer than ten of them had expired. The financial as well as the emotional toll on the surviving brothers was considerable, but they did what they could with the money at their disposal, dipping into the "charity box" and from time to time imposing special levies on the membership to help the widows and orphans of deceased members.

Tracking the African Masons by means of the federal census and the city directories clarifies one thing about the composition of the lodge: it did not draw its members from any one particular neighborhood. That reflected the general population pattern in Philadelphia: independent black households were to be found in every ward of the city and every one of its unincorporated suburbs. In some areas there were more African American families than in others; but at least at this stage of the city's history, segregation had more to do with economics than with race. Poorer people tended to cluster in Southwark and the Northern Liberties and on the southern fringes of the city, where rents were generally lower and real estate more affordable for those determined to become homeowners rather than renters. Some black Masons lived fairly close to one another. Every single brother, though, lived on a street where, for good or ill, he was obliged to interact on a daily basis with whites who did the same work as he did and contended with many, although admittedly not all, of the same hardships he and his family faced.[32]

Occupationally, the Philadelphia lodge was not the exclusive preserve of the economic elite of the African American community, yet neither were all its members mired in poverty. Some brothers were craftsmen and others small-scale entrepreneurs. Matthew Black was a brass founder, Henry Stuart was a nail maker—as was Absalom Jones at one point in his life—and George Bampfield was a cabinetmaker.[33] Thomas Mount and Nicholas Marks were grocers, and when he returned home safely from his last voyage, David Dunkin opened a grocery store. Samuel Saviel also sold food, specializing in West Indian limes, which added zest to everyday dishes and kept scurvy at bay. The street vendor John Coates cooked up and sold the spicy delicacy known as pepper-pot soup. James Forten was a sailmaker who operated his own loft. Peter Richmond was a hatter. William Harding Sr. was a gardener and John Trusty drove a coach. The lodge included shipwrights, carpenters, and barbers, some of whom doubled as doctors in an era when bloodletting was regarded as the cure for a host of ailments.[34] Collectively these men constituted the burgeoning African American middle class. However, the lodge also had its share of unskilled laborers.

A few of the brothers were prosperous by anyone's reckoning. Samuel Saviel held title to four thousand acres of unimproved land in western Pennsylvania, in addition to a house and lot in Philadelphia.[35] Absalom Jones owned real estate, as did James Forten, Robert Turner, and at least half a dozen more.[36] Though not yet able to rise to the ranks of property owners, others had at least a modicum of financial security. For this economic upper tier, paying their dues posed no real problem. Others, though, lived a hand-to-mouth existence. They fell woefully behind in their "quarterage" payments to the lodge, and one or two were in such dire straits that they had to ask their brothers for charity—requests the lodge complied with as best it could after ascertaining that the need was real.[37]

On the matter of unpaid dues the lodge was realistic. The officers knew some men who would pay if they could. Whether or not they should be expelled was a matter brothers determined on a case-by-case basis. And then there was the question of seafaring members. A man might be months in arrears simply because he had not been on hand to make payment. After much discussion, the members voted that sailors and others who had been absent from the city for a prolonged period of time should receive a statement of arrears once they returned and be given time—although not too much time—to balance accounts.[38]

Similarly, the brothers' educational attainments varied widely. A few of the lodge members were more than literate; they were decidedly well read. As a child, James Forten had received two years of formal instruction at the Society of Friends' African School. At the same time that he was ministering to his congregation at St. Thomas's and presiding over the lodge as master, Absalom Jones was operating his own school. Samuel Saviel and Peter Richmond left modest libraries, a fact that suggests they could do far more than stumble through a verse or two of the Bible. They were not alone. Jones, Forten, George Bampfield, and a handful of other members had sufficient discretionary income to purchase books. Publishers in this era often solicited subscriptions before they invested in publishing a costly work: they needed to be certain that they would at least be able to cover their expenses. In 1801, Forten, Jones, Bampfield, and Richmond were among the two dozen men of color who helped underwrite William W. Woodward's edition of a translation of a turgid French antislavery novel, which he paired with a reprinting of the selected works of the African-born poet Phillis Wheatley.[39]

If the lodge had its share of educated men with the money to become modest literary patrons, it had others who could not even sign their names. Nevertheless, the minute book evinces the high value it placed on education and enlightenment. Those more fortunate in literary attainments were expected to put their talents at the disposal of the lodge as an institution as well as their brother Masons. Lodge meetings regularly included addresses on the founding principles of Masonry from one of the officers, or an "apprentice lecture" by a man newly admitted to the craft.[40] The Philadelphia brethren honored the principles of Masonry with their reverence for learning and for moral worth, for crafting men of good repute to work together for the betterment of society as a whole, without regard to race, religion, or nationality.

In certain respects the African Lodge resembled the fledgling black churches and the network of benevolent societies. Brothers exercised a degree of moral stewardship over one another and came to the aid of fellow Masons and their families in times of need. Inevitably there was a certain degree of overlapping. However, the lodge was not simply another religious organization or another mutual welfare group. It attracted into the Masonic fold men from different churches. The master was an Episcopal priest, and a goodly number of men from his church were on the roster. Brother Richard Grey was the church's sexton. At various times James Forten and John Church served on the vestry. Robert Turner was buried at St. Thomas's when he succumbed to tuberculosis in 1807.[41] Henry Wilshire, Thomas Mount, Henry Stuart, John Livingston, and other lodge members took their children to St. Thomas's to be baptized. Of course, a man could change his religious affiliation. Nicholas Marks had *his* children baptized at St. Thomas's, but by the time he died in 1816, he had joined Mother Bethel.[42] Whereas Marks was a newcomer to Richard Allen's Methodist congregation, Brother Joseph Houston had been active in it almost from the time of its founding.[43] Others probably moved from one church to another, especially once their options

increased in the first decade of the new century with the formation of black
Presbyterian and Baptist congregations.

Although the hallmark of the lodge was unity across lines of origin, occupation, exposure to slavery, and denominational affiliation, harmony did not
always prevail in the craft. From time to time, tensions surfaced. What, for
instance, was behind Brother Davis's "heavy complaint" against Brother
Ross? Or Brother William Harding's formal complaint against the lodge
after he was denied a small sum of money he insisted it owed him?[44] Peter
Nixon, enraged over his expulsion for "improper Conduct," bombarded the
lodge with letters. Since this was an era when the recipient, rather than the
sender, was required to pay the cost of postage, the lodge members informed
their erstwhile brother that they would not receive any more of his missives
unless he footed the bill for them![45]

What lay behind these quarrels between brother and brother, or between
an individual brother and the lodge? The minute book is silent. It was sufficient to record that a parting of the ways had taken place. Men fell out with
one another for many reasons—a perceived slight, a dispute over money, a
difference of opinion that could not be resolved with a shake of the hand or
an agreement simply to disagree. The brothers were proud men, champions
of their community, ready to speak up when the need arose and defend themselves and other people of color when white lawmakers proposed discrimina-
tory legislation or white busybodies like Mathew Carey libeled them. That
they occasionally clashed with one another was hardly surprising. Wrangling
saddened the lodge and was quickly passed over in the official record. It was
far better to focus on fraternal feelings than to rehash who had said what to
whom and why. Why differences arose is occasionally hinted at, though. Not
every brother was prepared to take on every duty assigned him. In the early
weeks of 1798 James Forten missed a lodge meeting, only to learn that he
had been unanimously elected treasurer. He was far from happy, given that
the position demanded a great deal of time and attention. He had just entered
business for himself and could not afford such distractions. He declared that
he "would not Accept of it But...would rather pay his fine." He paid up,
and another brother was chosen to serve in his stead.[46]

Although the secretary liked to be able to record that "The Lodge Closed
in Harmony & Brotherly Love," such accord was not always the case. In the
summer of 1798 something happened that roiled the lodge. So acrimonious
was the dispute that the membership decided the record of the event should
not even be allowed to sully the minute book. A half page was neatly cut
out but not quite neatly enough to obliterate everything: a few lines remain.
Someone, possibly the master of the lodge, lamented that fraternal feelings

had given way to wrangling, "and the Brethren in general Wished that the Members would be more Condescending to Each other."[47]

Generally, though, fraternal feelings *did* prevail. The brothers assembled together and ate together at least once a week. "Called off from labour to Refreshment" was a frequent entry in the minute book. Sociability was a core element in the life of the lodge. On St. John's Day in the summer of 1798, for instance, a well-planned tasty but modestly priced dinner awaited the brothers after they had paraded. The following year it was much the same—a public procession, followed by a "Cold cut." The occasion was both solemn and festive. Any brother who failed to muster and march would still be expected to help pay for the meal his more dutiful brothers consumed.[48] The delinquency was not without cause: St. John's Day observances could occupy an entire day with the solemn procession, the address, the communal meal, and then the business of the Lodge. On a weekday this was a considerable sacrifice for workingmen to make. Lost hours of labor meant lost wages. Even for the self-employed a day of Masonic observance entailed a shifting of business commitments, and perhaps a reliance on wives and grown children to staff a shop or be on hand to inform customers that the man they had come to see would not be available until the following day. Yet the fraternal expectation remained that the brother would make the sacrifice and fulfill his Masonic duty for unity and for proud public procession.[49]

Parades, sermons, Masonic dinners, installations, rituals. Collectively they testified that Philadelphia's African Masons were asserting control over their lives when, in many cases, those lives had not long since been under the control of others. Page after page of the minute book describes the electing of officers, the hiring of a suitable meeting room, and the articulation of those values that Masons believed rendered a man worthy for admission to the brotherhood or unworthy to remain in fellowship. While some were expelled for infractions ranging from neglecting to pay dues to indulging in "vicious conduct," those who proved contrite were generally forgiven, and numerous other men pursued admission to the craft.[50] Applicants were carefully screened by committees appointed for that purpose. Not everyone was admitted on his first application, and one negative vote was enough to sink a would-be Mason.[51]

A major preoccupation of the lodge was what the minute book designated "the Business of the Warrant." Prince Hall had given the Philadelphians a permit and promised them a warrant, by virtue of his lodge's charter from England. The warrant was a long time coming. Without it the Philadelphians lacked the certification they required for proper Masonic expansion, yet they were unsure how best to approach Hall regarding it. Clearly they did not wish to push or alienate this eminent man, but they did want to expedite the matter. How should they proceed? Should they send an emissary? Much debate ensued about who should go to Boston, how his expenses should be covered, and how he should be compensated for weeks, perhaps months, missed from work. The lodge would have to commit to helping his family in his absence. Should they write instead? They determined to write, and Prince Hall replied, but not with the hoped-for warrant. Getting that would take many months of delicate negotiation. In March 1798 the brothers approved a motion by Absalom Jones "that a Letter should be wrote to Answer the one that Came from [B]oston." Brothers William Harding and James Forten composed the letter and submitted it to the entire lodge for approval, and seafaring member Jonathan Harding agreed to deliver it.[52] Nothing happened quickly. Prince Hall observed that the warrant would cost money and his lodge did not have the means to subsidize the Philadelphians. In March 1799 they agreed to pay Hall for "the expenses." Once more Brother Harding was asked if he might travel to Boston, and once more he agreed to go. Another letter was composed formally asking Hall to have the warrant prepared. Brother Bampfield presented the draft and it was unanimously approved. To facilitate the matter, the lodge authorized borrowing thirty dollars—an extraordinary measure— and James Forten and Peter Richmond, men of sufficient standing to secure credit from members of the white community, were commissioned to handle financial matters. Apparently they received a loan from "the Bank," probably Alexander Hamilton's newly created Bank of the United States, and at long last the matter of the warrant sailed toward a successful conclusion.[53]

The minute book records other concerns besides the central one of securing the warrant. What, for instance, should the lodge call itself? Brother Bampfield proposed "Moses African Lodge of Philadelphia." Although white lodges generally avoided taking any title for themselves that suggested affiliation with a particular faith, that was not the case with the early African lodges, and there was a certain ring to "Moses African Lodge." Black preachers often referred to the descendants of Africa as a people who, like the Israelites, had been chosen by God, and the image of a black Moses leading the enslaved and oppressed to freedom, just as Moses had led *his* people out of Egyptian captivity, was a tremendously powerful one. The brethren initially approved of Brother Bampfield's suggestion, but for whatever reason the name change was never carried into effect.[54] Although the records say nothing more about any wrangling over the issue of what to call the lodge, one or two brethren may have had their own suggestions to make. Ultimately, it was simpler and less contentious to continue referring to the lodge simply as "African." No one could quarrel with *that*.

The matter of finding a clean and commodious place in which to meet occupied a great deal of the lodge's attention. After searching for some time for a suitable room and moving from one meeting place to another, the lodge finally agreed to rent a room from Brother Nicholas Marks in the late spring of 1799.[55] Another decade would pass before the African Masons could afford to build a permanent lodge.

Moving from one place to another prompted concerns about the security of the furniture and the lodge's constitution. Absalom Jones took charge of the bylaws, which were apparently written on parchment, so that they could be "sewed together." To lose them or the constitution would compromise the very existence of the lodge and risk having the details of its "mysteries" fall into profane hands. The brothers also arranged to have the lodge's candlesticks, Bible, compass, and square properly stored.[56] The minute book repeatedly recorded the lodge's concern to maintain "good order" and "due form." Brother Bampfield proposed, along with the name change, "that the Lodge should Purchase a Model of our Certificate." And to further the lodge's validity, the brothers voted to pay the considerable sum of twenty dollars to have "the plate and Seal" decently engraved by one of their own members. To finance that expenditure the officers devised an ingenious plan: those who paid for their certificates early would get them first and at a discount.[57]

The degree of exchange with white lodges is not easy to gauge from the minute book, but white Masons did occasionally attend meetings of the African Lodge. The secretary duly noted their names and lodges and added a word or two about the pleasure the African Masons took in receiving them. In October 1799, for instance, five white brothers assisted in raising Thomas Mount "to the Sublime Degree of a Master Mason." John Cox, of Lodge No. 9, presented himself in December 1799, and George Springer, the master of Lodge No. 52, visited the African Lodge a few weeks later.[58] Hiram Levenstine of Lodge No. 88 came back so frequently that when the secretary of the African Lodge drew up the roster he inadvertently included Levenstine's name, confusing him with John Livingston, an African Mason. Obviously Levenstine was a welcome guest, a white brother who was prepared to defy whatever prohibitions his own lodge laid down and offer the hand of friendship to black brethren. And equally obviously the African Masons took pleasure in his attendance at their meetings.[59]

In his *History of Freemasonry* Harry E. Davis maintains that those white Masons like Levenstine who *did* extend a fraternal hand to the African Lodge did so at considerable risk to themselves. Supposedly, in 1797, when the African Lodge first came into being, the Pennsylvania Grand Lodge threatened with expulsion anyone in its own lodges who countenanced the African one, declaring it a "clandestine" or illegitimate lodge.[60] Davis's characterization accords with the account Peter Mantore and his friends gave Prince Hall about their rejection by the white lodges. On the other hand, the African Lodge obviously did have white friends. Moreover, on St. John's Day no one chased the African Masons from the streets.

Thanks to the observant Elizabeth Drinker, we know that the black and white Masons ended their parades in 1797 in different locations. What she does not tell us—most likely because she did not know—was where the brethren set out from. Possibly the Masons, black and white, had assembled at the same point, set out along the same route, and then separated to attend their own churches. But perhaps that was not the case. Perhaps the two processions began as they would end, with a distance between the brethren that was simply unbridgeable. The relationship between the African and the white lodges in Philadelphia in those early years defies easy categorization. The white Masons embraced no blanket acceptance of their black brothers, but neither did they repudiate them universally. Some tentative possibilities for fellowship between the two did exist during this transitional era.

If the relationship of the African Lodge with white Masons is difficult to gauge, so also is the degree of its interaction with various entities within the free black community. That the minute book seldom mentions other organizations is not surprising. Most of the members of the lodge were active in their churches and in numerous non-Masonic mutual benefit societies. Their circles of activity intersected, but they did not overlap completely. On one occasion, though, the African Lodge made a determined effort to reach out. In December 1799 the news reached Philadelphia that George Washington had died. A day of mourning was to be observed on February 22, 1800, President Washington's birthday. All the lodges, white and African, would hold what was essentially a Masonic funeral, albeit one without a body. Brother John Livingston proposed, if the lodge thought it "Consistan[t]," that the members of two other black organizations, the Friendly Society of St. Thomas and the Humane Society, be invited to march with them. The lodge agreed and appointed a six-man committee, including Master Absalom Jones, to communicate with the two societies. The lodge also settled the matter of primacy without rancor. The eldest society, the Friendly Society, would march first, with the other two falling in behind. The occasion was so solemn that every lodge member was told he was expected to march. Absences would simply not be excused.[61]

George Washington's passing led to a remarkable outpouring of grief and to an equally remarkable (if fleeting) moment of unity in Philadelphia, not only among the different African American organizations but between the races. Black preachers eulogized Washington as did white ministers. Richard Allen, not an African Lodge member at this point but known and respected by many of the brethren, publicly lamented "[o]ur father and friend." In his last will and testament Washington had "dared to do his duty, and wipe off the only stain with which man could ever reproach him"—he had decreed that his slaves would receive their freedom.[62] As for the men of the African Lodge, they had ample opportunity to express their grief. They almost certainly joined in the great procession that took place on December 28, 1799, when it seemed virtually every inhabitant of the City of Brotherly Love came out into the streets to honor Washington. On that day "the Grand Lodge" marched, and "Several private lodges" followed behind "according to Juniority."[63] Two months later, on the late president's birthday, the Masons held their own special observances, and the African Lodge once more turned out in force in a shared tribute to a fallen brother. It was a very visible display of what the craft truly *could* be if shared devotion overcame the barriers erected by racial distinctions and the long history of oppression.

With the finalizing of arrangements to honor Brother Washington on his birthday, the first minute book of the African Lodge concluded. Of course, the lodge's existence did not end with it. Perhaps fire, or simply the ravages of time, consumed the next two or three sets of minutes. Perhaps they did survive and are somewhere waiting to be found. As it stands, we simply do not know how the lodge developed between 1800, when the secretary blotted dry the ink on the last page of that first book, and 1813, when his successor took up his pen and began chronicling the lodge anew. By the time the minutes resume, it is clear that the Philadelphians had received their coveted warrant. Death had claimed some of the founding members of the lodge, while others had fallen away or been disowned. However, the inner circle remained much the same—Absalom Jones, Thomas Mount, Peter Richmond, Matthew Black, and others. To their number had been added dozens more African Masons. Some were the sons of the founders. Others were newcomers to Philadelphia, drawn by the increasing richness and vitality of what was indisputably one of the largest free communities of color in the nation. For both the old guard and the new arrivals, the African Lodge, within a generation renamed the Prince Hall Lodge, would remain a core organization within that greater whole. In terms of origins, occupations, religious affiliations, and the like, Philadelphia's African American Masons would continue to be a diverse group. Individually and collectively, they pressed for the end of slavery throughout the Union and for their own community's civil and political rights. And they would continue to find in the craft something that added another layer of meaning to their lives.

CHAPTER 4

Nation and Oration

The Political Language of African American Freemasonry in the Early Republic

COREY D. B. WALKER

> There were some strong words in the Masonic defense and justification: freedom versus slavery, innocence contrasted to vanity and self-interest. The implications of such language, had anyone wanted to draw them out, were subversive indeed.
>
> —Margaret C. Jacob

Three years after drafting the Declaration of Independence, Thomas Jefferson confronted one of the major obstacles to the establishment of a modern political community.[1] Joining such philosophers as Hume, Locke, and Spinoza, who each drafted formidable treatises inquiring into the political status of religion, Jefferson penned his *Virginia Act for Establishing Religious Freedom* in an effort to mitigate the coercive influence of organized religion and affirm the fundamental right of citizens to exercise religious freedom. He grounded the right of freedom of religion firmly on the secular foundations of political authority. While he recognized that religion could promote social restraint and moral improvement, he nevertheless feared that religious doctrines, hierarchies, and passions would threaten the cohesiveness of the political community. Jefferson's argument "that our civil rights have no dependence on our religious opinions" not only insisted on the secular foundations of political community but also reinforced the idea that proper political discourse did not depend on religious languages or ideas. That is, political language appropriate to a modern polity rightfully disavows sectarian religious claims, commitments, and guarantees of traditional religion. With the passage of Jefferson's act in 1786, the political problem of religion was seemingly resolved by asserting that religious *and* political freedom were grounded not in God, but in "the people." The founding of the American republic therefore stands as a watershed event in the modern world.

The bold assertion of the sovereignty of the people, however, fell short in at least two ways of resolving the tensions buried within it. First, although Jefferson grounded the principle of religious freedom in the sovereignty of the people, this did not insulate the political arena from the influences of religion. Indeed, though popular sovereignty came to serve as the legitimate and authorizing foundation for politics in the American nation, it was not able to absolutely restrict the use of religious language, metaphors, and ideas in the cause of politics. Puritan beliefs, New Divinity theology, covenant theologians, and teachers influenced by moral law had a profound impact on the development of political ideas and languages in America's evolving experiment with democracy. Second, recourse to the people opened up the very question of who properly constituted the people.[2] Ethnic and racial minorities, women, and indigenous peoples recognized the severe limitations of this political principle and developed critical strategies to expand its scope and meaning in an effort to reestablish the grounds of political community on a logic of inclusion rather than exclusion. In so doing, they fashioned political languages that did not adhere to the neat and clean divides between religion and politics that statesmen like Jefferson sought to maintain. Instead, they tarried on the boundaries of the religious and the political in advancing their claims for political inclusion.

This chapter investigates how African American Freemasons developed a language to negotiate this complex political landscape and to challenge the formal exclusion of free and enslaved blacks from the American polity. Crucial in this effort was the creation of a heterodox political language that critically blended religious *and* political ideas and pressed them simultaneously into service. African American Freemasons employed the moral universalism of the order as "a source for a particular use of nation language among African Americans as well as a metaphorical framework for understanding the middle passage, enslavement, and quests for emancipation."[3] Freemasonry provided the necessary framework in forming an alternative conception of the political, one that included African Americans as proper political subjects. Working within the interstices of the languages of religion and politics, the African American Freemasons of the early republic fashioned a language that advanced a broader conception of the nation and citizenship in American democracy.

Early African American Masonic orations highlight the complex political language of African Americans as they navigated the fractious early American republic. Freemasonry provided African Americans with a vocabulary and grammar that could be readily adapted to the exigencies of their existence in the early United States. As an integral expression of ideas and ideals of political community, Freemasonry offered African Americans an organization actually challenging American pretensions to a democratic universality. In addition, its "civil theology," free of traditional theological dogma and open to the requisite virtues that characterized membership in a modern polity, complemented the secular language that properly defined the political sphere of American democracy. Indeed, the language of Freemasonry with its appeal to "the brotherhood of man" echoed the universal—yet always already qualified—sentiments of the people and provided a distinctive platform for articulating and fashioning new political identities. By examining the orations of African American Freemasons we can recover a critical dimension of African American and American public life.

Political life in the early republic was far from living up to the democratic ideals espoused in the founding documents of the United States. A protean political language compounding ideas drawn from a vast spectrum of liberalism, republicanism, utilitarianism, Calvinism, Puritanism, and New Divinity theology only complicated this inaugural imperfection and how to navigate competing conceptions of rights, liberty, freedom, and justice.[4] Freemasons injected their own civil theology into this political and ideological maelstrom. It "was not a dogma; rather it marked the parameters of a conversation or debate which rested on the shared assumption that there was some correlation between" an individual, morality, politics, and community.[5] It was grounded in the dignity of human life and a nonsectarian conception of God that sought to align the individual's moral ideals and practices with the proper form of political community.[6]

African American Freemasonry highlighted the utility of this civil theology for contesting the dominant political ideas of the nation. The black lodge functioned as "a social and intellectual space in which the ruling pro-slavery and racist politic was critiqued and the needs of the black community debated and addressed."[7] From the associational medium of Freemasonry derived an African American conception of the nation incorporating them and countenancing their cultural solidarity and political subjectivity.

In an address delivered on the occasion of the Masonic celebration of St. John on June 25, 1797, Prince Hall, the founder and leader of African American Freemasons, used Freemasonry's civil theology to articulate an alternative vision of political community in the United States. Addressing himself to the members of African Lodge, Hall reminded those assembled in Menotomy (Cambridge), Massachusetts, of the time that had passed since his last address and the significance of the structure of Freemasonry: Beloved Brethren: "'Tis now five years since I deliver'd a Charge to you on some parts and points of Masonry. As one branch or superstructure on the foundation; when I endeavoured to show you the duty of a Mason to a Mason, and charity or love to all mankind, as the mark and image of the great God, and the Father of the human race." Hall echoes the sentiments expressed by many Masonic orators of the period who sought to instill Masonic virtues in the assembled members of the fraternity. The key themes of love and charity, so influential in the civil theology of Freemasonry, are equally pronounced in Hall's oration: "I shall now attempt to shew you that it is our duty to sympathise with our fellow men under their troubles, the families of our brethren who are gone: we hope to the Grand Lodge above." We are to have sympathy, but, he continued, "this is not to be confined to parties or colours; not to towns or states; not to a kingdom, but to the kingdoms of the whole earth, over whom Christ the king is head and grand master." Although Hall remained firmly within Masonic tradition at the onset of this oratorical ritual, he nevertheless moved to articulate his claim for African American membership in the political community of the United States.[8]

The memory and history of the African diaspora emerge as the critical ground for the elaboration of a political language derived from Freemasonry's civil theology. Later in his oratorical performance, Prince Hall reminds his fellow Masonic brethren: "Among these numerous sons and daughters of distress, I shall begin with our friends and brethren; let us see them dragg'd from their native country by the iron hand of tyranny and oppression, from their dear friends and connections, with weeping eyes and aching hearts, to a strange land and strange people, whose tender mercies are cruel; and there to bear the iron yoke of slavery & cruelty till death as a friend shall relieve them." Although their duty as Masons binds them to universal aims and goals of the fraternity—to see "our friends and brethren"—the fulfillment of those ideals is hindered by the institution of chattel slavery that ensnares Africans and their descendants in the New World. In the displacement and disjuncture produced by these experiences, Hall highlights the failure of the civil theology of Freemasonry to fulfill its claims to universality and equality. By first affirming the principles of that civil theology and then drawing attention to the existential and political realities of life for those on the underside, his doubled articulation calls into question the very concepts and meaning of Freemasonry and modern political society. Hall thus connects past and present in an attempt to raise the awareness of the members of the African Lodge as to the contradictory forces unleashed in the Atlantic world, forces that the rituals of African Freemasonry struggle to overcome and heal. In this scenario, the charge to African American Freemasons cannot be severed from the existential situation of Africans and their descendants throughout the diaspora. "And must not the unhappy condition of these our fellow men," Hall exhorts, "draw forth our hearty prayer and wishes for their deliverance from these merchants and traders, whose characters you have in the xviii chap. of the Revelations, 11, 12, & 13 verses."[9]

Hall then switches the focus of his oration from explicating the civil theology of Freemasonry to developing a distinct political language that functions to critique democracy in America. Prince Hall's political language is infused with the imagery and metaphors informing the African American jeremiad tradition.[10] Drawing on the deep textures of the African diaspora, Hall proclaims, "[I]t now begins to dawn in some of the West-India islands… God can and will change their conditions and their hearts too; and let Boston and the world know, that He hath no respect of persons; and that the bulwark of envy, pride, scorn and contempt, which is so visible to be seen in some and felt, shall fall." Hall's stinging rebuke of the empty rhetoric of the egalitarian principles of American democracy is conjoined in this political language with a gesture to a just political order resulting from the actions of those C. L. R. James termed "the Black Jacobins."[11] By creating the conditions for a new form of political community, the Haitian Revolution reverberated in Hall's invocation of divine action.

Hall grounds his claims not only within a radically expanded conception of the universals so central to the civil theology of Freemasonry but, more important, within a political language centering moral authority around the Grand Architect of the Universe who sits in judgment not only of the craft but also of the social and political order. To this end, Hall provides a biblical basis for the equality of all people, regardless of race:

> The great law-giver, Moses, who instructed by his father-in-law, Jethro, an Ethiopian, how to regulate his course of justice and what sort of men to choose for the different offices…. So Moses hearkened to the voice of his father-in-law, and did all that he said.—Exodus xviii. 22–24. This is the first and grandest lecture that Moses ever received from the mouth of man; for Jethro understood geometry as well as laws, *that* a Mason may plainly see:… We see that great and good men have, and always will have, a respect for ministers and servants of God. Another instance of this is in Acts vii. 27 to 31, of the European [*sic*] Eunuch, a man of great authority, to Philip, the apostle: here is mutual love and friendship between them. This minister of Jesus Christ did not think himself too

good to receive the hand, and ride in a chariot with a black man in the face of day; neither did this great monarch (for so he was) think it beneath him to take a poor servant of the Lord by the hand, and invite him into his carriage, though but with a staff, one coat, and no money in his pocket. So our Grand Master, Solomon, was not asham'd to take the Queen of Sheba by the hand, and lead her into his court.... [O]ur Grand Master Solomon did not divide the living child, whatever he might do with the dead one; neither did he pretend to make a law to forbid the parties from having free intercourse with one another, without fear of censure, or be turned out of the synagogue.

Barely veiled here is a characterization of the inability of Prince Hall's white American Masonic brothers to accept the humanity of African American Freemasons. If Jethro instructed Moses and if Philip and Solomon freely conversed and interacted with Africans, why would white American Freemasons object to Masonic relationships with their African American brothers? Hall's language challenges the efforts of American Freemasons "to give Freemasonry a genteel and honorable reputation, despite occasional jests and suspicions."[12] He advances the provocative idea that African American Masons possess the requisite knowledge to properly instruct American Freemasons on the *true* meaning of the principles and aims of the fraternity—and, by extension, the true meaning of democracy.

Hall exhorts his brothers to remain calm in the face of mounting racial violence: "[A] slave in the West-Indies, on Sunday or holidays enjoys himself and friends without any molestation," even though in Boston, on the supposed day of rest, "without any provocation—twenty or thirty cowards fall upon one man." He points to recent events in Haiti to reassure his listeners that freedom, equality, and vindication await the faithful:

My brethren, let us remember what a dark day it was with our African brethren six years ago, in the French West-Indies. Nothing but the snap of the whip was heard from morning to evening; hanging, broken on the wheel, burning, and all manner of tortures inflicted on those unhappy people.... But blessed be God, the scene is changed; they now confess that God hath no respect of persons, and therefore receive them as their friends, and treat them as brothers. Thus doth Ethiopia begin to stretch forth her hand, from a sink of slavery to freedom and equality.[13]

Hall embraced "the common wind" then coursing through the Afro-Atlantic world and refreshed the political language of African American Freemasonry.[14]

For African American Freemasons the sacred bonds of justice, love, and equality that were central to their civil theology were more than obligations of the initiated member. Their egalitarian rhetoric transcended the sacred confines of the lodge, embracing those outside its hallowed halls. African American Freemasons held in a constant dialectic the intertwined universal aims of the fraternity: nurturing benevolence, justice, and love among the brethren while extending these virtues to those in the diaspora encumbered with slavery, discrimination, and alienation. Thus, their spread of Freemasonry among Africans and their descendants in America marked both their Masonic *and* their political efforts.

African American Freemasons clearly recognized the limits of their social and political status as Freemasons and as citizens in the United States. To create a space for themselves, they articulated a *supranational* concept of citizenship—one that both embraced and transcended the boundaries of the United States. Freemasonry provided its African American adherents a particular vocabulary for connecting them with the peculiar political situation they confronted in a racist society. They claimed membership in both the global fraternity and the polity of the United States.

In many ways, the culture of Freemasonry gave vivid expression to the political ideals of American democracy. Far from being antithetical, Freemasonry's civil theology and American political culture resonated with one another. A leading scholar puts it this way: "If, as Thomas Jefferson argued, the Capitol represented 'the first temple dedicated to the sovereignty of the people,' then the [Masonic] brothers of the 1793 [cornerstone laying] ceremony served as its first high priests."[15] Yet in so reconfiguring that civil theology and political culture, African American Freemasons paradoxically became heretics, subverting the dominant coordinates of the political field of the early republic.

African American Freemasons were painfully aware of the paradox that the Quaker David Cooper described: "If these solemn *truths,* uttered at such an awful crisis, are *self-evident*: unless we can shew that the African race are not *men,* words can hardly express the amazement which naturally arises on reflecting, that the very people who make these pompous declarations are slave-holders, and by their legislative conduct, tell us, that these blessings were only meant to be the *rights* of *white-men* not of all *men*."[16] The egalitarianism available in the civil theology of Freemasonry enabled a new conception of United States citizenship—one that placed a moral imperative before the United States to adhere without restriction to the political principle that "all men are created equal."

African American Masons deployed the structures and culture of Freemasonry in an effort to articulate their fitness for citizenship. Prince Hall's letter of 1786 to the governor of Massachusetts, James Bowdoin, which addressed the emerging rebellion in western Massachusetts led by Daniel Shay, illustrates this posture:

> We, by the Providence of God, are members of a fraternity that not only enjoins upon us to be peaceable subjects to the civil powers where we reside, but it also forbids our having concern in any plot or conspiracies against the state where we dwell; and as it is the unhappy lot of this state at the present date, and as the meanest of its members must feel that want of a lawful and good government, and as we have been protected for many years under this once happy Constitution, so we hope, by the blessing of God, we may long enjoy that blessing; therefore, we, though unworthy members of this Commonwealth, are willing to help support, as far as our weak and feeble abilities may become necessary in this time of trouble and confusion, as you in your wisdom shall direct us. That we may, under just and lawful authority, live peaceable lives in all godliness and honesty, is the hearty wish of your humble servants, the members of the African Lodge.[17]

Prince Hall and the members of African Lodge based their civic action on their membership in Freemasonry more than on the obligations of formal citizenship. Their supranational citizenship as Freemasons, a form of citizenship within a global fraternal community transcending the boundaries of the nation, is here invoked as the foundation for their virtuous offer of service. As supranational citizens, they are bound by both the rituals and obligations of this international brotherhood "to be peaceable subjects to the civil powers where [they] reside." Yet their desired citizenship in the nation also prompts their offer to intercede on behalf of the state to restore order to the state. Although the formal parameters of the political culture do not include them as proper citizens, their supranational citizenship, by virtue of their standing as Freemasons, transforms them into citizens of the United States as well. The letter reassures the authorities that the "secret society" of Africans is not seeking to act against the state in any form. Indeed, they are willing to take up arms against those who fail to comply with the legally constituted state under which Hall and his brethren "have been protected for many years." With divine Providence and the guidance of Governor Bowdoin, Hall voluntarily submits the skill and lives of the members of the African Lodge to the service of the state.

Although Hall and the others highlighted their truncated position in the eyes of the state—"we, though unworthy, members of this Commonwealth"—

the members of African Lodge nevertheless sought to fulfill the requirements of formal political citizenship through service. While dressed in deference, the letter revealed a formidable political strategy designed to obtain favor from the political elite on behalf of those willing to submit to the dictates of the state. In return, they sought "to live peaceable lives" under the conditions of "just and lawful authority."

They wanted neither a return to the political status quo nor mere recognition as Freemasons. Their recognition of the state's "just and lawful authority" undergirded their claim for full citizenship. By invoking the universals that were ever present in the public philosophy of the early republic as well as those available in the civil theology of Freemasonry, they were able to develop a multifaceted argument that satisfied the claim for a national citizenship through an appeal to nonnational ideals—what I have termed a supranational citizenship.

In a world increasingly fractured along the lines of race wrought by the involuntary migration of millions of Africans, African American Freemasons invoked this supranational citizenship to begin to heal the horrible fissures from this enforced marginalization. Their status as Freemasons and free blacks did not dissolve the bonds they maintained with their enslaved counterparts, especially given that many of these Masons had themselves experienced enslavement and that they lived intimately among innumerable others who had also known it. Freemasonry was grounded in individual freedom, agency, and integrity. As Masons in America who uniquely had experienced slavery and knew its unavoidably caustic impact upon those who were apparently free, black Masons almost could not do otherwise than condemn this infamy in America and seek always to extirpate it. The logic of the system of chattel slavery recognized the status of free blacks insofar as it was derived from and dependent on the maintenance of the institution of chattel slavery. For African American Freemasons, the specter of slavery and the destiny of the enslaved were linked with their duties, obligations, and rituals as members of the fraternal order. Thus they could ill afford to ignore the plight of those enslaved Africans and descendants throughout the diaspora; supranational citizenship was not only for themselves, but for all Africans worldwide.

In a petition to the Senate and House of Representatives of Massachusetts, Prince Hall and his brethren lodged a formal complaint against the kidnapping and selling of free blacks in the slave trade.[18] The kidnapping of one of the members of African Lodge had incited this particular appeal. In a related letter from a member of Portland Lodge No. 1 of Maine, a fellow Freemason detailed the earlier turn of events:

The Negroes who were kidnapped from here [i.e., Boston] last winter have returned. They were carried to St. Bartholomew's and offered for sale. One of them was a sensible fellow and a Freemason. The merchant to whom they were offered was of this fraternity. They soon became acquainted. The Negro told his story. They were carried before the Governor, with his shipmaster and the supercargo. The story of the Negroes was, that they were decoyed on board, under pretense of working. The story of the others was, that they were purchased out of jail, where they were confined for robbery. The Governor detained them. They were kept within limits, in which a gentleman of the Island was bondsman for them for six months, in which time they sent proofs, which arriving, they were liberated.[19]

The February 27, 1788, petition was a response not only to this incident but also to the random kidnapping and enslavement of free blacks in Boston. The writers of this appeal invoked both the universals of humanity and the particulars of political citizenship in the first sentence: "That your petitioners are justly alarmed at the inhuman and cruel treatment that three of our brethren, free citizens of the town of Boston, lately received."[20] Echoing the inalienable rights of every citizen of the United States—"life, liberty, and the pursuit of happiness"—the petitioners demanded, "What then are our lives and liberties worth, if they may be taken away in such a cruel and unjust manner as this?"[21] Since they did not question their ability to appropriate the language of the nation—hence their querying the value of their "lives and liberties"—they were able to articulate their outrage with those who perpetrated such crimes.

Freemasonry's civil theology empowered them the petitioners to channel its universals to condemn not only the kidnapping but the whole of the Atlantic slave trade itself. The petition reinforced the linking of the destinies of free blacks with those of the enslaved:

One thing more we would beg leave to hint, that is, that your petitioners have for some time past, beheld with grief, ships cleared out of this harbor for Africa, and they either steal our brothers and sisters, fill their ship-holds full of unhappy men and women, crowded together, then set out for the best market to sell them there, like sheep for slaughter, and then return here like honest men, after having sported with the lives and liberty of their fellow-men, and at the same time call themselves Christians. Blush, O Heavens, at this![22]

The experiences of diaspora came to the forefront as the protest moved beyond the boundaries of the nation to encompass a global context. They yoked themselves—"honest men"—with "the lives and liberty of their fellow-men," the enslaved. Their membership in a larger civic world animated their complaint against the Atlantic slave trade. The universals of Freemasonry's civil theology grounded in human dignity transcended the boundaries of the nation-state and facilitated the opening of a political space for an expansive form of supranational citizenship. Such a conception of citizenship empowered African American Freemasons to advance a claim for full citizenship within the United States as well as political freedom for Africans and people of African descent throughout the diaspora.

The moral and political ideals expressed through African American Freemasonry's civil theology challenged the chattel slavery, racial discrimination, and political inequality that characterized the era of the early republic. African American Freemasons invoked the Masonic universals of charity, love, and fraternity to solicit their embrace within the American nation. African American Freemasonry emerged from this era's political ferment as it simultaneously enriched that culture's capacity for articulating alternative conceptions of democracy. In this vein, the 1828 statement by the African American Freemason John T. Hilton—"The day of our enrollment in the list of Lodges of the Grand Lodge of England was to us, as Masons, as great an event as the Declaration of Independence was to the people of the United States"—resonates not only within the registers of Freemasonry but also within the arena of politics proper.[23]

CHAPTER 5

Brotherhood Denied

Black Freemasonry and the Limits of Reconstruction

STEPHEN KANTROWITZ

Reconstruction would succeed through Free-masonry.[1] That was the message Lewis Hayden brought to the black Masonic brethren of Massachusetts in late 1865, as he reported what he had seen and done on his mission to establish lodges in the newly free states of Virginia and the Carolinas. Hayden did not underestimate the challenges that awaited him and his comrades. He had been a slave himself just twenty years before, and he understood that the legacies of slavery and caste would take time to overcome. "[I]n the emerging of nations or people from a state of oppression," he explained, "more especially when the oppressor is allowed to prey upon them, there must be jealousies and want of confidence in each other." Slavery had denied black southerners the right to organize their own lives, families, and communities. Now, even as newly freed blacks struggled to overcome "discord" in their communities, they faced stubborn resistance from whites—what Hayden grimly described as "a deep and unalterable purpose in the hearts of the old oppressors to blast, or at least to crush out, the rising hopes and dawning prospects of their late bondmen." In some places—Charleston, South Carolina, and Petersburg, Virginia—he found "united and harmonious" communities forging institutions and accumulating property. In Richmond, though, the people he met "did not present so hopeful an aspect, so intellectual nor so dignified a character" as at the other places. The black Masons there had only "obtained a room in which to form the Lodge with great difficulty," and among them, in the former capital of the Confederacy, Hayden sadly noted "jealousies and bickerings."[2]

Such discord, Hayden believed, could "only be removed by associations of the strongest possible ties known among men": the ties of Freemasonry. Though he was intimately familiar with the churches, mutual benefit and relief associations, schools, and literary societies that bound African Americans to one another in the free states, here he pinned his hopes on the lodges and principles of a secret ritual order.[3] "[A]s there are [no ties] known to men whose obligations and duties are so sacred or more holy than ours, we feel that when they have taken upon themselves such obligations, and as they progress in the lessons therein taught, confidence is restored, and each can trust the other with safety; and, in place of confusion, discord, and ruin, each heart is filled with those truly Masonic virtues, 'brotherly love, relief, and truth.'"[4]

In this, Hayden was in good company. Many black northern activists earnestly believed that no institution had more to contribute to the success of emancipation than did the brotherhood of Freemasonry. Leading men in every northern city—from Prince Hall, Richard Allen, and David Walker through John Jones, George T. Downing, and John S. Rock (as well as Hayden himself)—had invested themselves deeply in its rituals, language, and hierarchies. For them, the principles of brotherly love, relief, and truth offered an ethical compass whose needle pointed without reference to the sectarianism of denominational life or the outright hypocrisy of the slaveholder's democracy.

Freemasonry promised to help overcome both the external and the internal forces standing in the way of black advancement. Its cosmopolitan ideology and invocations of universal brotherhood offered a powerful challenge to white supremacy, particularly at a moment when the spirit of the age seemed to be firmly on the side of freedom and equality. Throughout Reconstruction, black Masons sought to leverage white Masons' commitments to their craft into a broader acceptance of them as men and brothers. At the same time, they hoped that the "mystic tie" might also work changes within and among men. The order's secret rites and lore established bonds of shared knowledge and experience, while the lodge itself—the small group of men at the heart of Masonic practice and governance—fostered mutual affection and obligation that could override the "jealousies and bickerings" fostered by oppression. In order to overcome the worst of these struggles within Freemasonry itself and to foster unity among the leading black men of the country, black Freemasons worked to bring the order together under a governing body—the National Grand Lodge.

These projects met with powerfully mixed results during the 1860s and 1870s. Freemasonry did extend its reach into the former slave states, as well as into the small but growing black communities of the west. At the same time, many black Masonic leaders came to feel that the rapid expansion of the order under the auspices of a powerful national grand master debased Masonic principles; what had formerly been local struggles rapidly became a national schism. And though some white Freemasons moved tentatively to accept black brethren, most rejected their overtures. Reconstruction, whether of the brotherhood or through its agency, turned out to be harder work than it had seemed.

By the 1850s black Freemasonry had spread across the North and even into the urban South, but its development was radically reshaped by the Civil War.[5] During and after the war, black Freemasons entered the former Confederacy as soldiers, missionaries, sojourners, and settlers. Military lodges among the black regiments in South Carolina—the 55th Massachusetts and the 1st North Carolina (part of the "African Brigade")—met to mourn departed brethren and execute their wills.[6] Reverend (later Bishop) James W. Hood of the AME Zion church brought Prince Hall to the freedpeople of occupied North Carolina.[7] Lodges in some of the Union slave states, taking advantage of the new wartime political climate even before slavery was formally abolished, joined in: an 1863 Union Christmas celebration in occupied Portsmouth, Virginia, included a local lodge organized by the black Grand Lodge of Maryland.[8]

At the end of the war black Masons sought, sometimes successfully, to incorporate themselves into national rituals of mourning and celebration.[9] Before a large Masonic audience in Chicago, the black civic leader and leading Mason John Jones publicly declared the U.S. flag "as being NOW the emblem of LIBERTY TO ALL."[10] Even in the former slave states, lodges emerged in freedpeople's collective public life. Nashville's black Masons announced their first public gathering in the summer of 1865.[11] Charleston, South Carolina, had several lodges by that fall,[12] and these were among the associations called to plan for a grand barbecue and procession in celebration of the upcoming anniversary of emancipation.[13]

As Freemasonry moved toward the freedpeople, they responded, and black Masonic lodges quickly grew up in every former slave state. In 1866, John Jones estimated there were seven thousand black Freemasons; by 1877 a newspaper in Jones's hometown put the number at about twenty-eight thousand, while another prominent black Mason offered the perhaps inflated figure of a hundred thousand.[14] At least some of these new lodges undertook programs of economic uplift and mutual benefit.[15]

But a specter haunted black Freemasonry in the decade after the Civil War: recurrent schisms and jurisdictional disputes that split grand lodges and pitted them against one another in contests over territory. These questions of the "origin and authorities under whom the different Lodges and Grand Lodges were then working"[16] had by the 1840s become serious enough to prompt leading black Masons from several of the existing grand lodges to initiate an ambitious experiment: the National Grand Lodge (NGL). They envisioned this national compact as a new "mother lodge" for black North Americans, which would bring the nation's leading black Masons together in periodic council and resolve disputes among state lodges. "[A]ll having received their authority from the same source," one of the founders explained, there would be no further cause for conflict.[17] Within a few years, Masonic author Martin Delany enthusiastically declared the project a success: "[T]he differences and wounds which long existed were all settled and healed," he wrote, "[and] a complete union formed."[18] Freemasonry did indeed flourish during the next decade, and by 1865 fourteen grand lodges, claiming jurisdiction over entire states, belonged to the national compact.[19]

But Delany's sunny portrait of unity was wildly unrealistic, for some of the existing grand lodges refused to join the compact. As a result, the NGL failed in its primary purpose of bringing black Masonry's schismatic history to an end. Indeed, the question of a lodge's relationship to the compact sometimes set Masons against one another. New York, for example, had two competing grand lodges in the 1860s, one of which did not belong to the compact; each organization's members were forbidden to recognize members of the other as brothers, leading some to rue publicly "[t]he misunderstanding which unhappily prevails among the craft."[20] Adherence to or rejection of the National Grand Lodge appears to have been the critical feature of this division: a St. John's Day celebration in June 1863 invited only those Masons "who acknowledged the jurisdiction of the National Grand Lodge."[21] And these divisions followed black Freemasonry into the former Confederacy. The first lodge in Augusta, Georgia, announced its welcome in these terms: "All brethren of good standing and members of Lodges working under the National Compact are invited to meet and participate in our meetings."[22]

Pro-compact Masons likened their cause to the defense of the federal union against secession, and even some critics of the National Grand Lodge described a national system of Masonic governance as the "true form."[23] In 1861, a group of New York Masons hoping to reunite their state's warring factions deployed the language of union to call for reconciliation, asking "[y]oung men and brothers" to "rise up in our might, and call upon our fathers to cast in oblivion the cause of dissension. . . . May God direct us, and may every brother's heart respond for the union, for our cause!"[24] But by the end of the war that elevated rhetoric of Masonic unity had given way to highly charged partisan condemnation. When a dissident group of black Masons in Pennsylvania rejected subordination to the NGL's rulings, officials dismissed their demands for a reorganization of the national body as "subversive of ... [its] purposes."[25] They declared that those who had "in violation of their most sacred and solemn covenant, rebelled against the rightful authority" of the NGL thereby forfeited their standing as Masons.[26] In that year—1865—the implications of this rhetoric would have been contextually unmistakable: the Union would be preserved; treason would be made odious and traitors punished—if only to the extent of reading them out of the fraternity.

More, the NGL soon challenged Freemasonry's traditional means of expansion, in which state grand lodges were free to establish lodges in states or territories lacking a grand lodge of their own. This had caused problems before the war. Ohio's grand lodge was perhaps uniquely evangelical: during the 1850s it chartered at least twelve lodges in five states.[27] This practice drew some criticism, but at the triennial session of the NGL in 1856 the right to establish lodges in areas without existing grand lodges was adopted by a two-thirds majority, with the caveat that this measure should be undertaken only by the "nearest Grand Lodge" to that unorganized state or territory.[28] Considering that Ohio's black grand lodge was geographically the nearest to virtually all western free black communities—from Chicago to San Francisco to New Orleans—this was hardly a meaningful limitation. Further east, where settlement was denser and grand lodges shared borders with unorganized territories, the regulation was unhelpful in another way: in 1865 the grand lodges of both Maryland and the District of Columbia claimed subordinates in Virginia, with which both shared a border.[29]

No ex-Confederate state boasted a grand lodge, which meant that the war's end opened a vast new field for expansion. As a result, questions of Masonic federalism quickly became urgent. Within months of the war's end, men representing several states as well as the NGL itself moved into the former Confederate states, chartering lodges among the freedpeople and antebellum free blacks of southern cities and towns. And when the NGL met for its triennial session late in 1865, one question preoccupied its members: with whom should the power to charter new lodges reside?[30] A proposal to restrict the right of chartering new lodges to the existing state grand lodges provoked several days of strenuous debate.[31] A measure granting exclusive power to the national grand master to "open or constitute any Subordinate Lodge or Lodges" in areas beyond existing jurisdictions failed to pass, but so did a subsequent motion to reaffirm the decade-old "nearest grand lodge" standard. Ultimately these thorny constitutional questions were deferred until the next triennial session, scheduled in 1868.[32]

The man who made the motion to put off that decision was the one who would profit most from the resulting uncertainty. The 1865 session's election of Richard Howell Gleaves to the office of national grand master brought to the fore the organizational genius of Ohio's grand lodge, a man with a remarkable aptitude for organizing fraternal orders (not limited to Freemasonry) as well as for making his home wherever the action was. After spending the late 1840s and early 1850s building Masonry in Ohio, he traveled throughout the Ohio and Mississippi valleys, establishing lodges wherever he went. Shortly before being elected grand master of Ohio in 1856, in fact, he was serving as master of a newly constituted lodge in New Orleans, one of the many subordinates Ohio claimed in other states.[33] He spent much of the early 1860s doing business and taking a leading role in various fraternal and sororal bodies in Philadelphia.[34] In the months just before his election as national grand master in 1865 he toured the former Confederate states, and after taking office he headed off for a career in the Masonic and Republican worlds of South Carolina; within a decade he was the state's lieutenant governor.[35]

Gleaves was determined to bring compact Freemasonry to the South by any means necessary. "We will endeavor, with our utmost exertions," he promised in his first speech as national grand master, "to cement the craft in every State of the Union . . . into one common band of Masonic workmen."[36] "The late war," Gleaves later explained, "opened a vast field of labor for the colored Masons among their race in the southern states."[37] He made plain his vision of executive power, promising (in the first person plural) to continue shaping the order in this way: during his term as president he would bring a majority of the states in the Union into the compact, and "None shall disagree, if it be in our power to prevent it."[38]

Between the triennial sessions of the NGL, Gleaves traveled the South, organizing lodges and even forging them into grand lodges. His efforts were remarkably successful: in 1867 the NGL reached its peak, with twenty grand lodges working under it.[39] Yet even for some Masons loyal to the NGL, this seemed a usurpation of authority and a fundamental misunderstanding of the nature of Masonic commitment. In the two years following the 1865 meeting, Virginia, Missouri, and Kentucky all formed grand lodges under Gleaves's guidance, and those grand lodges were admitted to the NGL. How, some asked, could these new lodges be part of the compact when the national body would not meet again until 1868?

Lewis Hayden, himself the second-ranking member of the NGL's elected leadership,[40] reflected on this question in an 1867 pamphlet that marked a public rupture with Gleaves's policies.[41] Freemasonry was unsafe in Gleaves's hands for several reasons, Hayden argued. First, he was moving too fast, prizing speed and numbers over spirit and quality. How could Gleaves promise to "turn over to your care and keeping State Grand Lodges from two-thirds of these United States"[42] within a single three-year term when many of those states at present contained not a single Mason or lodge? Only past grand masters of individual lodges could constitutionally serve as officers of new grand lodges; did Gleaves propose to conjure such officers out of thin air? Second, he was usurping authority never granted to the NGL, not only forming and admitting new grand lodges in unprecedented ways but also presuming to sit in judgment on conflicts involving both compact and noncompact lodges.[43] Third, Gleaves funded his activities out of his own pocket, establishing a precedent that only wealthy men would be able to follow though "we, as a body, have not many among us that can afford so to do."[44]

Hayden was not opposed to the NGL itself. He believed that Masonic government should approximate as closely as possible the government of the United States: "[T]he Government of the country being national, so should we be national also; and it is well for us that we are so organized as a National Grand Lodge, that the lessons we impart are and must be of a national character, to the end that the unity of the Government may be ever maintained: for all our hopes as a people are involved in the issue, extending even to that of life and liberty."[45] The NGL not only kept black Masons from being "divided into parties"; its example might help teach a lesson about the proper conduct of the national government.[46]

But this same belief led Hayden to the conclusion that the National Grand Lodge must be preserved and protected from Gleaves's tyranny. He soon began attacking Gleaves in the idiom of national Reconstruction politics. As he wrote his pamphlet in 1867, President Andrew Johnson was locked in a high-stakes struggle with congressional radical Republicans, who were Hayden's allies. Hayden explained that the process of admitting a new state grand lodge to the national compact was, like that of admitting a new territory or seceded state to the Union, properly a legislative power. If Gleaves persisted in claiming that authority for himself, then "the National Grand Lodge will overturn his policy, as Congress has that of Johnson, for they are alike, one and the same."[47]

Hayden had a point about the weakness and undemocratic features of a system that pitted triennial sessions of a legislative body against a vigorous (and self-funding) executive. Yet beneath this elevated language it is possible that a more earthly struggle was under way. In the early 1870s Massachusetts's black Freemasons were still fuming that their lodges in the southern seaboard states had "been gobbled up by the Nationals."[48] Hayden's trip south in 1865 had yielded subordinate lodges for the Prince Hall Grand Lodge of Massachusetts in Charleston, Richmond, and Petersburg, lodges that drew their Masonic legitimacy from that descent and paid their dues (as a substantial one-time fee in order to receive their charters) to Massachusetts. Later that winter, though, National Grand Master Gleaves traveled to Norfolk, where he organized the Union Grand Lodge of Virginia. When Virginia Masons later wrote to the NGL office to ask whether they were now entitled to a refund of the moneys they had sent to Boston, the national grand secretary replied by depicting Massachusetts's chartering of lodges as a selfish act: "[T]he authorities of the Prince Hall Grand Lodge seem to have regarded the *pecuniary interest,* much more than the harmony, prosperity, general interest, and welfare of the lodges which it had erected." Nonetheless, he admitted, the Prince Hall Grand Lodge's authority had been legitimate until the moment the state formed its own grand lodge, so there was no technical impropriety. Take the case up with the Boston men, advised the national secretary—but he could not say just who they might be, "not having received any communication from them for the last two years."[49]

Amid suspicion and division—"jealousies and bickerings," perhaps—relations between the original home of black Freemasonry and its national authority had broken down. Hayden, though in principle a supporter of national authority, now began to assert that lodges established in a new territory could remain subordinate to their original grand lodge even after a new grand lodge had been established for that territory if the lodge deemed it "inexpedient or unsafe to surrender their warrant and take another from the new Grand Lodge."[50] Unsafe, he must have been implying, because the new grand lodge was an extraconstitutional innovation, existing without proper Masonic authority and therefore casting doubt upon the Masonic legitimacy of any man working under it.

Perhaps the national grand secretary had it partly right when he charged the Massachusetts Grand Lodge with seeking to retain a subordinate lodge's allegiance for worldly reasons. Yet in some respects this battle over dues, charter fees, and bragging rights was a battle of principles after all. As Hayden warmed to his arguments against Gleaves's activities over the following years, he elaborated on the metaphysical shortcomings of Gleaves's approach to Masonic recruitment and organization. He began from the axiom that Masons must, above all, be men of independent thought and action, not the creatures of others. "It is a principle that all acts performed, whether by the individual Mason or as a body, must be his or their free act"; men were not to be aggressively recruited into Freemasonry—not even "leading questions" were to be offered.[51] "Self-controlling authority" was the mark of "*true* and *perfect*" Masonic craft.[52] He insisted on the rights of Masons "to establish, or not, a Grand Lodge for themselves, and that when a Grand Lodge is so established it should be the free act of the Masons whose Grand Lodge it is to be."[53] It was un-Masonic, in other words, to create an organization for a group of men (or Masons), heedless of whether they were "prepared or not prepared for such an organization."[54]

Such language might suggest that Gleaves was the Masonic democrat, seeking the rapid incorporation of men into the order's local, state, and national structures, while Hayden was the elitist, urging patience and worrying over whether or not men were "prepared." Yet in reality the contrast was far less stark than this. For men on both sides of this schism, to be a Freemason was to be special kind of man—one of particularly good character and ability. But part of that specialness was these men's ability, and indeed their obligation, to act as free-minded, responsible citizens of their Masonic polity. Having voluntarily entered into Masonry, they were bound by its obligations; should they, as members of individual lodges, take it upon themselves to form a grand lodge, they could do so. But that was a solemn undertaking, and one for which they did indeed have to be prepared. Hayden made sure to describe these obligations in nonpartisan terms: grand lodges could not, for example, simply throw off the NGL because they disapproved of its leaders "any more so than a State in this Union can release herself honorably and lawfully from the obligations she is under to the national government, and which she voluntarily assumed when she became part of the national compact."[55] But by the same token, no powerful central authority could impose that obligation upon them; they, as members of free and independent lodges, had to seek it out and take it upon themselves in their collective wisdom.

Gleaves, in Hayden's view, sacrificed a spiritual (even sacred) proof of Masonic manhood in the service of rapid recruitment and centralized authority. He made a mockery of the "ancient landmarks." To capture this, Hayden turned to satire, asking by what means a state such as Virginia or Kentucky could create a grand lodge virtually out of whole cloth. The answer, he suggested, was that Gleaves must have constructed a "portable lodge, moving through the country on wheels... propelled by steam."

When this heaved to a stop at some remote town ("Confederate Cross Roads, Kentucky," was Hayden's freighted invention) he imagined Gleaves grandly calling the meeting to establish a grand lodge to order, serving in turn as every officer at the meeting and finally submitting the report to himself.[56]

Hayden was by no means the only black Mason to sour on the NGL. In the years before 1874, when he finally called for its dissolution, numerous other state grand lodges withdrew from the compact.[57] Most notably, the Grand Lodge of Ohio in 1868 announced its withdrawal, describing the NGL as an un-Masonic "innovation" and pointing specifically to the unprecedented power it had assumed to establish new grand lodges and interfere in the affairs of existing ones. For their pains, they were suspended or expelled, denounced as schismatic by the NGL. Ohio's suspension began an exodus and marked the beginning of the end for the NGL's claim to national authority.[58]

As state after state disaffiliated, partisans of the now-independent grand lodges began to speak in louder and harsher terms. A scathing 1874 pamphlet denounced Gleaves as a "Masonic autocrat" and "inexorable tyrant" who had usurped powers that belonged to sovereign state grand lodges; his oppression through the NGL—a form of "Imperialism"—left them without any meaningful form of redress "but revolution." Under Gleaves, the author charged, the NGL was simply a financial scheme, bilking lodges of an annual fee for each member, as well as charging them to warrant each new lodge. Dissenting lodges were expelled and Masons loyal to the NGL forbidden from having any fellowship with them. This "Masonic centralization" was "repulsive to the cosmopolitanism of the Order, repulsive to the 'brotherhood of man,' and contrary to the teachings of 'the Fatherhood of God!'"[59] Hayden agreed, denouncing both Gleaves and the NGL as "these new despoilers who are of our own race and people...fraudulently obtaining the fruits of our toil by taking fees and receiving dues under the pretence" that they were practicing actual Masonry.[60]

The political resonance of this last charge might have been stronger than we can now easily intuit, for by 1874 Gleaves was not only national grand master but also the lieutenant governor of South Carolina, a state whose Republican government had recently become notorious for fiscal corruption. These misdeeds were part of the rationale offered by the resurgent white supremacist militias who had overthrown Reconstruction in many states and actively sought to do the same in those that remained under Republican governments: they were forced to this extreme, they claimed, by rampant corruption and incompetence, the inevitable consequence of black governance.

Northern periodicals during this period were replete with images of black elected officials as knaves and fools, inherently unfit to rule themselves, let alone entire states.[61] The anticompact forces were not blind to these challenges; they simply believed that the enforced unity of the NGL diminished Freemasonry without providing any meaningful benefits.[62]

In any case, the compact's days were numbered. In 1875, when Masons from around the nation met in Boston for a public celebration of black Masonry's centennial, they also held an assembly to try to find new common ground. Gleaves appeared on Hayden's home turf, not as the representative of the NGL but as a delegate from South Carolina; no one, though, misunderstood what was at issue in calls for "harmony of action" and a "united front" or in the acknowledgment that "dissentions have crept in."[63] These efforts failed, leading anticompact forces to propose an 1877 meeting in Chicago to reconcile the two wings of the fraternity. That meeting sought a "plan or regulation for the perfect union" of all the grand lodges, considering both the "legality" of the NGL and the "question of independent state Grand Lodges under our form of government."[64] Furious debate ensued over what to do about cases where two grand lodges claimed authority in a single state. The forces opposed to the NGL appear to have been in the ascendant, for a resolution emphasizing the importance of a "Masonic Union" was finally voted down, with a substitute adopted calling for competing lodges to meet and fuse into one lodge.[65]

Those compact men who did not accept the verdict of the Chicago meeting nonetheless agreed that reform was in order: they assembled in Delaware the following year in a National Union Convention in order "to heal the breach which had so long existed," as "our conditions as a race required the abolition of all dissension in our ranks."[66] Long-standing officers and members of the compact took part but sometimes under auspices that revealed how far their fortunes had fallen: Gleaves, now in political exile from South Carolina and having burned his bridges in Ohio when the NGL expelled its grand lodge a decade before, appeared as a delegate from Michigan. The heated discussions centered on the need to drop existing bars on fraternization with Masons from other factions. The NGL continued in attenuated fashion after that meeting, but it lacked legitimacy in the eyes of many black Freemasons.[67] As Reconstruction ended, so did the grand experiment in national Masonic governance.

Anticompact invective to the contrary, one did not have to be either a tyrant or a fool to believe that African Americans needed to face their foes with as much unity as possible. But during the most vibrant period of Reconstruction, during the late 1860s and early 1870s, it was also possible to imagine another alternative: acceptance by white Americans and a warm belonging in the United States. This too was part of black Freemasonry's vision of Reconstruction. Even as they struggled internally over questions of jurisdiction, expansion, and the compact, black Masons also actively sought fraternity with white Masons.

This story was as old as black Freemasonry itself. Beginning in Prince Hall's own era, Boston's black Masons had petitioned the white grand lodges for recognition and mutual visitation. Even as they constructed a freestanding National Grand Lodge in the late antebellum era, they also continued to press for recognition. Indeed, their desire for recognition was among the foremost features of the Declaration of Sentiments issued at the formation of the National Grand Lodge. "We do not know of any good reason" for separate white and black organizations, read the first sentiment. "Not that we have been wanting in attention to our White Brethren," the document continued; "We have from time to time solicited them to extend their jurisdiction over us, but to no effect."[68] Martin Delany's 1853 pamphlet on black Freemasonry suggested calling on the Grand Lodge of England "for settlement of [the] question of legality of Colored Masons in the U.S."[69] Now and again some visitation occurred across the color line, but when the question of membership or reconciliation was broached, black Masons were always rebuffed.[70]

White Masons pursued many strategies in denying the legitimacy of black Masons. They questioned the existence or validity of the charter Prince Hall had received from England in the 1780s; they claimed that the African Lodge had been stricken from England's records for irregularities; and they noted a common phrase in Masonic law restricting membership to those who were "freeborn." Both before and after the war, white Masonic bodies derided black Masons as "counterfeit" or "clandestine,"[71] "irregular" and "fraudulent,"[72] refused to consider their petitions for recognition, and aggressively swatted down the handful of whites who dissented from this policy. Black Masons offered strident replies. They recited Prince Hall's history and reproduced his antislavery writings and reminded all who would listen that they had received their charter from the same legitimating source, the Grand Lodge of England—which had, after British emancipation, amended its requirements for membership to men who were "freeborn, or no bondman."[73]

The end of slavery in the United States was supposed to change everything. Hayden expected the Civil War, once transformed into a war of emancipation, to lead white American Masons to a new set of conclusions. "We are now erecting a new fabric," he explained as the Republican governor of

Massachusetts lauded the state's black Masons for their wartime efforts; such expressions of regard "would be used as cement in the future to bind the black and white in this country into one common mass."[74] He had reasons to think so. The war had thoroughly delegitimized proslavery sentiment as a political position, and if white Masons now dismissed black Masons simply because they had not been born free, they were working against the emancipating spirit of the age and of the nation. The tendency of such arguments, it seemed to Hayden, was "to lead the Masonic fraternity against the government of the United States."[75] Instead, he reached out to "our friends among the white Masons, for there are such." He urged his white neighbors to be his brothers—to accept his right not only to sit in a first-class railway car or serve in a regiment but to enjoy a position of equality in the fraternal, non-state sphere of lodge meetings; to go beyond the formal inclusion represented by nondiscriminatory state policies and include black men in the supposedly universal brotherhood of the craft. This would be a victory of another order entirely: a victory not just in the streets but also in the intimate sphere of fraternal solidarity. It would match "the advancing civilization of this enlightened Christian age."[76]

This movement was already taking shape overseas. Freemasonry was international, and cosmopolitan in the sense that men of all nations and religions were in theory eligible for membership. Indeed, Freemasons who were not enmeshed in the United States' cultural and political history of race frequently proved willing to accept black American Masons as their brethren. When the Boston lawyer John S. Rock traveled to France for medical treatment in 1858, he reported visiting the Grand Orient, the highest assembly in French Freemasonry. "I was received in due and ancient form," he wrote, "and received the honors of the Lodge, and [was] invited to take a seat alongside of the Master." The sunlit dream of international brotherhood took on the colors of lived experience as Rock met "Masons from nearly every part of the globe." Visiting another Parisian lodge, one whose members were "rabidly anti-slavery," he discovered that the name just before his on the visitors' book belonged to a white Mason from York, Pennsylvania. Rock wondered whether the man would find himself in hot water upon his return to the United States should it become known that he had sat in a lodge "with a colored Mason." Perhaps not, he posited archly, for "the white Masons in America, after all, may not be such a set of savages as I have often been wicked enough to think they are."[77]

The establishment of full fraternal relations with brethren overseas had come during the Civil War, as the Grand Orient of Haiti entered into formal correspondence with the National Grand Lodge.[78] As the end of slavery in the United States offered an opportunity to revisit the historic basis of black men's exclusion from white lodges, black Masonic intellectuals and leaders called upon Europeans for aid. At war's end, John Jones called upon "the Masonic Fraternity dispersed around the globe" and especially "the Grand Lodge of England . . . to set this matter of the legitimacy of colored Masonry in the United States forever at rest" and "establish forever the constitutionality and legality of our Masonic existence."[79] A New York grand lodge received a high French Mason, who treated its members with respect and declared that "He knew no one by his color."[80] By the late 1860s, a few German grand lodges were making overtures of friendship, and an English translation had appeared of a German Masonic history that was generally supportive of the claims of the Prince Hall Masons.[81] From Italy, the high-degree Mason Garibaldi saluted one of his countrymen for "admitting all colored brethren into your lodge."[82] In 1875 the black grand lodges of Massachusetts and Ohio were officially recognized by the grand lodges at Hamburg, Germany, and Berne, Switzerland.[83] The following year a prominent Boston Mason received a jewel and warrant from the Grand Lodge of Hungary, naming him its representative to Boston.[84] Professor Richard Greener of the University of South Carolina—still then open to black students under the Republican Reconstruction government— lauded these "white brethren who believe in justice and right," asserting that "The unmasonic fabrics of caste are tottering under the strong blows, which these sturdy Liberals of Europe and the true masons of America are striking."[85]

If the destruction of caste was the test of true Masonry, however, then "true masons" were rare indeed in America. Although some non-Masonic white political allies recognized the importance of black Freemasonry, emancipation did not bring Masonic brotherhood to the Union. In 1864, for example, the Grand Lodge of Illinois apparently enacted new bylaws forbidding subordinate lodges from admitting any "negro or mulatto" and requiring the state grand master to seize the charter of any lodge that violated this principle."[86] Nor did the victory over the Confederacy bring about this millennium. Instead of Christian and Masonic union in service of peace and the nation, Hayden continued to see bigotry and treason. "[T]he Masons of Massachusetts, the white Masons I mean, have not yet caught the spirit of the age; they are still exclusive, intolerant, and proscriptive," he declared ruefully in 1865.[87]

Perhaps change would begin with one man. In October 1867, as the Reconstruction Acts brought hundreds of thousands of black men to the polls across the former slave states, Boston's St. Andrew's Lodge—one of the city's oldest and most prestigious white Masonic bodies—unanimously voted to make a Mason of a man of African descent: Joshua B. Smith, an antislavery militant who was also a famous and popular caterer to luminaries such as Charles Sumner.[88] It might be, as the lone white abolitionist among the brethren put it, "the dawn of a new era in fraternal association, and the first step" toward recognition of the black lodges.[89]

The very next year, perhaps encouraged by one of the white grand lodge's own members, Lewis Hayden and other black Masons from Boston, New Bedford, and Springfield petitioned the Grand Lodge of Massachusetts for recognition in the name of nearly 250 men working under the Prince Hall Grand Lodge.[90] Their petition presented their claim to Masonic legitimacy and noted their equality before the laws of the commonwealth; it claimed inspiration from both the egalitarian spirit of the age and the "'cosmopolitan' character of our fraternity"; and it left up to the white Masons the means by which they were to be acknowledged in their "equal Masonic manhood."[91] For the first time, the petition was heard, not tabled but referred to a committee of eminent Masons. Over the next year, the committee appeared to take its work seriously. It even examined the charter Prince Hall had received from England in the 1780s.[92]

But allies proved weak. A past grand master of Massachusetts's white grand lodge wrote to Lewis Hayden to praise one of his pamphlets on the legitimacy of black Freemasonry. "[I]f the door of our order was open to all irrespective of color," he wrote, "it would make it, as it should be, truly cosmopolitan." He signed himself "your friend and brother according to *my feelings*." But the final qualification turned out to be critical. When Hayden asked permission to publish this letter, as a rare crack in the facade of public opposition among the Bay State's white Masonic leadership, the old man demurred. "At present it would not be well to print my unimportant note," he offered in lieu of explanation. "Let us wait until a better state of things ensues."[93]

In the end the white grand lodge committee voted unanimously to reject the petition. Worse, it even refused to rule on the merits of the petition's arguments for black Masonic history and legitimacy: the seventy-two petitioners, they explained, asked admission for the whole of their fraternity, meaning that any ruling in the petitioners' favor would admit men unnamed therein and therefore unknown to the white brethren. "Under these circumstances," they explained, "it is not necessary to inquire into the validity of the proceedings of the persons named in the charter or whether the petitioners have any just claim to be considered their successors." It concluded by denying "Masonic intercourse" to the petitioners while noting that any individuals who were "worthy and well qualified" could of course "seek admission through duly organized lodges."[94] A dissident white Mason, Jacob Norton, dismissed this quibble as "a Bull-Run skedaddle"—a frantic and ignominious retreat from the "historical evidence of legitimacy of origin" that the black lodges provided.[95]

Under these circumstances, the admission of Joshua Smith seemed less overture than inoculation—a symbolic inclusion that made it appear as though the white lodges prized individual worthiness, not racial hierarchy. "It is not true," declared the *New England Freemason* in 1875, "that the Grand Lodges of this country refuse to recognize these spurious organizations because they are composed of black men. There are black men in good and regular standing in several of our jurisdictions," including Smith in Massachusetts, "and no Brother ever thinks of regarding or treating him any differently than if he were white." In language that smacked of the post–Civil War backlash against the enfranchisement of black citizens, the author continued, "No man—not even a black man—has an inalienable right to be made a Mason, nor to be recognized as a Mason."[96]

Smith, however unintentionally, served such white supremacists well. Prosperous, freeborn, very light-skinned, and courtly in manner, he was more than once the lone man of African descent in otherwise white surroundings.[97] Charles W. Moore, a leading white Boston Mason and editor of the *Freemason's Monthly Magazine,* devoted several pages to explaining the factors about Smith that made his admission so acceptable: his descent from "one of the most respectable white families of Virginia"; his free birth; his early education and economic success; his skin and features not being "of any decided African type"; and his "white wife and...children, who are indistinguishable in their complexion from the white children with whom they associate." Moore even alleged that Smith did not "look for intimate associates among the class to which his paternal ancestor belonged." In other words, Smith was anything but "a common 'negro'" and his initiation "therefore...does not strictly furnish any precedent for the admission of persons of the African race, however worthy they may be. It leaves that question untouched."[98]

Neither the original report of Smith's initiation nor the magazine's dismissal of it as a precedent escaped Hayden's notice.[99] He juxtaposed such "hatred of the negro"[100] with Garibaldi's call to admit "all colored brethren," noting "What a difference between the spirit of tyranny and that of liberty; more especially when the tyrant dwells in a land of liberty and the patriot in that of tyrants."[101] A few brave white souls asserted the universality of Masonic bonds, imagining a day when "the two bodies may peacefully unite, and Masonic universality will then become a reality, instead of being, as it is, a mere sham."[102] But the trend was in the other direction, as white grand lodge committees and publications across the North denounced European lodges that recognized black Masonry and continued to insist that Masons must be "free born," not simply "free men."[103] A Memphis Mason at an 1868 St. John's Day celebration considered the black Masons who assembled (presumably elsewhere) for the same Masonic holiday, then demanded of his audience, "What means that clandestine colored array that was called out to celebrate this day?—why assume they our name and form, and pretend to a work that has been denied them by the intelligence of our country and the landmarks of our order. Tell me, ye free-born sons of the white race."[104]

One white northern Masonic body went further. The committee of foreign correspondence of the Grand Lodge of New York, protesting a German lodge's plan to recognize the NGL, warned that such recognition would lead to violence. Many black Masons in the South were former slaves, it explained, "between whom and the whites there is irreconcilable and irradicable repugnance to social equality. A persistent attempt to enforce this equality would be very likely to result in the destruction of Masonry in the United States, or a war of races, ending in the extermination of the negro race."[105]

Lewis Hayden was aghast. Such rhetoric constituted "rather an incentive than a prediction" of racial violence, he knew, and he asked how Masons could square this call to violence with their principles.[106] His question was rhetorical, for the answers could be found frighteningly close to home. In 1865, President Andrew Johnson had made a similar prediction of "race war" if black Americans insisted on equality; in the years since, Johnson had betrayed the freedpeople's hopes that he would be Lincoln's worthy successor by siding again and again with the former slaveholders of the South and against the freedpeople and their Republican allies in Congress. Yet in 1867, as the struggle reached its climax, the white Grand Lodge of Massachusetts had hosted Andrew Johnson—their fellow Mason—at the dedication of their new Boston Temple.[107]

Instead of advancing together as brothers, Hayden came to understand, white Masons viewed black Masons as antagonists. Boston's white Masons refused the Prince Hall Masons' overtures for reconciliation because, like white Masons throughout the North, they hated the "advancement towards equality," evident in the "manly, upright, moral, and virtuous conduct" of African Americans, who were "fast advancing." This advancement was a point of particular pride, and pain: Hayden painted a bright and optimistic portrait of black southerners moving into new occupations, in trades and in "the humane support and protection of society." In the North, they were already hard at work at the highest levels of professional life and the minis-try.[108] But this self-reconstruction—this admirably Masonic commitment to "humane and manly acts"—had not brought respect and friendship.

Hayden turned his rage into an apocalyptic fantasy in which white Masons actually perpetrated a fratricidal "war of races." Bringing up to the present day the horrific events of the 1863 New York City draft riots, he reimagined them as the work of white Masons, emerging from their lodge at the call of scheming politicians to do the bloody work of race war. With their cer-emonial lambskin aprons still in place, they slaughtered a light-skinned black man—a man they had not recognized as a fellow Mason; a man who might have been the son or half-brother of one of their number, which made the fratricide simultaneously figurative and literal.[109]

Hayden's nightmare was not just catharsis; it was also politics. In depicting their white Masonic antagonists as enemies of the victorious Union, black Masons sought to recast the struggle within the order in sectional and party-political terms. They reached back to moments when many white Masons had stood for slavery and against the Lincoln government. Invoking slave emancipation as the gem in the nation's new crown, they linked the racial antagonism of white southern Masons to their recent status as slaveholders. When white Masons from slave states denounced northern white lodges for considering the claims of black Freemasons, one committee of black Masons asked, why did they not ask "the question in this form": "'Why will our Northern brethren persist in admitting our sons to fellowship in their Lodges, whom in the past we fathered, and afterwards kidnapped from their mothers' cradles?'"[110]

The spirit of the age did carry black Freemasons' cause a good distance, and the quest for recognition reached its apex in the mid-1870s. In Ohio, a proposal to recognize the state's black grand lodge came within a few dozen votes of success in 1875. The state's white grand master acknowledged the dif-ficulties inherent in such a move: "I am aware of the prejudice against the African race," he explained. "I am not entirely free from it myself." But this distaste, he continued, could not be the end of it. "We all have our passions and prejudices, and we should use our utmost endeavors to keep them within due bounds.... In this great centennial year, whilst liberty and equality are shed abroad through our great nation," he found it "right and proper" to unite the black and white grand lodges, heal the breaches, and recognize black Masons "as a part of the great Masonic family," to be "accorded their rights as such."[111] The vote was finally deferred for another year, but some felt the wind blowing in their direction. "Ohio has spoken," another state's grand master proclaimed, a bit prematurely.[112]

One leading white Mason, the former Confederate general Albert Pike, knew his Masonic history well and quietly acknowledged that his fellows stood on shaky ground. Boston's African Lodge was as legitimate in its origins as any of the mother lodges of Europe, he wrote in 1875. Yet for Pike this legitimacy could lead white Masonry in only one of two directions: a silent resolve to "let the thing drift" and protect white supremacy as long as possible or "full inclusion." In the latter case, this leading Masonic figure would depart. "I took my obligations to white men, not to Negroes. When I have to accept Negroes as *brothers* or leave Masonry, I shall leave it."[113]

Pike's view prevailed. In 1876 the motion to recognize a separate "African Grand Lodge" for Ohio finally came up for a vote in the white grand lodge. It lost by a margin of sixty votes out of more than seven hundred cast.[114] That September, as white supremacist militias in South Carolina and Louisiana saddled up to overthrow democratically elected governments, the leading lights of the white Massachusetts Grand Lodge affirmed the case against black Freemasonry. In a full-throated attack on Ohio's willingness to consider a dual system of white and black grand lodges, a committee rehearsed the past three decades of challenges to the legitimacy of any black Freemason who claimed Prince Hall origins.[115] Whatever opening Reconstruction had promised was now finally closed. Not until the turn of the twenty-first century would the nation's white lodges formally recognize black men as brothers.

Freemasonry did not, in the end, forge the ties Lewis Hayden had desired. Egalitarianism, unity, and central authority all found their racial and political limits within the brotherhood as surely as they did in the nation at large. Black Freemasons sought to shape Reconstruction, but try as they might to use its languages and principles to their benefit, neither they nor their projects escaped its tides and its tumult. In this, the brethren were in good company: no movement and no institution emerged from the crucible of those years without adjusting its sights downward from the jubilee of universal brotherhood. Indeed, when compared with the fate of the nearly four million freedpeople whose democratic aspirations fell before Democratic white supremacy during the late nineteenth century, the disappointments faced by some tens of thousands of black Freemasons might seem to merit no more than passing mention. But the goals toward which they struggled—unity in the face of adversity and the transformation of enemies into friends—represented impulses that would persist for a century and more to come in movements as various as Garveyism, labor unionism, black power, nonviolent resistance, and the black church. Lewis Hayden and his fellows dreamed of a "new fabric" for the postwar nation's social life, then worked tirelessly to make that vision real. How many, in any era, can say they did as much?

CHAPTER 6

"They Are Nevertheless Our Brethren"

The Order of the Eastern Star and the Battle for Women's Leadership, 1874–1926

BRITTNEY C. COOPER

In 1924, the national leadership of the Order of the Eastern Star (OES), the female auxiliary to the Prince Hall Masons, found itself embroiled in controversy over the male and female leadership of various local and state chapters of the order. Although both men and women could be members and leaders in the OES, the grand matron was constitutionally the presiding officer. This had led in many jurisdictions to a "lack of co-operation between the Grand Matron and the Grand Patron" because "in most cases the Grand Patron has overlooked the fact that the Grand Matron is the presiding officer," preferring to act not as "her legal adviser or assistant" but rather as "her superior dictator." Mrs. S. Joe Brown, international grand matron of the OES, recommended in her biennial address to the order that these overzealous grand patrons reacquaint themselves with the constitution and laws of the order so that they might "get a proper conception of the relative function of the offices" and "not attempt to perform both."[1] Within the bylaws of the International Conference of Chapters, the grand matron was the presiding officer and held financial signing power; the job of the grand patron was to "to assist and advise the International Grand Matron in the discharge of her duties."

Worse still than these internal squabbles within local chapters were the state-level cases in which the "Grand Master of the A.F. & A.M." acted as though he were "also Grand Master of the OES," going so far as to pursue litigation against OES chapters that refused to comply with Masonic directives. Although such OES court cases had previously been pursued in Washington, Louisiana, and West Virginia, the tensions between groups came to a head in 1920. Crittenden Clark, grand master of the African American Masons of Missouri, attempted to wrest power from the Missouri United Grand Chapter of OES by forbidding Masons to be members of the group and attempting to form and officially recognize a new OES body called Harmony Grand Chapter. The United Grand Chapter had recently amended its constitution to say that members could not hold leadership positions in other grand bodies. Clark rightfully perceived this language as an attempt by the women to gain more control of their organization. Mary Woods, grand matron of the United Grand Chapter, retaliated against Clark's efforts by filing a legal injunction to prevent him from removing files and other legal documents from the chapter's offices. For the next four years, the groups argued over which chapter was in fact the official OES body in that state. The struggle culminated at the 1924 biennial, when Brown called a joint session on cooperation between the A.F. & A.M. and the OES to attempt to mediate the feud.

Brown's position on the conflicts was clear: she supported women's right to lead. She viewed the attempt of black Masons and male Eastern Stars to override women's leadership as a sexist and racially divisive act that "prov[ed] to members of the other race either that our men have no confidence in their women or that we are not yet ready for our own leadership."[2] Although she reaffirmed the Masons' original intent to create the order "for the protection of their wives, widows, mothers, sisters, and daughters," she insisted that a spirit of "cordial co-operation" rather than male headship should guide the future leadership policies of the organizations.

The conflicts between male and female Eastern Stars illumine broader issues related to gender politics and leadership within African American communities in the first three decades of the twentieth century. Fraternal auxiliaries promoted social goals—care for children, widows, the sick, and the dead—that allowed black women to capitalize on gendered notions of care as feminine labor while upholding Christian notions of pious service and self-sacrifice. Through their work in fraternal auxiliaries, black women spearheaded a range of racial uplift projects, including creating homes for widows and orphans, offering life and burial insurance for local black communities, and financially supporting the building of churches and schools. These assignments indicate, however, that the relationship between fraternal orders and their female auxiliaries was not always clearly defined and that these relationships were continually contested and renegotiated in conflicts over gender roles.

Often, histories of feminist and womanist activism within black communities situate the emergence of these ideas and practices within institutional histories of the black church or of black women's organizations like the National Association of Colored Women (NACW). But black women's multiple organizational interactions were overlapping rather than discrete, and they pursued community agendas not just through club and church work but also through their membership in fraternities. While Evelyn Brooks Higginbotham argues that we can locate a nascent womanist theology emerging from the women's movement in the black Baptist Church between 1880 and 1920, in that same period—roughly between the founding of the first OES chapter in 1875 in Washington, D.C., and the 1924 biennial—these same battles over theology and leadership took place within black fraternal orders.[3] A closer look at the rituals of the fraternal orders offers additional insight into the ways that black women refashioned theological dictates around gender in order to expand their leadership roles within their communities.

Black women's organizational participation in fraternities provides another source for ascertaining their thinking about race and gender politics in the early twentieth century. As Elsa Barkley Brown has noted in her work on women in the Independent Order of St. Luke, "too often we have assumed that theory is to be found only in carefully articulated position statements." But as in the case of fraternal leaders like Maggie Lena Walker and Mrs. S. Joe Brown, "the clearest articulation of [their] theoretical perspective[s]" is to be found in their organizational affiliations and community and political activities.[4] The organizational leadership history of Sue M. Brown, international grand matron of the OES from 1922 to 1926, coupled with a critical reading and contextualization of her 1925 history of the order and her response to the Eastern Star legal cases, shows that the OES, and women's auxiliaries to fraternal orders more generally, served as both battleground and laboratory in the quest to train and employ African American women in racial leadership roles.

Racial Pride, Institution Building, and the Gendered Politics of History

The Order of the Eastern Star was originally founded in 1874 as the female auxiliary for the daughters, wives, sisters, and nieces of Prince Hall Freemasons. In its incipient stages, nine grand (state) chapters were founded in various eastern seaboard cities, including Washington, D.C. and Philadelphia.[5] Lacking a national coordinating body, all but two chapters had become defunct within a matter of years. In 1907, Mrs. Letitia L. Foy called together the few existing chapters of the Order of Eastern Star to form a national body known as the Supreme Grand Chapter of the OES. This national body, later designated the International Conference of Grand Chapters of the OES, sought "a better interpretation of and more uniformity in the ritualistic work" and to "encourage the organization of chapters," and facilitate female cooperation "in the great labors of Masonry, by assisting in and in some respects directing the charities and other work in the cause of human progress."[6]

Sue M. Wilson Brown published *The History of the Order of the Eastern Star among Colored Peoples* in 1925. Brown, also known as Mrs. S. Joe Brown, was no stranger to organizational leadership. Born in 1877 in Staunton, Virginia, she married University of Iowa graduate and attorney S. Joe Brown in 1902. She was an active member of the national club women's movement, serving as president of the Iowa Federation of Colored Women from 1915 to 1917 and Director of Fraternal Relations for the NACW in the 1920s. Brown's husband founded the first chapter of the National Association for the Advancement of Colored People (NAACP) in Iowa, and she succeeded him as president, serving from 1925 to 1931. She also served as first vice president of the National League of Republican Colored Women (NLRCW), a group founded by Nannie Helen Burroughs in 1924.[7]

Fraternal orders were bastions of financial capital in black communities. Under the auspices of fraternal leadership, black men and women often undertook major capital building projects with schools, temples, and churches. In fact, the fraternal temple in Fort Worth, Texas, housed not only the International Conference of Eastern Star but also the Temple Fraternal Bank and Trust Company, a financial institution worth over $100,000. Brown sought to ensure that women's participation in these building projects was part of the Masonic historical record. She argued that "woman has always been known as a home-builder, although the great world knows little of her deeds of heroism, her self-denial and her real devotion to suffering humanity. By experience she knows what it is to be widowed and homeless [;] therefore she has gladly contributed her part in furnishing and supporting homes for widows and orphans, and has constantly urged the fraternity to build such where there are none."[8] Brown's focus on the importance of black women's financial support to making Masonic building projects successful was also intended to suggest the need for their expanded participation in racial uplift work. Although Brown acknowledged building projects like the Masonic orphanage in Americus, Georgia, and the Widows and Orphans Home in Jacksonville, Florida, as projects spearheaded by Masons, she also claimed these endeavors as achievements of the Eastern Star. Brown was no stranger to institution building herself, having spearheaded the creation of a dormitory for African American women students at the University of Iowa through her work with the Iowa Federation of Colored Women's Clubs. Eventually that dormitory was renamed Sue Brown Hall in honor of her efforts to finance and maintain it. Richard Breaux notes that Brown and other women most likely used their training gained from work with the NACW and the OES to undertake these types of philanthropic projects.[9]

In his book *Manliness and Its Discontents* Martin Summers argues that Brown's invocation of domestic rhetoric in her speech relied on a "gender-essentialist framework"—a vision of the social order in which women and men had distinct and different abilities, roles, and responsibilities. Though he concedes that "Brown's invocation of the black woman as 'homebuilder' was not a complete acquiescence to the public-private organization of gender," he concludes that "Brown envisioned women's work in the home and in other private institutions as the avenue through which they would be best equipped to affect political change and race progress."[10] Summers's interpretation of Brown as a champion of domesticity constitutes a misreading of her gender politics. Brown's acknowledgment of women's work in the domestic sphere should not be automatically read as a capitulation to gender essentialism. She suggested that experience rather than biology positioned women socially to have an appreciation for the value of race work in the domestic sphere. Moreover, she argued that such appreciation was best demonstrated through women's concrete participation in institution-building projects. And though she claimed not to want to drag the order into politics, she actively encouraged women "to make use of their right of suffrage" in order to elect legislators who would "safeguard the interest of our group."[11] Thus she offered a multilayered conception of the various ways black women could participate in racial uplift work, moving from the domestic sphere into the public sphere through the promotion of healthy homes, political participation, and community institution building.

Brown's inclusion of Masonic building projects within her history of the Order of Eastern Star reflects a high degree of awareness among black women about the importance of history and historical interpretation. One of Brown's primary goals in starting new youth chapters of the OES and the NAACP was the teaching of "race history," which could be used to inculcate leadership ideals and racial pride in the forthcoming generation. In her 1924 address, Brown recommended that "a committee be appointed to publish a history of the Order of Eastern Star among Colored People," which would not only "preserv[e] a most important phase of our Race History" but would also "attract to our beautiful Order many who are ignorant of its glorious past of achievements...."[12] This documentary impulse has a long history among African American women. Beginning in the 1890s, black women like Anna Julia Cooper and Gertrude Mossell published works that documented the contributions of their forebears.[13] Race women like Mary Church Terrell and Ida B. Wells also wrote explicitly about the importance of race history in their autobiographies. The writing of race histories was not new, but black women's participation in the enterprise was, and their impulse to do so reflected a commitment to ensuring that the role of black women in racial uplift and advancement was not struck from the history of black achievement.[14] Given her prior experience with organizational histories and her leadership of her local NAACP chapter, Brown would have been an invaluable resource to her husband, who authored the organizational history of the Iowa NAACP in the late 1920s.[15]

Brown's explicit support of black institution building and the inculcation of racial pride through teaching black history place her and the work of the OES squarely within the complicated tradition of black nationalism. With regard to black women, this tradition is complicated in large part because black women's participation in multiple organizational networks suggests at best a pragmatic rather than an ideological commitment to black nationalism. As Kate Dossett argues, black women took a "flexible approach [to their] political groupings, economic initiatives, cultural protests and organizational strategies, which challenged the integrationist versus black nationalist dichotomy constructed by their contemporaries and built up by later narratives of American history."[16] Brown was equally, if not more, committed to the integrationist aims of the NAACP. Her complex allegiances to these competing ideological aims confirm Dossett's argument that historians must mine all these traditions in order to adequately and comprehensively characterize black women's race work. Black women's own commitment to authoring women-centered histories acted as a specific form of resistance to the masculinist tenor of black men's nationalist historical writing, which failed to acknowledge female contributions or marginalized those contributions through paternalistic rhetoric.

These women-centered histories, particularly their documentation of women's activism, offer rich intellectual genealogies, which situate black women's contributions at the intersections of both racial theory and practice. For instance, Brown notes that the OES was invited to participate in the Third Pan-African Congress in 1923 in London, although prohibitive costs prevented her from attending. She was also invited to attend the Negro

Sanhedrin or All-Race Conference spearheaded by Kelly Miller, a Howard University sociologist, in 1924. Pledging her full support for the confer-ence, Brown sent a representative to the event, which was held in Chicago. She suggested that the collaborative underpinnings of this group—which brought together all major racial organizations, church groups, sororities, and fraternities—reflected her own commitment to collaboration within the OES. This desire for cooperation led Brown to organize the Inter-Fraternity Council in Iowa, with "an object quite similar to that of the Sanhedrin, namely closer contact between different of our groups."[17] The OES's participation in the Sanhedrin Conference and support of the Pan-African Conference reflected a much broader history of black female participation in apparently male-led racial endeavors than has been recognized.[18] Brown's support for Pan-African efforts in addition to her work as "foreign correspondent" for the Iowa OES also reflects evidence of the diasporic consciousness that per-meated black political and cultural organizations in the 1920s. Moreover, the OES's participation in these various racial groups exemplified the large degree of cross-pollination between black women's organizations and larger race-based groups, particularly in major cities like Chicago and New York.

Black Women's Overlapping Organizational Networks

Brown's own history of organizational leadership reflected the scope of black women's overlapping organizational participation in the first three decades of the twentieth century. Within varied groups like the NACW, women's fraternal orders, and the black church, black women learned and extended leadership for the cause of racial advancement. While much contemporary scholarship has considered the role of race women within the church and the NACW, little scholarship has considered the role that fraternal organizations played in nurturing black women for leadership and for the work of uplift among black women.[19] Black women recognized the dialogic nature of their organizational interactions, however, and used their positions and connec-tions within these groups to advance the cause of the race on many different fronts. Fannie Barrier Williams, a prominent clubwoman from Chicago and a public intellectual, wrote in a 1900 article on the history and purpose of the NACW that two institutions had been essential in equipping black women for national club leadership—churches and secret societies. Secret societies had served as "another school of preparation for colored women." Quoting from an unattributed source, Williams wrote that "'the ritual of the secret societies is not without a certain social value.'" In line with the elitist tenden-cies that had come to characterize the club movement, Williams noted that secret societies "demand a higher order of intelligence than is required for church membership." In other words, they were more discerning in selecting members. In addition, however, secret societies inculcated the types of values—"care for the sick, provisions for the decent burial of the indigent dead, the care for orphans, and the enlarging of the sense of sisterhood"— that were central to the work of women's clubs. Inculcating these values led to the "development of the very conditions of heart that qualify women for the more inclusive work of those social reforms that are the aim of women's clubs." Both churches and secret societies had acquainted "colored women . . . with the general social condition of the race and the possibilities of social improvement."[20] Notwithstanding the elitism of Williams's statement, her historical assessment of the important role of secret societies as a training ground for black female leadership demands consideration.

In particular, her observations point to the ways that powerful networks allowed black female leaders to deal with multiple aspects of both race and gender discrimination by working simultaneously in a variety of groups. For instance, many of the women who made up the NLRCW were also members of the NACW. In fact, the NLRCW held its biennial meetings immediately following the biennial conferences of the NACW in the same city. Whereas the NLRCW was explicitly partisan in its work, the NACW attempted to remain nonpartisan in order to have the broadest possible coalitions of women.[21] Fraternal groups were also generally nonpartisan, and Brown insisted that the order should not be "tak[en] into politics." At the same time, however, she urged that "in this new day our women everywhere should be urged to make use of their right of suffrage, where they are permitted to do so and that when they vote not to fail to place in office men and women who will safeguard the interest of our group," particularly with regard to the passage of the Dyer Anti-Lynching Bill.[22] Brown understood the importance of a politicized racial body attentive to critical acts of legislation that could improve black life, and she deftly negotiated the advocacy of such politics under the nonpartisan agenda of the OES. Most important, her comments—and her committed participation in the Republican Party—reveal the critical role Brown believed women played in the politics of racial issues.[23]

Race women also often advocated for gender equality by framing black women's activism as critical to racial progress as a whole. While working as youth director for a local NAACP branch, Brown was approached by the national NAACP leadership to assist them in securing a speaking engagement before the Masons and the Eastern Stars at their 1924 national convention. Although she was not yet president of her local NAACP, Brown was considered a critical point of contact for both groups because of her position as international grand matron. She had transformed a female leadership tradition of supervising organizational youth initiatives into a key OES organizational leadership position. The NAACP leadership believed that collaborative efforts with the Masons and Eastern Stars would offer a critical avenue for disseminating information on racial progress and for drawing more black people into racial struggles. Despite her gender, NAACP leaders used their contact with Brown to cement relationships with both fraternal groups.[24]

William Pickens, the field secretary of the NAACP, had addressed the previous conference in 1922, and his address had spurred OES members to support the NAACP's anti-lynching efforts financially. Brown noted that the local OES chapters in her home state had raised nearly $200 on behalf of OES to support the campaign. Most important for Brown, she wanted to make sure that "our organization" was "on record in a more tangible way" in support of the Dyer Anti-Lynching Bill.[25] Her efforts culminated in an invitation to make a formal statement for the International Conference of Grand Chapters on the anti-lynching measure in an NAACP publication. It was the conjunction of her work with the Iowa OES and the NAACP that brought Brown to the attention of national NAACP leaders such as Joel Spingarn and James Weldon Johnson. Her work at the intersections of these many groups exemplified how race women used a variety of organizational connections—local and national—to contribute financial, intellectual, and political leadership in the advancement of African Americans.

Brown applied her training in establishing youth branches of the NAACP in Iowa to building similar branches within the OES. In her biennial address to the OES, she instructed the chapters that "wherever it is practicable the various Grand Jurisdictions establish some form of Juvenile Department...and that in those jurisdictions where such is not thought practicable, there be organized a Junior Division of the National Association for the Advancement of Colored People in which Race History is taught and black ideals instilled into our young people."[26] Brown joined with black female educators who were calling for the teaching of race history in a comprehensive and systematic way in schools and community institutions; race women relied on multiple organizations including the NACW, the NAACP, the OES, and the International Council of Women of the Darker Races, founded by Margaret Murray Washington in 1922, to implement and sustain these black history education programs.

The scale and success of black women's organizational affiliations in the first three decades of the twentieth century undoubtedly infused race women with confidence and made them reluctant to submit to a male leadership model. Fannie Barrier Williams and other race women routinely asserted the importance of women's clubs and women's work more generally for racial uplift, and they often argued that women were more effective at race work than men.[27] The struggles for women's leadership within the OES happened in tandem with similar struggles in other racial and religious organizations intertwined with the OES; together their web of interactions furthered their capacity to assert the importance of women's racial work.

The Role of Fraternal Orders in Shaping Conceptions of Black Female Leadership

Black activist women's participation in the OES and similar orders shaped their understanding of what black female leadership could and should look like. Those who wanted to lead had to be intelligent, have broad social sympathies, a commitment to sisterhood, and a broad knowledge of different facets of the race problem. Moreover, these women had to be committed to the work of social reform. These values constitute a kind of credo for race women's definition of black womanhood in the early twentieth century. In Williams's view, the rituals and values that characterized secret societies made them apt training ground for preparing women to do race work and to lead lives of acceptable black womanhood.

Summers argues that Prince Hall Freemasonry was "instrumental in contributing to the gender identity formation of large numbers of middle-class black men." The OES had similar implications for black women. On the basis of numbers alone, the Masons and Eastern Stars, along with other fraternal groups, had a significant ability to impact conceptions of masculinity, womanhood, and leadership among black people. By the 1920s, the Masons had nearly 300,000 members, while the Eastern Stars approached 120,000.[28] With regard to leadership models, Summers notes that "the order drew links between production, providership, respectability, and racial progress and conflated them with manhood. Moreover, Masons framed these relationships as natural and transhistorical." Through these constructions, "women became subordinated within this gendered framework of racial progress."[29] Women and youth, according to Summers, became "negative referents in the rhetoric, organizational framework, and rituals of their respective movements." Masons used "their relationships with the women's auxiliaries of local lodges, the national independent order of Eastern Star, [and] various youth departments within the fraternal organization," to articulate "a gender identity that was grounded in notions of providing for, and protecting, black families, black communities, and the race in general."[30] As a result, assertive attempts at leadership among black women met varied responses among black Masons. Some men attempted to fully suppress black women's leadership; conversely, others "recognized women's authority even as they sought to contain that authority within a traditional women's sphere that was still ancillary to the 'real' work of men."[31]

These conflicting ideological views of women's roles in the order came to a head in the 1920 Missouri conflict. Female members of the United Grand Chapter of OES successfully revised their constitution to limit the power of male members by including language that forbade OES leaders from holding positions in "other grand bodies."[32] Crittenden Clark reacted with an open letter prohibiting Masons from becoming members of that chapter. If Masons could not hold leadership positions, then they simply would not participate. In his discussion of the conflict, Martin Summers notes that the two bodies framed their attempts at arbitration very differently. After forming a committee to resolve the dispute, Clark argued that OES participation in the committee was "an act of contrition," in which OES members ought to make amends for transgressing proper roles and boundaries. The female members of OES viewed committee participation as an opportunity to plead their case and gain support for more autonomous operation.[33] Initially the OES members of the committee planned to capitulate to Clark's rhetoric and attempts to bring the OES under subordination, but other members of the Eastern Star, particularly the past grand matron Mary Woods, obtained an injunction barring committee members and Masons "from taking records from Grand Chapter offices" for use in the committee's adjudication.[34] Eventually several independent chapters of the OES were formed in Missouri, but only one, Harmony Grand Chapter, was recognized by the Missouri Grand Chapter of Prince Hall. In stark contrast to the leadership of the United Grand Chapter, the new female leadership of Harmony Grand Chapter affirmed their belief in and acceptance of "the Masonic rights that were given to [them] by [their] fathers, husbands, sons and brothers."[35] Summers notes that even after the disintegration of the United Grand Chapter of OES, Clark still engaged in a level of "paternalistic posturing," in which he characterized the splinter OES groups as "wayward children," unlike the Harmony Chapter, which submitted to his unquestioned authority. Such characterizations met with continued resistance from the original OES leadership, who declared the Harmony chapter to be illegitimate.[36] The schism led to several court cases in Missouri as chapters battled "over who held the legal rights to retain the extant records, property and other assets of the organization."[37]

For Brown, these attempts at male domination were not only exasperating but embarrassing. She worried that this "airing of dirty laundry" created a damaging public spectacle for both groups. She juxtaposed the irony of black men taking black women to court to gain leadership against the original purposes of the OES to protect their female family members. Clearly, this protectionist impulse had become somewhat obsolete, and Brown conceded as much, arguing instead for a spirit of cooperation. Her inversion of the rhetoric of protection in favor of an ethic of collaboration signaled a significant shift among black women in the quest for leadership. Whereas earlier women like Anna Julia Cooper had called on race men to protect black women, Brown believed that the internal bickering among the two groups had distracted both from the larger goal of racial progress. Furthermore, in her estimation, black men's zeal for power over the OES actually impaired their ability to act as its true protector.

To demonstrate her own leadership power, Brown informed the audience that she had called for a session at the conference on the topic "Cooperation between the A.F. & A.M. and the OES." Brown hoped that this session, which included among its presenters several Masons at the heart of the controversy, would allow the two groups to reach a consensus concerning the role of women. Because the courts were "slow to step in and attempt to arbitrate between" fraternal and religious factions and because such lethargy had left the Missouri cases unresolved for over three years, Brown argued that the international conference, while not possessing binding authority, was still the "proper place for representatives of these rival grand chapters to come together and confer."[38] Brown's husband, S. Joe Brown—along with Crittenden Clark, Mary Woods, and several others—participated in the conversation. Several members voiced disdain over the inclusion of the offending parties, but Brown reminded them that the accused grand masters "are nevertheless our brethren. We are their wives, mothers, sisters, and daughters and believe that no harm and unquestionably much good might result from this symposium."[39] Interestingly, Brown invoked familial language in order to foster reconciliation between the two groups. During the conflicts in Missouri, Clark had done the same thing, but his invocations were couched in a controlling paternalism. Brown's invocation of family, however, reflected the deft rhetorical negotiations that black female leaders had to make in order to establish authority and rapport in their public leadership role. In this respect, they invoked a horizontal relational ethic that placed high priority on maintaining productive relationships among members. Clark, by contrast, insisted on a relational hierarchy with men on top and women on bottom. Ultimately Brown assumed the role of mediator in this conflict, offering the opposing parties the opportunity to rationally resolve their issues. Because logical and rational negotiation was generally viewed as the province of men, Brown couched her move in a relational language that would prove more acceptable to an audience with strong investments in gender roles.

Even though the OES had initially been created to support the work of the Masons, by 1925 Brown had made it clear that women planned not only to *assist* in the work but also to *direct* certain projects, particularly as they related to charitable work. Her views illustrate the ways in which black women entered into and transformed these spaces into sites for the performance of race womanhood and into preparatory ground for racial leadership. For instance, while men used black women's auxiliaries and youth groups as a "negative referent" upon which to construct notions of masculinity, women like Brown transformed these groups into powerful organizations that prepared women and youth to grapple with and provide solutions for major racial questions. Rather than viewing the OES in opposition to Freemasonry, Brown pushed for and obtained collaboration between the two groups. The question, then, is what conceptions of leadership and female subjectivity black women fashioned for themselves through their participation in the OES.

In Brown's address, she explicitly charged her audience that membership in the OES "should be a greater force in stimulating its members to a more intelligent participation in civic, national, and international affairs, each standing out in our several communities for a practical application of the principles and ideals exemplified in the characters of our five heroines."[40] The five points of the Eastern Star logo symbolize five biblical women: Jephtha's daughter Adah, Ruth, Esther, Martha, and Electa. Each woman symbolized particular characteristics that constituted an all encompassing system of female virtue based on fidelity, friendship, sisterhood, kindness, love, philanthropy, and sacrifice.[41] Cheryl Townsend Gilkes argues that the biblical figures associated with Eastern Star are unique primarily because they "symbolize and affirm dependence and submission."[42] There does not seem to be a consensus on the particular value that each woman represents, as differing publications of the ritual vary, especially over time. According to Gilkes, however, Jephtha's daughter symbolizes fidelity; Ruth, kindness and love; Esther, truth and purity; Martha, sincerity and immortality; and Electa, fervency and commitment.[43] Whereas men were "admonished to be builders and leaders, like the characters in their part of the Biblical story, the women are encouraged to be the heroines in their part of the story through their devotion and support of their men and communities."[44] The central symbolic figures of the OES were designed to inculcate an appreciation for the biblical helpmate model of leadership in which women viewed their roles as complementary and ancillary to the work of men.

Although promulgation of this model might have been the primary goal of the original authors of the OES ritual, black women, employing their own budding experience with feminist theology, resisted those theological notions that confined them to a subordinate role within the organization.[45] For instance, some rituals interpret Electa, or the "elect lady" addressed in 2 John, as a philanthropist. Given race women's long history of building orphanages, schools, and convalescent homes to address the lack of social welfare provisions for black people in need, it is more believable that black OES members adopted this interpretation. Black women also adopted Esther as a fearless crusader for racial justice rather than for her more sedate characteristics of truth and purity.

Evelyn Brooks Higginbotham has argued that between 1880 and 1920 black women advanced a nascent form of feminist theology that "invoked biblical passages that portrayed positive images of women and reinforced their claim to the public realm."[46] Moreover, "they rejected a model of womanhood that was fragile and passive."[47] Race women often compared themselves to women like Esther, Deborah, and Mary, the mother of Jesus, as exemplars of female virtue and godly leadership. Higginbotham locates a central site of this emergent black womanist theology within the black Baptist women's movement, but black women simultaneously participated in fraternal orders that heavily invoked biblical imagery in their organizational rituals. The church and the secret society should properly be viewed, then, as complementary sites in which black women challenged prevailing conceptions of womanhood.

The five heroines, as interpreted by black fraternal women, provided models for the active, self-directing roles undertaken by OES women. Brown highlighted those roles in her address when she recounted the membership and financial status of the organization, noting that there were thirty-five grand jurisdictions and over one hundred thousand members, with a combined financial base of nearly half a million dollars. Many OES chapters owned property and/or assisted the Masons with the maintenance of their temples. Several chapters also operated burial funds and owned printing presses.[48] Although Brown's address invoked the rhetoric of "assistance," her celebration of black women's myriad business endeavors bespoke a commitment to women's direct leadership of the OES.

Here, as elsewhere, Brown directly challenged the notion that women should be relegated to the private or domestic sphere. Summers notes that Masons also "utilized the trope of heroic womanhood" but for very different ends. For Masonic purposes, "female activism [while] indispensable to the efforts of men" ultimately found its motivations in "a desire to sacrifice oneself to the greater cause of men's activism."[49] On the other hand, the order provided an additional organizational mechanism for women to affect large-scale questions serving racial advancement. In this respect, Brown's rhetoric fits within a much larger tradition of race women like Anna Julia Cooper, Ida B. Wells, Mary Church Terrell, and Pauline Hopkins, who suggested that black women and their organizations had a critical role to play in racial and national advancement. Moreover, she explicitly challenged the theology of female domestication and submission, arguing instead that the lives of the Eastern Stars' biblical heroines should rightly be read as supporting female participation in public life. Her call for a pragmatic application of these biblical models of leadership also fits within a long-standing tradition among black women of merging theory with practice in their community work.[50]

If the use of biblical figures indicates the ways in which OES members conceptualized female leadership, their use of rituals further illumined their negotiation of gender roles within the fraternity. According to the religious historian John Giggie, the Prince Hall Masons located the roots of black Masonry in the history of King Solomon, "who integrated the knowledge of the ages into a new physical science that became the moral and intellectual basis for sustaining human civilization."[51] At each level of initiation, Masons gained access to more of Solomon's truths. It is significant that much of Masonic lore located Solomon's wisdom in the "African cultures that preceded him."[52] Unlike its white counterparts, the Prince Hall OES incorporated a degree called the "Queen of the South" which referred explicitly to the biblical Queen of Sheba, who visited King Solomon in her quest for knowledge. Sue M. Brown indicated the importance of the Queen of the South degree to the OES during her address. She called for a uniformity of rituals among orders, suggesting that each order confer only the five degrees agreed upon by the OES and refrain from creating other rituals and degrees. The one exception was the degree of the Queen of the South, which she supported wholeheartedly because of its uniquely symbolic value for black women. The ritual script for initiation into the Queen of the South called for an initial resistance on the part of the Mason to the woman seeking additional knowledge, but "the candidate/queen eventually answered each of his objections to sharing with her the secrets—and the labor—of the Masonry."[53] The role playing involved in the degree of the Queen of the South points to two significant observations about the role of the OES in shaping black women's leadership. First, because of the frequent collaboration between Masons and Eastern Stars, the OES provided a significant space of negotiation between black men and women over women's leadership, even within the rituals that determined membership and rank. Second, in their pursuit of the degree of the Queen of the South, black women could ascend within the ranks of black cultural organizations to the position of intellectual, a role normally reserved for men. Their self-fashioning as intellectuals was a critical political intervention in larger discourses about black intellectual inferiority that excluded black men from participation in white intellectual networks and black women from participation in black male intellectual networks.

Black women could also become a part of a powerful history of racial achievement that began in Africa, again reinforcing a diasporic and transhistorical notion of black culture. Their experience in feminist theologizing would have made them aware that a critical part of Solomon's story lay in his interaction with the presumed African Queen of Sheba. In this respect, black women in the OES invoked their own biblical knowledge and helped to transform those stories into rituals that directly corresponded to black women's attempts to situate themselves as race leaders and intellectuals in the larger black public sphere. The ritualistic impulses of fraternal orders thus provided a unique mechanism whereby women could take a biblical character and actively inculcate values associated with that character into their own conceptions of leadership.

When faced with a rift that could have severely undercut the social and political impact of both the Prince Hall Masons and the Order of Eastern Star, Sue Brown drew upon a long tradition of black female leadership to reunite the rival groups. Her unapologetic assumption of the role of mediator within the conflict provided the most public signal of black women's move from an auxiliary role within black Freemasonry to a more central role in its progress. Brown's leadership was important because her commitment to women's rights and recognition did not occur at the expense of organizational unity. She understood that however sexist her male counterparts might be, they were "nevertheless [her] brethren."

Fraternal rituals and the commitment to notions of fraternity actually proved fertile ground in which black women could assert themselves as leaders and proprietors of racial uplift, not merely as assistants or helpmates to their male relatives. This training ground was itself a site of contestation among male and female African American activists. Brown's willingness to first expose and then challenge the faulty conceptions of male OES leaders and Masons about the capacity of women for leadership placed the OES squarely within the center of racial debates about the "woman question" that raged from the 1890s through the early twentieth century. In order to make more than incremental gains within these battles, black women like Brown demonstrated intellectual prowess, mediation skills, an aptitude for public debate, and a commitment to forthright, if friendly, confrontation over expanding gender norms.

Brown used her leadership role in the OES to engineer a set of important conversations about the role of women in racial uplift that then became critical for her work in other, more prominent organizations like the NAACP. In fact, in 1926, the NAACP director of branches, Robert Bagnall, solicited Brown as a consultant for establishing women's auxiliaries to local NAACP branches. In particular, the director wanted Brown's comments on the constitutional articles that would establish these auxiliaries, in order to "define carefully the relationship of the women's auxiliary to the branch."[54] Evidently Brown had considerable expertise in this area. Bagnall's insistence that the relationship of female-led auxiliaries to the larger organizational body be properly defined reflected growing challenges by black women to black men's patriarchal control of racial leadership, not just in fraternal orders but also in churches and in groups focusing on various aspects of the race problem. In many instances, black men were reluctant to relinquish power to women because much of their status as men in the broader public depended to a large extent on the control they were able to exert within race-based organizations.

Spurred by an emerging womanist theology that challenged women's subordination to men within the church, fraternal women added and transformed organizational rituals based on female biblical characters in ways that expanded racial conceptions of women's leadership. By adding additional degrees like the Queen of the South, the Order of Eastern Star created an institutional platform whereby race women could gain the additional knowledge that would equip them to be considered effective race leaders. The continual interplay of religion and fraternity suggests that these two institutions had complementary but distinct functions within African American communities. In many communities, fraternal orders acted as the social welfare arm of the church, providing financially for orphans, widows, and those who were sick. Specifically with regard to gender politics, black women found more freedom to pursue racial uplift agendas through their fraternal auxiliaries than they found in the male supremacist cultures of the church, largely because theology could not be used to demand their silence within the fraternal community.

Among African American women, perhaps what is more important is how fraternal memberships helped to constitute a nexus of race-based organizational connections. Brown's leadership history in the OES and her use of that connection in her work with the NAACP and the NACW reflect the numerous overlapping networks in which race women both received leadership training and performed racial uplift work. They understood that racial leadership was not a solitary or singular undertaking, and they drew on a wealth of shared experience in multiple local and national networks of black women. Their fraternal work helped establish and maintain a rich culture of organizational leadership and created additional opportunities for black women to do the important work of racial uplift.

CHAPTER 7

The Prince Hall Masons and the African American Church

The Labors of Grand Master and Bishop
James Walker Hood, 1831–1918

DAVID G. HACKETT

During the late nineteenth century, James Walker Hood was bishop of the North Carolina Conference of the African Methodist Episcopal Zion Church and grand master of the North Carolina Grand Lodge of Prince Hall Masons. In his forty-four years as bishop, half of that time as senior bishop of the denomination, Reverend Hood was instrumental in planting and nurturing his denomination's churches throughout the Carolinas and Virginia. Founder of North Carolina's denominational newspaper and college, author of five books including two histories of the AMEZ Church, and assistant superintendent of public instruction and magistrate in his adopted state, Hood represented the broad mainstream of black denominational leaders who came to the South from the North during and after the Civil War. Concurrently, Grand Master Hood superintended the southern jurisdiction of the Prince Hall Masonic Grand Lodge of New York and acted as a moving force behind the creation of the region's black Masonic lodges—often founding these secret male societies in the same places as his fledgling churches. At his death in 1918, the *Masonic Quarterly Review* hailed Hood as "one of the strong pillars of our foundation."[1] If Bishop Hood's life was indeed, according to his recent biographer, "a prism through which to understand black denominational leadership in the South during the period 1860–1920,"[2] then what does his leadership of both the Prince Hall Lodge and the AMEZ Church tell us about the nexus of fraternal lodges and African American Christianity at the turn of the twentieth century?

Scholars have noted but not substantially investigated the significance of fraternal orders in African American religious life. At the turn of the century, W. E. B. DuBois saw in these secret societies hope for the uplift of blacks through "mastery of the art of social organized life."[3] In 1910, Howard Odum ranked black fraternal orders equal in membership to the black church and "sometimes" more important.[4] In fact, according to *Who's Who of the Colored Race for 1915,* two-thirds of the most prominent African Americans held membership in both a national fraternal order and the black church. Forty-two percent of those holding joint memberships were Prince Hall Masons, one-third of whom were clergymen or church officers.[5] Subsequent research has explored the economic, class, and political importance of these orders while continuing to document their pervasive presence in African American society.[6] Yet none of these investigators have ventured into the meaning of fraternal beliefs and rituals for their members, and rarely have they explored the relationship between secret societies and the black church.[7]

In addition to the tendency among historians to underemphasize rites and beliefs, the study of the religious life of black fraternal orders has suffered from a paucity of evidence. The otherwise prolific Bishop Hood left few references to his lodge membership. Unlike the study of white lodges, which poses a problem not so much of finding materials as of making sense of them,[8] research into Prince Hall lodges is difficult because primary materials are harder to locate. This has partly to do with the scarcity of these records and partly with the still enforced "secrecy" of this secret society.[9] Nevertheless, in Hood's case some of the annual proceedings of the North Carolina Grand Lodge are available, and these records along with the minutes of the AMEZ North Carolina Conference allow us to observe similarities and differences between the two organizations and the role Hood played in each. Also available are several Prince Hall histories, some state-by-state proceedings, and a scattered national array of lodge information, members' writings, and newspaper accounts. Together these materials shed light on Hood's Masonic career while offering insight into the relationship between the lodge and the black church.

This chapter argues that for James Walker Hood the activities of the Prince Hall Masons complemented the work of the AMEZ Church. A considerable portion of the membership of Hood's North Carolina Prince Hall fraternity was drawn from the rolls of his North Carolina denomination. Though different in their beliefs and ritual lives, the two organizations were structurally similar. The origins of this relationship can be traced to the postrevolutionary era, when both mutual benefit societies and the black church provided seedbeds of autonomy and bulwarks against the racism of white society. After the Civil War, these two interwoven social institutions came to the South offering black southerners similar race histories that countered white racial images while providing meaning and hope for their lives. Bishop Hood appropriated from Masonry beliefs that complemented his missionary efforts, while his fraternity's practices created bonds among black men and helped them to become responsible members of the community. This marriage between the church and the lodge was not without conflicts with outsiders in the Holiness movement, between church and lodge members, and between men and women. Still, compared with white Masons, Bishop Hood's Prince Hall members were active supporters of the church in a common struggle against racism and for the self-determination of the African American community.

Church and Lodge

In late November of 1874, Bishop James Walker Hood presided over the week-long eleventh annual gathering of the ministers of the North Carolina Conference of the African Methodist Zion Church in New Berne, North Carolina. Reared in Pennsylvania and ordained in New England, Hood was pastor of a congregation in Bridgeport, Connecticut, when he was sent by his denomination as a missionary to the freedpeople in the South. He arrived in the city of New Berne in coastal North Carolina in 1864, was appointed bishop in 1872, and by 1874 had overseen the planting of 366 churches with over twenty thousand members.[10] As a northern missionary and church organizer, Hood operated in a milieu where most of the newly freed slaves were either completely unchurched or, in their exposure to religious teaching under slavery, were in need of additional structure and organization, at least from the northern perspective, in order to purify their Christianity from the distortions of southern white religion.[11] A religious conservative whose social activism stemmed from his belief that Christian conversion would lead to the downfall of oppression and social injustice, Hood urged his followers to pursue a "profound" commitment to Christ. This was especially important for ministerial candidates, whom the conference examined carefully for their "literary qualifications, their intemperate habits and filthy practices," and to whom the bishop directly appealed to honor the dignity of the ministry by living "holy and spotless lives." After these remarks Hood announced that, prior to the evening's "love feast," the Masonic fraternity would lay the cornerstone at New Berne's new brick church.[12]

Five days later, the Zion leader journeyed to Raleigh, where he was feted as "Most Worshipful Grand Master" at the fifth annual proceedings of the

Prince Hall Grand Lodge of Free and Accepted Ancient York Masons for the State of North Carolina. Shortly after his arrival in New Berne in 1864, Hood followed through on his commission as superintendent of the southern jurisdiction for the Prince Hall Masonic Lodge of New York by establishing King Solomon Lodge No. 1 in the same town where he organized his first AMEZ church.[13] The next three lodges were organized in the towns of Wilmington, Fayetteville, and Raleigh, sites of the largest AMEZ congregations.[14] In 1870, these four lodges formed themselves into the North Carolina Grand Lodge and unanimously elected Bishop Hood as their grand master. By 1874, there were eighteen Prince Hall lodges in the state with 478 members. In his address that year to his "dear Brethren," Grand Master Hood sounded notes of encouragement concerning the "state of the craft" that echoed—though in different language—the remarks he had made one week earlier to the AMEZ faithful regarding the state of their church. Appealing first to the "Supreme Grand Master" to bless their gathering "within these sacred walls," the Prince Hall leader pronounced that "the state of the craft in this jurisdiction is good." Most lodges were "composed of good, solid material, and, when the master's hammer has given [them] the necessary polish, [they] will form a beautiful structure." A few, notably his namesake J. W. Hood Lodge No. 8 in Goldsboro, "lacked Masonic ability," while the grand master reported that his best visit was to Pythagoras Lodge No. 6 in Smithville where most of "its members are professors of Christianity."[15] In assessing candidates for "the mysteries of Masonry" Hood urged that they be "men of active minds" who had, according to the grand lodge bylaws, "a desire for knowledge, and a sincere wish of being serviceable to [their] fellow-creatures." A candidate must also be "free," "of good standing as a citizen," and have no physical deformity "so as to deprive him from honestly acquiring the means of subsistence." On the last day of the gathering, Grand Master Hood prayed to the "Supreme Architect of the Universe" to "guide and govern all we do."[16]

Accompanying Bishop Hood in his journey from New Berne to Raleigh were several of his ministers who also served under his direction as leaders in Prince Hall Masonry. The 1874 AMEZ conference minutes list 192 ministers as members. Sixty-four, or one-third, of these conference members also appear in the available Prince Hall proceedings for the 1870s. These include one-third of the conference's ruling elders, some of whom held similar leadership positions within the grand lodge. Thomas H. Lomax, for example, was appointed presiding elder for the Charlotte district—one of six districts in the conference—by Bishop Hood in 1875. In that same year, Hood appointed Lomax district deputy grand master for the Charlotte district, one of five districts overseen by the grand lodge. Similarly, R. H. Simmons, a ruling elder throughout the 1870s, was appointed grand pursuivant within the grand lodge, in charge of instructing members in the lore and practice of Freemasonry. Several elders held important committee positions within both the conference and the grand lodge. Still others were both ministers of churches and leaders of their local lodges. In sum, in 1874 one-third of the AMEZ ministers in North Carolina were members and often leaders in Prince Hall Masonry. They in turn accounted for more than 13 percent of the state's 485 Prince Hall members. Since these figures do not include an untold number of church members who, like their ministers, followed their leader into the lodge, it appears that Grand Master Hood had forged a substantial portion of the leadership and membership of North Carolina's Prince Hall lodges from the leaders and members of his AMEZ denomination.[17]

Indeed, there were similarities between these two organizations. Not only did they share the same leader and an overlapping membership and exist in many of the same towns,[18] but they had similar organizational structures and appealed to the same broad cohort of young African American men. In both instances the annual meetings took place over several days and followed a rhythm of worship, business, and recreation. Central to each meeting was the bishop or grand master's address and report on his preceding year's visit to individual churches or lodges. Both were rational, hierarchical societies governed by bylaws and central committees. Enduring committees within the conference included credentials, finance, bylaws, and complaints, which had their parallels in the committees on credentials, finance, bylaws, and grievances within the grand lodge. Considerable time in each annual meeting was given over to complaints or grievances concerning existing members. AMEZ complaints involved intemperance, adultery, irregular credentials, and "preaching erroneous doctrine." Grand lodge penitents were more often assailed for being "dull and inactive," holding irregular credentials, or challenging Masonic doctrine. Finally, a major concern of both groups was the recruitment of able young men with "active intellects." AMEZ ministerial candidates were particularly scrutinized for their "clean" habits and Christian learning, while "good citizenship" and adequate employment were important criteria for becoming a Prince Hall Mason.[19] Taken together, the AMEZ conference and the Prince Hall Grand Lodge were structurally similar organizations.

And yet there were fundamental differences. The conference was the ruling body of a denomination of Christian men and women who believed in the literal Gospel and worshiped according to the practices of Methodism. The grand lodge, in contrast, was the governing body of a secret group of men whose beliefs stemmed from a variety of medieval, esoteric, and early Christian sources and who regularly passed their members through three successive rites of initiation. Hymn singing and sermons pervaded the Zion conference activities. Invocations of the Supreme Architect, esoteric rites, and flamboyant public processions distinguished the grand lodge gatherings. Church records marked time by the Christian calendar. Lodge minutes predated the Christian calendar by four thousand years to what Masons believed to be the beginning of time and Masonry. The December 1874 grand lodge proceedings, for example, are actually dated December 5874. The lodges themselves were named Hiram, Pythagoras, Widow's Son, Morning Star, Rising Sun, and even J. W. Hood to recognize important men and moments in Masonic lore. Unlike the Christian churches, which met to worship every Sunday, the lodges enacted their rituals twice a month on a weekday night, sometimes "before the full moon."[20] In moving from Sunday morning church services to weekday evening lodge meetings, Bishop Hood and other leading ministers left their sanctuaries; took off their ecclesial robes and entered lodge rooms decorated to resemble King Solomon's Temple; donned cloth aprons displaying the "All-Seeing Eye," embroidered collars, and jeweled pendants signifying their office; and assumed positions in a rectangle of elders. Despite their apparent structural similarities, there were significant differences of belief and ritual that separated the AMEZ church from the Prince Hall Lodge. How did Bishop Hood and his followers come to live in these mingled worlds? To try to answer this question we need first to consider the origins of the Prince Hall Lodge and the AMEZ Church and how each adapted to the needs and desires of African Americans.

Origins

Both the Prince Hall Lodge and the AMEZ Church emerged from the distinctive social milieu of free, urban African Americans after the Revolution. The earliest African American social institutions resulted from a mixture of black initiative and white discrimination. In Philadelphia, for example, Absalom Jones and Richard Allen created the Free African Society in 1787 as a mutual aid organization as well as a nondenominational religious association. Several years later, in perhaps the most famous event in African American religious history, Jones and other black members were forcibly removed from their prayer benches in St. George's Methodist Church. Subsequently, Jones and Allen created the African Episcopal and the African Methodist Episcopal churches. This incident of discrimination has influenced historians to emphasize white racism as the reason for the development of black churches. Albert Raboteau, in contrast, points to the earlier desires on the part of Jones and Allen to create a separate religious association as of equal importance with white racism in the creation of the black church.[21]

The close relationship between mutual benefit societies and the black church as both resources for black autonomy and barricades against white racism continued throughout the nineteenth century. African mutual aid societies assisted the needy, especially widows and their children, in return for modest dues. They also provided social networks for a community in flux by offering information on jobs, mobilizing public opinion, and cultivating social bonds. Many of Philadelphia's societies were associated with black churches, and many of their names indicate the continuing identity of blacks with their African heritage—the Daughters of Ethiopia, Daughters of Samaria, Angola Society, Sons of Africa, and the African Lodge of the Prince Hall Masons.[22] By the second quarter of the nineteenth century, Christian names predominated.[23] Out of the post-1820s Baltimore Mutual Aid Society, for example, grew at least three national societies: the Good Samaritans, the Nazarites, and the Galilean Fishermen.[24] By 1848, Philadelphia alone had over one hundred variously named small mutual benefit societies with a combined membership of more than eight thousand,[25] while in the South similar groups, like the Burying Ground Society of the Free People of Color of the City of Richmond (1815), had appeared. Many of the later societies, such as the New York Benevolent Branch of Bethel (1843), grew out of churches.[26] Yet the example of the African mutual benefit society preceding the Christian church suggests the weaving of African and Christian, secular and sacred, within and between these two primordial social institutions of African American culture.[27] These mutual influences were again on display in 1797 when Absalom Jones and Richard Allen—founders of the Free African Society and founding bishops of the African Episcopal and African Methodist Episcopal churches, respectively—established Philadelphia's African Lodge of Prince Hall Masons. In 1815, Absalom Jones became Pennsylvania's first grand master.

Masonry among African Americans began in Boston and spread to Philadelphia. In 1785 Prince Hall, an Indies-born artisan, along with fourteen other black Bostonians, was inducted into an English army lodge. Though their Masonic credentials were legitimate, the Grand Lodge of Massachusetts denied them admission, after which they applied to the Grand Lodge of England, which had recognized them as a valid Masonic lodge. Soon thereafter the growing number of black lodges created the African or Prince Hall Grand Lodge and, like their white counterparts had done after the Revolution, declared independence from the Grand Lodge of England.[28] From these beginnings, the Prince Hall lodges developed and, from the outset, reinforced their claims to authenticity in the eyes of European Americans

by largely following the beliefs and practices of European American lodges
while asserting to African Americans the ultimately African origins of the
Masonic fraternity.

Whatever their differences, all Masons trace their medieval origins to the
time of the Norman Conquest,[29] when guilds of stonemasons were essential to the building carried on by kings, nobles, and churchmen. When the
first grand lodge was formed in London in 1717, "Free," or independent,
Masonry[30] took on the character of a nobleman's club while retaining the
traditional features of medieval institutions connected to an artisan culture.
These included a secret brotherhood and the central importance of ritual,
initiation, and myths of origin.[31] When it migrated to the Continent and to
North America, the newly formulated Masonic order continued to alter its
beliefs and practices as it encountered different social and political contexts.[32]
By the middle of the eighteenth century, changes in the North American fraternity reflected shifting definitions of power and hierarchy embodied in the
American Revolution. Beginning in the 1750s, groups of mechanics, lesser
merchants, and military men—some of whom had been rejected by existing
lodges—transformed the social and intellectual boundaries of the fraternity.
By the 1790s, as the order spread rapidly through the countryside, these ambitious and politically active men began to describe the fraternity as embodying
the new republic's values of education, morality, and Christianity.[33]

Like the European Americans who joined this English society and adapted
it to their circumstances, African Americans found in the American Masonic
fraternity a useful "tool kit"[34] of social forms and ideals for adaptation to their
social environment. Like other mutual benefit societies, Prince Hall Masonry
offered its members economic aid and social connections. Unlike most other
societies, the first black Masons appear to have drawn their members from the
most "respectable" black families. The men who joined Philadelphia's First
African Lodge, for example, were among the most affluent and long-standing
black residents, even if their occupations did not measure up to bourgeois
status in their white neighbors' eyes.[35] Moreover, as the black equivalent of a
prestigious white society, Prince Hall leaders gained public recognition that
provided a stage for addressing the larger society. Until that time, usually
only black ministers received such public acknowledgment. Like the many
African American religious leaders who used the Declaration of Independence's trumpeting of equality to challenge racial inequality,[36] Prince Hall
and his followers employed the fraternity's ideals of unity and brotherhood
across racial and national lines to confront racism. "Live and act as Masons,"
Prince Hall charged his brothers, "give the right hand of affection and fellowship to whom it justly belongs; let their color and complexion be what it

will, let their nation be what it may, for they are your brethren and it is your indispensable duty so to do."[37] By asserting the egalitarian ideals of an international brotherhood, Prince Hall employed its moral authority to confront the contradictions of an American society that embraced equality yet denied rights of citizenship and humanity to black people.

At the same time, Prince Hall, the statesman Martin Delaney, and other early Masonic leaders created a history of the order that provided a powerful moral vision for the emerging African American community. While historians see the first Masons emerging from medieval stonemason guilds, Masons themselves, both white and black, trace the mythic origins of the fraternity to King Solomon, who, they believe, synthesized all previous wisdom into physical science and manifested it through the building of the Temple of Jerusalem. The three Masonic rites of initiation of Entered Apprentice, Fellow Craftsman, and Master Mason are intended to mark a deepening knowledge of the wisdom of this temple and, by analogy, the stages of life's journey. Masons, white and black, generally agree on this basic story and the rites that accompany it. Black Masons, however, claimed that the deeper truths presented by Solomon originated in the African civilization that preceded him. It was "the Africans," said Martin Delaney, "who were the authors of this mysterious and beautiful Order."[38] By this interpretation, black Masons were able to claim the legacy of Masonic history as their own and to contend that it was not a slave heritage but a glorious history in which Masonry was synonymous with freedom, liberty, and democratic government.

Though we do not know for certain when and where James Walker Hood entered into the "mysteries of Masonry," the evidence suggests that it was in 1855 when, as a young man of twenty-four, he first traveled from rural Pennsylvania to New York City and found work as a waiter. "Soon after I became of lawful age," he states in the North Carolina Grand Lodge proceedings, "I petitioned a regular Lodge, in due form, and my prayer was granted."[39] In the mid-nineteenth century, New York, Boston, and Philadelphia were the principal centers of the less than thirty Prince Hall lodges then in existence.[40] In joining the fraternity, the young Hood gained entrance into an influential society of African American men that encouraged his self-determination and opposed the racism of white society. Around the same time that the future grand master became a Mason, he also entered the ministry of the black church.

Hood had been born in 1831 into a religious family in rural southeastern Pennsylvania. His father, Levi, was a minister in the African Union Church, the very first black denomination, and his mother, Harriet, was a member of Richard Allen's Bethel AME Church. In 1855, during the young Hood's

sojourn in New York City, he joined a small congregation of the African
Union Church. In 1856, the Reverend Williams Councy, pastor of the congregation, granted Hood a preaching license. During the autumn of 1857
Hood relocated once again, to New Haven, Connecticut, but this time he
was unable to locate a branch of the African Union Church. So he joined a
quarterly conference of the Zion connection, which accepted his license to
preach. The following conference year, nearly two years after his affiliation
with the New Haven Quarterly Conference, that body recommended to
the June 1859 New England Annual Conference that it accept the young
minister on a trial basis. The annual conference consented to this request
and gave Hood an appointment of two stations in Nova Scotia. The AMEZ
Church, like most independent black denominations during these years, was
interested in the salvation of African people wherever they might be found.
After two years in Nova Scotia, Hood assumed the pastorate of a congregation in Bridgeport, Connecticut. Then, in 1863, members of the New
Haven conference, many of whom were from New Berne, North Carolina,
called on their bishop to send someone down to New Berne and surrounding areas to serve the newly emancipated people in areas captured by Union
forces. Shortly thereafter, in 1864, Reverend Hood set out on his mission to
the South.[41]

Like many black denominational leaders, Bishop Hood believed that the
black church in the United States had a providential role to play in society.
In his 1895 history of the African Methodist Episcopal Zion Church, the
Zion leader placed his denomination's story into the larger epic of the African exodus from white churches after the Revolution. The particular history
of the AMEZ denomination dates from 1796, when it was organized by a
group of black members protesting discrimination in the Methodist John
Street Church in New York City. Their first church, Zion, was built in 1800,
and from there emerged an African American denomination that continued
to follow Methodist polity. Like contemporary scholars, Hood saw the emergence of the African American church as both a reaction to white discrimination and an act of black self-determination. While decrying the particular
efforts of white Methodists to "maintain the inferiority of the Negro" in
the John Street Church, Bishop Hood also saw the late eighteenth and early
nineteenth-century movement of "colored members of all denominations"
into "the Negro Church" as guided by a "divine purpose." As he put it, "In
the unfolding of that Providence that underlay the human meanness which
produced the general exodus of the Afro-American race from the white
Church, there have come and still are coming to the proscribed race benefits
so rich, abundant, and glorious that the sufferings incident are not worthy

of mention." Without the black church, Hood proclaimed, the black man "would have had no opportunity for the development of his faculties, nor would he have had any platform on which to exhibit his vast possibilities."[42]

Though the founders of the new AMEZ denomination had, according to Hood, "no fault to find with the doctrine or form of government" of Methodism,[43] both he and other nineteenth-century "race historians" adapted the history of the Christian Church to serve the needs and desires of African Americans. As Laurie Maffly-Kipp has argued, during the nineteenth century a new genre of race history emerged among African Americans intent on providing a significant moral and spiritual purpose to the history and future of the race. Race historians hoped to counter white racial images by reimagining the story of the African American community in such a way that their narratives would provide both prophetic indictments of contemporary racial practices and self-fulfilling prophecies of racial unity.[44] Like most black Christians during his lifetime, Bishop Hood believed in the literal truth of Scripture. Using the genealogical tables of the Bible, the Zion minister identified Ham as the ancestor of blacks and traced the origins of major ancient civilizations, such as Egypt, Ethiopia, and Babylon, to Hamitic ancestry. Indeed, the Zionite insisted that the African race stood at the front ranks of the earliest civilizations of the world.[45] Like Prince Hall with his reworking of Masonic history, Hood and other race historians employed their understanding of the Bible to provide a positive vision for the emerging black community.

When James Walker Hood left Connecticut for North Carolina, he went as an emissary for perhaps the two most prominent and deeply interwoven social institutions of the northern African American community, the Prince Hall Masons and the black church. Both had emerged after the Revolution, and each provided the emerging black society with resources for its development and a defense against white racism. Both Hood's Masonic fraternity and his AMEZ denomination continued to observe the doctrines and practices of their white counterparts, yet each adapted its society's history to remove the stigma of slavery and endow its past and future with a significant spiritual and moral purpose. Bishop Hood was among the many northern missionaries who saw the black church as a means through which God was acting in history to uplift the black race. Grand Master Hood, in turn, saw in the Masonic fraternity an opportunity to embrace the dignity and humanity of a universal brotherhood. During the last decades of the nineteenth century, both societies became southern institutions. As senior bishop of the AMEZ Church, Hood presided over the growth of his denomination from 4,600 members in 1860 to 700,000 by 1916. At the same time, Grand Master

Hood contributed to the southern expansion of the Prince Hall Masons. By the turn of the century there were over 117,000 Prince Hall Masons nationally with nearly two-thirds of the membership concentrated in the South.[46] Despite the common commitment of each of these prominent social institutions to the uplift of black Southerners, there remained substantial differences. What was the relationship between the theology of the black church and the beliefs of Prince Hall Masons? And what were the practice and the purpose of Masonic rituals? Here again, James Walker Hood's story provides some insights.

Beliefs and Rites

Bishop Hood's theology reflected the thinking of an era prior to the rise of science and the professionalization of history, when biblical paradigms and sacred histories pervaded the religious worldview. By the 1880s the scientific and intellectual currents that had given rise to Protestant liberalism were filtering into black religious communities through such journals as the *AME Church Review*.[47] Hood was one among many of his contemporary black denominational leaders who defended the literal understanding of the Bible and stood against all changes in Christian doctrine. During the post-Civil War period, the Zion leader opposed Darwinian scientific theories, historical and critical study of Scripture, and the idea that salvation was possible outside Christianity.[48] By the turn of the century, the progressive "New Negro," who had little use for sacred stories and biblical worldviews, was gaining currency among African American intellectuals.[49] Prior to that time, and outside intellectuals' circles continuing for some time to come, Bishop Hood and his fellow race historians, many of whom were ordained ministers, provided their congregations with a vision of the historical world that placed the story of African American suffering into a temporal context that gave their lives meaning and hope. Emerging at a time when the power of sacred history had yet to be undercut by historical-critical methods, these histories offered African Americans representations of their race that countered disparaging white narratives.[50]

Like many of these accounts, Bishop Hood's sacred history parted company with European American narratives by asserting "the ancient greatness of the Negro race." The Zion leader began by accusing "modern historians of the Caucasian race" of trying to "rob" the Negro of a "history to which he can point with pride." Against this treachery, Hood proclaimed, "the Holy Bible has stood as an everlasting rock in the black man's defense." Employing the Bible and the work of selected white historians to buttress his case, the

Zion leader argued that "Ethiopia and Egypt were the first among the early monarchies and these countries were peopled by the descendants of Ham, through Cush and Mizraim, and were governed by the same for hundreds of years." More than an identification of African people in a white narrative, Hood's history identified the contributions of particular African cities and heroes to ancient culture. "Caucasian civilization can point to nothing that exceeds" the "gallantry" and "generosity" of the black city of Carthage nor the "persons of St. Augustine and St. Cyprian...two of the ablest ministers of which the Christian Church can boast." In this way, the Zion bishop underscored an African historical legacy that refuted white beliefs that Africans were an inferior race.[51]

Although Bishop Hood argued that white people had misrepresented the past by portraying Africans as a degraded race, he did not advise abandoning Christianity because of its contamination by white prejudice. Rather, he outlined what he saw as God's true plan. While realizing the original greatness of the race of Ham, Hood also recognized that Ham, through his son Nimrod, "forsook God and took the world for his portion." In retaliation, God at Babel "confounded" the language of Ham's people and "scattered them abroad from thence upon the face of all the earth." Hood's narrative then moved to America, ignored the era of slavery, and asserted the special destiny of the black church. Though God punished the followers of Ham for their idolatry, he also gave them a "promise," Hood told his followers, that the sons of Ham "shall cast aside idolatry and return unto the Lord." The African American church was now leading the way in this redemption. "That this promise is now in the course of fulfillment," he proclaimed, "the Negro Church stands forth as unquestionable evidence." The black church, in sum, was "the morning star which precedes the rising sun," leading all Christians toward the "millennial glory"[52]

Bishop Hood's race history must not be read as that of an uneducated man. Though he was largely self-taught, his writings reflect a lifetime of intelligent reading. Yet consistent with his faith in the Bible's literal truth, the Zion bishop interpreted Scripture in a manner that provided encouragement to his people. Beyond the inroads that scientific and biblical criticism was making into religious authority, the black orthodox response to these new intellectual currents was rooted in racial as well as religious concerns. Black religious leaders and other learned African Americans like James W. Hood were additionally burdened with the reality that black history was given insufficient attention by most scholars. Some feared that the Darwinian theory and biblical criticism employed in the liberal assault upon Scripture and traditional Christianity would be used to deny the humanity and rights of the black race.[53] In the face of these difficulties, Hood and his fellow denominational leaders turned to the Bible and found in it a more complete and compassionate presentation of the history and humanity of black people. Despite a reliance on Scripture's literal truth for accurate historical details, black traditionalists' understanding of the Bible as the inerrant word of God played a critical role in a period when there were few professionally trained African American scholars.[54] Beyond the Bible, the bishop turned especially to the race histories of his fellow black churchmen to support his beliefs. The most famous of these, the Baptist Rufus Perry's *The Cushites, or the Descendants of Ham,*[55] he endorsed as a work of "profound learning" that should become essential reading "respecting the ancient greatness of the descendants of Ham, the ancestors of the American Negro."[56] The sacred history of the Prince Hall Masons provided further support for the "truth" of the African American past.

Although Grand Master Hood left no Masonic race history of his own, the history written by Martin Delaney was likely passed down to him by Masonic orators through the lore of the lodge. Delaney's history asserts that the institution of Masonry was created by Africans and "handed down only through the priesthood" in the earliest period of the Egyptian and Ethiopian dynasties "anterior to the Bible record." These early Egyptians, Delaney continued, adduced and believed in a trinity of the Godhead that later became "the Christian doctrine of three persons in one—Father, Son, and Holy Ghost." Moses, "the recorder of the Bible," Delaney states, "learned all of his wisdom and ability from Egypt." "Africans," therefore, "were the authors of this mysterious and beautiful Order" and "did much to bring it to perfection" prior to the writing of the Bible.[57]

Though Bishop Hood never addressed the African origins of Masonry in his public writings, he did import elements of the Masonic tradition into his Christian race history. In his sermon "Creation's First-Born, or the Earliest Gospel Symbol," for example, he asserted the Masonic belief that the world had begun four thousand years before the birth of Christ. "We live in a period, by all accounts, not much less than six thousand years from that in which Jehovah spake and said, 'Let there be light.'"[58] Certain turns of phrase, like "morning star" and "rising sun," used to herald the future of the Negro church, held such symbolic significance in the Masonic beliefs that the grand master gave them as names for his first North Carolina lodges. The bishop's essay "God's Purpose in the Negro Church as Seen in the History of the Movement," moreover, refers to the "ancient and honorable" Prince Hall fraternity's maintenance of its "rites and benefits" as part of the larger effort of black people to respond to "Jehovah's plan for the Negro's development."[59] Aside from these and other occasional instances where the bishop mentions the Masonic fraternity or its catchwords and ideas, the Zion leader's public writings remain silent on the relationship between his Christian and Masonic beliefs. Within the confines of the lodge, however, Grand Master Hood provided more insight.

In his 1880 annual address to the North Carolina Grand Lodge, the most worshipful grand master instructed the gathered brethren on the relationship between the beliefs and rites of Masonry and what he considered religion. On one hand, Hood stated that he did not believe Masonry was a religion. Yet on the other hand, he did hold that the fraternity was older than Christianity and Judaism and—through its oral tradition—passed on an ancient knowledge born at the beginning of time. "Most Masonic writers admit that Masonry does not claim to be a religion. I admit that it is not a religious sect, yet I am fully persuaded that it is the offspring of the only genuine religion known to man in the early history of the world. This I gather from tradition.... For hundreds of years tradition was the only channel through which the knowledge of events was handed down from generation to generation.... Oral instruction was the universal mode in ancient times. Masonry is the only Order that retains and adheres strictly to the ancient mode."[60] Masonry, then, was heir to an oral transmission of ancient knowledge that originated at the beginning of the world. It was not itself a religion, yet it was the "offspring" of the only genuine religion available to ancient peoples. Since nowhere in either his Christian or Masonic writings did Hood speak of a conflict between Christianity and Masonry, the bishop appears to have believed that the orally transmitted, ancient knowledge passed through Masonry was complementary to Christian teachings. Since the content of this knowledge constituted that which was most secret in Masonry, Hood understandably did not divulge it. Yet he did begin to explain the process of its transmission.

According to the beliefs of Masonry, Grand Master Hood continued, King Solomon synthesized this esoteric knowledge into physical science and manifested it through the building of the Temple at Jerusalem. The Masonic lodge, in turn, symbolically represented the temple.

There are many symbols which identify the Freemason's Lodge with the city and Temple at Jerusalem. (1)—The city was built on the high hills of Zoria and Moria, and near the Valley of Jehosaphat. Our lodge is symbolically situated upon the highest hills and lowest valleys. (2)—The Temple was built due east and west. So is our Lodge. (3)—The Temple was an oblong square, and its ground was holy. Such is the form

and ground of our Lodge. . . . Like the Temple, our Lodge is founded
on the mercies of Jehovah: consecrated in His name dedicated to His
honor; and from the foundation to the capstone it proclaims, "Glory to
God in the highest, peace on earth and good will to man."[61]

Masonic wisdom, therefore, was symbolically represented in the lodge's repli-
cation of King Solomon's Temple in Jerusalem. Access to this knowledge in
turn came through an understanding of these symbols through participation
in rites of initiation.

Though Hood did not believe that Masonry was either a religion or
opposed to Christianity, nevertheless he did believe that "Masonic symbol-
ism, from beginning to end, was capable of instructing us in the truths of
evangelical religion."[62] For example, as Hood explained it, when the "candidate was initiated into the ancient mysteries" he was "invested with a
white apron in token of his newly attained purity." The grand master then
interpreted the symbolic meaning of the Mason's lambskin or white leather
apron through biblical references.

From the Book Divine we learn that it was the most ancient piece of
apparel ever worn. It was worn by Adam and Eve before they were
turned out of the Garden. . . . The apron, or girdle, was universally
received as an emblem of truth among the ancients. Paul so styles it.
'Having your loins girded with truth.'. . . He, therefore, who wears the
white apron as a badge of a Mason, is continually reminded of that
innocence and purity which ought to be the distinguishing characteristic of every Mason.[63]

How the brother came truly to understand the apron's symbolic meaning came
through "the peculiar circumstances in which he receives it."[64] Here Hood
appeared to be saying that the Christian idea of innocence and purity was most
deeply apprehended through the Masonic ritual of initiation. The apron was
not, however, a token of the initiate's entrance into the Christian community
but rather a sign through which the novice "was made to feel his relationship
to the fraternity."[65] Whether Masonic rituals deepened the candidate's understanding of Christian truths, as Hood stated, or of Masonic fellowship, as his
remarks might be interpreted, the fraternity's secret ceremonies clearly set the
brotherhood apart from the practices of Christian congregations.

Exclusive to all American Masons, white and black, were two or more
monthly gatherings on weekday evenings for long and complex rituals of
initiation into the three degree stages of Entered Apprentice, Fellow Craft,
and Master Mason. A 1903 Prince Hall national inventory highlighted the

importance of these stages by categorizing the membership according to which of these three rites they had completed.[66] Each of these ceremonies lasted an hour or more and plunged the candidate into the mysteries of the order. At the moment the lodge was "opened," the initiate lost his sense of time. Ceremonies were said to begin at "daybreak," although meetings were actually held in the evening. While he was prepared, the evening's actors changed into costumes. Others arranged the setting, lit candles, and extinguished the lights. The lodge room itself was rectangular in imitation of the shape of the Ark of the Covenant. The Bible was placed on an altar in the middle of the room beside replicas of a craftsman's square and compass and laid open to a passage appropriate for the evening's "labor." Seated around the room were the members, in formal attire with aprons displaying a picture of the All-Seeing Eye (like the one on the American one-dollar bill). The major officers sat in designated chairs, each wearing an embroidered collar and jeweled pendant representing the special insignia of his position. Slowly the present faded from view, and before the members' eyes an imagined scene from the past appeared.

Each major ritual took the form of a journey through the good and evil of human life. As the candidate proceeded in his travels, he was stopped at certain points to hear a lecture, to pray, or to be subjected to a dramatic presentation designed to link his mind and emotions through physical stimulation. For example, the Entered Apprentice ritual began when the partially undressed and blindfolded initiate entered the lodge room and was met by the sharp point of the drafter's compass against his exposed left breast, accompanied by the senior deacon's stern words not to reveal the secrets of the order. Through similar trials the initiate was taught the history of the order and the meaning of its key symbols and instructed in his moral responsibilities as a Mason. After the initiation the lodge was "closed" with a prayer or song and the announcement that, because the sun had set, their Masonic labors had ended. The lodge now returned to ordinary time.[67]

Within each ritual, the candidate learned that the Bible was the "cornerstone" of Masonry and that he must be obedient to God, but the major thrust of the rite was to teach Masonic tenets. As the Methodist minister and deputy Prince Hall grand master William Spencer Carpenter explained in a Masonic sermon, "The traveling as a Master Mason is symbolic of the journey through life to that Celestial Lodge eternal in the Heavens, where God is the Worshipful Master, Jesus Christ is the Senior Warden, and where the Holy Ghost is the Junior Warden, whose duty it is to . . . call the craft [the assembled Masons] from labor to refreshment and from refreshment to labor again at the will and pleasure of the Master."[68] As in Grand Master Hood's explanation of the Mason's apron, Carpenter was not entirely clear whether Christianity or Masonry had the upper hand. In fact, Masonic rituals contained a grab bag of religious elements. The frequent Masonic reference to God as the "Grand Architect of the Universe" underscored the order's embrace of reason and science. Like natural laws, moral laws could be discerned, and it was the Mason's duty to obey them. Similarly, commitment to the brotherhood of all men and the truth of all religions suggested an opposition to sectarian divisions. At the same time, the rituals borrowed extensively from the Bible and the Judeo-Christian tradition. As a result, Freemasonry contained an ambiguous religious content, open to several interpretations.[69] For many men, the fraternity's rituals succeeded primarily in creating a lasting, meaningful bond between members infused with religious overtones.

In addition to these private rituals, Prince Hall Masons conducted public parades that proclaimed the identity and dignity of the order. These processions were the highlight of the North Carolina Grand Lodge's annual meetings. Preceded by a brass band, the members of the fraternity, dressed in their regalia, marched through the town's principal streets usually to a Zion Methodist church. There a minister offered prayers, a Masonic anthem was sung, Grand Master Hood addressed the craft, the band played some music, all sang a Masonic ode, and a minister offered a benediction. After these "usual ceremonies," the "procession again was formed" and paraded back to the lodge.[70] Prince Hall parades had their origins in the practices of the European American Masonic tradition yet had particular meaning in the African American community.[71] Carried out with the rehearsed self-consciousness of public theater complete with ornamented clothing and polished gestures, this public performance of fraternal life enacted racial dignity and pride for a people derided as unruly by some white southerners. Louis Armstrong captured the heart of this positive function for fraternal orders when he remembered watching his father march by as the grand marshal of the New Orleans Odd Fellows parade: "I was very proud to see him in his uniform and his high hat with the beautiful streamer hanging down. . . . Yes, he was a fine figure of a man, my Dad. Or, at least that is the way he seemed to me as a kid when he strutted by like a peacock at the head of the Odd Fellows parade."[72] Wearing an apron or sash and making a "show in a procession" was admittedly one of the attractions of fraternal orders, but as Virginia's grand master Harrison Harris remarked, "[W]e do not want a Masonry that makes a man anxious to shine in a procession" but a "Masonry that goes into the family and makes a man a better husband, a kinder father, a more devoted patriot and . . . a more liberal and devoted Christian."[73] It was this understanding of Masonry that attracted James Walker Hood.

Complement and Conflict

We cannot say for certain how significant Masonic beliefs and rituals were for Bishop Hood. We do know that he spent considerable time throughout his career attending to the fraternity's affairs and presiding over its ritual life. After thirteen years as grand master, he continued to serve in such capacities as grand orator and supervisor of Masonic jurisprudence, guiding the brotherhood's beliefs and practices. Late in life, when he was too feeble to attend the annual grand lodge meetings, he wrote letters to the assembled brethren that were printed prominently in their proceedings. Yet despite his annual unanimous reelection while he served as grand master, Hood had finally chosen to step down from the position because of his more pressing "ecclesial labors."[74] In fact, any comparison between the time and effort involved in Hood's work for the church and his labor for the lodge would show that his church work was more important.

What does seem clear is that Bishop Hood appropriated from Masonry beliefs that complemented his missionary efforts. Given his Christian conservatism, it seems unlikely that the Zion leader would have been attracted to the liberal Masonic ideals of interreligious brotherhood or scientific progress that, some scholars have argued, helped bring modernizing late nineteenth-century European American men into the order.[75] In addition to his biblical literalism, Hood remained opposed to non-Christian paths to salvation. He viewed Islam, for example, as a "corrupting influence" operating "against the Christian Church."[76] Instead, Bishop Hood's Masonic teachings emphasized universal values like "purity of heart" and "rectitude of conduct." The Mason was an honest, upright man, a good citizen and responsible member of the community. Moreover, as one member put it, Masonry, "having fewer doctrines, can reach some that Christianity cannot reach, and not until Christianity shall cover the earth...will the demand for Masonry cease."[77] The best lodges, the grand master believed, were those in which "all its members are professors of Christianity, and are men whose lives accord with their profession."[78] Further displaying his evangelical Christian ideals, Hood's grand lodge enforced a code of behavior forbidding alcohol, tobacco, and any illegal behavior. Similarly, the Zion leader spoke to his brothers of the need to "soften our hearts" by giving our love to Jesus. In 1885 and subsequent North Carolina Grand Lodge gatherings, the members sang Hood's Masonic hymn "The Feast of Belshazzar," which ended with the following chorus:

> See our deeds are all recorded,
> There is a Hand that's writing now:
> Sinners give your hearts to Jesus–

At His royal mandate bow;
For the day is fast approaching—
It must come to one and all,—
When the sinner's condemnation,
Shall be written upon the wall.[79]

In this way, Grand Master Hood emphasized the Christian teachings within Masonic beliefs. Moreover, though he did not share in the Masonic embrace of non-Christian religions, the Prince Hall leader did see the lodge as a vehicle for building Christian unity across black denominational lines. "It was my purpose," he reflected near the end of his life, "to invite the best men in all the Churches in this State in the Masonic Fraternity. In this our success has been all that could have been expected. Every denomination having a considerable membership has been represented in this Grand Lodge. Nearly all have been represented in the office of Grand Officers."[80] Hood's appropriation of Masonic beliefs complemented his Christian efforts to uplift and unite his people.

An emphasis on discipline and respectability was similarly central to both organizations. As we have seen, Hood and his fellow northern missionaries who established most southern black churches brought with them a formal organization, governed by published rules that stipulated adherence to standards of moral conduct and punished those who transgressed. Duty-bound to teach the values of religion, education, and hard work, these respectable people equated restrained public behavior with individual self-respect and the advancement of the race. Prince Hall emissaries—again, often the same people—imposed a similar organizational structure and had similar behavioral expectations for their members. Admissions committees were looking for intelligent, clean-living, sober, and industrious young men, preferably married and able to provide for their households. In both cases, expectations of respectable deportment and threats of expulsion conditioned behavior that encouraged racial uplift.[81] In these efforts, fraternal members claimed, "Masonry does not aspire to the office of Christianity. It provides no atonement, and consequently cannot save the soul; but it seeks to elevate man, to beautify and adorn his character with domestic virtues. It teaches him the lessons of sobriety, and industry, and integrity. But Christianity teaches him to prepare for a higher life, a future state, and a brighter world."[82]

Taken together, Prince Hall lodges and Christian churches were central to the southern institution building that freedom demanded. After emancipation, African Americans quickly adopted the voluntary associational conventions of American life to suit their specific needs. Moreover, as an institution brought to the South by a northern AMEZ missionary, Hood's North Carolina lodges shared with his churches a desire to bring discipline and respectability to the newly freed slaves. Broadly interdenominational in membership within the framework of the post-Reconstruction South, the lodges supported the mainstream churches in this common effort to purify the beliefs and uplift the practices of black southerners. Though there is little evidence of regional consciousness in Hood's behavior and writings or of tensions between the North Carolina lodges and their northern elders, future studies of southern fraternalism may reveal a regional distinctiveness and perhaps, as with the churches, disputes over resources and relative power within institutional structures that straddled the regions. In addition, studies of other southern black Masonic leaders may suggest a greater willingness to follow liberal Masonic traditions, though not at the expense of the church institution, given the critical role it played in the post–1865 black world.

The marriage of church and lodge was not always harmonious. By the 1890s, leaders of the new Holiness movement emerging from the Mississippi Delta began to speak out against the involvement of the black church with fraternal orders. Responding to the social estrangement experienced by some African Americans, Holiness leaders attacked "worldly" Baptists and Methodists for their fashionable standards of consumption and their allegiance to secret societies, calling them back to the simplicity of the early Christian Church. Followers of Charles Price Jones's new Church of Christ, for example, were encouraged to mark their spiritual birth as sanctified Christians by "pitching their secret order pins . . . out the church windows."[83] Though Bishop Hood did not directly address the Holiness attack on fraternal orders, as we have seen, his Prince Hall lodges followed stringent rules of ethical conduct. At the same time, the Zion bishop resisted a growing worldliness within mainstream black Methodism by retaining earlier emphases on a holy ministry, morally pure and free of scandal. As a participant in the Holiness movement within black Methodism, Hood and his contemporaries insisted that freedom from sin was attainable in this life and that every Christian should strive for this sanctification. Belief in the possibility of sanctification in one's lifetime was not shared by all Methodists, but Hood and other bishops insisted that their candidates for ministry adhere to this teaching.[84] Though the rapid growth of the Holiness movement likely influenced Prince Hall membership elsewhere, Hood's emphasis on high ethical conduct and striving for sanctification may have worked against both church and lodge defections in North Carolina.[85]

In addition to these attacks from outside the church-lodge nexus, there is also scattered evidence of tensions within the black church between fraternal members and church leaders. Writing in the *Indianapolis Freeman* in 1891, a Baptist minister complained that fraternal "members took more interest in their societies than their church."[86] Such behavior, echoed Methodist H. T. Keating in the *Christian Recorder,* led secret society members to "neglect their duties" to the church "in order to be regular in their attendance upon lodge meetings."[87] These complaints were often couched in conciliatory language that recognized the power of the orders within the church. "It will be observed that we do not enter into a discussion of whether secret societies are right and good in principle," Keating continued, "but simply protest against the neglect of the church in the slightest degree for these societies. Assuming both church and society right, which is most right and worthy of support?"[88] In response, Mason and AME minister S. H. Coleman, writing in the *AME Church Review,* defended the lodge as "not a substitute for the church but an handmaid of religion." The teachings of the order, he claimed, supplemented rather than replaced the truths of the Bible by teaching "us our social and political duties."[89] Other Prince Hall members pointedly rebuked the church for its criticisms. G. L. Knox specifically warned that "[d]id it so desire, [the lodge] could destroy the power of the pulpit." He then added "but such is not its mission.... Instead of being in antagonism with the church, it is content to draw its inspiration from God's holy house, and as an humble handmaiden, to do its Master's work, as it shall see it and understand it."[90] Though this evidence suggests some power struggles in the black church between lodge members and church leaders, these differences can hardly be compared with the successful evangelical effort to shut down the white Masonic order during the anti-Masonic campaign of the 1820s or the late nineteenth-century threat of excommunication posed by conservative white churches against those members who dared join fraternal orders.[91] White Masons were far less likely than black Masons to be church members;[92] by contrast, fraternal orders and the black church were deeply interwoven social institutions.

Gender tension between black lodge members and women was another potential area for conflict, but there appears to have been less of it among black Masons than among white. Not only did the rituals of the Prince Hall Masons set them apart from the African American church, but exclusive male membership separated the brothers from black women. In his study of the late nineteenth-century black Odd Fellow Amos Webber, Nick Salvatore remarks on Webber's relationship with his wife: "It was not that Amos thought Lizzie unimportant or that, after thirty years of marriage, he did not care for her. Rather his formal distancing from her suggested the overwhelming maleness of the world he inhabited."[93] In bearing witness to the powerful influence of nineteenth-century gender roles, black fraternal members inhabited a distinctly male sphere. Fraternal rites, unlike those of the Protestant churches, celebrated a man's bonds with his brothers while neglecting the event of his marriage. Even within the predominantly female churches these distinctions continued, with men controlling the visible, public positions of authority and women providing for the church's social activities through Sunday school, prayer meetings, missionary work, social events, and care for the needy.[94] And yet underlying both the lodge and the church was a tangled thicket of male-female relationships—intimately joined by kinship ties between sisters and brothers, wives and husbands—that formed a common social framework for community activities. Within the church, acceptance of male religious leadership did not prevent women from creating their own influential networks, while within the lodge, women's auxiliaries participated in social activities and found meaning in the order's larger purposes.[95]

James Walker Hood was instrumental in efforts to include women in both lodge and church activities. As Mark Carnes has shown, late nineteenth-century white Masons were very reluctant to include women in their affairs, even going so far as to threaten members with fearful punishment if they should "tell their wife the concerns of the order."[96] In contrast, shortly after founding the North Carolina Grand Lodge, Hood encouraged the establishment of a ladies' auxiliary—the Order of the Eastern Star[97]—which became involved in the maintenance and support of the order.[98] At the same time, Bishop Hood supported the full ministerial rights of women within the AMEZ denomination. He acted on this conviction, first by ordaining Mrs. Julia A. J. Foote as deacon at the New York Annual Conference in 1894 and then, during the ultimately successful struggle for women's ordination that engulfed the denomination at the turn of the century, by supporting full equality for women in all aspects of church life.[99] All this is not to deny the probability of gender tensions in an African American community where the male role remained dominant. Evelyn Higginbotham and others have identified some of these tensions within the black church.[100] Doubtless there were conflicts as well between some black women and the Prince Hall Masons. Yet in contrast, most white Masons were not members of their wives' churches and discouraged the creation of ladies' auxiliaries.[101] Compared with the separation of the male lodge and the female church among the white Protestant middle class, there was substantially more interaction between the male world of Prince Hall men and the activities of black women.

James Walker Hood believed that his labors for the Prince Hall Masons complemented his work for the AME denomination in a common effort to provide encouragement and hope to black southerners facing debilitating circumstances. In his view the church was more than a means for spiritual renewal—it was a providential movement acting in history to uplift the black race. As part of this larger movement of God, the Zion leader appropriated from Masonry beliefs and practices that complemented his missionary efforts. As part of the effort of African Americans to respond to the indignities and racial violence that formed the fabric of everyday life, the fraternity provided a mediating institution to defy the racism of American society. Membership in the order provided responsible and industrious men with public recognition, moral authority, and an alternative history with which to buffer and respond to potentially disabling images of the black man. Denied all but the most menial jobs and pushed to the margins of white society, the fraternity recognized each man's dignity and nurtured his growth by providing outlets for leadership and avenues for gaining status. At the same time, rites of initiation secured a lasting, meaningful bond with other men, while the fraternity's eclectic ideology provided a framework for a moral commitment that drew broadly upon the spiritual values of the Judeo-Christian tradition. Though rarely recognized by white Americans, after the Civil War the Prince Hall Masons flourished among African American men, providing, alongside the black church, a separate male sphere that reinforced a collective sense of African American identity and pride.

The study of the Prince Hall Masons as a fraternal organization whose beliefs and activities intermingled with those of the AMEZ Church has larger implications for the study of Christian history. Since the early 1700s, Masonically inspired fraternal orders have spread throughout European and American Christianity, providing men with an eclectic tool kit of cultural resources for adapting to their social world. Recent scholarship has begun to explore the ways in which fraternal beliefs and rituals have paralleled, supported, and subverted the activities of Christian churches. From the appropriation of Masonic practices by upstart Mormons to the creation of a separate male sphere of sympathetic feeling, scholars have argued for the inclusion of Masonic resources in efforts to broaden our understanding of the Christian religious world.[102] Bishop Hood's Christian conservatism had no difficulty incorporating Masonic beliefs and rites in this larger worldview. More important, Hood's racial identity shaped relationships between lodge and church to serve a larger racial purpose. By including fraternal beliefs and rituals in a larger understanding of religious culture, students of Christianity may continue to find a rich resource for insight into the gender, racial, and ritual dynamics of post-Enlightenment Christianity.

CHAPTER 8

"Arguing for Our Race"

*The Politics of Nonrecognition and the Public
Nature of the Black Masonic Archive*

MARTIN SUMMERS

> Future historians will bear us out when we assert,
> that, with every impediment placed in the march of
> our progress by such anti-masonic spirits whence
> emanated that unchristian-like article, our record of
> morality, in proportion to the disadvantages which we
> encounter on every hand, heightens in comparison
> with our more favored white brothers.
>
> —Lewis Hayden, *Grand Lodge Jurisdictional Claim*

In the early summer of 1868, the prominent
black Massachusetts Freemason Lewis Hayden delivered an address before
his fellow members of the Prince Hall Grand Lodge. Much of his address
challenged charges by white Masons that Prince Hall Freemasonry was an
illegitimate tradition. Instead he exposed the hypocrisy of those who pur-
portedly subscribed to the universal values of brotherhood, love, and belief
in the unity of humankind while refusing to recognize or interact with
black Masons. "As for American Masonry," Hayden intoned, "we know
of no kind or generous deed performed by it, at any time or under any
circumstances, towards the colored men of our land." Hayden's comments
were part of a long tradition of African American Masons staking claims
to legitimacy and eminence for themselves, and by extension for the race
as a whole, in the face of persistent white racism.[1]

Ever since the provincial grand master of Massachusetts had refused to
act on a request by Prince Hall and his brethren for a charter, and for more
than a century after Hayden's protest, Prince Hall Freemasonry had to contend with a variety of approaches and postures by white Freemasons. These
ranged from indifferent tolerance of its existence to active hostility toward

it. The governing bodies of white American Masonry tended either not to recognize Prince Hall Freemasonry as a legitimately constituted tradition or, if they did recognize it, to follow a segregationist policy toward it.[2]

Prince Hall Freemasons' responses to nonrecognition were by no means uniform. From the postemancipation period through at least the mid-twentieth century, they exhibited a wide spectrum of opinions regarding their relation to white Freemasons and their own legitimacy as inheritors of the enlightened principles of the craft. Some articulated an uncompromising commitment to integration, while most acquiesced in the official policy of nonrecognition as long as American Freemasonry was governed by an unofficial "separate but equal" principle. Many pointed to their relations with European lodges as confirmation of their legitimate status even as some invoked ethnocentric arguments to claim the traditions of Freemasonry as their own.

Even as they responded in various ways to the challenges to their legitimacy, Prince Hall Freemasons were scrupulously attentive to the importance of historical documentation and argument. Hayden's confidence that future historians would corroborate Prince Hall Freemasons'—and, by extension, the black race's—perseverance in the face of racially motivated barriers was matched by his and others' conviction that their own role as historians was critical to the stability and strengthening of their fraternal tradition. Individuals from a range of socioeconomic backgrounds and levels of education—men including, among others, Hayden, Martin R. Delany, Samuel W. Clark, William H. Grimshaw, George W. Crawford, John E. Bruce, Arthur Schomburg, Harry Williamson, and Harry E. Davis—assumed the responsibilities of historical documentation and preservation and "by weight of evidence balanced the scales of unprejudiced opinion to the credit of [Prince Hall Freemasons'] claim to unquestionable and legitimate descent from the original Grand Lodge of England."[3]

But these acts of chronicling were not limited to the esoteric writings of black Masons, nor were they confined to the exclusive sites of the lodge or the Masonic library. One could see them in the reprinting of Masonic speeches in the black-owned *Pacific Appeal* and proceedings of various grand lodge annual meetings in the postemancipation period; in regular columns and the serialization of published histories of Prince Hall Freemasonry in the *Colored American Magazine* and the *New York Age* from the turn of the century through the 1930s; and in the creation of a collection of black Masonic historical materials at the 135th Street Branch of the New York Public Library on the eve of World War II. In this sense, the "public" nature of the black Masonic archive belied the premium that Prince Hall Freemasonry, as a fraternal association, placed on inscrutability and exclusiveness.[4] Indeed, the production and circulation of historical knowledge by black Masons confirms the arguments that some scholars—both Masonic and non-Masonic—have made regarding the order: that it is not, in the strictest sense, a secret society.[5]

Through an examination of their responses to nonrecognition from approximately the 1860s to the 1940s, this chapter seeks to uncover how black Masons used history—as argument and practice—to establish their legitimacy as both Masons and leaders of the race. In doing so, it places as much emphasis on the form of those responses as it does on their content. That is, it considers the extent to which the arguments for the legitimacy of Prince Hall Freemasonry constituted acts of collective remembering—recalling the struggles and progress not only of the fraternal order but of the race itself. The historical knowledge that these black Masons produced and circulated, then, was as much about the present and the future as it was about the past.[6]

What follows is not a comprehensive cataloging of the various positions black Masons took regarding recognition and integration or a complete reconstruction of the intellectual defense of their authenticity. The regional, ideological, and generational differences within black Masonry during this period resist any easy characterization.[7] The question of whether, and to what degree, non-Masons within the African American community engaged in this collective remembering is also beyond the scope of this chapter. The sources do not allow for any definitive statements about how the non-Masonic public may or may not have consumed histories of black Masonry or news items about the latest recognition controversies. However, this chapter argues that through this collective remembering, which in many ways collapsed the trials and struggles of the fraternal order into the trials and struggles of the entire race, Prince Hall Freemasons sought to establish their own legitimacy as race leaders.[8]

Interracial Masonic relationships in the antebellum United States were much more complicated than one might expect, given the existence of entirely separate fraternal traditions. Black Masons at the turn of the nineteenth century in Boston, one of the centers of Masonic activity in early republican America, were met with a fair amount of indifference from white Masons. Indifference led to interaction and, in some cases, collaboration between black and white Masons in New England and beyond. Visitation between lodges was not unknown in Boston, and white Masons were reported to have violated a Grand Lodge of Pennsylvania's directive on at least one occasion when they visited an African American lodge in Philadelphia in October of 1799. Black and white Masons also cooperated in various interlodge fraternal rituals, as when, for example, members of Boston's African Lodge No. 459 participated with white Masons in the Masonic funeral rites for George Washington in 1800. Collaboration between white and black Masons even extended to cooperation in efforts to root out lodges that made illegitimate claims of having descended from the Grand Lodge of England. Richard H. Gleaves of the African Independent Grand Lodge of Pennsylvania, for instance, assisted the (white) Grand Lodge of Ohio's investigation of a fraudulent charter that had led to the formation of a black (non-Prince Hall) lodge in the mid-1840s.[9]

This kind of fraternal collegiality, however, was overshadowed by white antipathy. Enmity toward African American Masons was generally expressed in the exclusionary practices of white lodges, which became more and more pervasive in the decades preceding the Civil War. In 1851, for instance, a subordinate lodge in New York made it official policy that no "Negro" should be initiated under its auspices. That same year, the (white) Grand Lodge of Illinois issued a directive to all its subordinate lodges "to admit no negro or mulatto, as visitor or otherwise, under any circumstances whatever."[10] White Masons also stepped up their challenges to the fundamental legitimacy of Prince Hall Freemasonry in the decade and a half before the Civil War, prompting the physician, abolitionist, emigrationist, and Mason Martin R. Delany to assert the African roots of Freemasonry in his widely read 1853 publication, *The Origin and Objects of Ancient Freemasonry*.[11] Although white Masons in the early national period occasionally asserted that Prince Hall Freemasonry was irregularly constituted, as the black Masonic historian Harry E. Davis argued, "It was a later generation of Masons who attempted to attaint the birth-right of the Prince Hall sodality."[12]

The racially specific exclusionary policies of some grand and subordinate lodges notwithstanding, white Masons rarely questioned the legitimacy of the Prince Hall tradition on the basis of race. Rather, they relied on abstruse procedural arguments and the historical record to challenge African American Masons' claims to be legitimate descendants of the Grand Lodge of England. One argument invoked "territorial jurisdiction," the idea that a grand lodge could not charter a subordinate lodge in a territory over which another grand lodge had authority. Many white Masonic authorities asserted that the Grand Lodge of England had violated the Provincial Grand Lodge of Massachusetts's territorial prerogative by chartering African Lodge No. 459. Another argument held that the African Lodge had failed to obtain a new charter after a schism between the Ancient and Modern factions was healed in England in the early nineteenth century. Other authorities asserted that shortly after Prince Hall's death in 1808, the African Lodge became dormant and was subsequently removed from the Grand Lodge of England's rolls. They further argued that its reconstitution in the 1820s did not conform to proper Masonic procedure.[13]

Another argument against their legitimacy that African American Masons felt compelled to refute rested on the purported requirement that Masons be free men whose mothers had not been bondwomen. This argument was used extensively, but whether, and to what extent, it supplanted the more procedural arguments is unclear. It is likely that white American Masons began to make this case more strenuously with the maturation of the abolitionist movement in the United States and in response to developments within the British Empire. In 1847, nine years after the abolition of slavery in British imperial possessions, the Grand Lodge of England substituted "free" for "freeborn" as a qualification for becoming a Mason.[14] With increasing challenges to slavery in the southern United States, white American Masons who opposed recognizing Prince Hall Freemasonry as a duly constituted tradition might have latched on to the freeborn qualification even more tenaciously. Regardless, African American Masons vigorously met these arguments with their own counterarguments, ones that ranged from culturally chauvinist and religious to secular. Indeed, African American Masons often *moved among* all three lines of argument in rejecting the freeborn qualification as a spurious reason for doubting the authenticity of the Prince Hall tradition.

Many African American Masons pointed to the history of the Jewish people in order to expose the fallacious logic of the freeborn requirement. In doing so, they reiterated genealogies of modern Freemasonry in which the secrets of the craft had made their way from God through Moses to King Solomon. Because Freemasonry itself had been transmitted through a historically enslaved people, they argued, it was disingenuous to now use the freeborn requirement as a means of excluding African Americans. In arguing for the "expurgation from the ritual of the word 'free born,'" Hayden reminded his fellow Masons that the "Israelites, a people doomed to perpetual slavery were Masons." Delany agreed that bondmen were not worthy material for initiation into Freemasonry in the present age, yet he also pointed out that the original intent behind this proscription was to exclude from the order those individuals who voluntarily became servants and those who were subjected to servitude as a result of criminal punishment. This did not preclude the enslaved African American, the "kindred brother in humanity…with panting aspirations for liberty," from joining the craft once he was freed because of either abolition or his own initiative. "Does Masonry, then, contemplate the withholding of its privileges from such applicants as these?" Delany asked. "Certainly not; since Moses, (to whom our great Grand Master Solomon, the founder of the temple, is indebted for his Masonic wisdom,) was born and lived in captivity eighty years, and by the laws of his captors a slave."[15]

Within the context of Masonic history, the invocation of the Israelite origins of the craft was a deft refutation of the freeborn criterion for admission to the order. Within the larger context of United States slavery and race relations, however, this invocation also underscored the historical association that African Americans had with the Jewish people. Delany's and Hayden's arguments reflected a dominant strain within antebellum black religious thought—particularly present in the sacred worldview of enslaved blacks—that equated African American enslavement with Hebrew enslavement within Egypt and emphasized that just as Moses had delivered his people from Pharaoh, blacks would be delivered from bondage within their lifetime. Even though there were some, Delany included, who claimed that African Americans were inheritors of the Egyptian and Ethiopian civilizations (and who located the roots of Freemasonry within those civilizations), African Americans persistently identified with the children of Israel. As Thomas Wentworth Higginson, the abolitionist and Union Army officer, opined after spending time with African American soldiers under his command, "Their memories are a vast bewildered chaos of Jewish history and biography; and most of the great events of the past, down to the period of the American Revolution, they instinctively attribute to Moses."[16] His hyperbole notwithstanding, few would argue with Higginson's reading of the importance of the historical experiences of Jews in the spiritual life of African Americans in the nineteenth century.

Indeed, I suggest that Hayden and Delany invoked the Israelite origins of Freemasonry in part to connect the experiences of African American Masons in particular to the experiences of African Americans in general. This was a rhetorical strategy that saw more use in the antebellum and immediate postemancipation period than it would in the late nineteenth and early twentieth centuries. By the turn of the twentieth century, African American Masons were making more secular arguments to refute the freeborn qualification as a justification for white Masons' policy of nonrecognition. To be sure, being a generation or two removed from emancipation, African American Masons felt less compelled to take on the freeborn qualification as an issue. When they did, however, it was often on grounds that relied more on procedural or secular arguments than on romantic and religious analogizing of the historical experiences of Jews and blacks. Samuel W. Clark invoked the Declaration of Independence to argue that all people were born free and also questioned the legal right of white Masons to change the Masonic principles to exclude African Americans on the basis of their history of enslavement. George Crawford's defense of the superiority of the free-man over the freeborn qualification was elegant in its simplicity when he wrote that "it is at once apparent that it matters little whether a candidate for the mysteries was born free, or not, so long as he is free when he presents himself for initiation."[17] But the absence of references to Old Testament Jews may have signaled more—a reluctance to invoke the actual history of African American slavery. Just as the emergent African American middle class in the late nineteenth and early twentieth centuries sought to distance itself from the historical stigma of slavery through the suppression of folk cultural forms such as spirituals and ecstatic religious worship, African American Masons— as part of that middle class—may have for the same reasons abandoned the black-Hebrew parallel that had been a critical part of an antebellum African American worldview. In other words, they may have sought to establish their credentials as Masons and race men on rational arguments that were commensurate with their status as actual and aspiring members of a black professional class rather than on religious arguments that acknowledged the history of black slavery.[18]

But this was a turn-of-the-century development. During and in the immediate aftermath of the Civil War, African American Masons routinely situated their critiques of the freeborn argument within the larger context of slavery and linked white Masons who advocated nonrecognition on these grounds with proslavery segments of American society. Hayden pulled no punches in an 1862 address before a meeting of the Prince Hall Grand Lodge in Boston. After praising the Grand Lodge of England's modification of the initiation requirement, Hayden lambasted white American Masons for continuing to adhere to the idea that an initiate had to be freeborn. "Because it strikes at the foundation upon which the institution is said to be founded," Hayden argued, "it being that of common brotherhood, and the denial of which gives aid and comfort to Human Slavery, in that it admits that man can be otherwise *born* than *free*."[19] Six years later, Hayden made an even more explicit charge that white American Masons had been complicit in the maintenance of slavery. The premise of his charge was that since the Enlightenment principle of natural rights applied to everyone regardless of his racial background, to continue to adhere to the freeborn qualification was no less proslavery and un-Masonic than holding or trading slaves themselves. Hayden reminded his audience that "the child is free at birth, and virtually that *all men are born free,* and that before you can enslave you must kidnap, nevertheless, they, of the American Masonic Institutions are ready to recognize the validity of such kidnapping, notwithstanding the penalty pronounced by God against the crime."[20] To suggest that white Masons who clung to the freeborn qualification tacitly endorsed the illegal act of enslavement was a harsh indictment, and in making this charge, Hayden clearly imported an abolitionist argument into the larger recognition debate. In doing so, he not only sought to shame white Masons but also framed the experiences of African American Masons within a larger history of antiblack racism, at the center of which stood slavery.[21]

In addition to disputing the specific spurious charges of irregularity leveled by their white counterparts, Prince Hall Freemasons addressed the underlying motivations behind nonrecognition. As in the case of their challenges to the freeborn qualification, they situated the racial divide in Masonry within the historical narrative and contemporary context of race relations in the United States. While some expressed a desire for racial integration, most African American Masons recognized, and were comfortable with, the necessity of maintaining separate social spheres as long as there was recognition of the legitimacy of the Prince Hall tradition.[22] Indeed, they pointed to the existence of separate churches as an appropriate model of race relations within the world of Freemasonry. There were distinct religious traditions and little intermingling between whites and blacks in the sacred world, but no one questioned the authenticity of the Christian faith of African Americans.[23] In fact, black Masons acknowledged the importance of having strong institutions that would guide the development of the postemancipation black community, of which Prince Hall Freemasonry would be one. White Masons' "fears" that recognition would lead to organizational "amalgamation" were as unfounded as the "social equality" canard that whites would use to justify segregation and disenfranchisement. A. W. A. De Leon, an officer of the Prince Hall Grand Lodge of Massachusetts, expressed this idea succinctly in a letter to the editor of the *Pacific Appeal*. "As a race we are too exquisitely sensitive, and as individuals too exquisitely punctilious to 'crowd' ourselves where we are not wanted," De Leon wrote; "all we ask and shall continue to *demand* as our inherent right, is a recognition upon the broad, cosmopolitan and indistructible basis of Masonry which knows neither clime nor color, accepting man for his merit and virtue alone."[24]

Acknowledgment of separate institutional development did not translate into a tacit acceptance of white supremacy. In his letter to the editor, De Leon clearly attributed the need for African Americans to build separate institutions to the racism of whites. "Church and State, notwithstanding the abolition of the accursed system of slavery," he declared, "are still loth to accord to him equality, which is but the counterpart of freedom." De Leon even more explicitly yoked white Masons to the reactionary forces that sought to blunt, and even turn back, the tide of African American progress that emancipation promised. He did so by equating white Masons' nonrecognition policy with the attitudes and actions of the most ardent white supremacists, whether or not they tangibly participated in, and benefited from, slavery. De Leon rhetorically asked why African American Masons were so reviled by their white counterparts. He assured his readers that no African American Mason had ever been responsible for an anti-Masonic exposé. He went further by reminding his audience that "[n]ever have we applied incendiary torches to the school houses, asylums, churches and dwellings of those in whose interest the writer vouchsafes to wield his influence, nor butchered cradled infants *simply because they were white!*"[25] By rhetorically playing with the historical—and contemporary—narrative of white-on-black violence, De Leon implicitly associated white Masons with the antiabolitionist mobs and the antidraft rioters of the antebellum and Civil War eras. The racism that African American Masons faced in the nonrecognition policy, in other words, was cut from the same cloth as the racist violence that African Americans faced on a daily basis.

But De Leon and others expressed confidence in the inevitability of the true spirit of Freemasonry overpowering the prejudices of "localized" (i.e., white American) Masons, just as they expressed confidence that more liberal ideas about race would prevail in the wake of emancipation.[26] Here again they conflated the experiences of African American Masons with the experiences of the race as a whole. "[W]e are prompted to think that their [white Masons'] endeavors in building up a Masonic hierarchy will be abortive," De Leon asserted, "and that the genius of universal liberty and a religious discountenance of caste by the better informed Masons of the country, will triumphantly demolish the repugnant parts of the old institution, built partly on slavery and color-exclusion."[27] Reactionary white Masons would eventually be swept aside by a union of Prince Hall Freemasons and their progressive white Masonic allies, just as the Democratic Party in the former Confederacy had been defeated by an alliance of radical Republicans, southern white Unionists, and freedpeople. Indeed, Hayden, De Leon's fellow grand lodge officer, could not have been more explicit in framing the racial politics of Freemasonry within the larger narrative of postemancipation politics. Pointing to the passage of "civil rights laws in order to protect the black men of the country from the prejudices growing out of slavery," Hayden argued that these would serve as a precedent for Masons. "Equality before the [Masonic] law will then be a fact," he predicted, "and, until that day shall arrive, contention, as now, will continue."[28]

When they drew parallels or illustrated convergences between nonrecognition, slavery, antiabolitionism, and the postemancipation white backlash, black Masons both accessed and contributed to a larger collective memory among African Americans. But the historical record also served to establish their own authenticity within the Masonic world as much as it served to secure their status as race men. Outraged by the refusal of the (white) Grand Lodge of Massachusetts to grant a petition to Prince Hall Freemasons on a technicality, an unidentified writer for the *Pacific Appeal* argued, with a great degree of certainty, that a proper investigation of the Masonic archive would vindicate African American Masons of the charges that they were bogus. "The historical evidence of legitimacy of origin of these colored Lodges would prove overpowering and decidedly too conclusive," the author wrote. He further delivered a gendered challenge to white Masons, admonishing them for "quibbling" when "the manly and rational settlement of a living question is called for by all intelligent men and Masons."[29] This "living question" that would consistently be taken up by African American Masons prompted exchanges of the historical record in the pages of the *Pacific Appeal* and other black newspapers into the twentieth century; it also prompted collaborative efforts to preserve that record.

In the midst of the postemancipation period, African American Masons recognized the need to construct and preserve a comprehensive black Masonic archive. Most of the historical renditions of the origins and early decades of Prince Hall Freemasonry—including the controversial formation of the National Grand Lodge in 1847—that circulated in the black press were responses to white Masons' charges of illegitimacy.[30] In these cases, they were usually included in reprints of the speeches of indignant African American Masons. Occasionally historical information was circulated in response to requests by African American Masons themselves. These requests might accompany the proceedings of a grand lodge meeting (which might or might not have been printed in the newspaper), as was the case with Samuel W. Clark of Ohio. As the chairman of that state's Committee on Foreign Correspondence, Clark sent the "private transactions" of Ohio's grand lodge meeting along with a request for any information regarding the "higher degrees of Masonry among colored Masons in America." Peter Anderson, the editor of the *Pacific Appeal,* obliged with a lengthy discourse on the introduction of Royal Arch and York Rite degrees into the African American community. He cautioned at the end of the article, however, that his history should not necessarily be considered the definitive one. "This tradition we make partly from memory and partly from records, which we have seen and been in our possession, but not at present at our immediate command," Anderson wrote, "and if any defects I will gladly stand corrected by any one who has been contemporaneous with us in the Masonic Order."[31] Others expressed concern that the scattered and evanescent nature of the historical record regarding the legitimacy of the Prince Hall tradition would continue to impede African Americans from enjoying full equality within the Masonic world. Even as he pointed to the recognition of Prince Hall's legitimacy by various European grand lodges, William T. Boyd, Samuel Clark's predecessor, argued that without more formal histories, white American Masons would persist in denying the authenticity of Prince Hall Freemasonry. As a possible solution, Boyd urged more collaborative relationships between African American Masons from various states. "It would be a praiseworthy enterprise if the several Grand Lodges were to agree," he suggested, "that if the P. H. Grand Lodge would write out a good and reliable history of its 'Rise and Progress,' such history to be predicated upon reliable documents in the archives of the Grand Lodge of England, as well as such other reliable papers as may be found in its own archives...then we, the other Grand Lodges, would pay all necessary expenses of printing and the obtaining of documents."[32]

Boyd's specific proposal was not taken up by African American Masons, but his overall point about the need for more collaborative efforts to document the historical record of Prince Hall Freemasonry did not fall on deaf ears. In addition to the overall coverage of fraternal and associational life among African Americans, by the turn of the twentieth century, some black newspapers had regular columns explicitly devoted to Masonry. The history of the Prince Hall tradition was prominently featured in these columns, including the serialization of, and advertisement for, published historical texts. Moreover, as in the case of the *Pacific Appeal* in the postemancipation period, this very public presentation and circulation of information about the Prince Hall tradition was aimed at establishing African American Masons' legitimacy as Masons and race leaders.

Challenges to the legitimacy of Prince Hall Freemasonry did not subside by the early twentieth century. If anything, they intensified, occasionally manifesting in legal suits initiated by white Masons seeking injunctions against African American Masons using names similar to theirs.[33] Even progressive white lodges were prevented from fully recognizing and sanctioning the interaction of their members with African American Masons by the white supremacist attitudes that pervaded the Masonic world and the larger American culture. The (white) Grand Lodge of Washington State, for instance, officially recognized Prince Hall Freemasons in 1898 but refrained from endorsing visitation. Using language that evoked Booker T. Washington's Atlanta compromise speech three years before, the Grand Lodge gave as its reason "'the fact that the white and colored races in the United States have in many ways shown a preference to remain in purely social matters, separate and apart.'" A fear of alienating southern white lodges also probably played a role in the Washington Masons' evasion of full recognition. Even the decision to recognize but not endorse visitation, however, drew criticism and censures from southern white lodges.[34]

The allusion of the Grand Lodge of Washington State to Booker T. Washington's formulation of race relations was apt, for it represented a view that was shared by many, if not most, African American Masons. While Prince Hall Freemasons certainly hoped for the day when the principles of brotherhood and equality would become truly realized within American Freemasonry, they clamored neither for integration nor even for visitation. In language that was reminiscent of De Leon's rejection of the "social equality" canard thirty years earlier, S. R. Scottron, editor of the *Colored American Magazine*'s "Masonic Department," argued that white Masonic fears that recognition would lead to efforts by African Americans to infiltrate white lodges were completely unfounded. "The white Mason may turn the deaf ear to the Negro's appeal and knock, fully assured in his own mind, that the appeal comes from one particularly anxious to introduce himself, socially or otherwise, into company where he is not wanted," Scottron wrote. "But he is wrong."[35] Indeed, African American Masons perceptively understood that white Masons' use of social equality drew on the same cultural codes that animated hard-line segregationists. That is, they understood its deployment as a spurious metaphor for interracial sex that would potentially alarm white Masons who were otherwise open to greater contact with black Masons. "Another objection against the recognition of the Prince Hall organizations or the admission of black men into the Lodges of the whites..." wrote Harry A. Williamson, in an article for the *American Freemason,* "is the consequent social intermingling among the Lodge members, particularly the possibility of black members coming into active contact with the wives and daughters of their white brethren at the various social functions." Williamson reminded his readers, however, that given the history of coerced sexual relations between white men and African American women in the United States, it was African American Masons who had more to fear from greater social contact.[36]

The realities of Jim Crow led to divergent, sometimes contradictory, opinions about recognition among African American Masons. Williamson, a Brooklyn Mason who would become one of the most important historians and archivists of the Prince Hall tradition, pointedly informed the editor of the *American Tyler-Keystone* that "the Prince Hall Mason has no desire for social equality outside the Lodge room. Within the sanctum sanctorum," he continued, "he desires only the social recognition that is the inherent right of a Master Mason."[37] On the other hand, George W. Crawford, an African American Mason and an attorney from New Haven, Connecticut, offered an equally strident yet more audacious challenge in his history of Prince Hall. For him, recognition would mean nothing without a larger transformation in racial attitudes in the United States. "So far from considering ultimate white recognition as an indispensable end to be sought," Crawford wrote, "the writer believes that it is not even an end to be desired, unless it is preceded by a complete reversal of the attitude of white folk on many points in the race question." It is not clear whether this was a committed position for Crawford or merely rhetorical flourish, given that elsewhere in his history he advocated cooperation between African Americans and whites in the Masonic world. In doing so, he particularized the Washingtonian dictum to speak directly to members of the craft: "[I]f in all things Masonic the white and black Americans could be one, and yet in matters social be as separate as the fingers of the hand, then no one would ever hear impugned the Masonry of Prince Hall and his followers."[38] Crawford's reference to Washington's famous speech at the 1895 Atlanta Exposition illustrated a clear acceptance of the "separate but equal" doctrine advocated by progressive white Masons.

Others expressed comfort with the doctrine and did so in public as well as private communications. Williamson, for instance, in 1930 told a white Masonic correspondent that "[n]either side is ready for group social contact in Masonry . . . any more than they are ready for group social contact otherwise." In a delicately worded admission, Williamson confessed that Prince Hall Freemasons were "not ready for 'de facto' recognition," but he blamed the situation less on African Americans themselves than on the larger American culture. "Unfortunately, the social fabric of American civilization is not of the proper texture for the experiment."[39] Williamson went further, suggesting to a fellow African American Mason that the right of visitation was not only unnecessary but potentially detrimental. It was not they who would begin seeking admission to white lodge meetings in large numbers but, rather, white Masons who would begin "inspecting" Prince Hall lodges "merely out of curiosity." Indeed, Williamson felt that the value of formal recognition was overstated and the benefits limited. The only immediate benefit he could see was that the formal acknowledgment of the legitimacy of the Prince Hall Masons by white grand lodges would assist them in their efforts to attract prospective initiates away from bogus black Masonic organizations. The correlation that Williamson drew between the imprimatur of white American Freemasonry and the appeal of Prince Hall was unfounded and perhaps reflected his own class bias.[40] Nonetheless, his pragmatic approach to the question of formal recognition reflected more of a commitment to parallel institutional and group development than any kind of integrationist desire.[41]

In short, while not deferring to white Masons on the question of their legitimacy, Prince Hall Freemasons in the early twentieth century adopted a gradualist position with respect to the relationship with their white counterparts. Separate associational worlds would eventually yield to a more integrated Masonry, as long as white Masons accepted the authenticity of the Prince Hall tradition and allowed for occasional interaction between the two groups. "All that my group desires at this time is an 'acknowledgement' by Caucasian grand jurisdictions, that the Prince Hall organizations are 'regular,'" Williamson wrote to the editor of the *Trestle Board,* "then leave us to continue our way unmolested so that in time to come our progress will so convince the Caucasian Mason,—[that] he will seek closer relationship."[42] Another, unidentified writer rejected the social equality argument of white Masons as a red herring but appealed to "our brethren on the opposite side . . . for a gradual lessening of the gulf which now divides, that ere long we may meet at that sacred and hallowed plot of God's green earth, there kneeling upon both knees give praise to the Great Creator of the Univeres as brothers one and all."[43] In the end, African American Masons held no uniform position on recognition or integration. Yet they fiercely defended the Prince Hall tradition from charges that it was a bogus or spurious one. In doing so, they relied on the historical record and the archive and, in the process, validated their status as Masons and race men.

In the fall of 1904, the *Colored American Magazine* began a column entitled Masonic Department. According to the magazine's publisher, Fred R. Moore (who would also go on to publish the *New York Age*), the column was needed for several reasons. One was to educate African American Masons about their Masonic history. Moore, as well as others, believed that Prince Hall Freemasons knew too little of their genealogy and therefore were not prepared to rebut white Masonic charges that they were irregular. The column was intended to "put the record of Masonry authoritatively . . . upon the table of every member of the craft." A second objective of the column was to expose white Masons to the history of the Prince Hall tradition. And finally, Moore and the column's editor hoped that the material contained in its pages would be edifying for non-Masons. "[T]o be in the largest sense useful to the people, and to aid in the spread of information desired by all classes and professions," Moore wrote, in announcing the column's launch, "we have determined to enter a field of hitherto quite unoccupied by any of our race periodicals."[44] The "people" to whom Moore referred encompassed more than existing, or prospective, members of the fraternal order. It also consisted of the larger African American community, which would benefit from exposure to the history and, by extension, the contemporary role of Freemasonry in the civic life of the race.

As the cultural studies scholar Hazel Carby points out, the *Colored American Magazine,* which ran from 1900 to 1909, was part of a "revolution" in print journalism, in which publishers of magazines sought to maintain a mass audience through inexpensive subscriptions and advertising that cultivated a mass consumer market. Even though the magazine's content catered to the African American professional class, Carby suggests that its audience probably included literate members of the working class, including skilled laborers and domestics. Moreover, the publisher and editors envisioned the magazine's fulfilling the black middle class's responsibility to uplift the race. "The pedagogic role of the journal was considered by the staff as a significant aspect of its function," Carby writes; "the possibility of being able to 'educate' and expand the horizons of its audience was fully exploited."[45] As Moore's comment suggests, he and the editor, Scottron, not only felt an obligation to provide historical knowledge to African American Masons as a tool to combat racist accusations of their illegitimacy; they also wanted to expose the African American community in general to the virtues of Freemasonry. Scottron articulated this dual mission in his introduction to the Masonic Department:

> A race able to sustain organizations such as these above a century, with never flagging interest and industry, has already shown the highest capacity of mankind. We wish to place facts,—dates and quotations,—before our young men, and all others, who may not have at hand the history of the Order, that each may speak as with authority, fortified with indisputable references; a source of pride to himself and confusion to his enemy.[46]

Scottron firmly situated the history of Prince Hall Freemasonry within the larger narrative of race progress and wanted Masons and non-Masons alike to appreciate its significance.

The same motivation undoubtedly animated the editor of a similar column for the *New York Age* some thirty years later. Edited by Bertram Baker, Masonic Notes ran regularly in the African American newsweekly in the mid-1930s. Both the Masonic Department and Masonic Notes columns certainly promoted Prince Hall Freemasonry by emphasizing the respectable, middle-class character of its members and their families. They did this through features on individual Masons, the entrepreneurship and community work engaged in by lodges and their ladies' auxiliaries, and the stateliness and elegance of lodges' social affairs. But one common feature of both these columns deserves particular attention: the serialization of histories of Prince Hall Freemasonry. From October 1904 to March 1906, the *Colored American Magazine* reprinted in serial form the 1886 publication by Samuel W. Clark, "The Negro Mason in Equity." The *New York Age* serialized Harry A. Williamson's "A Chronological History of Prince Hall Masonry, 1784–1932," from April to December of 1934.

To be sure, the editorial decisions to serialize the work of these Masons were not completely driven by an altruistic motivation to share the history of Prince Hall Freemasonry with non-Masonic African Americans. Monetary considerations—in terms of both increasing subscriptions and selling books—played a considerable role. Early in the Clark series, for instance, Scottron reminded the magazine's agents to promote the Masonic Department in their solicitations to potential subscribers. "We certainly trust that our people are alive to the importance of the widest possible circulation of our Masonic history," Scottron appealed, "and that no effort will be spared in that direction."[47] For Harry Williamson, however, the value of having his Masonic history see print far exceeded what could be gained in sales receipts. In announcing the upcoming serial, Bertram Baker proudly informed the *New York Age* readers that he had "prevailed upon Brother Williamson" to allow him to print chapters of his history "[i]n the interest of the Craft and for the benefit of those—the average Mason, into whose hands the completed volume may never reach, but who nevertheless reads [t]his newspaper."[48] Williamson probably did not need a lot of arm-twisting. He confided to a fellow Mason that he had finished the manuscript some time ago and had intended to publish it but was prevented from doing so by the "depression which all but wrecked the Masonic book market." He decided to permit its serialization "because it was simply becoming 'moth eaten' waiting for conditions to improve" and he "felt the printing might prove of interest and value to our men although few of them comprise much of a reading public."[49] Even though this reflected a limited idea of what constituted a public that could benefit from his historical knowledge, at other points he and other Masons envisioned a more expansive public. At the conclusion of the serialization, Williamson expressed the hope that "the data presented will prove both interesting and valuable to all those who may be interested in the perpetuation of the history of the progress of Prince Hall Masonry." A similar hope was articulated in a follow-up article by Williamson's fellow

Mason Arthur A. Schomburg. The fact that Williamson eventually deposited his extensive collection of materials related to black Freemasonry in
Schomburg's archive of Negro literature and history, housed at the New
York Public Library, suggests that he had a more wide-ranging view about
the potential beneficiaries of Masonic historical information.[50]

While the histories that were circulated in the *Colored American Magazine* and the *New York Age* were different in their scope and express intent,
both drew on historical and contemporary narratives to position Prince
Hall Freemasons as Masons, Americans, and race men. "The Negro Mason
in Equity" was originally a pamphlet-sized publication of an 1886 public
address. Clark's address was explicitly directed at refuting white Masonic
accusations that the Prince Hall tradition was illegitimate. As such, the
publication was not a narrative per se but rather a point-by-point defense
of Prince Hall Freemasonry through a methodical rebuttal of the facts and
logic behind white Masonic arguments. "A Chronological History," on the
other hand, was more conventional historical narrative, providing a state-
by-state recounting of the formation and activities of Prince Hall lodges.
The historical dispute between white and African American Masons hardly
surfaced in the pages, suggesting that Williamson thought the best way to
combat charges of illegitimacy was to simply ignore them.

But there were significant parallels between the two histories, even taking
into account the differences in content and rhetorical style. In a rhetorical move that was common from the immediate postemancipation period
through the mid-twentieth century, both works emphasized that African
American Masons were the true embodiment of the Masonic spirit and that,
indeed, they would deliver American Freemasonry from its racial parochial-
ism. Equally important, they stressed the fundamental Americanness of the
black Mason and, by extension, the African American community. In an
embellishment that Clark probably would not have disagreed with, Scottron
argued that the typical Prince Hall Freemason "hopes for himself, hopes
for his country, desiring with his every pulse-beat that America shall attain
to that high elevation consistent with the eloquent words of the fathers, to
be found in the orations past and present of Americans, who dwell upon
the great mission of our country to bring liberty, fraternity and equality to
all mankind."[51] Scottron, like an earlier generation of Masons, linked the
principles of the craft to what he considered to be the radical egalitarianism
of the American republican tradition. Others did so by highlighting the
patriotism of black Masons. Prince Hall's service in the Continental Army
as well as his offer to assist the Massachusetts militia in suppressing Shay's
Rebellion shortly after the Revolution was consistently referred to in print

and oratorical histories of the fraternal order.[52] When Williamson pointed to the proliferation of military lodges that were attached to the black regiments in the United States Army throughout the West or when he explained the significance behind the naming of a lodge in Augusta, Georgia, after the black astronomer, mathematician, and surveyor Benjamin Banneker, he was accessing, and contributing to, a collective memory that celebrated African Americans' contribution to national development and progress.[53]

But if these histories emphasized the fundamental Americanness of black Masons and the African American community as a whole, they also reflected the middle-class bearings of the fraternal order. As such, they reiterated the naturalness of African American Masons' capacity for race leadership. References to Prince Hall consistently included descriptors such as "leading free colored citizen of Boston" and "leader among his people," whereas contemporary Masons were regularly described as "illustrious," "progressive," and the "best citizens" of their respective communities. Moreover, the "Chronological History," in particular, documented the importance of Prince Hall Freemasons to the economic well-being of the African American community, often detailing how much property, in dollar terms, a subordinate or grand lodge in any individual jurisdiction owned.[54] The message was clear: by virtue of their character, their respectability, and their entrepreneurial aptitude, African American Masons were best equipped to shepherd the race toward group development and collective progress.

The very public nature of these histories of Prince Hall Freemasonry and their circulation were aimed, in part, at engaging a white Masonic reading public that doubted African American Masons' legitimacy. Historians of Prince Hall probably felt that they could reach more white Masons by circulating the true historical record through the black press than by communicating with individual progressive white Masons. And there is some anecdotal evidence that, at least in the case of the serialization of "The Negro Mason in Equity" in the *Colored American Magazine,* white Masons were reading and seeking more information about the history of the Prince Hall tradition. As Scottron pointed out in one of his columns, "We are not only gratified at the interest manifested by white Masons, but somewhat surprised that they give evidence of a deeper interest in the history than our colored brethren."[55] But the public nature of the Prince Hall archive also served to link African American Masons with the larger African American community, both as fellow victims of a history of white supremacy and as fellow protagonists in an ongoing narrative of group advancement, a narrative in which they would play the leading part.

On a winter evening in 1936—some sixty-eight years after Lewis Hayden predicted that future historians would document the collective struggles and progress of Prince Hall Freemasons—Harry A. Williamson officially presented his collection of material on Negro Masonry to the New York Public Library's Department of History, Print and Literature, located at its 135th Street Branch in Harlem. The department had its origins in the library's purchase of the massive collection of books, pamphlets, manuscripts, and images owned by Arthur Schomburg in 1926. An Afro-Puerto Rican bibliophile, historian, and writer, Schomburg, the first curator of the department, was also a Prince Hall Freemason and a friend of Williamson's.[56]

Williamson, who had been collecting material related to Prince Hall Freemasonry and Masonry as a whole, first began exploring the possibility of preserving his documents and artifacts in the late 1920s. He approached Sumner Furniss, an African American Mason from Indianapolis and an officer in the Ancient and Accepted Scottish Rite, Northern Jurisdiction, about having the Supreme Council serve as a repository for the materials. "Life at best is brief and I have often wondered what would eventually become of this great effort after my death," Williamson wrote to Furniss. "The members of my own grand jurisdiction have taken very little interest in and place very little value upon my efforts toward a preservation of the history of our branch of the great Fraternity [;] consequently I desire to arrange for the disposal of the result of those years of time and money spent in getting the items together where they will be appreciated and do the greatest number the most good." Williamson requested that the collection be called the Harry A. Williamson Memorial Library and that the material be used only for reference and not for circulation. Despite an affirmative response from Furniss, and for unknown reasons, Williamson canceled the bequest six years later.[57]

By 1934, Williamson had intensified his search for a suitable repository. He informed Schomburg that he and his wife were moving to a smaller apartment that would not be able to accommodate his collection. Because of his friendship with Hugo Tatsch, the progressive white curator of the Iowa Masonic Library, Williamson had considered depositing his considerable set of materials there. However, he had "not adopted this idea because the collection would not be accessible to our group; in fact, some of the items unfavorable to the whites might be destroyed for obvious reasons."[58] It was very important to Williamson that African American Masons have access to the historical record that would in fact document their legitimacy. But he also felt that the material should be accessible to more than just Masons. As he mentioned to his friend Harry E. Davis, a Mason from Cleveland, Ohio, and a prominent historian of the Prince Hall tradition himself, "It is my desire to have my collection placed where it will be accessible to our group. Should it go into a private collection, all of the material will disappear and be of no service to any who might be inclined to research."[59]

Given the constant assaults on their legitimacy as a fraternal tradition, the preservation, production, and circulation of historical knowledge were critical for Prince Hall Freemasons. In a coda to the "Chronological History" series, Schomburg put as fine a point on this sentiment as possible when he wrote that the "links of real brotherhood continue uninterrupted to this day because knowledge is power."[60] For a fraternal association that placed as much premium on genealogy as Freemasonry did, it was imperative that African American members of the order be able to demonstrate everywhere and always that they had in fact descended from the Grand Lodge of England. They understood nonrecognition as but a "break between principle and practice"[61] within the world of Freemasonry, just as slavery and Jim Crow were, to their minds, breaks within the liberal democratic tradition of the United States. While they were confident that principle and practice would eventually be reconciled, they knew that in the meantime they would have to defend the authenticity of their credentials.

But from African American Masons' perspective, knowledge of Prince Hall history was not only for their own benefit. It promised to also benefit the larger African American community by binding the historical experiences of the race with those of the fraternity and creating a collective narrative of mutual progress. Regarding nineteenth-century African American historiography, John Ernest argues that "the purpose of historical research and writing was to identify the historical contours of the African American community, and in that way to aid in the ongoing realization of the historical agency of that community."[62] With the historical narratives that they produced and circulated, the African American Masons did precisely this, by positioning themselves as the principal agents of community advancement. In this regard, they understood their historical role as fundamentally different from that of their white counterparts. Most African American Masons surely would have agreed with A.W.A. De Leon's comparison between the Prince Hall and white Masonic traditions. White Masons "would have us believe that they are not prompted by prejudice or ill-feeling, but by arguments 'fairly and squarely' based upon the ground of incompatibility and capability as a race, and not against individuals," De Leon wrote. "Our power is not derived by arguing for ourselves individualy, but we assume the right, and that right gives us the power of arguing for our race."[63]

Three Key Texts of Prince Hall Masonry

African Lodge No. 459 Charter

(September 29, 1784)

To all and every one of our Right Worshipful and loving Brethren, we, Thomas Howard, Earl of Effingham, Lord Howard, &c., &c., &c., Acting Grand Master, under the authority of His Royal Highness, Henry Frederick, Duke of Cumberland, &c., &c., &c., Grand Master of the Most Ancient and Honorable Society of Free and Accepted Masons, send greetings:

KNOW YE THAT WE, that we, at the humble petition of our right trusty and well-beloved Brethren, PRINCE HALL, BOSTON SMITH, THOMAS SANDERSON and several other Brethren, residing in Boston, New England, in North America, do hereby constitute that said Brethren into a regular LODGE OF FREE AND ACCEPTED MASONS, under the title or denomination of the AFRICAN LODGE, to be open in Boston aforesaid, and do further, at their said petition, and of the great Trust and hereby appoint the said PRINCE HALL to be Master, BOSTON SMITH, Senior Warden, and THOMAS SANDERSON, Junior Warden, for the opening of the said LODGE, and for such further time only as shall be thought proper by the Brethren thereof, it being our will that this our appointment of the above officers shall in no wise affect any future election of officers of the LODGE, but that such election shall be regulated agreeable to such by-laws of said LODGE as shall be consistent with the general laws of the society, contained in the Book of Constitutions; and we hereby will require you, the said PRINCE HALL, to take especial care that all and every one of the said Brethren are, or have been regularly made masons, and that they do observe, perform and keep all the rules and orders contained in the Book of Constitutions; and, further, that you do from time to time, cause to be entered in a book kept for that purpose, an account of your proceedings as a LODGE, together with such rules, orders and regulations, as shall be made for the good government of the same; that in no wise you omit once in every year to send to us, or our successors, Grand Master, or to Rowland Holt, Esq., or Deputy Grand Master, for the time being, an account in writing of your said proceedings, and copies of all such rules, orders and regulations, as shall be made as aforesaid, together with a list of the members of the LODGE, and such sum of money as may suit the circumstances of the Lodge, and reasonably be expected toward the Grand Charity.

Moreover, we hereby will and require you, the said PRINCE HALL, as soon as conveniently may be, to send an account in writing of what may be done by virtue of these presents.

(seal)
Given at London, under our
hand and seal of Masonry,
this 29th day of September,
A.L., 5784, A.D. 1784
"By the GRAND MASTER'S command,
Witness: W. M. White, G.S.
R. Holt, D.G.M."

Declaration of Independence (published in the *Columbian Centinel* [Boston], June 26, 1827)

Greetings:

Be it known to all whom it may concern. That we, the Master, Wardens, members of African Lodge No. 459, City of Boston (Mass.), U.S. of America, hold in our possession a certain unlimited Charter granted September 29, A. L. 5784, A.D. 1784 by Thomas Howard, Earl of Effingham, ★★★ Whether the conditions have been complied with by our ancestors, we are unable to say; but we can add that, in consequence of the decease of the above-mentioned Brother, the institution was for years unable to proceed, for the want of one to conduct its affairs agreeably to what is required in every regular and well-educated Lodge of Masons. It is now, however, with great pleasure we state that the present age has arrived to that degree of proficiency in the art, that we can at any time select from among us many whose capacity to govern enables them to preside with as much good order, dignity, and propriety as any other Lodge with our knowledge. This fact can be proved by gentlemen of respectability, whose knowledge of Masonry would not be questioned by any one well acquainted with the art. Since the rise of the Lodge to this degree of proficiency, we conclude that it was best and proper to make it known to the Most Worshipful Grand Lodge from when we derived our charter, by sending written documents and monies, to fulfill the agreement of our ancestors giving information of the low state to which it had fallen, its cause, &c., with its rise and progress; and also soliciting favors, whereby we might be placed on a different and better standing than we had theretofore. And notwithstanding this has long since been done, and more than sufficient time has lapsed for returns, yet we have never received a single line or reply from that Hon. Society. In consequence of that neglect, we have been at a stand what course to pursue. Our remote situation prevents us from making any verbal communication whatever. Taking all of these things into consideration, we have come to the conclusion that with what knowledge we possess of Masonry, and as people of Color by ourselves, we are, and ought by rights, to be free and independent of other Lodges. We do therefore, with this belief, publicly declare ourselves free and independent of any Lodge from this day, and that we will not be tributary, or be governed by any other lodge than that of our own. We agree solemnly to abide by all proper rules and regulations which govern the like Fraternity, discountenancing all imposition to injure the Order, and to use all fair and honorable means to promote its prosperity, resting in full hope that this will enable us to transmit it in its purity to our posterity for their enjoyment.

Done at the Lodge, this 18th day of June A.D. 1827.
In full testimony of what has been written we affix our names:
John T. Hilton, R.M.W.
Thomas Dalton, Sen. Ward.
Lewis York, Jun. Ward.
J. H. Purron, Secretary

Declaration of Sentiments of the Great National Convention, Held at the City of Boston, Mass., June 23, 1847, A. L., 5847 (reprinted in *Minutes of Proceedings of the Triennial Session of the National Grand Lodge, A. Y. M., Held in Philadelphia, July, 1856* [Philadelphia: Brown's Steam-Power Book and Job Printing Office, 1856], 5–6)

Sentiment 1—The question has been asked, the cause of separate organizations of White and Colored Masons in the United States of America. We do not know any reason why there should be, and we have made several attempts, without any success, to have but one. We are, and always have been, in possession of all the Ancient Landmarks and Regulations of the Craft; and we do acknowledge all the genuine Masons, of all nations and shades of complexion, to be our brethren.

Sentiment 2—Therefore, in pursuance of the above call, we have met in the City of Boston, State of Massachusetts, in the year and date above-mentioned, and do form in solemn Convention, and say [*sic*] before the world our sentiments thereon.

Sentiment 3—In all stages of oppression, we have petitioned for redress, but found none; *therefore,* in solemn convention assembled, we do, in the name of the Great Masonic Body, of Free and Accepted A. Y. Masons, declare ourselves a free and Independent Body of Masons, to be known as the National Grand Lodge of Color of these United States of America, and Masonic Jurisdiction thereunto belonging, with full power and authority to grant Letters of Dispensation and Warrants to all State Grand Lodges under our jurisdiction, and that the said State Grand Lodges shall have full power and authority to grant Letters of Dispensation and Warrants to the Subordinate Lodges under the several Jurisdictions, and to establish as many Lodges as they may deem most expedient.

Sentiment 4—Not that we have been wanting in attention to our White Brethren. We have from time to time solicited them to extend their jurisdictions over us, but to no effect.

We, therefore, the delegates of the several lodges through these United States, in Convention assembled, appealing to the Supreme Judge of the World for the rectitude of our intentions, do in the name, and by the authority of our constituents, declare and publish the said National Grand Lodge of Color of the United States to be a *Free and Independent Body,* with full power as named in the third article of this declaration, and for the support of this declaration, with a firm reliance on the protection of Divine Providence, we mutually pledge ourselves to each other in the solemn ties of BROTHERHOOD.

Your Committee most respectfully recommend to your honorable body the Free Masons' Library and General Ahimans' [*sic*] Rezon, as published by Samuel Cole, second edition, published in 1826, for your government for the next ensuing six months, or the time being, and that the 8th Article of the 8th Section shall in no case or instance be departed from.

DELEGATES.

Boston—John T. Hilton, George Gaul, William E. Ambush, Nathan Lewis, George C. Willis, Henry Harris, James H. Holt, Jonas [sic] Dalton.

Pennsylvania—J. J. Gould Bias, M.D., James J. Richmond, Samuel Van Brakle, Emery Conakin, James Newman, Philip Buchanan, Jonathan Lopeman, J. W. Powell, Wm. H. Bruce, John Anderson.

New York—Alexander Elston, William H. Clark, Lewis Hayden.

Providence—Nathan C. Willis.

Appendix B

Glossary of Basic Masonic Terminology

This glossary was compiled by Mark A. Tabbert, Director of Collections at the George Washington Masonic National Memorial Association. Below are the principal sources consulted.

Coil, Henry. *Coil's Masonic Encyclopedia.* Rev. ed. Richmond, VA: Macoy Publishing and Masonic Supply Company, 1996.

Hodapp, Christopher. *Freemasons for Dummies.* Hoboken, NJ: Wiley, 2005.

Roundtree, Alton G. *The National Grand Lodge and Prince Hall Freemasonry: The Untold Truth.* Camp Springs, MD: KLR Publishing, 2010.

Roundtree, Alton G., and Paul M. Bessel. *Out of the Shadows: The Emergence of Prince Hall Freemasonry in America.* Camp Springs, MD: KLR Publishing, 2006.

Voorhis, Harold V. B. *Masonic Organizations and Allied Orders and Degree.* Red Bank, NJ: Press of Henry Emerson, 1952.

General Terms

accepted Refers to the acceptance of non-stonemasons (e.g., gentlemen) into British stonemasons' guilds in the seventeenth and eighteenth centuries. In theory all Freemasons are accepted stonemasons.

A.F. & A.M. Ancient Free & Accepted Masons.

affiliated masonic body An organization that has a historic relationship with Freemasonry and may require a person to have a family member who is a Freemason in order to join. Examples: Knighthood of Pythagorus, Daughters of Isis, Heroines of Jericho, and the Order of the Eastern Star.

Ahiman Rezon The constitutions of the Ancient Grand Lodge of England, written by Laurence Dermott and published in London in 1756. The title is usually translated from Hebrew to mean "a help to a brother." The Grand Lodge of Pennsylvania also titles its grand constitutions Ahiman Rezon.

A.L. "Anno Lucis" or "in the year of light." The Masonic dating system from the creation of the world. Add four thousand years to the current year: A.D. 2011 equals A.L. 6011.

American Doctrine Or "doctrine of exclusive territorial jurisdiction," the presumption that there can be only one recognized grand lodge within a prescribed geographical area, and especially a state. The doctrine developed between 1786 and 1796 after the creation of the U.S Constitution and formation of the independent Grand Lodge of Pennsylvania. This doctrine is the major Masonic reason that Prince Hall grand lodges were not recognized by other grand lodges. Over time the doctrine was reinterpreted so that two grand lodges could coexist in the same territory if they recognized each other. Only after mutual recognition could a grand lodge outside the territory recognize both grand lodges.

ancient Also spelled "antient," refers to something of antiquity or without known origin; specifically refers to the Ancient Grand Lodge of England, formed in 1756, in contrast to the premier or so-called Modern Grand Lodge formed in 1717 in London.

appendant Masonic body An organization whose membership is open only to Master Masons (third-degree Masons) in good standing. Examples: the Royal Arch, the Scottish Rite, and the Shrine.

blue lodge A local Masonic lodge, the smallest unit of Freemasonry. Blue is the standard color associated with the three degrees in Masonry and symbolizes fidelity. This is in contrast to a so-called red lodge, which refers to Royal Arch Masonry. A blue lodge is also called a symbolic Lodge or craft lodge.

bogus Masonry Or "spurious masonry." A group of men, women, or both who lack any authenticity or lineage to a regular and recognized grand lodge; essentially any group who attempt to usurp grand lodge authority or conduct plagiarized Masonic rituals.

charter A Masonic legal document that grants a group of Freemasons the right to meet, initiate new members, and engage in other activities. A lodge cannot meet without holding a charter from a grand lodge. Also called a warrant. See **lodge**.

clandestine Masonry A group of Freemasons meeting without the legal consent of a grand lodge.

communication A lodge meeting. A grand communication is a meeting of a grand lodge

Compact Grand Lodge See **National Grand Lodge**.

constitutions Or "grand constitutions." The book of rules and regulations that governs a grand lodge and its subordinate lodges. The first Masonic book ever published was Reverend James Anderson's *The Constitutions of the Free-Masons* in London in 1723.

the Craft Another name for Freemasonry; also used to designate a type of lodge, such as a craft lodge, as compared with a grand lodge or red lodge.

DDGM district deputy grand master. The senior Masonic official in a subunit of a grand lodge jurisdiction. A DDGM is like a middle manager between several lodge masters and a grand lodge grand master.

degree A ceremony of membership initiation. Freemasonry consists of three initiation degrees: Entered Apprentice (EA), Fellowcraft (FC), and Master Mason (MM). Other Masonic organizations confer additional initiation degrees, but these are contained in appendant or affiliated Masonic organizations.

DGM Deputy grand master. The second-highest officer in a grand lodge, similar to a vice president. When a grand master is absent, the deputy grand master presides.

doctrine of exclusive territorial jurisdiction. See **American Doctrine.**

east Where the sun rises and the master of a lodge presides. A grand master presides in the grand east. Because all lodges are a representation of the First Jerusalem Temple built by King Solomon, all lodges are, or should be, situated due east and west.

F.A.A.M. Free and Accepted Masons.

F. & A.M. Free and Accepted Masons.

Freemasonry A private fraternal organization. Defined in Masonic ritual as a "peculiar system or morality conveyed through allegory and illustrated by symbols." Also called the Craft, Symbolic Freemasonry, or Blue Lodge Masonry. Freemasonry confers three initiation degrees: Entered Apprentice, Fellowcraft, and Master Mason.

GAOTU Grand Architect of the Universe, a Masonic name for God.

grand A term applied to a governing body and the officers thereof, such as a grand lodge that governs local lodges and a grand master who is superior to a lodge master.

grand lodge Represents a geographical area and regulates local lodges in that area. A grand lodge is composed of the grand master, deputy grand master, and grand senior and junior wardens and the masters and wardens of the lodges within the jurisdiction. The first grand lodge was formed in London in 1717. In the jurisdiction of the United States there are grand lodges for each state and the District of Columbia, as well as for Puerto Rico.

grand master As a master rules his local lodge, a grand master governs his state grand lodge. A grand master has authority over all Masonic activities and organizations within his jurisdiction.

Great Lights The Holy Bible (or other recognized Volume of Sacred Law), Square, and Compasses. Without the three Great Lights no lodge or grand lodge can open and work. The three lesser lights are the sun, moon, and master of a lodge (represented by three burning tapers around the three Great Lights).

Hiram Abif The master craftsman who built the Temple of God in Jerusalem. The Bible states he was sent to Solomon by Hiram, King of Tyre. He is the "widow's son," and all Masons assume the role of Hiram in the Master Mason degree. The junior warden also represents Hiram Abif.

Hiram, King of Tyre King Solomon's principal ally in building the Temple in Jerusalem. According to the Bible, King Hiram provided the men and materials for construction. The senior warden represents King Hiram.

irregular Masonry The operation and unauthorized practice of a lodge or grand lodge, in particular a so-called Masonic body that performs nonrecognized rituals and practices, such as performing Masonic weddings or initiating children.

J&B Jachin and Boaz, the names of the two great bronze pillars that stood before the Temple in Jerusalem built by King Solomon.

junior warden The third principal officer of the lodge. The "second vice president," subordinate to the master and senior warden. He also represents Hiram Abif.

jurisdiction The geographical area or areas under the authority of a grand lodge. Usually within a US state, but some grand lodges have additional lodges in various territories. For example, the Grand Lodge of Massachusetts also has lodges in Cuba, Panama, Chile, and Japan.

lodge A local assembly of Freemasons and also the place where Masons assemble. Like a church, a lodge may refer to the congregation or the building. Masonic lectures define, "A lodge is a certain number of masons duly assembled with a Holy Bible (or other VSL), Square and Compasses and a charter or warrant empowering them to work." Every Freemason must belong to a lodge, and all lodges are under the authority of a grand lodge.

lodge officers A lodge is presided over by a worshipful master (WM) and senior and junior wardens (SW, JW). Other officers are the secretary treasurer, senior and junior deacons (SD, JD), senior and junior stewards (SS, JS), chaplain, and tyler. Lodges may have a marshal or master of ceremonies, organist, soloist, inside sentinel, almoner, electrician, and orator, to name a few.

Mainstream Masonry In the United States and Canada, the regular, recognized, and predominately white grand lodges. These trace their lineage to the grand lodges of England, Scotland, or Ireland. The term gained prominence in the 1980s to distinguish predominately white from predominately black, or Prince Hall, Freemasonry.

master The senior officer of the lodge, or the president. His formal title is worshipful master (WM). He is a representation of Solomon, King of Israel.

Master Mason A man who has received all three degrees in Masonry and is a full member of a lodge in good standing.

Moderns Refers to the premier grand lodge formed in 1717 in London. When the Ancient Grand Lodge formed in 1756, it derogatorily called the elder grand lodge "modern," thereby suggesting it had fallen away from the "ancient and true Masonry."

National Grand Lodge Also known as Compact Grand Lodge. Formed in 1847 by the Massachusetts and Pennsylvania Prince Hall grand lodges to help spread Freemasonry within African American communities.

Negro Freemasonry Outdated term once used to describe any regular or bogus Masonic organization composed of African Americans. The term "Prince Hall Masonry" is now used to identify regular and recognized predominately black lodges. See **Prince Hall Freemasonry.**

operative masonry Stonemasonry, as distinct from speculative Masonry/Freemasonry.

past grand master (PGM) A Mason who has served as a grand master of a grand lodge.

past master (PM) A Freemason who has served as a worshipful master of a lodge.

Prince Hall Freemasonry Also known as Prince Hall Affiliated (PHA). Masonic organizations that are directly related to, in amity with, or descended from African Lodge No. 459, Boston, or the Prince Hall Grand Lodge of Massachusetts. The term is used to identify regular and recognized, predominately black Freemasonry. It replaced the term "Negro" or "Colored" Freemasonry, especially since the 1990s, when both white and black men have been able to join either Mainstream or Prince Hall lodges.

recognition The acceptance by one grand lodge of another grand lodge as regular, holding legitimate Masonic authority and proper lineage. Once grand lodges recognize each other, members of one grand lodge may usually visit the other.

regular Freemasonry Freemasons working in a duly constituted lodge under a regular and recognized grand lodge, especially a lodge that adheres to all "ancient established customs and usages" and strictly confers recognized rituals.

Saints John Saint John the Baptist and Saint John the Evangelist, who, in the United States, are by tradition "the patron saints of Freemasonry." Lodges are "erected to God and dedicated to the Holy Saints John."

senior warden The second principal officer of the lodge, the "first first vice president," subordinate to the master and senior to the junior Warden. In the absence of the master, the senior warden presides over meetings. He also represents Hiram, King of Tyre.

Solomon King of Israel who built the first Temple to God in Jerusalem. According to the Bible, he was assisted by Hiram, King of Tyre, who sent him Hiram Abif the master craftsman. In Freemasonry the master of a lodge represents King Solomon.

So Mote It Be "So may it be." The closing phrase for all Masonic prayers but also used after speeches, announcements, or other declarations.

speculative Masonry Freemasonry, contrasted with operative masonry, or stonemasonry.

symbolic lodge A local Masonic lodge. This is in contrast to a lodge of operative stonemasons, who work with real tools and stone. Freemasons work with symbols and allegory.

the Temple Built in Jerusalem by King Solomon. According to the Bible, the Temple was the "House unto the Name of the Lord," a sanctuary for the Ark of the Covenant and the place of worship for the tribes of Israel. All Masonic lodges are representations of the Temple, and all Freemasons are symbolically stonemasons working on the Temple.

tenets of Freemasonry Brotherly Love, Relief, and Truth.

volume of sacred law (VSL) Any sacred writing or text recognized as such. Most common in the United States is the Christian Bible, but a VSL can be any book chosen by the lodge members and approved by the grand lodge. It is possible to have more than one VSL open during a meeting, but a lodge cannot work without an open VSL.

warrant See **charter**.

working tools The gavel, twenty-four-inch gauge, plumb, level, square, and trowel. These tools are used by operative masons to prepare stone and build buildings. Freemasonry applies symbolic meaning to each tool to prepare men to be better human beings.

Prince Hall Affiliated and Appendant Masonic Organizations

Daughters of Isis. A female auxiliary to the Shriners. It is a social fraternal order founded in 1910.

Heroines of Jericho A cogender organization for women and Royal Arch Masons, similar to the Order of the Eastern Star.

Knights Templar The third body of the York Rite. Local Knights Templar bodies are called commanderies. To join, a Mason normally must have received the degrees of the Royal and Select Cryptic Masons. Each commandery confers three orders (or degrees): the Red Cross, the Knight of Malta, and the Order of the Temple. The Knights Templar is the only appendant Masonic body that is specifically Christian.

Order of the Eastern Star A cogender organization started by Rob Morris in 1853. It is open to all women who believe in a Supreme Being and to Master Masons in good standing. The first Prince Hall Eastern Star chapter was founded in Washington, D.C., in 1873. The order has one degree that teaches the virtues of five biblical heroines: Adah, Ruth, Esther, Martha, and Electa.

Order of Pythagorans A boys' organization founded in 1936, sponsored by Freemasons. Similar to the Order of Demolay. The Order of Demolay is for boys; local Demolay chapters are sponsored by "mainstream" Masonic lodges.

Royal Arch Masonry The first of three bodies that comprise the York Rite. Also referred to as "Red Lodges," Royal Arch Masons meet in chapters and are presided over by a high priest. To join the Royal Arch a man must be a Master Mason. Chapters confer the Mark Master, the Past Master, Most Excellent Master, and Royal Arch degrees.

Royal and Select Masons Also known as Cryptic Masons. The second body that comprises the York Rite. Royal and Select Masons meet in councils and are presided over by an illustrious master. To join, a Freemason must be a Royal Arch Mason. Councils confer the royal master, the select master, and the super excellent master degrees.

Scottish Rite Formally called the Ancient and Accepted Scottish Rite of Freemasonry (A.A.S.R.). The Scottish Rite confers the fourth through the thirty-second degree and honors the most active members with the thirty-third degree. The degrees are usually conferred on groups of Masons as allegorical plays. To join the Scottish Rite, a man must first be a Master Mason. The Scottish Rite is composed of four bodies: lodge of perfection, princes of Jerusalem council, rose croix chapters, and a consistory. The governing body is a supreme council, 33° presided over by a sovereign grand commander.

Shriners Members of the Ancient Egyptian Arabic Order Nobles of the Mystic Shrine (A.E.A.O.N.M.S.). The Shrine is an appendant body of

Freemasonry. It is a social and philanthropic organization founded in Chicago in 1893. To be a Shriner, a man must first be a Freemason.

York Rite   Composed of three bodies: the Royal Arch, Royal and Select Cryptic Masons, and the Knights Templar. Each body is independent in its governance, but they are confederated in the progress and uniformity in the York Rite system. The York Rite has no national headquarters.

Major Repositories of Prince Hall Masonic History

The Iowa Masonic Library

Grand Lodge of Iowa, A.F. & A.M.
813 First Avenue SE
P.O. Box 279
Cedar Rapids, IA 52406-0279
Ph.: 319-365-1438
Fax: 319-365-1439
http://www.gl-iowa.org/library.html

Considered one of the largest repositories of Prince Hall–related materials in the United States, the Iowa Masonic Library includes more than six hundred titles relating to Prince Hall Masonry. Many of those are proceedings of Prince Hall grand lodges in the United States and Canada. The Prince Hall proceedings include materials from nearly all states in the United States and several provinces in Canada. Included in the proceedings collection are those related to appendant bodies such as York Rite, Scottish Rite and Shrine. Prince Hall–related periodicals include the *Phylaxis, Plumb Line, Prince Hall Sentinel,* and many others. The archival collection includes approximately 3 linear feet of material, including reports and histories of various Prince Hall jurisdictions, papers by Henry A. Williamson, and various Prince Hall–related addresses. The library is the repository of the Joseph

Walkes Collection of Prince Hall Masonry, which includes approximately 150 titles, approximately 9.5 linear feet of archival materials, and microfilm copies of the Henry A. Williamson collection of the New York Public Library. Finally, the rare book collection of the Iowa Masonic Library contains many addresses by Prince Hall–related authors, including Prince Hall, Lewis Hayden, and Alexander Clark.

Livingston Masonic Library

Grand Lodge of New York, F. & A.M.
71 W 23rd Street, 14th Floor
New York, NY 10010-4171
212-337-6620
nfo@nymasoniclibrary.org

The Chancellor Robert R. Livingston Masonic Library collection includes approximately 140 cataloged items devoted to African American Freemasonry, with half the titles relating specifically to Prince Hall Freemasonry. Archival holdings include the collection of African American Masonic material assembled by Edward R. Cusick, focusing on the late nineteenth and early to mid-twentieth centuries. A finding aid for the Cusick collection appears on the library's web page. Other ephemera consisting of newspaper articles, programs, and lodge notices are held in vertical files.

Several folders of correspondence by Harry E. Davis (author of *A History of Freemasonry among Negroes in America*); Harry A. Williamson (a leader of Prince Hall Masonry, scholar, and author); and Arthur A. Schomburg (grand secretary, Prince Hall Grand Lodge, New York) are available.

The Masonic Library and Museum Association (of North America)

http://www.masoniclibraries.org/

Moorland-Spingarn Research Center

Founders Library
Howard University
500 Howard Place, NW
Washington, DC 20056
http://www.howard.edu/msrc/default.htm

Since 1987 the MW PHGL of DC has deposited approximately twenty-five linear feet of grand lodge archival material, as well as but not limited to official grand lodge proceedings, photographs, grand lodge program memorabilia, lodge trestle boards, lodge histories, grand lodge regalia, and monographs pertaining to Freemasonry.

Every two years the MW PHGL of DC deposits new material in MSRC.

Schomburg Center for Research in Black Culture

New York Public Library
515 Malcolm X Blvd.
New York, NY 10037-1801
202-491-2200
http://www.nypl.org/research/sc/sc.html

The Schomburg Center for Research in Black Culture, New York Public Library, is the primary repository in New York City for material relating to Prince Hall Masonry. Its collections include the works of Harry A. Williamson as well as his papers, photographs, and scrapbooks.

Van Gorden-Williams Library and Archives

National Heritage Museum
33 Marrett Road
Lexington, MA 02421
718-861-6559
http://nationalheritagemuseum.org/Default.aspx?tabid=466

Collections related to Prince Hall Freemasonry include nearly 150 titles, including 15 serials titles and proceedings (often single issues) from various Prince Hall organizations, published in the nineteenth and twentieth centuries. The archives house a small collection of ephemera related to Prince Hall organizations, including souvenir programs, invitations, and postcards. Highlights include three speeches by Lewis Hayden published in the 1860s; research notes of Harold V. B. Voorhis related to Prince Hall Freemasonry, which include facsimile and transcribed summaries of the minutes of African Lodge No. 459 of Boston and its successor, the Independent African Grand Lodge of Boston (1807–28), as well as research notes related to Philadelphia African Lodge No. 544.

Prince Hall Grand Lodge
Contact Information

This directory was compiled by Mark A. Tabbert, Director of Collections at the George Washington Masonic National Memorial Association. Below are the principal sources consulted.

Henderson, Kent, and Tony Pope. *Freemasonry Universal: A New Guide to the Masonic World.* 2 vols. Victoria, Aus.: Global Masonic Publications, 1998.

Hodapp, Christopher. *Freemasons for Dummies.* Hoboken, NJ: Wiley, 2005.

List of Lodges Masonic. Bloomington, IL: Pantagraph Printing & Stationery Co., 2011.

In the United States

Alabama

Prince Hall Grand Lodge F. & A.M.
  of Alabama
1630 N. 4th Ave
Birmingham AL 35203
205-328-9078

Alaska

Prince Hall Grand Lodge F. & A.M.
  Alaska and Its Jurisdiction, Inc.
1200 East 9th Avenue, Suite 101
Anchorage, Alaska 99501-3959
907-646-2210
(fax) 907-646-2217

Arizona

Prince Hall Grand Lodge F. & A.M.
  Arizona and Jurisdiction, Inc.
Masonic Temple
6035 S. 24th Street

Phoenix, AZ 85042
602-268-8511
http://www.azmwphgl.com/

Arkansas
Prince Hall Grand Lodge F. & A.M.,
  Inc., Jurisdiction of Arkansas
119 E. Fourth Ave
Pine Bluff, AR 71601
870-534-5467
(fax) 870-535-3581
http://arkphagrandlodge.com/

California
Prince Hall Grand Lodge, F. &
  A.M., State of California, Inc.
9027 S. Figueroa St.
Los Angeles, CA 90003
323-242-2393
(fax) 323-754-2930
http://www.mwphglcal.org/ph/

Colorado
Prince Hall Grand Lodge of
  Colorado, Wyoming, Utah, and
  Parts of South Korea
2921 S. Vaughn Way
Aurora, CO 80014
303-671-0046 or 303-884-0055
http://mwphglco.com/

Connecticut
Prince Hall Grand Lodge of
  Connecticut, Inc., F. & A.M.
66 Montville Street
Hartford, CT 06120
203-329-9957
(fax) 203-329-9957

Delaware
Prince Hall Grand Lodge F. & A.M.
  of Delaware
623 S. Heald St

Wilmington DE 19801
302-652-9283
http://www.mwphglde.org/

District of Columbia
Grand Lodge, F. & A.M., PHA,
  Jurisdiction of the District of
  Columbia Inc.
1000 U Street NW
Washington, DC 20001
202-462-8878; 202-462-8877
(fax) 202-265-5620
http://mwphgldc.com/

Florida
Union Grand Lodge Most Ancient
  and Honorable Fraternity Free
  and Accepted Masons PHA
  Florida & Belize, Central
  America Jurisdiction Inc.
410 Broad St.
Jacksonville, FL 32202
904-354-2368
(fax) 904-355-8667
http://www.mwuglflorida.org/

Georgia
Prince Hall Grand Lodge Free and
  Accepted Masons Jurisdiction of
  Georgia
330 Auburn Ave NE
Atlanta, GA 30335
404-521-1358
(fax) 404-525-1341
http://www.mwphglga.org/

Hawaii
Prince Hall Grand Lodge
  F. & A.M. of Hawaii and Its
  Jurisdiction, Inc.
P.O. Box 89-3553
Mililani, HI 96789
http://www.phglofhawaii.org/

Illinois

Prince Hall Grand Lodge F. & A.M.
  State of Illinois and Jurisdiction
809 E. 42nd Place
Chicago, IL 60653
773-373-2725
(fax) 773-523-1793
http://www.mwphglil.com/

Indiana

Prince Hall Grand Lodge Free and
  Accepted Masons Jurisdiction of
  Indiana
5605 E. 38th St
Indianapolis, IN 46218
317-546-8062
(fax) 317-546-8071
http://www.mwphglin.org/

Iowa

Prince Hall Grand Lodge of Iowa
  and Jurisdiction, Inc.
1351 Christie
Davenport, IA 52803

Kansas

Prince Hall Grand Lodge F. & A.M.
  of Kansas and Its Jurisdiction
PO Box 300463
Kansas City, MO 64130-0463
913-621-4300
(fax) 913-621-4330
http://www.phglks.com/

Kentucky

Prince Hall Grand Lodge F. & A.M.
  of Kentucky, Inc.
1304 S. 28th St.
Louisville, KY 40211
502-776-5560
(fax) 502-773-0355
http://www.phglky.com/

Louisiana

Prince Hall Grand Lodge F. & A.M.
  for the State of Louisiana and
  Jurisdiction
1335 N. Blvd., Suite 301
Baton Rouge, LA 70802
504-387-0996
(fax) 504-343-0366
http://www.mwphglla.com/

Maine

Prince Hall Lodge in Maine is
  chartered by Prince Hall Grand
  Lodge of Massachusetts.

Maryland

Prince Hall Grand Lodge F. & A.M.
  State of Maryland and
  Jurisdiction
1307 Eutaw Place
Baltimore, MD 21217
410-669-4966
(fax) 410-462-4642
http://www.mwphglmd.org/

Massachusetts

Prince Hall Grand Lodge F. & A.M.
  Jurisdiction of Massachusetts
24 Washington St.
Dorchester, MA 02121
617-445-1145
(fax) 617-445-8698
http://www.princehall.org

This grand lodge has lodges in
Maine and New Hampshire, the
Netherlands, and Belgium.

Michigan

Prince Hall Grand Lodge Free and
  Accepted Masons Jurisdiction of
  Michigan

3100 Gratiot Ave
Detroit, MI 48207
313-579-3333; 313-579-3336
(fax) 313-579-0507
http://www.miphgl.org

Minnesota

Prince Hall Grand Lodge of
  Minnesota and Jurisdiction
Minneapolis Urban League
Sabathani Community Center
310 East 38th Street, Suite 224
Minneapolis, MN 55409-1337
http://www.mwphglmn.net/page1.
html

  This grand lodge also has lodges
in North Dakota.

Mississippi

Stringer Grand Lodge F. & A.M.
  (Prince Hall Affiliations)
  Jurisdiction of Mississippi
1072 John R. Lynch St.
Jackson, MS 39202
601-354-1403; 601-354-1404
(fax) 601-354-4881
http://www.mwstringergl.org/

Missouri

Prince Hall Grand Lodge F. & A.M.
  of Missouri and Jurisdiction
4525 Olive St.
St. Louis, MO 63108
314-361-3044

Montana

Lodges in Montana are chartered by
  the Grand Lodge of Oregon.

Nebraska

Grand Lodge F. & A.M. of
  Nebraska and Its Jurisdiction
2418 Ames Ave.

Omaha, NE 68111
402-451-5177
(fax) 402-451-8087
http://mwphglne.org

Nevada

Prince Hall Grand Lodge, F. &
  A.M., of Nevada, Inc.
2700 Colton St.
North Las Vegas, NV 89032
702-647-2095
(fax) 702-783-7093
http://www.phanv.org/

  This PHGL also has a lodge in
Idaho.

New Hampshire

The lodge in New Hampshire is
  chartered by the Grand Lodge of
  Massachusetts.

New Jersey

Prince Hall Grand Lodge F. & A.M.
  State of New Jersey
180-192 Irvine Turner Blvd.
Newark, NJ 07108
973-824-6457
http://www.mwphglnj.org/

New Mexico

Prince Hall Grand Lodge F. & A.M.
  of the State of New Mexico, Inc.
525 San Pedro Drive NE
Albuquerque, NM 87108-7638
505-268-5823
(fax) 505-254-7638
http://www.mwphglnm.org/

New York

Prince Hall Grand Lodge of the
  Most Ancient and Honorable
  Fraternity of Free and Accepted

Masons of the State of
New York
454 W. 155th St.
New York, NY 10032
212-281-2211
http://princehallny.org/

North Carolina

Prince Hall Grand Lodge of Free
and Accepted Masons of North
Carolina and Jurisdictions, Inc.
315 E. Main Street
Durham, NC 27701
919-683-3147
(fax) 919-683-9636
http://www.mwphglnc.com

North Dakota

Lodges in North Dakota are
chartered by the Grand Lodge of
Minnesota

Ohio

Prince Hall Grand Lodge of Ohio
F. & A.M.
50 Hamilton Park
Columbus, OH 43203
614-221-6197 or 614-221-9982
(fax) 614-221-7760
http://www.phaohio.org/

Oklahoma

Prince Hall Grand Lodge F. & A.M.
Jurisdiction of Oklahoma
1304 W. Broadway
Muskogee, OK 74401
918-683-3123

Oregon

Prince Hall Grand Lodge F. & A.M.
of Oregon, Inc.
115-118 NE Russell St.
Portland, OR 97212
503-218-2225

(fax) 503-698-4253

This grand lodge also has a lodge
in Idaho.

Pennsylvania

Prince Hall Grand Lodge of
Pennsylvania F. & A.M.
4301 N. Broad St.
Philadelphia, PA 19140
215-457-6110; 215-457-6111
http://www.princehall-pa.org/

Rhode Island

Prince Hall Grand Lodge F. & A.M.
of the State of Rhode Island
883 Eddy St.
Providence, RI 02905-4705
401-461-2600
(fax) 401-461-2600

South Carolina

Prince Hall Grand Lodge of F.
& A.M. of the State of South
Carolina
2324 Gervais St.
Columbia, SC 29204
803-254-7210
http://www.mwphglsc.com/

South Dakota

The lodge in South Dakota is
chartered by the Grand Lodge of
Kansas.

Tennessee

Prince Hall Grand Lodge F. & A.M.
of Tennessee
253 South Parkway
Memphis, TN 38109
901-774-7230

Texas

Prince Hall Grand Lodge of Texas
3433 Martin Luther King Freeway

Fort Worth, TX 76101
http://www.mwphglotx.org/

Utah

Lodges in Utah are chartered by
the grand lodges of Texas and
Colorado.

Vermont

There are no Prince Hall lodges in
Vermont.

Virginia

Prince Hall Grand Lodge of
Virginia, Inc.
906 N. Thompson St.
Richmond, VA 23230
804-359-1111
(fax) 804-359-8123
http://www.MWPHGL-VA.org

Washington

Prince Hall Grand Lodge F. & A.M.
Washington and Jurisdiction
306 24th Ave S.
Seattle, WA 98144
206-323-8835
(fax) 206-325-7079
http://www.mwphglwa.org/

This grand lodge has lodges in
Canada, South Korea, Germany, and
Japan.

West Virginia

Prince Hall Grand Lodge of West
Virginia, F. & A.M., Inc.
PO Box 233
Whitman, WV 25652-0233
304-239-2731

Wisconsin

Prince Hall Grand Lodge F. &
A.M. of Wisconsin, Inc.
600 W. Walnut St

Milwaukee, WI 53212
414-265-6555
(fax) 414-265-6994

Wyoming

Lodges in Wyoming are chartered
by the Grand Lodge of Colorado.

Outside the United States

Alberta, Canada

Prince Hall Grand Lodge of Alberta
1802-70 Street
Edmonton, Alberta T5B 1T7
Canada

Ontario, Canada

Prince Hall Grand Lodge of
Ontario F. & A.M. Province of
Ontario and Jurisdiction
414 Parent Avenue
Windsor, Ontario N9A 2C1
Canada
519-258-8350
(fax) 519-258-5638

Bahamas

Prince Hall Grand Lodge of the
Commonwealth of the Bahamas
P.O. Box N78216
Nassau, Bahamas
809-328-1662

Caribbean

Prince Hall Grand Lodge F. &
A.M. of the Caribbean and
Jurisdiction
Prince Hall Memorial Centre
Graeme Hall, Christ Church
Barbados, West Indies
246-437-0375
(fax) 246-437-2013

NOTES

Introduction

1. Sidney Kaplan and Emma Nogrady Kaplan, *The Black Presence in the Era of the American Revolution,* rev. ed. (Amherst: University of Massachusetts Press, 1989), 16–17.

2. Some reasonable dispute exists as to whether this initiation actually occurred in March 1775 or in March 1778. A further possibility advanced is that Prince Hall, the leader of the black men, was initiated in March 1775, but the other fourteen men were not until March 1778. That a soldier named John Batts was the Masonic agent setting the initiations in motion at whatever date is not disputed. The principal historians doubting the 1775 date—as well as the legitimacy of black Freemasonry as a whole—are Henry Wilson Coil and John MacDuffie Sherman in *A Documentary Account of Prince Hall and Other Black Fraternal Orders* (Fulton: Missouri Lodge of Research, 1982), 24–28, 132–40. Yet despite their extensive research, they never prove that the initiation did not happen in March 1775—or that Prince Hall and other local blacks did not mingle with British soldiers at the same time, only that it may not have happened until March 1778. Coil and Sherman deny the Masonic legitimacy of the procedure altogether, but that dubious charge need not concern us here. Following the chronology of other respected historians of black Freemasonry, including Charles Wesley and William Upton, the editors accept the March 1775 date as at least responsibly plausible.

3. James Anderson, *"The Constitutions of the Free-Masons* (1734). An Online Electronic Edition," ed. Paul Royster, 2006, http://works.bepress.com/paul_royster/33.

4. Joanna Brooks, "The Early American Public Sphere and the Emergence of a Black Print Counterpublic," *William and Mary Quarterly,* 3rd ser., 62, no. 1 (January 2005): 67–92.

5. Chernoh Sesay, "Freemasons of Color: Prince Hall, Revolutionary Black Boston, and the Origins of Black Freemasonry, 1770–1807" (PhD diss., Northwestern University, 2006), and Sesay, chapter 1 of this book.

6. See, for example, Joanna Brooks and John Saillant, eds., introduction to *"Face Zion Forward": First Writers of the Black Atlantic, 1785–1798* (Boston: Northeastern University Press, 2002), 10–12.

7. See John Marrant, *A Sermon Preached on the 24th Day of June 1789,…at the Request of the Right Worshipful the Grand Master Prince Hall, and the Rest of the Brethren of the African Lodge…* (Boston, 1789) in Brooks and Saillant, *"Face Zion Forward,"* 90, and Peter P. Hinks, "John Marrant and the Meaning of Early Black Freemasonry," *William and Mary Quarterly,* 3rd ser., 64, no. 1 (January 2007): 105–16.

8. Leigh Eric Schmidt, "'A Second and Glorious Reformation': The New Light Extremism of Andrew Croswell," *William and Mary Quarterly*, 3rd ser., 43, no. 2 (April 1986): 237–38.

9. See Sesay, chapter 1 of this book.

10. See Julie Winch, chapter 3 of this book, and Harry Davis, "Documents Relating to Negro Masonry in America," *Journal of Negro History* 21 (1936): 425–26.

11. See Julie Winch, chapter 3 of this book.

12. *Complete History of Widow's Son Lodge No. 11, F. & A.M. (Prince Hall)* (Brooklyn, 1970?).

13. *Massachusetts Centinel,* May 5, 1787.

14. See the discussion by Peter P. Hinks in chapter 2.

15. John Telemachus Hilton, *An Address Delivered before the African Grand Lodge, of Boston, No. 459. June 24th, 1828, by John T. Hilton: On the Annual Festival, of St. John the Baptist* (Boston: David Hooton, 1828).

16. *Liberator,* March 25, 1864.

17. Samuel Van Brakle, "Masonic Oration Delivered 27th of December, A.L. 5852, A.D. 1852. At Bethel Church, at Philadelphia, for the Benefit of the Poor of Said Church (n.d.), 3–4. See Appendix B in this volume for an explanation of these dates and of other Masonic terminology.

18. Frederick Douglass, "What Are the Colored People Doing for Themselves?," *North Star,* July 14, 1848.

19. Martin Delany, "The Origin and Objects of Ancient Freemasonry: Its Introduction into the United States, and Legitimacy among Colored Men. A Treatise Delivered before St. Cyprian Lodge, No. 13, June 24th, A.D. 1853—A.L. 5853," in *Martin R. Delany: A Documentary Reader,* ed. Robert S. Levine (Chapel Hill: University of North Carolina Press, 2003), 60.

20. Luis F. Emilio, *A Brave Black Regiment: History of the Fifty-Fourth Regiment of Massachusetts Volunteer Infantry, 1863–1865* (Boston: Boston Book, 1891), 129, 313.

21. See "Regimental Warrant" in Records of Prince Hall Freemasonry, Samuel Crocker Lawrence Library, Grand Lodge of Masons, Boston, Massachusetts.

22. For the low estimate, see Theda Skocpol and Jennifer Lynn Oser, "Organization despite Adversity: The Origins and Development of African American Fraternal Associations," *Social Science History* 28 (Fall 2004): 385. For the high estimate, see John Jones, *An Argument in Relation to Freemasonry among Colored Men in This Country, Showing Its Regularity, Legality and Legitimacy* (Chicago: Tribune Co., 1866), 5. On wartime initiation, see, e.g., David Hackett's discussion in chapter 7.

23. William A. Muraskin, *Middle-Class Blacks in a White Society: Prince Hall Freemasonry in America* (Berkeley: University of California Press, 1975), 29. Grimshaw claimed that there were more than sixty-six thousand in 1901; he also offers state-by-state figures or estimates. William H. Grimshaw, *Official History of Freemasonry among the Colored People in North America* (1903; repr., New York: Negro Universities Press, 1969), 304–5.

24. Jones, *An Argument in Relation to Freemasonry,* 12.

25. Lewis Hayden, *Caste among Masons: Address before Prince Hall Grand Lodge of Free and Accepted Masons of the State of Massachusetts, at the festival of St. John the Evangelist, December 27, 1865* (Boston: Edward S. Coombs, 1866), 10.

26. Lewis Hayden, *Letters in Vindication of the National Grand Lodge of Ancient, Free, and Accepted Masons of the United States of North America* (Boston: Edward S. Coombs, 1867), 6–11.

27. Hayden, *Caste among Masons,* 7; Hackett, chapter 7 of this book. See Stephen Kantrowitz, "'Intended for the Better Government of Man': The Political History of African American Freemasonry in the Era of Emancipation," *Journal of American History* 96, no. 4 (March 2010), and chapter 5 of this book.

28. See Kantrowitz, "'Intended for the Better Government of Man,'" and *More Than Freedom: Fighting for Black Citizenship in a White Republic, 1829–1889* (New York: Penguin Press, 2012); David A. Gerber, *Black Ohio and the Color Line, 1860–1915* (Urbana: University of Illinois Press, 1976), 162–63; Ronald David Snell, "Indiana's Black Representatives: The Rhetoric of the Black Republican Legislators from 1880 to 1896" (PhD diss., Indiana University, 1972), 50–78. On John Langston, see Charles H. Wesley, *The History of the Prince Hall Grand Lodge of Free and Accepted Masons of the State of Ohio, 1849–1971: An Epoch in American Fraternalism* (Washington, DC: Association for the Study of Negro Life and History, 1972), 44; Julius Eric Thompson, "Hiram R. Revels, 1827–1901: A Biography" (PhD diss., Princeton University, 1973).

29. See, e.g., Elsa Barkley Brown, "Uncle Ned's Children: Negotiating Community and Freedom in Postemancipation Richmond, Virginia" (PhD diss., Kent State University, 1994); Peter J. Rachleff, *Black Labor in Richmond, 1865–1890* (Urbana: University of Illinois Press, 1989).

30. *Proceedings of the Sixth Triennial Session of the Most Worshipful National Grand Lodge of Free and Accepted Ancient York Masons of the United States of America. Held in the City of Baltimore, October, A.D. 1865.–A.L. 5865* (Philadelphia: D. E. Thompson, 1866), 47.

31. Lewis Hayden, *A Letter from Lewis Hayden, of Boston, Massachusetts, to Hon. Judge Simms, of Savannah, Georgia.* (Boston: Committee on Masonic Jurisprudence, Prince Hall Grand Lodge, 1874), 24.

32. *Proceedings of a Grand Semi-Annual Communication of the Union Grand Lodge of Virginia…and the Grand Annual Communication … A.D. 1870* (Lynchburg: Evening Press Print, 1871), 21–22. Stephen Kantrowitz thanks Corey D. B. Walker for his generosity in making this item available.

33. See, for example, Alton G. Roundtree and Paul M. Bessel, *Out of the Shadows: The Emergence of Prince Hall Freemasonry in America; Over 225 Years of Endurance* (Camp Springs, MD: KLR Publishing, 2006); Tony Pope, "Our Segregated Brethren, Prince Hall Freemasons," *Phylaxis,* September 1994, http://www.freemasons-freemasonry. com/popefr.html; Grimshaw, *Official History;* and Matthew Brock, *History of the National Grand Lodge* (Columbus: n.p., 1980).

34. For earlier articulations of the "woman question" in black Freemasonry, see Martha S. Jones, *All Bound Up Together: The Woman Question in African American Public Culture, 1820–1900* (Chapel Hill: University of North Carolina Press, 2007), 111–13.

35. Elsa Barkley Brown, "Womanist Consciousness: Maggie Lena Walker and the Independent Order of Saint Luke," *Signs* 14 (Spring 1989): 610–33.

36. Jones, *All Bound Up,* 169–70; Paul Ortiz, *Emancipation Betrayed: The Hidden History of Black Organizing and White Violence in Florida from Reconstruction to the Bloody Election of 1920* (Berkeley: University of California Press, 2005), 134.

37. Martin Summers, *Manliness and Its Discontents: The Black Middle Class and the Transformation of Masculinity, 1900–1930* (Chapel Hill: University of North Carolina Press, 2004), 145.

38. Cooper, chapter 6 of this book.

39. Quoted in Summers, *Manliness,* 143.

40. Jones, *An Argument in Relation to Freemasonry,* 4.

41. Mark C. Carnes, *Secret Ritual and Manhood in Victorian America* (New Haven: Yale University Press, 1991); Mary Ann Clawson, *Constructing Brotherhood: Class, Gender, and Fraternalism* (Princeton: Princeton University Press, 1989); Summers, *Manliness;* Maurice Wallace, "'Are We Men?' Prince Hall, Martin Delany, and the Masculine Ideal in Black Freemasonry, 1775–1865," *American Literary History* 9 (Fall 1997): 396–424.

42. Compare Carnes, *Secret Ritual and Manhood,* and Beito, *From Mutual Benefit to the Welfare State: Fraternal Societies and Social Services, 1890–1967* (Chapel Hill: University of North Carolina Press, 1999), esp. 2–3.

43. For some starting points on the relationships among Freemasonry and the AME and AME Zion denominations, see David Hackett's discussion in chapter 7; John M. Giggie, *After Redemption: Jim Crow and the Transformation of African American Religion in the Delta, 1875–1915* (New York: Oxford University Press, 2008); and Matthew James Zacharias Harper, "Living in God's Time: African American Faith and Politics in Post-emancipation North Carolina" (PhD diss., University of North Carolina, 2009), 58–109. John M. Giggie's important essay "For God and Lodge: Black Fraternal Orders and the Evolution of African American Religion in the Postbellum South" appeared after this volume had gone to press; readers may find it in Orville Vernon Burton, Jerald Podair, and Jennifer L. Weber, eds., *The Struggle for Equality: Essays on Sectional Conflict, the Civil War, and the Long Reconstruction* (Charlottesville: University of Virginia Press, 2011).

44. Richard Theodore Greener, *An Oration Pronounced at the Celebration of the Festival of Saint John the Baptist, June 24, 1876, at the Invitation of the Eureka Lodge No. 1, F.A.M., in the Savannah Georgia Theatre* (Savannah: D.G. Patton, [1877]), 15.

45. See Kantrowitz, chapter 5 of this book; Muraskin, *Middle-Class Blacks in a White Society,* 195.

46. Letter of A. W. A. De Leon, Boston, to "Worshipful Sir & Brother," February 10, 1869, GBR 1991 HC 28 A (21), Library of the United Grand Lodge of England, London.

47. Jones, *An Argument in Relation to Freemasonry,* 4; Delany, "Origins and Objects."

48. See Muraskin, *Middle-Class Blacks in a White Society,* 188–90; *Proceedings of the Prince Hall Grand Lodge of Massachusetts* (1885), 10.

49. Summers, *Manliness,* 33.

50. Muraskin, *Middle-Class Blacks in a White Society,* 29.

51. Beito, *Mutual Aid,* 50.

52. Quoted in Summers, *Manliness,* 34–35.

53. Quoted ibid., 41.

54. Quoted in Muraskin, *Middle-Class Blacks in a White Society,* 221.

55. Ibid., 222–23.

56. Ortiz, *Emancipation Betrayed,* 102.

57. See ibid., 103–14. Robin D. G. Kelley reflects that "[t]he bonds of fellowship developed in these fraternal orders played an important role in consolidating black union support, even if some of the orders' middle-class leadership opposed unionization." *Race Rebels: Culture, Politics, and the Black Working Class* (New York: The Free Press, 1994), 38.

58. Theda Skocpol, Ariane Liazos, and Marshall Ganz, *What a Mighty Power We Can Be: African American Fraternal Groups and the Struggle for Racial Equality* (Princeton: Princeton University Press, 2006), 135–67.

59. Muraskin, *Middle-Class Blacks in a White Society,* 221–22.

60. Summers, *Manliness,* 38–39.

61. See, e.g., Ortiz, *Emancipation Betrayed,* 134.

62. Muraskin, *Middle-Class Blacks in a White Society,* 227–31.

63. Skocpol, Liazos, and Ganz, *What a Mighty Power,* 177; Muraskin, *Middle-Class Blacks in a White Society.*

64. Muraskin, *Middle-Class Blacks in a White Society,* 224ff., 237.

65. Skocpol and Oser, "Organization despite Adversity," 225.

66. Muraskin, *Middle-Class Blacks in a White Society,* 230.

67. Quoted in Skocpol, Liazos, and Ganz, *What a Mighty Power,* 177–78; Muraskin, *Middle-Class Blacks in a White Society,* quote on 230.

68. Skocpol, Liazos, and Ganz, *What a Mighty Power,* 178.

69. Alferdteen Harrison, *A History of the Most Worshipful Stringer Grand Lodge: Our Heritage is Our Challenge* (Jackson: Most Worshipful Stringer Grand Lodge Free and Accepted Masons Prince Hall Affiliate of the State of Mississippi, 1977).

70. Stephen Kantrowitz's observation of recognition ceremonies, May 10, 2003.

1. Emancipation and the Social Origins of Black Freemasonry, 1775–1800

I am indebted to Stephen Kantrowitz and Peter Hinks for their expert and insightful commentary. I thank Donald Yacovone, Mark Tabbert, and Conrad Wright for their support at various stages in the writing and revision of this essay. I am grateful to the Massachusetts Historical Society and the Boston Athenaeum for their generous financial support. I thank Cynthia Alcorn of the Samuel Crocker Lawrence Library, and the staff at both the New England Historic Genealogical Society and the Rare Books Department of the Boston Public Library. I also thank the reviewers and editors of this volume.

1. *Massachusetts Centinel,* August 19, 1786.

2. Ibid.

3. This is an elaboration on an argument made by Ira Berlin, *Many Thousands Gone: The First Two Centuries of Slavery in North America* (Cambridge, MA: Harvard University Press, 1998), 62, 251–52. A search using the *Early American Newspapers, Series 1, 1690–1876* digital database for the funerary descriptions and obituary notices of other black Freemasons before 1807 turned up three other notices. In addition to the Belcher notice, the author found four others that did not include the detail of his. These included notices for Thomas Saunderson in the *Boston Gazette and Country Journal,* September 7, 1789; for James Hawkins, *Farmer's Museum, or Literary Gazette,* February 24, 1800; and for Prince Hall in the *New England Palladium,*

December 8, 1807, the *Newburyport Herald,* December 8, 1807, and the *Providence Gazette,* December 12, 1807.

4. *American Recorder and Charlestown Advertiser,* December 18, 1786.

5. Negro elections were slave celebrations that evolved partially from the General Election Day, the seventeenth- and eighteenth-century spring colonial holiday marking the installation of the new governing body. Slaves who attended the public ceremony while waiting on their masters were encouraged and supported in performing their own elections. In New York and New Jersey, among those slaves owned by the Dutch a different kind of black crowning festival took place. Where the Dutch celebrated Pentecost, or Whit Sunday, Africans evolved the celebration of Pinkster. By the mid-eighteenth century, Negro Election Day in New England had grown from a minor occurrence during the General Election Day to become its own festive and widely anticipated event. On the transition from Negro Election Day celebrations performed during slavery to parades organized by free blacks, see Shane White, "'It Was a Proud Day': African Americans, Festivals and Parades in the North, 1741–1834," *Journal of American History* 81, no. 1 (June 1994): 13–50. For an investigation of Pinkster see Shane White, "Pinkster: Afro-Dutch Syncretization in New York City and the Hudson Valley," *Journal of American Folklore* 102, no. 403 (January–March 1989): 68–75. Also see William D. Piersen, *Black Yankees: The Development of an Afro-American Subculture in Eighteenth-Century New England* (Amherst: University of Massachusetts Press, 1988), 117–43, and Lorenzo Johnston Greene, *The Negro in Colonial New England, 1620–1776* (1942; repr., New York: Atheneum, 1974), 255, 328.

6. For mention of Prince Hall as a founding father of free black American life, see Richard S. Newman and Roy E. Finkenbine, eds., "Forum: Black Founders" *William and Mary Quarterly,* 3rd ser., 64, no. 1 (January 2007): 83–167.

7. For a discussion of Prince Hall and black Freemasonry's origins and disputes concerning its dating, see the introduction to this volume.

8. For work critical of black Freemasonry, see Joanne Pope Melish, *Disowning Slavery: Gradual Emancipation and "Race" in New England, 1780–1860* (Ithaca: Cornell University Press, 1998), 81; Gary Nash, *Forging Freedom: The Formation of Philadelphia's Black Community, 1720–1840* (Cambridge, MA: Harvard University Press, 1988), 218–19; William A. Muraskin, *Middle-Class Blacks in a White Society: Prince Hall Freemasonry in America* (Berkeley: University of California Press, 1976); and Loretta J. Williams, *Black Freemasonry and Middle-Class Realities* (Columbia: University of Missouri Press, 1980). Also see Joanne Lloyd, "Beneath the 'City on the Hill': The Lower Orders, Boston 1700–1850" (PhD diss., Boston College, 2007), 299–312.

For work commending African American Freemasonry, see Joanna Brooks, *American Lazarus: Religion and the Rise of African-American and Native American Literature* (New York: Oxford University Press, 2003); Brooks, "Prince Hall, Freemasonry, and Genealogy," *African American Review* 34, no. 2 (Summer 2000): 197–216; Joanna Brooks and John Saillant, eds., *"Face Zion Forward": First Writers of the Black Atlantic, 1785–1798* (Boston: Northeastern University Press, 2002); Stephen C. Bullock, *Revolutionary Brotherhood: Freemasonry and the Transformation of the American Social Order, 1730–1840* (Chapel Hill: University of North Carolina Press, 1996), 158–62; Peter P. Hinks, *To Awaken My Afflicted Brethren: David Walker and the Problem of Antebellum Slave Resistance* (University Park: Pennsylvania State University Press, 1997), 70–74; Hinks, "John Marrant and the Meaning of Early Black Freemasonry," *William and Mary Quarterly* 64, no. 1 (January 2007): 105–16; Stephen Kantrowitz, "'Intended for the Better Government of Man': The Political History of African American Freemasonry in the Era of Emancipation" *Journal of American History* 96, no. 4 (March 2010): 1001–26; Richard Newman, *Freedom's Prophet: Bishop Richard Allen, the AME Church, and the Black Founding Fathers* (New York: New York University Press, 2008), 119–22; Harry Reed, *Platform for Change: The Foundations of the Northern Free Black Community, 1775–1865* (East Lansing: Michigan State University Press, 1994), 63–69; John Saillant, "'Wipe Away All Tears from Their Eyes': John Marrant's Theology in the Black Atlantic, 1785–1808," *Journal of Millennial Studies* 1, no. 2 (Winter 1999), http://www.mille.org/publications/winter98Word%20docs/saillant.doc; Theda Skocpol, Ariane Liazos, and Marshall Ganz, *What a Mighty Power We Can Be: African American Fraternal Groups and the Struggle for Racial Equality* (Princeton: Princeton University Press, 2006); Corey D. B. Walker, *A Noble Fight: African American Freemasonry and the Struggle for Democracy in America* (Urbana: University of Illinois Press, 2008); Charles H. Wesley, *Prince Hall: Life and Legacy* (Washington, DC: United Supreme Council, Southern Jurisdiction, Prince Hall Affiliation, 1977); Julie Winch, *A Gentleman of Color: The Life of James Forten* (Oxford: Oxford University Press, 2002), 146; Craig Wilder, *In the Company of Black Men: The African Influence on African American Culture in New York City* (New York: New York University Press, 2001), 111–16; and Maurice Wallace, "'Are We Men?' Prince Hall, Martin Delany, and the Masculine Ideal in Black Freemasonry, 1775–1865," *American Literary History* 9, no. 3 (Autumn 1997): 396–424.

9. I use the term "orders" rather than "classes" to acknowledge the importance of debates about the definition and analytical usefulness of class in examinations of early national northern cities. For recent work on the importance of class to understanding issues of status, economic inequality, community consciousness, and social and political activism see Simon Middleton and Billy G. Smith, eds., *Class Matters: Early North America and the Atlantic World* (Philadelphia: University of Pennsylvania Press, 2008); Sean Wilentz, *Chants Democratic: New York City & the Rise of the American Working Class, 1788–1850* (Oxford: Oxford University Press, 1984); and Billy G. Smith, *The "Lower Sort": Philadelphia's Laboring People, 1750–1800* (Ithaca: Cornell University Press, 1990). Also see Lloyd, "Beneath the 'City on the Hill,'" 299–312.

10. The literature on abolition is extensive. A sample of recent work with a broad transatlantic scope includes David Brion Davis, *The Problem of Slavery in the Age of Revolution, 1770–1823* (New York: Oxford University Press, 1999), and Christopher Brown, *Moral Capital: Foundations of British Abolitionism* (Chapel Hill: University of North Carolina Press, 2006). A short list of excellent examinations of the ambiguities and limits of gradual emancipation in the North includes David Gellman, *Emancipating New York: The Politics of Slavery and Freedom, 1777–1827* (Baton Rouge: Louisiana State University Press, 2006); Melish, *Disowning Slavery;* Gary B. Nash and Jean R. Soderlund, *Freedom by Degrees: Emancipation in Pennsylvania and Its Aftermath* (New York: Oxford University Press, 1991); Richard Newman, *The Transformation of American Abolitionism: Fighting Slavery in the Early Republic*

(Chapel Hill: University of North Carolina Press, 2002); John Wood Sweet, *Bodies Politic: Negotiating Race in the American North* (Baltimore: Johns Hopkins University Press, 2003); and Shane White, *Somewhat More Independent: The End of Slavery in New York City, 1770–1810* (Athens: University of Georgia Press, 1991). Also see Eva Sheppard Wolf, *Race and Liberty in the New Nation: Emancipation in Virginia from the Revolution to Nat Turner's Rebellion* (Baton Rouge: Louisiana State University Press, 2006).

11. This information comes from the author's database compiled by recording all the entries in the Boston Taking Books between 1780 and 1801 that were labeled "black," "negro," or "colored." Taking Books were the eighteenth-century Boston tax rolls that listed the polls in Boston. Polls were males over twenty-one who qualified for paying the poll tax. These records are organized in volumes. See Boston Taking Books, vols. 1780–1801, Rare Books Department, Boston Public Library. For a more detailed explanation of the Boston Taking Books database see Chernoh Momodu Sesay Jr., "Freemasons of Color: Prince Hall, Revolutionary Black Boston, and the Origins of Black Freemasonry, 1770–1807" (PhD diss., Northwestern University, 2006), 55–155. For other work using the Boston Taking Books database to examine black Boston see Jacqueline Carr, "A Change 'as Remarkable as the Revolution Itself': Boston's Demographics, 1780–1800," *New England Quarterly* 73 (December 2000): 583–602.

12. On the Quok Walker case see Arthur Zilversmit, "Quok Walker, Mumbet, and the Abolition of Slavery in Massachusetts," *William and Mary Quarterly,* 3rd ser., 25, no. 4 (October 1968): 614–24. For an examination of why and how northern abolition moved so gradually see Melish, *Disowning Slavery.*

13. Thomas Pemberton, Response to the Queries of St. G. Tucker, March 12, 1795, Documents related to Slavery in Massachusetts (microfilm P-380 reel 4), Jeremy Belknap Papers, Massachusetts Historical Society, Boston.

14. This Felix might have been one of two people. A Felix served Mary Needham and Abia Holbrook the elder, who passed away on January 28, 1769, while master of the Boston South Writing School. At some point before 1769 Felix began to work for the Holbrooks. See Robert J. Dunkle and Ann S. Lainhart, eds., *Boston Deaths, 1700–1799,* vol. 1 (Boston: New England Historic Genealogical Society, 1999); and *The Records of the Churches of Boston and the First Church, Second Parish, and Third Parish of Roxbury: Including Baptisms, Marriages, Deaths, Admissions, and Dismissals,* transcr. Robert J. Dunkle and Ann S. Lainhart (Boston: New England Historic Genealogical Society, 2001), CD-ROM. Another Felix is described as the servant of a Mr. Holbrook who married the free black woman Susannah Kater on April 21, 1772. See *Inhabitants and Estates of the Town of Boston, 1630–1800 and the Crooked and Narrow Streets of Boston, 1630–1822* (Boston: New England Historic Genealogical Society and Massachusetts Historical Society, 2001), CD-ROM, reference code 35589.

15. See "January 6, 1773. The humble Petition of many Slaves, living in the Town of Boston, and other Towns"; Boston, April 20th, 1773 Petition; "To the Honourable his Majestys Council and the Honourable House of Representatives in General Court assembled May 25 1774," in *Documentary History of the Negro,* ed. Herbert Aptheker (New York: Citadel Press, 1951), 1:5–10. See "To the Honorable

Counsel & House of [Representa]tives for the State of Masssachusetts Bay in General Court assembled, January 13, 1777," Massachusetts Archives, Massachusetts State Archives, Boston, 212:132. See "To his Excellency Thomas Hutchinson, Esq; Governor of said province; to the Honourable his MAJESTY'S COUNCIL, and the Honourable HOUSE OF REPRESENTATIVES in General Court assembled, June, A.D. 1773," and "To the honourable his Majesty's Council and the honourable House of Representatives of the Province of Massachusetts-Bay, in General Court assembled, at Boston, the 20th day of January, 1774," in *Insights and Parallels: Problems and Issues of American Social History,* ed. William L. O'Neill (Minneapolis, MN: Burgess Publishing Co., 1973), 45–48. See Ceasar Sarter, "Essay on Slavery," *The Essex Journal and Merrimack Packet,* August 17, 1774.

In addition to black-authored petitions addressed to the Massachusetts legislature, other appeals appeared in print. For example, see *The Appendix: or, some Observations on the expediency of the Petition of the Africans, living in Boston, &c., lately presented to the General Assembly of this Province, To which is annexed, the Petition referred to. Likewise, Thoughts on Slavery with a useful extract from the Massachusetts Spy, of January 28, 1773, by way of an Address to the Members of the Assembly. By a Lover of Constitutional Liberty* (Boston: E. Russell, 1773); and An African, "For the Massachusetts Spy," *Massachusetts Spy* (Boston), February 10, 1774, reprinted in *Insights and Parallels,* 48–49.

16. Gary Nash attributed this difference to the initial trust of black Philadelphians in white abolitionist efforts and the lack of organized white abolitionist activity in Boston. See Nash, *Forging Freedom,* 59.

17. Black petition, January 13, 1777.

18. Records of African Lodge No. 1, Minutes and Accounts, 1779–1786, Boston, microfilm Records of African Lodge, Samuel Crocker Lawrence Library, Grand Lodge of Massachusetts, Boston.

19. "To the Honorable Counsel & House of [Representa]tives for the State of Masssachusetts Bay in General Court assembled, January 13, 1777," Massachusetts Archives, 212:132.

20. For an insightful examination of the varied meanings of freedom during the late eighteenth century see François Furstenberg, "Beyond Freedom and Slavery: Autonomy, Virtue, and Resistance in Early American Political Discourse," *Journal of American History* 89, no. 4 (March 2003): 1295–1330.

21. William Bentley, *The Diary of William Bentley, D. D., Pastor of the East Church, Salem Massachusetts* (1905; repr., Gloucester, MA: Peter Smith, 1962), 2:329. Also quoted in Wesley, *Prince Hall,* 89. Wesley incorrectly dated the creation of the "East Indian Marine Society," in Salem, as 1799. Osgood must have been a member of the East India Marine Society, established in 1766. South Fields probably identified a location in Salem. The Marine Bible Society and the East India Marine Society were both founded in Salem. See Conrad Edick Wright, *The Transformation of Charity in Postrevolutionary New England* (Boston: Northeastern University Press, 1992), 62, 274.

22. Bentley, *Diary of William Bentley,* 2:329. For a brief description of the relationship between Bentley and Freeman see Richard Brown, *Knowledge Is Power: The Diffusion of Information in Early America, 1700–1865* (New York: Oxford University Press, 1989), 203.

23. Prince Hall Letter, November 26, 1786, Letters and Sermons by Prince Hall, 1787–1802, microfilm Records of African Lodge. For an edited copy of this letter, see Wesley, *Prince Hall,* 43; and Sidney Kaplan, "Blacks in Massachusetts and the Shay's Rebellion," *Contributions in Black Studies* 8 (1986–87): 5–14.

24. Petition to the General Court of Massachusetts, January 4, 1787, the African Petition, Unenacted Legislation: House Document 2358, Massachusetts Archives, Massachusetts State Archives, Boston, reprinted in Kaplan and Kaplan, *Black Presence,* 207.

25. Blackman petition, Boston, October 17, 1787, Ms. Bos. II, Boston Town Records, July–December 1788, Rare Books Department, Boston Public Library. In 1796 Hall also sent a message to the Boston selectmen asking them to fund the education of black children. See Prince Hall Letter, October 4, 1796, Letters and Sermons by Prince Hall, 1787–1802, microfilm Records of African Lodge. This letter is copied in Wesley, *Prince Hall,* 200.

26. This protest was printed in the *New York Packet,* February 26, 1788, and August 29, 1788, and the *Massachusetts Spy,* April 24, 1788.

27. For more about this rivalry see Bullock, *Revolutionary Brotherhood,* 85–108; Mark A. Tabbert, *American Freemasons: Three Centuries of Building Communities* (New York: New York University Press, 2005), 24–28, 44–45; David Stevenson, *The Origins of Freemasonry: Scotland's Century, 1590–1710* (Cambridge: Cambridge University Press, 1993), 4–5, 213–233; and John Hamill, *The Craft: A History of English Freemasonry* (Wellingborough, UK: Crucible imprint of the Aquarian Press, 1986), 41–60. Debate about the legitimacy and competition of these early grand lodges has some scholars to describe the first English grand lodge as the Grand Lodge. For example, Hamill describes the eighteenth-century English grand lodge as the Grand Lodge of England. See Hamill, *The Craft,* 41. Other scholars, describing the first English grand lodge in a more neutral way, use either the London grand lodge or the Modern grand lodge. See Bullock, *Revolutionary Brotherhood,* 41–45, 343n12. In 1813 the Ancient and Modern grand lodges merged to from the Grand Lodge of England.

28. See letter from John M. Sherman to Edward R. Cusick, December 1, 1961, John Batt Folder, Prince Hall Hanging File, Samuel Crocker Lawrence Library at the Grand Lodge of Massachusetts, Boston.

29. For a description of this older American Masonic cohort see Bullock, *Revolutionary Brotherhood,* 50–85, and Tabbert, *American Freemasons,* 33–48.

30. Bullock, *Revolutionary Brotherhood,* 97.

31. Massachusetts Grand Lodge, *Proceedings in Masonry: St. John's Grand Lodge, 1733–1792; Massachusetts Grand Lodge, 1769–1792. With an appendix, containing copies of many ancient documents, and a table of lodges* (Boston: Grand Lodge of Massachusetts, 1895), 449, quoted in Bullock, *Revolutionary Brotherhood,* 97.

32. *Sketches of Boston, Past and Present, and of Some Places in Its Vicinity* (Boston: Phillips, Sampson, and Co.; Crosby and Nichols, 1851), 74. For marriages performed by Eliot see *Inhabitants and Estates.*

33. John Eliot, Response to the Queries of St. G. Tucker, ca. 1795, Documents related to Slavery in Massachusetts, Jeremy Belknap Papers. Given that Elliot was not a Freemason and that records do not reveal the extent to which he understood the circumstances from which black Freemasonry arose, it seems that he used the

term "clandestinely" in a loose sense. Harold Van Buren differentiated between unrecognized but regular, irregular, and clandestine Masonic lodges. A regular Masonic body referred to a lodge born of the proper authority and origins. A regular lodge, in possession of its original and legitimate charter and active only to the limits of its certified powers, might exist in isolation and therefore be regular but unrecognized. A regular lodge if guilty of certain infractions could become irregular. Voorhis explained that a "clandestine Masonic body is one that has been set up since organized Grand Lodge Freemasonry was formed, without any authority of any kind, by individuals grouping themselves into such a body." Harold Van Buren Voorhis, *Negro Masonry in the United States* (1945; repr., Whitefish, MT: Kessinger Publishing, 1997), 3–5).

34. Eliot, "Slavery in Massachusetts." Scholars of Prince Hall Freemasonry have made this point. See William H. Upton, *Negro Masonry Being a Critical Examination of the Objections of the Legitimacy of the Masonry Existing Among the Negroes of America* (Cambridge: M.W. Prince Hall Grand Lodge of Massachusetts, 1902), 119–120, and Harry E. Davis, *A History of Freemasonry among Negroes in America* (Philadelphia: United Supreme Council, Northern Jurisdiction, 1946), 40–50. For the most recent scholarship on the flexible terms under which new lodges and quasi-lodges sometimes formed themselves, see Bullock, *Revolutionary Brotherhood,* 114–21; and Tabbert, *American Freemasons,* 33–34.

35. Eliot, Response to the Queries of St. G. Tucker, ca. 1795, Documents related to Slavery in Massachusetts.

36. "A Coppey of a Letter from Philadelphia 2 March 1797," Letters and Sermons by Prince Hall, 1787–1802, microfilm Records of African Lodge.

37. Ibid. In addition to ties between Philadelphia and Boston, this letter suggests a series of networks that might have allowed black Masons in the north to spread the craft among former slaves in the mid-Atlantic and southern states.

38. See Winch, *Gentleman of Color,* 149, and chapter 3 of this book. Also see Davis, *History of Freemasonry among Negroes,* 96.

39. Prince Hall to London grand lodge, June 30, 1784, GBR 1991 HC 28 A 2 1784, The Library and Museum of the United Grand Lodge of England, London, United Kingdom. Also reprinted in Upton, *Negro Masonry,* 208–9, and Davis, *History of Freemasonry among Negros,* 33–34.

40. On October 5, 1768 at the age of fifty-three, John Rowe became the provincial grand master of the Massachusetts Grand Lodge. For more information on Rowe see Bullock, *Revolutionary Brotherhood,* 77.

41. By 1801, approximately forty-two men belonged to the lodge.

42. Horton and Horton and Stapp argue that even by the mid-nineteenth century, the spectrum of wealth among African Americans was small and far less than that for whites. James Oliver Horton and Lois E. Horton, *Black Bostonians: Family Life and Community Struggle in the Antebellum North* (1979; rev. ed., New York: Holmes and Meier, 1999), 10; and Carol Buchalter Stapp, *Afro-Americans in Antebellum Boston: An Analysis of Probate Records* (New York: Garland, 1993), 154–58.

43. These figures are compiled from the Boston Taking Books, vols. 1783–1798.

44. African American Bostonians formed the African Society in 1796. See *Laws of the African Society, instituted at Boston, anno domini, 1796* (Boston: African Society, 1802).

45. For African Americans who did own property see *The Statistics of the United States Direct Tax of 1798, As Assessed on Boston; and The Names of the Inhabitants of Boston in 1790, as Collected for the First National Census,* reprinted in *A Report of the Record Commissioners of the City of Boston,* vol. 22 (Boston: Rockwell and Churchill, 1890).

46. Assessors noted taxes on Hall's property in the Taking Books for eight years between 1784 and 1801. See Boston Taking Books, vols. 1784–1801.

47. Boston Taking Books, vols. 1780–1801.

48. *Statistics of the United States Direct Tax of 1798.*

49. Minutes of the African Lodge, Boston 1807–1846, microfilm Records of African Lodge.

50. *Laws of the African Society, 1796.*

51. Middleton married Alice Marsh sometime before the 1780s and had at least three children with her. See *Inhabitants and Estates,* reference code 40073. Middleton is listed as a coachman in tax records for 1784 and 1792. See Boston Taking Books, vols. 1784, 1792.

52. *Inhabitants and Estates,* reference code 30243.

53. The two men owned 1,925 square feet of land on which stood a "1 story" "wooden dwelling" valued at $345. See *Statistics of the United States Direct Tax of 1798.* African Lodge records do not describe Glapion as a member of the lodge.

54. *Independent Ledger and American Advertiser,* December 30, 1782.

55. *Independent Chronicle,* January 1, 1778.

56. Prince Hall to London grand lodge, June 30, 1784, Library and Museum, United Grand Lodge of England.

57. During the Revolutionary War, James Ross, the rum major for Colonel Crafts's Regiment of Artillery wrote a bill certifying that by April 24, 1777, Crafts's regiment had received, from Prince Hall, "5 drumheads deliver'd at sundrey times" worth £1.19.8. The original bill is located in the Massachusetts Archives, 151:375 1/2.

58. For a microanalysis of antebellum probate records to discern varied relationships between personal property and real estate ownership, consumption, and status among African Americans see, Stapp, *Afro-Americans,* 57–60, 127–160.

59. Boston Taking Books, vols. 1794–1797.

60. For more on Boston's postwar economy see Jacqueline Barbara Carr, *After the Siege: A Social History of Boston, 1775–1800* (Boston: Northeastern University Press, 2005), 88–147; and Alan Kulikoff, "The Progress of Inequality in Revolutionary Boston," *William and Mary Quarterly,* 3rd series, 28, no. 3 (July 1971): 409.

61. On African American sailors and seafaring in the Early National period, see Jeffrey Bolster, *Black Jacks: African American Seamen in the Age of Sail* (Cambridge, MA: Harvard University Press, 1997.)

62. *Pennsylvania Packet, and Daily Advertiser,* April 11, 1788.

63. *Laws of the Sons of the African Society, Instituted at Boston, Anno Domini, 1798* (Boston: African Society, 1802). The 1798 rules were updated from the *Laws of the African Society, 1796.*

64. *Laws of the Sons of the African Society, 1798.*

65. Boston Taking Books, vols. 1780–1801. For the migration of southern blacks into Philadelphia see Nash, *Forging Freedom,* 134–243; and Nash, "Forging Freedom: The Emancipation Experience in the Northern Seaport Cities, 1775–1820,"

in *Slavery and Freedom in the Age of the American Revolution,* ed. Ira Berlin and Ronald Hoffman (Charlottesville: University of Virginia Press, 1983; Urbana: University of Illinois Press, 1986).

66. For example, see Records of African Lodge No. 1, Minutes and Accounts, 1779–1786, Boston, microfilm Records of African Lodge.

67. Dalton had become a Freemason at least as early as 1789 and Buffom in 1775. See Records of African Lodge No. 1, Minutes and Accounts, 1779–1786; and Records of African Lodge, Boston, Accounts, 1782–1809/Minutes, 1809–1816, microfilm Records of African Lodge. Buffom and Dalton were listed as having gone to sea in 1790 and 1796, respectively. Also see Boston Taking Books, vols. 1790, 1796.

68. Most scholars of Prince Hall Freemasonry have either ignored or missed this point. Most studies identify the March 6, 1775, date simply as the time when Prince Hall and his fourteen colleagues became Freemasons. See Jeremy Belknap to St. George Tucker, Response to the Queries of St. G. Tucker, ca. 1795, Documents related to Slavery in Massachusetts. Also see Wesley, *Prince Hall,* 10.

69. Records of African Lodge No. 1, Minutes and Accounts, 1779–1786, Boston, microfilm Records of African Lodge.

70. For a description of these rites see Hamill, *The Craft,* 41–46.

71. Some scholars have looked at this payment as evidence that these blacks were simply duped for their money by a British officer and were not legitimate Masons. For this perspective see Voorhis, *Negro Masonry;* and Henry Wilson Coil and John MacDuffie, *A Documentary Account of Prince Hall and Other Black Fraternal Orders,* ed. John M. Sherman (Trenton: Missouri Lodge of Research, 1982). From their creation, Prince Hall Freemasons have had to defend their legitimacy against white Freemasons who have questioned the origins and authenticity of black Freemasonry.

72. "A Coppey of a Letter from Philadelphia 2 March 1797," microfilm Records of African Lodge. My inserted brackets indicate the difficulty of discerning the handwriting. It seems that the authors mistakenly wrote "Masons" instead of Masters. Some controversy surrounds this letter. I have used the copy from the African Lodge microfilm. However, Davis used a slightly different version of this letter, which he said was "the more reliable and accurate of the two." Davis wrote that the second version stated, "We number eleven, of which number five are Masters." See Davis, *History of Freemasonry among Negroes,* 73–74. The author has not seen the second letter referred to by Davis. Davis argues that between 1797 and 1818, thirty-seven black Philadelphians became Freemasons "in Europe or the West Indies." See Davis, *Freemasonry among Negroes,* 290–91. Davis included some of these names from the March 2, 1797, letter that blacks in Philadelphia wrote to African Lodge No. 459. However, it seems that he took the liberty to name some of these men without giving proof that they were made Masons outside North America. For example, he listed James Forten as one of the thirty-seven. However, Julie Winch has argued that it is not clear where and when the prominent black Philadelphian and Freemason entered into the fraternity. See Winch, *Gentleman of Color,* 146.

73. For mention of Rowe's black man, "Adam," having been taken by the British, see John Rowe, April 8, 1776, *Letters and diary of John Rowe: Boston merchant, 1759–1762, 1764–1779,* ed. Anne Rowe Cunningham (Boston: W. B. Clarke Co., 1903), 447. This Adam might have been the black Mason Adam Row.

74. Boston Taking Books, vols. 1780–1801.

75. Ibid.

76. For Spooner appearing in Boston in 1791 see Records of African Lodge, Boston, Accounts, 1782–1809/Minutes, 1809–1816, microfilm Records of African Lodge; and Boston Taking Books, vol. 1791.

77. See Hinks, "John Marrant," 105–16; Saillant, "Wipe Away All Tears"; and Brooks, *American Lazarus*, 87–113.

78. John Marrant, *A Sermon Preached on the 24th Day of June 1789, … at the Request of the Right Worshipful the Grand Master Prince Hall, and the Rest of the Brethren of the African Lodge*(Boston: Bible and Heart, 1789), in Brooks and Saillant, "*Face Zion Forward*," 77–92.

79. Prince Hall to Countess of Huntingdon, reprinted in *Prince Hall's Letter Book*, ed. William H. Upton, *Ars Quatuor Coronatum: Being the Transactions of the Quatuor Coronati Lodge No. 2076*, 13 (London: The Lodge, 1900), 7.

80. Patrick Rael demonstrates these demographic patterns to argue persuasively for the origins of black identities specific to the northern states. Moreover, he argues not that all northern blacks thought alike but that a particular notion of what it meant to be black underlined much of northern public discourse about racial distinctions and the relationships between race and class. See Patrick Rael, *Black Identity and Black Protest in the Antebellum North* (Chapel Hill: University of North Carolina Press, 2002), 12–26.

81. Most historical evidence of black governors describes them as slaves; however, sources do not demonstrate that every black governor was held in bondage.

82. Diana, baptized in Trinity Church in 1780, worked as a servant for a Phebe Borland. See *Inhabitants and Estates*, reference code 9135. For mention of Louisa Belcher see *Proceedings of the Massachusetts Historical Society*, 2nd ser., vol. 16 (Boston, Massachusetts Historical Society, 1902), 68.

83. On the connection between West African secret societies and African American Freemasonry see Wilder, *In the Company of Black Men*, 111–16; and Michael A. Gomez, *Black Crescent: The Experience and Legacy of African Muslims in the Americas* (Cambridge: Cambridge University Press, 2005), 238–50.

84. Bullock, *Revolutionary Brotherhood*, 52.

85. *Massachusetts Centinel*, August 19, 1786.

86. Records of African Lodge No. 1, Minutes and Accounts, 1779–1786, Boston, microfilm Records of African Lodge.

87. For an insightful analysis of how the expense and show of colonial funeral practices took on new political and social importance during the American Revolution see T. H. Breen, *The Marketplace of Revolution: How Consumer Politics Shaped American Independence* (New York: Oxford University Press, 2004), 213–17. Breen shows how, in the era of the Revolution, the seriousness of bereavement ceremonies heightened the significance of consumer decisions surrounding the changing rules for a "politically correct" funeral.

88. On African American burial practices see Berlin, *Many Thousands Gone*, 61–62, 251–52; Piersen, *Black Yankees*, 77; and David R. Roediger, "And Die in Dixie: Funerals, Death, and Heaven in the Slave Community, 1700–1865," *Massachusetts Review* 22, no. 1 (1981): 163–83. The prominent white Freemason and Salem minister William Bentley described a 1797 interment in Salem as the "funeral of a young Black, born of African Parents, according to the rites of the Church

of England." Quoted in Piersen, *Black Yankees,* 77. Though the selectmen had to approve sextons to work in public burial spaces, individual churches also chose their own custodians to maintain their facilities, tombs, and vaults. Hence Boston church records reveal African Americans who were accorded private burials because of their membership in white congregations. For various examples of this see *Records of the Churches of Boston.*

89. *A Report of the Record Commissioners of the City of Boston, Containing the Selectmen's Minutes from 1776–1786* (Boston: Rockwell & Churchill, 1894), 25:186. The Rare Books and Manuscript Department at the Boston Public Library also holds the loose manuscript papers of the Boston selectmen, the documentary basis for the bound manuscript volumes of the selectmen's minutes, which were further consolidated and formed the printed series *Report of the Record Commissioners of the City of Boston.*

90. *Selectmen's Minutes 1787–1798,* 27:103.

91. Ibid., 327. Faddy was Boston Faddy and Stephenson was probably Henry Stevenson. Boston Faddy is mentioned in the records of African Lodge No. 459. See Records of African Lodge No. 1, Minutes and Accounts, 1779–1786, Boston, microfilm Records of African Lodge. The Taking Books listed Stevenson as a "gravedigger" in 1796. See Boston Taking Books, vol. 1796.

92. *Selectmen's Minutes 1787–1798,* 27:159.

93. Ibid., 189.

94. *Inhabitants and Estates of the Town of Boston,* reference code 30243.

95. Boston Taking Books, vols. 1789 and 1798–1801. It is not clear whether Faddy continued as a groundskeeper after 1798; however, from 1798 to 1801 assessors described him as a bell ringer and carpenter.

96. Brooks, *American Lazarus,* 116.

97. Ibid. Brooks's emphasis on secrecy is important for understanding the significance of black Freemasonry. However, the efforts of the African Lodge to gain a warrant, to maintain a correspondence with the Grand Lodge of London, to display respectability, and to confer with white Masonic authorities about the content of public black Masonic orations illustrate its desire to maintain a degree of transparency for white Masons. For evidence of Hall's giving a charge to the esteemed white Freemason William Bentley for comment, see Bentley, *Diary of William Bentley,* 2:279. For evidence that whites visited the black lodge in Philadelphia in 1797, see Winch, *Gentleman of Color,* 149, and chapter 3 of this book.

98. Records of African Lodge, Boston, Accounts, 1782–1809/Minutes, 1809–1816, microfilm Records of African Lodge.

99. Bullock, *Revolutionary Brotherhood,* 247.

100. These numbers are compiled from Letters and Sermons by Prince Hall, 1787–1802; and Records of African Lodge No. 1, Minutes and Accounts, 1779–1786, microfilm Records of African Lodge.

101. On Abolition Day parades see Rael, *Black Identity,* chap. 2; Len Travers, *Celebrating the Fourth: Independence Day and the Rites of Nationalism in the Early Republic* (Amherst: University of Massachusetts Press, 1997); David Waldstreicher, *In the Midst of Perpetual Fetes: The Making of American Nationalism, 1776–1820* (Chapel Hill: University of North Carolina Press, 1997), 308–23; White, "It Was a Proud Day"; William B. Gravely, "The Dialectic of Double Consciousness in Black American

Freedom Celebrations, 1808–1863," *Journal of Negro History* 4 (Winter 1982): 302–17; and Lloyd, "Beneath the 'City on the Hill,'" 329–39.

102. "African Independence," *New England Galaxy & Masonic Magazine,* July 14, 1820.

2. "To Commence a New Era in the Moral World"

1. *An Address Delivered Before the African Grand Lodge, of Boston, No. 459, June 24th, 1828, by John T. Hilton: On the Annual Festival, of St. John the Baptist* (Boston: David Hooton, 1828), 8, 9, 12–13, 14.

2. For example, one of the most important general contemporary studies of American abolitionism, James Brewer Stewart, *Holy Warriors: The Abolitionists and American Slavery,* rev. ed. (New York: Hill and Wang, 1996), makes no mention whatsoever of black Freemasonry. Nor does Patrick Rael in his probing work, *Black Identity and Black Protest in the Antebellum North* (Chapel Hill: University of North Carolina Press, 2002). Save for a very brief discussion, African American Freemasonry does not figure at all into James and Lois Horton's *In Hope of Liberty: Culture, Community, and Protest Among Northern Free Blacks, 1700–1860* (New York: Oxford University Press, 1997). While Benjamin Quarles in *Black Abolitionists* (New York: Oxford University Press, 1969) notes the important involvement of John T. Hilton and Lewis Hayden in antebellum abolitionism, he neither treats the centrality of their Masonry to their abolitionism nor the broader impact of black Freemasonry upon the development of the abolitionist movement in the antebellum North.

3. The origins of black Freemasonry in North America are explored in Charles H. Wesley, *Prince Hall: Life and Legacy* (Washington, DC: United Supreme Council, Southern Jurisdiction, Prince Hall Affiliation, 1977); Chernoh Sesay, "Freemasons of Color: Prince Hall, Revolutionary Black Boston, and the Origins of Black Freemasonry, 1770–1807" (PhD diss., Northwestern University, 2006); and Corey D. B. Walker, *A Noble Fight: African American Freemasonry and the Struggle for Democracy in America* (Urbana: University of Illinois Press, 2008). See also an array of documents in Henry Wilson Coil and John MacDuffie Sherman, eds., *A Documentary Account of Prince Hall and Other Black Fraternal Orders* (Fulton: Missouri Lodge of Research, 1982). This volume, however, must be supplemented by an extraordinary transcription in typescript of nearly all of the earliest original manuscript records of African Lodge No. 459—denoted African Lodge No. 1 until the receipt of its charter in 1787—held at the Samuel Crocker Lawrence Library, Grand Lodge of Masons in Massachusetts, Boston. Coil and Sherman compiled this complete transcription and drew from it for the more compact *A Documentary Account of Prince Hall and Other Black Fraternal Orders.* Various sections of the complete transcription are assigned titles such as "The Earliest Records of African Lodge" and the page numbering is not consecutive throughout. When referring to documents from the complete transcription, I will cite it as *A Documentary Account of Prince Hall* (typescript), along with any further information necessary for locating the reference. See the discussion of these two compilations in this volume's preface.

John T. Hilton observed in June 1828 that Prince Hall and other members of the original military lodge of 1775 had petitioned "the Grand Lodge of Massachusetts" at some point prior to 1784—an exact date was not given. "[A]lthough their petition appeared in proper form, it was rejected. The cause of which, sprang from that difference which colour has established." The problem with this recollection is that the Grand Lodge of Massachusetts, reconstituted after independence from England, did not officially exist until 1792. See *An Address Delivered before the African Grand Lodge, of Boston, No. 459. June 24th, 1828, by John T. Hilton,* 4.

4. Prince Hall, "A Charge Delivered to the African Lodge, June 24, 1797 at Menotomy," in Dorothy Porter, ed., *Early Negro Writing, 1760–1837* (Baltimore: Black Classic Press, 1995), 77.

5. For white Masons visiting African Lodge No. 459, see Wesley, *Prince Hall,* 98–100. For Hall visiting white lodges, see, for example, his letter to the grand secretary in England in William H. Upton, *Negro Masonry, Being a Critical Examination of Objections to the Legitimacy of the Masonry Existing among the Negroes of America* (Cambridge, MA: The M. W. Prince Hall Grand Lodge of Massachusetts, 1902), 212–13. For visitations in Philadelphia, see Winch, chapter 3 of this book. White Masons would continue to visit African Lodge No. 459 into the 1820s: see "Records of African Lodge, Boston. Minutes, 1806–1816," *A Documentary Account of Prince Hall* (typescript), 16, 20, 27.

6. Samuel Bell, *An Oration, Delivered at Amherst, June 25, A.L. 5798, before the Benevolent Lodge of Free and Accepted Masons…*(Amherst, NH, 1798), 8.

7. "The Columbian Parnassiad. The African Lodge," *Columbian Magazine,* August 1788, 467–69. The black Huntingdonian minister John Marrant similarly argued for the roots of Freemasonry in Cain and his descendants in *A Sermon Preached on the 24th Day of June 1789, … at the Request of the Right Worshipful the Grand Master Prince Hall, and the Rest of the Brethren of the African Lodge…*(Boston, 1789), 10. Other powerful evidence for a late eighteenth-century embrace by whites of black Freemasonry is also available: see the poem "Masonry" with the lines "No more shall COLOURS disagree; / But hearts with hands unite; / For in the wond'rous mystery, / There's neither BLACK nor WHITE," in *Massachusetts Centinel,* May 5, 1787, and the highly respectful description of the funeral for a leading black Mason, Luke Belcher, in *Massachusetts Centinel,* August 19, 1787.

8. John Eliot to Jeremy Belknap, in "Queries Relating to Slavery in Massachusetts," *Collections of the Massachusetts Historical Society,* 5th ser., 3 (1877): 382–83.

9. Ibid., 383.

10. For a further discussion of this organizational character, see Peter P. Hinks, "John Marrant and the Meaning of Early Black Freemasonry," *William and Mary Quarterly,* 3rd ser., 64, no. 1 (January 2007): 105–16. See also Joanna Brooks, "The Early American Public Sphere and the Emergence of a Black Print Counterpublic," *William and Mary Quarterly,* 3rd ser., 62, no. 1 (January 2005): 67–92. Both Wesley, *Prince Hall,* and Sesay, "Freemasons of Color," discuss Hall's labors to advance public education of black children and protect the community from threats of kidnapping and violent assault.

11. For a justification of this "unlimited" character, see Upton, *Negro Masonry,* 106–10.

12. For Philadelphia, see Wesley, *Prince Hall,* 124–29, and Julie Winch, *A Gentleman of Color: The Life of James Forten* (New York: Oxford University Press, 2002), 144–49. See also "Extracts from Minutes of African Lodge, Philadelphia, 1797–1800,"

A Documentary Account of Prince Hall (typescript), 6. Six of the first black Masons in Philadelphia—all of whom appear to have been mariners—probably were originally initiated into the brotherhood at Golden Lodge No. 22 in London: See Wesley, *Prince Hall,* 127, and Winch, chapter 3 of this book, at page 70. African Lodge No. 459 had had members from Providence for several years by 1790. In 1797, the lodge issued them a charter to create their own, more convenient lodge. See Floyd J. Miller, *The Search for a Black Nationality: Black Emigration and Colonization, 1787–1863* (Urbana: University of Illinois Press, 1975), 16; Wesley, *Prince Hall,* 124–26, 141; and William H. Robinson, ed., *The Proceedings of the Free African Union Society and the African Benevolent Society, Newport, Rhode Island 1780–1824* (Providence: Urban League of Rhode Island, 1976).

13. See Prince Hall, "A Charge Delivered to the Brethren of the African Lodge on the 25th of June, 1792 at the Hall of Brother William Smith in Charlestown," in Porter, *Early Negro Writing,* 63–69.

14. See Hall, "Charge Delivered to the African Lodge, June 24, 1797 at Menotomy," 70–78.

15. See William Grimshaw, *Official History of Freemasonry among the Colored People in North America* (1903; repr., New York: Negro Universities Press, 1969), 84–88. Grimshaw transcribed two seminal documents apparently from 1791 to substantiate the date: first, an official authorization from the Grand Lodge of England of Hall's deputation as a "Provincial Grand Master" enabling him to charter new lodges, and second, a formal synopsis of the creation of the African Grand Lodge in Boston on June 24, 1791, a ceremony at which white Masons from the local St. Andrew's Lodge assisted. The first document, he stated, "was found among the old manuscripts of African Lodge, No. 459, of Pennsylvania," but he did not indicate who observed and reported it. Nevertheless, Grimshaw asserted that "[t]here is no doubt but what Prince Hall gave them a copy of his authority when he established the Lodge in 1797" (p. 87). For the second document, he offered no source, although he placed the relevant summary in quotation marks (pp. 84–85). Neither of these documents is in *A Documentary Account of Prince Hall* (typescript). Sherman in fact disputes the existence of the provincial grand master designation. See John MacDuffie Sherman, "The Negro 'National' or 'Compact' Grand Lodge," typescript, 4, Samuel Crocker Lawrence Library. He claims Grimshaw "invented" the designation. Charles Wesley, citing earlier twentieth-century Prince Hall Masons, doubts Hall's designation as grand master because no Grand Lodge of Massachusetts then existed, although he acknowledges that "friendly terms" did exist then between the African Lodge and St. Andrew's. Wesley, *Prince Hall,* 100–101. While it is true that the first postrevolutionary grand lodge in Massachusetts—St. John's—was not created until 1792, Sherman's and Wesley's disavowals of Grimshaw's assertion do not grapple with the likely fact of the deputation from the Grand Lodge of England or the likelihood of St. Andrew's endorsement. The very scrupulous William Upton argued that "there are *traces* of an earlier organization [i.e., of a grand lodge], in the life time of Prince Hall—and *possibly ante-dating the organization of the white Grand Lodge of Massachusetts*" in 1792. To substantiate this likelihood, he noted that Prince Hall placed "G.M." (abbreviation for "Grand Master") after his signature on an official document in 1792. He also observed that in 1795 the Reverend Jeremy Belknap referred to Hall as a "Grand Master." Upton, *Negro Masonry,* 133–34. While not directly referring

to 1791, even the virulently negrophobic General Albert Pike, Confederate war hero and Sovereign Grand Commander of Virginia Masons (he emphasized in 1875 that "[w]hen I have to accept negroes as *brothers* or leave Masonry, I shall leave it") asserted nevertheless that "Prince Hall Lodge was as regular a Lodge as any lodge created by competent authority, and had a perfect right...to establish other lodges, making itself a Mother lodge." "Views of General Albert Pike, Sovereign Grand Commander, A. & A. Scottish Rite," September 13, 1875, in Upton, *Negro Masonry,* app. 12, 214–15.

16. See Grimshaw, *Official History,* 96, where he records the presence as well of black Masons from Philadelphia, Providence, and New York. "Records of African Lodge, Boston. Minutes, 1806–1816," *A Documentary Account of Prince Hall* (typescript), 1, document the meeting on December 28, 1807, but make no reference to the presence of Masons from elsewhere. Wesley, while aptly criticizing Grimshaw for claiming the presence of the other Masons without documenting it, incorrectly charges that "there is now no documentation for this meeting." Wesley, *Prince Hall,* 152. Upton, however, also accepted that a meeting did occur at which the Masons from elsewhere were present and the grand lodge organized—or reorganized. Upton, *Negro Masonry,* 134–35.

17. See Grimshaw, *Official History,* 112–13; Upton, *Negro Masonry,* 12; "African Grand Lodge, Philadelphia," *A Documentary Account of Prince Hall* (typescript).

18. See Grimshaw, *Official History,* 124. Craig Steven Wilder, *In the Company of Black Men: The African Influence on African American Culture in New York City* (New York: New York University Press, 2001), 112–16. The sole extant public reference to a lodge in New York City prior to 1826 is a newspaper announcement placed by "Sandy Lattion, R.W. Master" for a meeting of the "African Lodge" on October 6, 1818. See [Harry A. Williamson], "Here and There," unpublished typescript, microfilm reel 5, box 10, Harry A. Williamson Collection on Negro Masonry, Schomburg Center for Research in Black Culture, New York Public Library. At least one Prince Hall Masonic historian has speculated that the original African Lodge in New York City had been chartered by the African Grand Lodge in Philadelphia: see Harold A. Wilson, "Pieces of My Thinking," unpublished typescript, box 2, folder 2/24, 2, Boyer Lodge No. 1 Records, 1849–1980, Schomburg Center. Another—William T. Boyd in 1883—suggested that "seafaring men who received their Masonic degrees abroad" created the lodge in 1813 or 1814: see *Complete History of Widow's Son Lodge No. 11* (Brooklyn, 1970), 12. The minutes of African Lodge No. 459 record deliberations on the lodge in New York City: see "Records of African Lodge, Boston, Minutes, 1809–1816," January 23, 1826–January 11, 1828, A *Documentary Account of Prince Hall* (typescript), 31–42. Yet a reproduction from a page of the lodge's minute book for December 6, 1814, in *Complete History of Widow's Son Lodge No. 11,* 13, records that "[t]here was a letter written by a gentleman in New York to us for a warrant in which there was expressed the only terms on which they would accept one." No further related commentary was recorded and Coil and Sherman recorded the date for the meeting but chose not to enter the statement for that date: "Records of African Lodge, Boston, Minutes, 1809–1816," 8–9. Further evidence from the reproduction indicates its authenticity. As discussed later in this chapter, the appellation "Boyer African Lodge" was almost certainly not assigned until 1825 or soon after.

19. See "Records of African Lodge, Boston. Minutes, 1806–1816," 1–15. Regarding a possible lapse in administration, John T. Hilton stated in 1828 that after Hall's "decease the government fell into various hands, and consequently was subject to alternate changes... [and] it was difficult to ascertain its precise condition." *An Address Delivered before the African Grand Lodge, of Boston, No. 459,* 6. See also [John M. Sherman?], "Memo regarding the Situation of African Lodge in 1821, and the Influence of Thomas Paul and J. T. Hilton in Reviving the Lodge," typescript, Samuel Crocker Lawrence Library.

20. The following biographical summary of Hilton is drawn largely from Peter P. Hinks, *To Awaken My Afflicted Brethren: David Walker and the Problem of Antebellum Slave Resistance* (University Park: Pennsylvania State University Press, 1997); James O. Horton and Lois E. Horton, *Black Bostonians: Family Life and Community Struggle in the Antebellum North* (New York: Holmes & Meier, 1979); *Liberator,* March 25, 1864; C. Peter Ripley, ed., *The Black Abolitionist Papers,* vol. 3: *The United States, 1830–1846* (Chapel Hill: University of North Carolina Press, 1991), n. 12, 305–6. Regarding Hilton's initiation into the African Lodge, see "Records of African Lodge, Boston. Minutes, 1809–1816," 19.

21. "Records of African Lodge, Boston. Minutes, 1809–1816," 34.

22. See Alton G. Roundtree and Paul M. Bessel, *Out of the Shadows: The Emergence of Prince Hall Freemasonry in America: Over 225 Years of Endurance* (Camp Springs, MD: KLR Publishing, 2006), app. 14, "Request to the Grand Lodge of England for Permission to give Four Additional Degrees," 355–56.

23. See "Records of African Lodge, Boston. Minutes, 1809–1816," January 23, 1826, 30–31.

24. "African Independence," *New England Galaxy and Masonic Magazine,* July 14, 1820. See also the cartoons of David Claypool Johnston, "A splendid procession of free Masons" (ca. 1819) in *David Claypool Johnston: American Graphic Humorist, 1798–1865: An Exhibition held by the American Antiquarian Society* (Worcester, MA, 1970), and of Edward Clay, "Morgan's Deduction" in his *Life in Philadelphia* (Philadelphia: S. Hart, 1830) and reprinted in Gary Nash, *Forging Freedom: The Formation of Philadelphia's Black Community, 1720–1840* (Cambridge: Harvard University Press, 1988), 257. See also the screed and cartoon printed as a broadside, *Grand Masonic Bobalition. At de Consecratium ob de Masonic Tumble. Bosson, May Dirty, Five Tousan Eight Hundred and Sumptin. Dialogue between Cuffee and Sambo* (Boston: [John Marsh?], 1832).

25. See the useful discussion in Sherman, "Negro 'National' or 'Compact' Grand Lodge," 9–11.

26. *Columbian Centinel,* June 26, 1827. The full text of the declaration is reprinted on pages 176–77 of this volume and in Roundtree and Bessel, *Out of the Shadows,* app. 13, "Declaration of Independence," 353–54. The following quotations are drawn from this text.

27. Grimshaw, *Official History,* 100.

28. Martin Delany, "The Origin and Objects of Ancient Freemasonry: Its Introduction into the United States, and Legitimacy among Colored Men. A Treatise Delivered Before St. Cyprian Lodge, No. 13, June 24th, A.D. 1853—A.L. 5853," in *Martin R. Delany: A Documentary Reader,* ed. Robert S. Levine (Chapel Hill: University of North Carolina Press, 2003), 63.

29. These negotiations with Boyer Lodge No. 1 had been ongoing since early 1826—see n. 19. However, not until June 1827 was the resolve within Number 459

achieved to extend the charter. Nevertheless, by mid-July, Boyer Lodge "refused to accept the Charter" and Boston wrote Boyer "for further Explanation of the Conduct." After this entry for July 18, 1827, the minutes are silent—save for a fleeting reference on January 11, 1828—regarding any further negotiations with Boyer. "Records of African Lodge, Boston, Minutes, 1809–1816," 38–42.

30. *Columbian Centinel,* January 27, 1827. See also "Records of African Lodge, Boston, Minutes, 1809–1816," 37.

31. *Freedom's Journal,* March 16, 1827.

32. Hinks, *To Awaken My Afflicted Brethren,* 91–115.

33. See Terry Alford, *Prince among Slaves* (New York: Harcourt Brace Jovanovich, 1986), 136–41; Philip J. Staudenraus, *The African Colonization Movement, 1816–1865* (New York: Columbia University Press, 1961), 162–65; *Freedom's Journal,* September 5 and October 24, 1828. For a full list of the members of African Lodge No. 459 in 1828–29, see Hinks, *To Awaken My Afflicted Brethren,* app. C, 265–66.

34. *Freedom's Journal,* October 24, 1828.

35. Hall, "Charge Delivered to the African Lodge, June 24, 1797, at Menotomy," 74.

36. J. Marcus Mitchell, "The Paul Family," *Old-Time New England* 53 (Winter 1973): 73–77; Arthur O. White, "Prince Saunders: An Instance of Social Mobility among Antebellum New England Blacks," *Journal of Negro History* 60 (January 1975): 526–35.

37. Susan Paul, *Memoir of James Jackson, the Attentive and Obedient Scholar,* ed. Lois Brown (1835; repr., Cambridge, MA: Harvard University Press, 2000), 113.

38. The most thorough treatment of this very important but neglected movement is Sara Connors Fanning, "Haiti and the U.S.: African American Emigration and the Recognition Debate" (PhD diss., University of Texas, 2008). See also Winch, *Gentleman of Color,* 209–20, and Julie Winch, "American Free Blacks and Emigration to Haiti, 1804–26," *Documentos de Trabajo,* Centro de Investigaciones del Caribe y America Latina, Universidad Interamericana de Puerto Rico, 33 (August 1988): 1–22; [Loring Dewey], *Correspondence Relative to the Emigration to Haiti, of the People of Colour, in the United States. Together with the Instructions to the Agent Sent Out by President Boyer* (New York: Mahlon Day, 1824), letter of the Rev. Thomas Paul opposite the title page. Prince Saunders was closely attached to Boston's African Lodge, where he had served as secretary from at least early 1810 through 1814. See also the very important 1824 letter from Joseph-Balthasar Ingernac, secretary-general to President Boyer, to Paul encouraging his emigration and that of the other "descendants of Africa who groan in the U. States in misery and humiliation" in *Lincoln Intelligencer* (Wiscasset, Maine), August 6, 1824. See "Records of African Lodge, Boston: Minutes, 1809–1816," 3–8. For Benjamin Hughes, see *New York Observer,* December 18, 1824, and *United States Gazette,* April 18, 1825.

39. James E. McClellan, *Colonialism and Science: Saint Domingue in the Old Regime* (Baltimore: Johns Hopkins University Press, 1992), 105–6, 183–205; John D. Garrigus, *Before Haiti: Race and Citizenship in French Saint-Domingue* (New York: Palgrave Macmillan, 2006), 37, 126, 149, 232–33, 267, 291–96; Alain Le Bihan, "La Franc-Maçonnerie dans les Colonies Françaises du XVIIIe siècle," *Annales Historiques de la Révolution Française* 46 (January–March 1974), 39–47. Regarding the relationship of Toussaint and the black generals around him to Freemasonry, see also Jacques

de Cauna, "Autour de la Thèse du Complot: Franc-Maçonnerie, Rèvolution et Contre-Rèvolution á Saint-Domingue (1789–1791)" in *Franc-Maçonnerie et Politique au Siècle des Lumières: Europe-Amériques,* ed. Cecile Revauger (Bordeaux: Pessac, 2006), 310–14.

40. Harry Davis has argued that between 1797 and 1818, thirty-seven black Philadelphians became Freemasons "in Europe or the West Indies." However, the reliability of some of these figures has been questioned. Davis, *A History of Freemasonry among Negroes in America* (Philadelphia: United Supreme Council, Northern Jurisdiction, 1946), 290–91. For Courtmanche and Glapion, see "The Earliest Records of African Lodge," *A Documentary Account of Prince Hall* (typescript), 8, 10, 14.

41. Brenda Gayle Plummer, *Haiti and the Great Powers, 1902–1915* (Baton Rouge: Louisiana State University Press, 1988), 18–19; Jacques de Cauna, "Quelques Aperçus sur l'Histoire de la Franc-Maçonnerie en Haiti," *Revue de la Société Haïtienne d'Histoire et de Géographie* 52 (September–December 1996): 20–34; *Report by a Joint Committee of the Legislature of Massachusetts, on Freemasonry, March, 1834* (Boston: Dutton and Wentworth, State Printers, 1834), 48. A further distant possibility for the designation of Haiti as the progenitor of the grand lodge in Boston is that African Lodge No. 459 had never proclaimed its grand lodge status as decisively or publicly as it had in its 1827 declaration of independence. This event occurred, of course, after the collapse of the publicized emigration movement to Haiti and Haiti's own admittedly less publicized declaration of Masonic independence. This context could have conjoined with the real possibility that the two grand lodges exchanged official recognition. Regarding the Masonry of Granville, see Jonathas Henri Theodore Granville, *Biographie de Jonathas Granville* (Paris: Imprimerie de E. Briere, 1873), 318n1.

While both Grimshaw, *Official History,* 124, and Wilder, *In the Company of Black Men,* 113, indicate that Boyer African Lodge was so named in 1812, Harry A. Williamson, an eminent early twentieth-century historian of black Freemasonry, suggested that the name Boyer African Lodge actually only attached to the earlier New York lodge in 1825 or 1826 after its negotiations with the Boston grand lodge. Another Prince Hall historian, Harold A. Wilson, has speculated that "[i]n all likelihood the styling African was the patent name of the Lodge until 1824. Between the years 1824–1826 the name of the Lodge was changed to the patent name of Boyer... in honor of the Haitian soldier-statesman, Jean Boyer." See "The Saga of Boyer Lodge," in *1812–1962 Sesquicentennial of Boyer Lodge No. 1, F. & A.M.,* box 2, folder 2/25, Boyer Lodge No. 1 Records, 1849–1980, Schomburg Center. Neither Upton in *Negro Masonry* nor Wesley in *Prince Hall* discusses the creation of this lodge in the teens. The lodge was apparently named after Boyer (1775–1850), who had been a deputy and close adviser to Alexandre Petion. Boyer had also allied with the mulatto general Andre Rigaud in the south of Saint-Domingue during the revolutionary upheavals of 1791–1804. In 1812, Boyer in fact would have been little known among African Americans, thus making the denomination of the lodge then somewhat curious. By 1818, however, with the passing of Petion, Boyer became much more prominent as he assumed the presidency of the south and reunited the country in 1820 after the death of King Henri-Christophe in the north. In 1818 and much more extensively in 1824, as Boyer encouraged African American emigration to the island nation, he became renowned in black communities all along the

American eastern seaboard. John Edward Baur, "Mulatto Machiavelli: Jean-Pierre Boyer and the Haiti of His Day," *Journal of Negro History* 32 (July 1947): 307–53. See also Winch, *Gentleman of Color,* 209–20.

42. See "Records of African Lodge, Boston. Minutes, 1809–1816," 2, 8, 13, 15, 21, 24, 28, 29, 41; letter of October 15, 1829 in "Miscellaneous Papers," in *Correspondence Relative to the Emigration to Haiti,* 16–17. For a discussion of similar commercial initiatives undertaken in Haiti by African American emigrants between 1824 and 1826, see Fanning, "Haiti and the U.S.," chap. 5 ("The Push and Pull in Emigration").

43. *Address Delivered before the African Grand Lodge, of Boston, No. 459. June 24th, 1828,* 3–5, 11–13, 14. See also *Freedom's Journal,* November 7, 1828. For a discussion of the relative weakness of black Masonic identification with America in the late eighteenth century, see Hinks, "John Marrant and the Meaning of Early Black Freemasonry," 114–16.

44. *Address Delivered before the African Grand Lodge, of Boston, No. 459. June 24th, 1828,* 12–14.

45. Ibid., 5, 9, 15.

46. The 1829 mandate of David Walker, a close Masonic brother of Hilton's, to "Men of colour, who are also of sense…[to] *go to work and enlighten your brethren*" resonates richly with Hilton's summons. *David Walker's Appeal to the Coloured Citizens of the World,* ed. Peter P. Hinks (University Park: Pennsylvania State University Press, 2000), 30.

47. *Liberator,* March 25, 1864.

48. *Freedom's Journal,* April 25 and September 5, 1828. *Liberator,* August 13, 1831.

49. *Liberator,* April 20, 1833.

50. William Lloyd Garrison, *Thoughts on African Colonization: or An Impartial Exhibition of the Doctrines, Principles and Purposes of the American Colonization Society. Together with the Resolutions, Addresses and Remonstrances of the Free People of Color* (Boston: Isaac Knapp, 1832), pt. 2, 17–21.

51. See, for example, *Liberator,* March 23, 1833, February 14, 1835, and July 24, 1846.

52. *Liberator,* March 25, 1864. See, for example, *Liberator,* June 28, 1844, and September 14, 1849, and Carleton Mabee, *Black Freedom: The Nonviolent Abolitionists from 1830 through the Civil War* (New York: Macmillan, 1970), 164–81. Hilton in fact may have moved to Cambridgeport so his children could be educated in integrated schools in Cambridge.

53. See *Liberator,* August 3, 1838, August 16, 1839, August 14, 1840, and July 9, 1841.

54. *Liberator,* October 19, 1833. Benjamin Hughes also pronounced a eulogy for Wilberforce in the same month: see Hughes, *Eulogium on the Life and Character of William Wilberforce, Esq.: Delivered and Published at the Request of the People of Color of the City of New York, Twenty-Second of October, 1833* (New York: Printed at the office of the *Emancipator,* 1833).

55. *Liberator,* August 4, 1843.

56. *Liberator,* October 20, 1848.

57. *Liberator,* October 11, 1850.

58. *Liberator,* September 17 and December 10, 1831.

59. See Grimshaw, *Official History,* 124–213. See also Charles H. Wesley, *The History of the Prince Hall Grand Lodge of Free and Accepted Masons of the State of Ohio, 1849–1971: An Epoch in American Fraternalism* (Washington, DC: Association for the Study of Negro Life and History, 1972).

60. Grimshaw, *Official History,* 202–3.

61. See "Lewis Hayden—Contacts with Freemasonry," typescript, 1, Samuel Crocker Lawrence Library. See also *Grand Lodge of the Most Ancient and Honorable Fraternity of Free and Accepted Masons, of the Commonwealth of Massachusetts… M.W. Simon W. Robinson, G.M.* (Boston: Office of the Freemasons' Magazine, 1847).

62. Grimshaw, *Official History,* 189–205. Although it is overwhelmingly oriented toward establishing the illegitimacy of the Freemasonry initiated by Prince Hall and thus all ensuing black Freemasonry, the following typescript does provide a useful chronology of immediate events precipitating the crisis that in 1847 led to the creation of the National Grand Lodge by Hilton and others: see Sherman, "The Negro 'National' or 'Compact' Grand Lodge," 16–18.

63. "Declaration of Sentiments" of the National Grand Lodge, adopted June 24–26, 1847. See pages 178–79 of this volume and also Matthew Brock, *History of the National Grand Lodge* (Columbus, OH: s.p., 1980).

64. See *New York Tribune,* June 21, 1848; *New York Herald,* June 26, 28, 1848.

65. Samuel Van Brakle, "Masonic Oration Delivered 27th of December, A.L. 5852, A.D. 1852. At Bethel Church, at Philadelphia, for the Benefit of the Poor of Said Church," [Philadelphia, 1853?], 3–4.

66. Regarding the bitter dispute between the New York lodges and the NGL, see the broadside *Address to the Public in the State of New-York, and to All Others Whom It May Concern…from "The United Grand Lodge of the State of New-York* ([New York?], 1849) and *Circular Issued 30 July 1849 by the United Grand Lodge of the State of New-York* (New York, 1849). See also the excellent summary of these New York rivalries in *Complete History of Widow's Son Lodge No. 11,* 14–17.

67. Lewis Hayden, *Letters in Vindication of the National Grand Lodge of Ancient, Free, and Accepted Masons of the United States of North America* (Boston: Edward S. Coombs, 1867), 6–11.

68. Ibid., 30–32.

69. For a detailed discussion of the troubled history of conflict within the NGL and more broadly between black and white Masons over the years after 1865, see Kantrowitz, chapter 5 of this book.

70. *Liberator,* March 25, 1864.

71. *Address Delivered before the African Grand Lodge, of Boston, No. 459. June 24th, 1828,* 9.

3. "A Late Thing I Guess"

1. Elaine Forman Crane, ed., *The Diary of Elizabeth Drinker* (Boston: Northeastern University Press, 1991), 2:935.

2. Minutes of the African Lodge, Philadelphia, 1797–1800, 1, Samuel Crocker Lawrence Library, Grand Lodge of Massachusetts, Boston. I am grateful to the Grand

Lodge of Massachusetts, AF and AM, and to Cynthia Alcorn, the librarian of the lodge's Samuel Crocker Lawrence Library, for giving me access to the microfilm of the minute book.

3. Edward R. Turner, *The Negro in Pennsylvania: Slavery—Servitude—Freedom, 1639–1861* (Washington, DC: American Historical Association, 1912), 253.

4. The Philadelphia press often carried letters and articles conjuring up alarming images of the city's future if the African American population were allowed to continue to grow unchecked. (For fairly typical examples see *Freeman's Journal and Philadelphia Daily Advertiser,* July 7 and July 9, 1804.) Those fears were voiced even by individuals like Thomas Branagan, who claimed to be well disposed toward black people in general and to abhor slavery. His *Avenia; or, A Tragical Poem on the Slavery and Commerce of the Human Species* (Philadelphia: S. Engles, 1805) contained an early call for the separation of the races to avert the twin "horrors" (as he saw them) of racial warfare and interracial unions.

5. For an overview of the social and economic prospects of black Philadelphians in the 1780s and 1790s, see Gary B. Nash, *Forging Freedom: The Formation of Philadelphia's Black Community, 1720–1840* (Cambridge, MA: Harvard University Press, 1988), 134–71.

6. On the demise of slavery in Pennsylvania, see Gary B. Nash and Jean R. Soderlund, *Freedom by Degrees: Emancipation in Pennsylvania and Its Aftermath* (New York: Oxford University Press, 1991), esp. chaps. 3–5.

7. For the text of the 1780 law, see Roger Bruns, ed., *Am I Not a Man and a Brother: The Antislavery Crusade in Revolutionary America, 1688–1788* (New York: Chelsea House, 1977), 446–50.

8. On the diverse elements that constituted Philadelphia's free community of color in the 1790s, see Julie Winch, *A Gentleman of Color: The Life of James Forten* (New York: Oxford University Press, 2002), 126–35, and Ashli White, *Encountering Revolution: Haiti and the Making of the Early Republic* (Baltimore: Johns Hopkins University Press, 2010), chap. 1.

9. On the pioneering work of the Pennsylvania Abolition Society, see Richard S. Newman, *The Transformation of American Abolitionism: Fighting Slavery in the Early Republic* (Chapel Hill: University of North Carolina Press, 2002), esp. chap. 1.

10. For the history of the Free African Society, see William Douglass, *Annals of the First African Church in the United States of America, Now Styled the African Episcopal Church of St. Thomas* (Philadelphia: King & Baird, 1862), 12–49, and Richard S. Newman, *Freedom's Prophet: Bishop Richard Allen, the AME Church, and the Black Founding Fathers* (New York: New York University Press, 2008), esp. chaps. 2–3.

11. Mathew Carey, *A Short Account of the Malignant Fever, Lately Prevalent in Philadelphia: With a Statement of the Proceedings That Took Place on the Subject in Different Parts of the United States,* 2nd ed. (Philadelphia: The Author, 1793); Absalom Jones and Richard Allen, *A Narrative of the Proceedings of the Black People during the Late Awful Calamity in Philadelphia* (Philadelphia: William W. Woodward, 1794).

12. *Gazette of the United States,* June 22, 1797.

13. Charles H. Wesley, *Prince Hall, Life and Legacy* (Washington, DC: United Supreme Council, Southern Jurisdiction, Prince Hall Affiliation, 1977), 127.

14. William Henry Grimshaw, *Official History of Freemasonry Among the Colored People in North America* (1903; repr., New York: Negro Universities Press, 1969), 110; Douglass, *Annals of the First African Church,* 31; Wesley, *Prince Hall,* 127.

15. African Lodge of Philadelphia to African Lodge of Boston, March 2, 1797, Records of the African Lodge at Boston, Part A, Letters and Sermons (microfilm), Samuel Crocker Lawrence Library.

16. Ibid.

17. Wesley, *Prince Hall,* 216.

18. Grimshaw, *Official History,* 90, 110.

19. *James Robinson's Philadelphia Directory for 1803* (Philadelphia, 1803), 188. Absalom Jones delivered a charity sermon to raise money to help the "poor and distressed citizens" who had suffered as a consequence of the epidemic. *Claypoole's American Daily Advertiser,* October 5, 1797.

20. Minutes of the African Lodge, 1, 59.

21. *North American Daily Advertiser,* December 15, 1843.

22. *Poulson's American Daily Advertiser,* February 18, 1818; Ruth Dixon Priest and Katherine George Eberly, comps., *Index to Seamen's Protection Certificate Applications for the Port of Philadelphia, 1796–1823* (Baltimore: Clearfield, 1995), 24, 118; Port of Philadelphia. Alphabetical List of Masters and Crews, 1798–1880, transcription, 1802, p. 32; 1804, p. 74; 1805, pp. 243, 389, Historical Society of Pennsylvania, Philadelphia, PA (hereafter cited as HSP).

23. Christ Church, Baptisms, 1769–94, p. 915, HSP; Philadelphia County Wills, Book Y (1800), no. 101, Philadelphia City Archives (hereafter cited as PCA).

24. Alphabetical List of Masters and Crews, 1802, p. 32; 1804, p. 74; 1805, pp. 243, 389. In 1796 Congress authorized the issuing of "protection certificates" for American sailors as a means of safeguarding them from impressment into the British and French navies. The British were the worst offenders in this regard, claiming as British subjects thousands of American sailors before the final peace with France in 1815. For a black sailor the "seaman's papers" assumed an even greater importance than they did for his white shipmates. A certificate described the bearer as not only an American citizen but a free man. A man of color whose ship put in to a strange port, especially in the South, could easily find himself claimed as a slave. Of course, seaman's papers could all too easily be lost, stolen, or simply ignored.

25. Philadelphia County Wills, Book Y (1800), no. 41.

26. For a wide-ranging discussion of the role of African American men as sailors, see W. Jeffrey Bolster, *Black Jacks: African American Seamen in the Age of Sail* (Cambridge, MA: Harvard University Press, 1997).

27. Minutes of the African Lodge, 5.

28. *Poulson's American Daily Advertiser,* February 18, 1818. On the status of the Forten family, see Winch, *Gentleman of Color,* 8–19.

29. Nash, *Forging Freedom,* 36.

30. Philadelphia County Wills, Book Y (1800), no. 307.

31. Ibid., nos. 41 and 101; ibid., Book 6 (1818), no. 23; St. Thomas's African Episcopal Church, Baptismal Registers, vol. 1 (unpaginated); Winch, *Gentleman of Color,* 107–8. I thank the congregation of St. Thomas's African Episcopal Church, especially the members of its historical society, for giving me access to the church's manuscript records.

32. The first and second federal censuses (1790 and 1800) are available online at Ancestry.com and HeritageQuest.com. City directories exist for Philadelphia for virtually every year from 1790 to 1800.

33. Philadelphia County Wills, Book Y (1800), no. 43; ibid., Book 7 (1822), no. 164; *Cornelius William Stafford's Philadelphia Directory for 1801* (Philadelphia, 1801).

34. *Edmund Hogan's Prospect of Philadelphia, and Check on the Next Directory* (Philadelphia, 1795); *Cornelius William Stafford's Philadelphia Directory for 1797* (Philadelphia, 1797); *Cornelius William Stafford's Philadelphia Directory for 1798* (Philadelphia, 1798) *Cornelius William Stafford's Philadelphia Directory for 1799* (Philadelphia, 1799) *Cornelius William Stafford's Philadelphia Directory for 1800* (Philadelphia, 1800); *Cornelius William Stafford's Philadelphia Directory for 1801* (Philadelphia, 1801); *James Robinson's Philadelphia City Directory, City and County Register for 1802* (Philadelphia, 1802); Philadelphia County Wills, Book 17 (1844), no. 46.

35. Philadelphia County Wills, Book Y (1800), no. 101.

36. Ibid., Book 2 (1807), no. 77.

37. See, for instance, Minutes of the African Lodge, 8 (Quam Butler), and 9 ("Distressed Brother").

38. Ibid., 22, 23.

39. *The Negro Equaled by Few Europeans. Translated from the French. To Which Are Added, Poems on Various Subjects, Moral and Entertaining; by Phillis Wheatley, Negro Servant to Mr. John Wheatley, of Boston, in New England,* vol. 2 (Philadelphia: William W. Woodward, 1801), end pages (unnumbered). Jones's name appears on the subscription lists of various publications, most (but not all) of them religious in nature. On Forten's literary interests, see Winch, *Gentleman of Color,* 159.

40. See, for example, Minutes of the African Lodge, 16, 18, 51. In December 1799 the lodge was so pleased with its St. John's Day oration that the brothers voted to have it printed. Unfortunately, no copies have survived.

41. *Stafford's Philadelphia Directory for 1797;* Douglass, *Annals of the First African Church,* 106–7; Philadelphia County Wills, Book 2, no. 77 (1807); Cemetery Returns for African Church of St. Thomas (1807), Philadelphia Board of Health Records, PCA.

42. St. Thomas's African Episcopal Church, Baptismal Registers; Philadelphia Wills, Book 6, no. 111 (1816), p. 324.

43. *Colored American,* October 14, 1837.

44. Minutes of the African Lodge, 26, 31–33.

45. Ibid., 11–12.

46. Ibid., 10.

47. Ibid., 18.

48. See, for example, ibid., 13, 14, 36.

49. See, for instance, the arrangements for the Feast of St. John the Baptist in ibid., 14.

50. See, for instance, ibid., 12.

51. William Wiltshire, for example, was turned down when one lone brother expressed doubts about his candidacy. Ibid., 15. He reapplied and was admitted.

52. Ibid., 3, 6, 35.

53. Ibid., 27, 28–29.

54. Ibid., 24.

55. Ibid., 30.

56. Ibid., 2, 4–5, 46.

57. Ibid., 24, 38, 39.

58. Ibid., 49, 52.

59. Ibid., 40–41, 49, 52, 58.

60. Harry E. Davis, *A History of Freemasonry among Negroes in America* (Philadelphia: United Supreme Council, Northern Jurisdiction, 1946), 96.

61. Minutes of the African Lodge, 56–57. For an account of the observances, see *Pennsylvania Gazette,* February 26, 1800.

62. *Philadelphia Gazette,* December 31, 1799.

63. *Herald of Liberty,* January 13, 1800.

4. Nation and Oration

1. This chapter draws on parts of my book *A Noble Fight: African American Freemasonry and the Struggle for Democracy in America* (Urbana: University of Illinois Press, 2008).

2. See J. C. D. Clark, *The Language of Liberty, 1620–1832: Political Discourses and Social Dynamics in the Anglo-American World* (New York: Cambridge University Press, 1994).

3. Eddie S. Glaude Jr., *Exodus! Religion, Race, and Nation in Early Nineteenth-Century Black America* (Chicago: University of Chicago Press, 2000), 3.

4. See James T. Kloppenberg, "The Virtues of Liberalism: Christianity, Republicanism, and Ethics in Early American Political Discourse," in *The Virtues of Liberalism* (New York: Oxford University Press, 1998), 21–37. For an understanding of how African Americans negotiated these turbulent political and religious currents, see Peter P. Hinks, "John Marrant and the Meaning of Early Black Freemasonry," *William and Mary Quarterly,* 3rd ser., 64, no. 1 (January 2007): 105–116, and John Saillant, *Black Puritan, Black Republican: The Life and Thought of Lemuel Haynes, 1753–1833* (New York: Oxford University Press, 2002).

5. Colin Kidd, "Civil Theology and Church Establishment in Revolutionary America," *Historical Journal* 42, no. 4 (1999): 1010.

6. On the "radical" dimensions of Freemasonry and modern political thought and history, see Margaret C. Jacob, *The Radical Enlightenment: Pantheists, Freemasons, and Republicans* (1981; repr., Lafayette, LA: Cornerstone, 2006).

7. Craig Steven Wilder, *In the Company of Black Men: The African Influence on African American Culture in New York City* (New York: New York University Press, 2001), as quoted in Joanna Brooks, "The Early American Public Sphere and the Emergence of a Black Print Counterpublic," *William and Mary Quarterly* 62, no. 1 (2005): 67–92.

8. Prince Hall, "A Charge Delivered to the African Lodge, June 24, 1797 at Menotomy," in Dorothy Porter, ed., *Early Negro Writing, 1760–1837* (Baltimore: Black Classic Press, 1995), 70–71.

9. Ibid., 71.

10. See Wilson Jeremiah Moses, *Black Messiahs and Uncle Toms: Social and Literary Manipulations of a Religious Myth* (University Park: Pennsylvania State University Press, 1993), and David Howard-Pitney, *The Afro-American Jeremiad: Appeals for Justice in America* (Philadelphia: Temple University Press, 1990).

11. Hall, "A Charge Delivered to the African Lodge, June 24, 1797," 71. C. L. R. James, *The Black Jacobins: Toussaint L'Ouverture and the San Domingo Revolution* (1938; repr., New York: Penguin, 2001).

12. Hall, "A Charge Delivered to the African Lodge, June 24, 1797," 72–73. Steven Bullock, *Revolutionary Brotherhood: Freemasonry and the Transformation of the American Social Order, 1730–1840* (Chapel Hill: University of North Carolina Press, 1996), 82.

13. Hall, "A Charge Delivered to the African Lodge, June 24, 1797," 74.

14. Julius S. Scott, "The Common Wind: Currents of Afro-American Communication in the Era of the Haitian Revolution" (PhD diss., Duke University, 1986).

15. Bullock, *Revolutionary Brotherhood,* 137.

16. Cited in A. Leon Higginbotham Jr., *In the Matter of Color: Race & the American Legal Process: The Colonial Period* (New York: Oxford University Press, 1978), 385.

17. William H. Grimshaw, *Official History of Freemasonry among the Colored People in North America* (1903; repr., New York: Negro Universities Press, 1969), 81.

18. On the kidnapping and (re)enslavement of free blacks in Boston, see Peter P. Hinks, "'Frequently Plunged into Slavery': Free Blacks and Kidnapping in Antebellum Boston," *Historical Journal of Massachusetts* 20 (1992): 16–31.

19. William H. Grimshaw, *Official History,* 83. Winston C. Babb has noted:

Lavasseur, who served as Lafayette's secretary on the tour of the United States in the 1820's, said that he was told by a Frenchman that there was a connection between Masonry in the West Indies and in America. It seemed that mariners in those waters were in constant danger of falling into the hands of pirates who, while they might "rob and hang all without distinction of religion, have a particular respect for Free masons, whom they almost always treat like brothers."

Winston C. Babb, "French Refugees from Saint Domingue to the Southern United States: 1791–1810" (PhD diss., University of Virginia, 1954), 363.

20. William H. Grimshaw, *Official History,* 81–82.

21. Ibid., 82.

22. Ibid.

23. Ibid., 100.

5. Brotherhood Denied

1. This chapter draws on research for the author's book *More Than Freedom: Fighting for Black Citizenship in a White Republic, 1829–1889* (New York: Penguin, 2012). For a companion piece covering a broader swath of nineteenth-century African American history, see the author's "'Intended for the Better Government of Man': The Political History of African American Freemasonry in the Era of Emancipation," *Journal of American History* 96 (March 2010): 1001–26.

2. Lewis Hayden, *Caste among Masons: Address before Prince Hall Grand Lodge of Free and Accepted Masons of the State of Massachusetts, at the Festival of St. John the Evangelist, December 27, 1865,* 2nd ed. (Boston: Edward S. Coombs, 1866). For more on

Hayden and on the antebellum history of black Freemasonry, see Kantrowitz, *More Than Freedom.*

3. See Patrick Rael, *Black Identity and Black Protest in the Antebellum North* (Chapel Hill: University of North Carolina Press, 2002).

4. Hayden, *Caste among Masons,* 10

5. See, e.g., the list of lodges warranted by Ohio Masons during the 1850s in Charles H. Wesley, *The History of the Prince Hall Grand Lodge of Free and Accepted Masons of the State of Ohio, 1849–1971: An Epoch in American Fraternalism* (Washington, DC: Association for the Study of Negro Life and History, 1972), 36; *Proceedings of the National Grand Lodge,* 1856, 1862, and 1865, Van Gorden-Williams Library, National Heritage Museum, Lexington, Massachusetts; and the state histories in William Grimshaw, *Official History of Freemasonry among the Colored People in North America* (1903; repr., New York: Negro Universities Press, 1969). Key works on the nineteenth-century history of black Freemasonry include Chernoh Sesay, "Freemasons of Color: Prince Hall, Revolutionary Black Boston, and the Origins of Black Freemasonry, 1770–1807" (PhD diss., Northwestern University, 2006); Steven C. Bullock, *Revolutionary Brotherhood: Freemasonry and the Transformation of the American Social Order, 1730–1840* (Chapel Hill: University of North Carolina Press, 1996); Peter Hinks, *To Awaken My Afflicted Brethren: David Walker and the Problem of Antebellum Slave Resistance* (University Park: Pennsylvania State University Press, 1997); Wesley, *History;* and Martin Summers, *Manliness and Its Discontents: The Black Middle Class and the Transformation of Masculinity, 1900–1930* (Chapel Hill: University of North Carolina Press, 2004); and chapters 1 and 2 in this volume. A vast insider scholarship on black Freemasonry is rife with controversy; a deeply flawed but essential starting point is Grimshaw, *Official History;* see also Alton G. Roundtree and Paul M. Bessel, *Out of the Shadows: The Emergence of Prince Hall Freemasonry in America: Over 225 Years of Endurance* (Camp Springs, MD: KLR Publishing, 2006). For a general introduction to the order, see Mark A. Tabbert, *American Freemasons: Three Centuries of Building Communities* (Lexington, MA.: National Heritage Museum, 2005).

6. *Weekly Anglo-African* (New York), February 20, 1864, 1D.

7. See chapter 7 in this volume.

8. *Weekly Anglo-African* (New York), January 16, 1864, 4C–4D. For further details of the state of subordinate-lodge organization in late 1865, see *Proceedings of the National Grand Lodge,* 1865, 12ff.

9. See, for example, their efforts to participate in funeral observances for Abraham Lincoln: Corey D. B. Walker, "'The Freemasonry of the Race': The Cultural Politics of Ritual, Race, and Place in Postemancipation Virginia" (PhD diss., College of William and Mary, 2001), 272; *Weekly Anglo-African* (New York) May 6, 1865, 2F–3A.

10. *Weekly Anglo-African* (New York), May 13, 1865, 1E–F. This was not an untroubled achievement: black Masons' participation in the opening of the Chicago Sanitary Fair that spring caused white Masons to boycott the proceedings; *Weekly Anglo-African* (New York), June 24, 1865, 4E.

11. *Colored Tennessean* (Nashville), August 12, 1865.

12. *Christian Recorder* (Philadelphia), November 4, 1865 (Accessible Archives).

13. *South Carolina Leader* (Charleston), December 15, 1865, 3B.

14. John Jones, *An Argument in relation to Freemasonry among Colored Men in This Country* (Chicago: Tribune Company, 1866), 5; "Colored Masonry," *Chicago Daily Tribune,* September 5, 1877 (ProQuest Historical Newspapers); Richard Theodore Greener, *An Oration Pronounced at the Celebration of the Festival of St. John the Baptist, June 24, 1876, at the Invitation of the Eureka Lodge No. 1, F. A.M., in the Savannah Georgia Theatre* (Savannah: D. G. Patton, [1876?]), 8. Greener's figure may have been high, but hostile white commentators did sometimes offer it as well; see "Masonic," *Chicago Daily Tribune,* July 11, 1875, 9 (ProQuest Historical Newspapers).

15. See Walker, "'Freemasonry of the Race.'"

16. Lewis Hayden, *Letters in Vindication of the National Grand Lodge of Ancient, Free, and Accepted Masons of the United States of North America* (Boston: Edward S. Coombs, 1867), 28–29.

17. Ibid.

18. M. R. Delany, *The Origin and Objects of Ancient Freemasonry: Its Introduction into the United States, and Legitimacy among Colored Men. A Treatise Delivered Before St. Cyprian Lodge, No 13, June 24th, A.D. 1853—A.L. 5853* (Pittsburgh: W. S. Haven, 1853), 21.

19. *Proceedings of the Sixth Triennial Session of the Most Worshipful National Grand Lodge of Free and Accepted Ancient York Masons...Baltimore, October A.D. 1865...* (Philadelphia: P. E. Thompson, 1866) (hereafter cited as *NGL 1865*), 2–3.

20. *Weekly Anglo-African* (New York), January 21, 1860, p. 1, col. 6.

21. *Weekly Anglo-African* (New York), July 4, 1863, p. 2, cols. 2–3.

22. *Loyal Georgian* (Augusta), October 13, 1866, p. 4, col. 4.

23. Hayden, *Caste among Masons,* 53–54.

24. *Weekly Anglo-African* (New York), November 30, 1861, p. 3, col. 1.

25. *NGL 1865,* 8–9.

26. Ibid., 11.

27. Wesley, *History,* 36.

28. *Minutes of Proceedings of the Triennial Session of the National Grand Lodge, A. Y. M., Held in Philadelphia, July, 1856* (Philadelphia: Brown's Steampower Book and Job Printing Office, 1856) (hereafter cited as *NGL 1856*), 32.

29. *NGL 1865,* 14.

30. See reference to debate over National Grand Master Drayton's (as yet unfound) 1865 address in ibid., 24–5.

31. *NGL 1865,* 18–19.

32. Ibid., 20–22.

33. *NGL 1856,* 44.

34. See, e.g., Gleaves's roles as recorded in the *Christian Recorder* (Philadelphia), October 22, 1864 (master of a Masonic lodge), June 25, 1864 (chief of a district grand lodge of the Good Samaritans and Daughters of Samaria), and October 10, 1863 (member of the state Grand Tabernacle of the Independent Order of Brothers and Sisters of Love and Charity) (all Accessible Archives).

35. There is no biography of Gleaves and, so far as I can determine, no collection of his papers. Wesley, *History,* and Grimshaw, *Official History,* contain much of what is known about his Masonic career. The South Carolina Department of Archives and History, Columbia, has a few records of his service as lieutenant governor and of his trial for corruption; see Richland County Court of General Sessions, Indictments,

1877–1881. Some of his exploits can be traced through the columns of African American newspapers such as the *Christian Recorder.*

36. *NGL 1865,* 47.

37. Gleaves's speech at the Prince Hall Centennial, 1875, reprinted in *Proceedings of the Prince Hall Grand Lodge…1875* (Boston: Prince Hall Grand Lodge, 1876), 48–49.

38. *NGL 1865,* 47.

39. Roundtree and Bessel, *Out of the Shadows,* 65.

40. *NGL 1865,* 38.

41. Hayden, *Letters in Vindication,* 9–10.

42. Ibid., 18.

43. Ibid., 23–24. Others noted the impropriety of Gleaves's formation of grand lodges; see the polemic by A. W. A. De Leon, *An Appeal to the Masons Working under the Jurisdiction of the "National Grand Lodge"* (San Francisco: n.p., [1874]), 5.

44. Hayden, *Letters in Vindication,* 27.

45. Ibid., 32.

46. Lewis Hayden, *Grand Lodge Jurisdictional Claim; or, War of Races. An Address before the Prince Hall Grand Lodge of Free and Accepted Masons for the State of Massachusetts, at the Festival of Saint John the Baptist, June 24, 1868* (Boston: Edward S. Coombs, 1868), 36.

47. Hayden, *Letters in Vindication,* 6–7.

48. *Proceedings of the M. W. Grand Lodge of the Most Ancient and Honorable Fraternity of Free & Accepted Masons for the State of Ohio . . .* [1871?], incomplete photocopy, Van Gorden-Williams Library (hereafter cited as *Proceedings of Ohio, 1871*).

49. *Proceedings of a Grand Semi-Annual Communication of the Union Grand Lodge of Virginia . . . and the Grand Annual Communication . . . A.D. 1870* (Lynchburg: Evening Press Print, 1871), 21–22. I thank Corey D. B. Walker for his generosity in making this item available to me.

50. Hayden, *Letters in Vindication,* 12.

51. Ibid., 26.

52. Hayden, *Grand Lodge Jurisdictional Claims,* 35.

53. Ibid., 34–35.

54. Hayden, *Letters in Vindication,* 26.

55. Hayden, *Grand Lodge Jurisdictional Claims,* 35.

56. Hayden, *Letters in Vindication,* 19–20.

57. Lewis Hayden, *A Letter from Lewis Hayden, of Boston, Massachusetts, to Hon. Judge Simms, of Savannah, Georgia.* (Boston: Comm. on Masonic Jurisprudence, PHGL, 1874), 24; see also *Proceedings of the Prince Hall Grand Lodge . . . 1874* (Boston: Prince Hall Grand Lodge, 1875), 12–16.

58. *Proceedings of the M. W. Grand Lodge of the Most Ancient and Honorable Fraternity of Free & Accepted Masons for the State of Ohio and its Jurisdiction…1868* (Cincinnati: Moore & McGrew, 1868), 7ff; Wesley, *History,* 51–56; Grimshaw, *Official History,* 209–11.

59. De Leon, *Appeal to the Masons,* 2–6.

60. Lewis Hayden, *A Letter,* 24.

61. See James Pike's classic anti-Reconstruction work, *The Prostrate State.*

62. See De Leon, *Appeal to the Masons,* 7.

63. *Transactions of the General Assembly of Masons, Held at Boston, Mass., June 23, A. L. 5875, A.D. 1875* (New York: Tobitt & Bunce, 1875), 10–11.

64. *Chicago Daily Tribune,* September 5, 1877, 3 (ProQuest Historical Newspapers).

65. *Chicago Daily Tribune,* September 6, 1877, 8; September 7, 1877, 8 (ProQuest Historical Newspapers).

66. "Report of the Proceedings of the Convention of Colored Masons…" *Christian Recorder,* May 23, 1878 (Accessible Archives).

67. Some Masonic historians assert that the NGL voted to dissolve, but this claim is challenged by the adherents of a present-day "National Grand Lodge" that claims Masonic descent from Gleaves's organization, asserting that it was never legally abolished and that its members are the legitimate bearers of the Masonic legacy. One of this body's leading members makes the case that Grimshaw's *Official History* offers a partisan "State Rightist" (i.e., anti-NGL) account of the 1860s and 1870s, Matthew Brock, *History of the National Grand Lodge* (Columbus, OH: s.p., 1980). See also http://mwnationalgrandlodge.org/ and the discussions throughout Roundtree and Bessel, *Out of the Shadows.*

68. 1847 "Declaration of Sentiments" reprinted in the *Proceedings of the National Grand Lodge,* 1856, 5–6.

69. Delany, *Origin and Objects,* 6.

70. Delany recounted stories of black Masons in Pennsylvania and elsewhere in the North being refused Masonic recognition by whites, though he contrasted this unfavorably with what he claimed was the fact that on many occasions "Southern Masons recognize and fellowship colored men, as such, wherever they meet them as Masons," citing as evidence his own attendance at a lodge in a border city (probably Cincinnati) at the same time as leading white Masons from Kentucky. Ibid., 22. Such visitation was unusual enough that a white Masonic lodge's invitation to members of the NGL in 1856 brought a vote of thanks "for the hospitality extended toward this M.W.N.G. Lodge, for which our hearts will ever feel the most unbounded gratitude." *NGL 1856,* 20.

71. For full statements of the position of each side, compare Hayden's arguments in *Caste among Masons* with "A Question Settled," *Masonic Review* (Cincinnati) 2, no. 3 (December 1846): 55–58.

72. See De Leon, *Appeal to the Masons.*

73. Hayden, *Caste among Masons.*

74. "Affairs about Boston," *Weekly Anglo-African* (New York), January 7, 186[5], p. 1, cols. 5–6, original newspaper in Executive Letters, Series 567x, vol. W100, Commonwealth of Massachusetts Archives, Boston. This issue is dated 1864, but internal evidence makes it clear that this is a typographical error.

75. Hayden, *Caste among Masons,* 45.

76. Ibid., 28–29.

77. *Frederick Douglass' Paper,* December 31, 1858, 1.

78. *NGL 1865,* 37, 39.

79. John Jones, *Argument in Relation to Freemasonry among Colored Men in This Country…* (Chicago: Tribune Company, 1866), 5.

80. *Weekly Anglo-African* (New York), February 18, 1865, 1.

81. J. G. Findel, *History of Freemasonry* (London: Asher & Co., 1866); see Hayden, *Grand Lodge Jurisdictional Claims,* 92.

82. "Colored Masons—Letter from Garibaldi," *New York Times*, August 6, 1867, 1 (Proquest Historical Newspapers). The fact that the Louisiana Mason he thanked was generally considered schismatic is suggestive but not, for these purposes, crucial.

83. *Proceedings of the Prince Hall Grand Lodge...1875*, 53–54, 58.

84. *Proceedings of the Prince Hall Grand Lodge...1876*, December 21, 1876.

85. Richard T. Greener, *An Oration Pronounced at the Celebration of the Festival of Saint John the Baptist, June 24, 1876, at the Invitation of Eureka Lodge No. 1, F.A.M.,...* (Savannah: D. G. Patton, [1876]), 9.

86. Jones, *Argument*, 16.

87. Hayden, *Caste among Masons*, 28–29.

88. *Boston Commonwealth*, October 19, 1867, 3. The following discussion of the ensuing controversy is based on *Freemason's Monthly Magazine*, December 1, 1867, 37–39.

89. *Boston Commonwealth*, October 19, 1867, 3. This exceptional Mason was Charles Slack, a leading Republican politician and editor of the *Commonwealth*.

90. *Proceedings of the Most Worshipful Grand Lodge of Ancient Free and Accepted Masons of the Commonwealth of Massachusetts* (Boston: Caustic-Claflin, n.d.; hereafter cited as *PGLM*), 454–61 (December 9, 1869).

91. Ibid., 459–60.

92. Ibid., 462.

93. In "1776–1876—New Day—New Duty," *Proceedings of the Grand Lodge of the Most Ancient and Honorable Fraternity of Free and Accepted Masons of the State of Ohio. Sixty-sixth Annual Grand Communication begun and held at Columbus, October 19, A. L. 5875.* (Cincinnati: John D. Caldwell, 1875), 51. This man was Massachusetts grand master Winslow Lewis, whom Hayden called out in 1868 for having seen and authenticated the original warrant of the African Lodge but, though regarded "as a friend," not speaking out. Hayden, *Grand Lodge Jurisdictional Claims*, 32.

94. *PGLM*, 462–63.

95. *Proceedings of Ohio, 1871*, 21–30.

96. "Colored Lodges," *New England Freemason*, November, 1875, 394–95.

97. Smith was the only nonwhite initiated into the Boston Anti-Man-Hunting League, an antebellum secret society whose purpose was to foil slave catchers; see Stephen Kantrowitz, "Fighting Like Men: Civil War Dilemmas of Abolitionist Manhood," in *Battle Scars: Gender and Sexuality in the U.S. Civil War*, ed. Catherine Clinton and Nina Silber (New York: Oxford University Press, 2006), 19–40.

98. "A Negro Made a Freemason," *Freemason's Monthly Magazine*, December, 1867, 37–38.

99. Hayden, *Grand Lodge Jurisdictional Claims*, 25–28.

100. Ibid., 5, 25, 45.

101. Ibid., 28.

102. [Lewis Hayden], *Masonry among Colored Men in Massachusetts; to the Right Worshipful J. G. Findel, Honorary Grand Master of the Prince Hall Grand Lodge, and General Representative thereof to the Lodges upon the Continent of Europe* (Boston: Lewis Hayden, 1871), 48.

103. Hayden, *Grand Lodge Jurisdictional Claims*, 52, 60–63.

104. "St. John's Day," *Memphis Daily Avalanche*, June 25, 1868, 3 (America's Historical Newspapers).

105. Hayden, *Grand Lodge Jurisdictional Claims,* 63.

106. Ibid., 69.

107. Ibid., 71–72; William D. Stratton, comp., *Dedication Memorial of the New Masonic Temple, Boston* (Boston: Lee and Shepard, 1868), 191–92.

108. Hayden, *Grand Lodge Jurisdictional Claims,* 72. In this passage, without using names, Hayden made unmistakable reference to the legal services provided to poor people, white and black, by his friend and Masonic brother Robert Morris, and to the succor given the poor of all colors by their comrade Dr. John V. DeGrasse. His pride and his fears were general but also intensely personal.

109. Ibid., 73–74.

110. *Proceedings of the Prince Hall Grand Lodge … 1874,* 23.

111. *1776–1876—New Day—New Duty,* 6–8.

112. *Proceedings of the Prince Hall Grand Lodge … 1875.*

113. Quoted in George Crawford, *Prince Hall and His Followers* (1914; repr., New York: AMS, 1971), 84–86.

114. "The Caucasian Masonic Order in the United States versus the Prince Hall or Negro Masonic Fraternity and Related Matters," reel 14, Henry Albro Williamson Masonic Collection, reel 14, Schomburg Center for Research in Black Culture, New York Public Library, New York.

115. *Proceedings of the Grand Lodge … of Free and Accepted Masons of the Commonwealth of Massachusetts: Quarterly Communication, September 13, 1876* (Boston: Rockwell & Churchill, 1876), 58–91. After hearing this report the members of the lodge voted to have five hundred copies printed for distribution.

6. "They Are Nevertheless Our Brethren"

I thank Susana Morris, Mia Bay, and the Working Group at the Rutgers Center for Race and Ethnicity for their generous comments on various versions of this chapter.

1. Sue M. Brown, *The History of the Order of Eastern Star among Colored People* (1925; repr., New York: G.K. Hall, 1997), 177.

2. Ibid.

3. See Evelyn Brooks Higginbotham, *Righteous Discontent: The Women's Movement in the Black Baptist Church, 1880–1920* (Cambridge, MA: Harvard University Press, 1993). See also Martha S. Jones, *All Bound Up Together: The Woman Question in African American Public Culture* (Chapel Hill: University of North Carolina Press, 2007), for a discussion of women's ordination in the African Methodist Episcopal Church.

4. Elsa Barkley Brown, "Womanist Consciousness: Maggie Lena Walker and the Independent Order of Saint Luke," *Signs* 14, no. 3 (1989): 631.

5. Brown, *History of the Order,* 151.

6. Ibid., 155.

7. Elizabeth Lindsay Davis, *Lifting as They Climb* (New York: G.K. Hall, 1996), 198.

8. Brown, *History of the Order,* 193.

9. Richard Breaux, "'Maintaining a Home for Girls': The Iowa Federation of Colored Women's Clubs at the University of Iowa, 1919–1950," *Journal of African American History* 87 (Spring 2002): 238.

10. Martin Summers, *Manliness and Its Discontents: The Black Middle Class and the Transformation of Masculinity, 1900–1930* (Chapel Hill: University of North Carolina Press, 2004), 132.

11. Brown, *History of the Order,* 174.

12. Ibid., 189.

13. Anna Julia Cooper's *A Voice from the South* was published in 1892. Gertrude Mossell published her own history of race women, *The Work of the Afro-American Woman,* in 1894, under the name Mrs. N. F. Mossell.

14. Laura Maffly-Kipp, "Redeeming Southern Memory: The Negro Race History, 1874–1915," in *Where These Memories Grow: History, Memory, and Southern Identity,* ed. W. Fitzhugh Brundage (Chapel Hill: University of North Carolina Press, 2000), 169–89. "Race histories" refers to a genre of texts that proliferated in the years 1874–1915 in which "several dozen writers authored studies of the Negro past, present, and future, in an effort to … record 'the many brave deeds and noble characteristics' of the race," 170.

15. For access to S. Joe Brown's history of the Iowa NAACP, see the Papers of the NAACP: Selected Branch Files, 1913–1939, Part 12, Series C—The Midwest, ed. John H. Bracey Jr. and August Meier. Microfilm finding aid: http://cisupa.proquest.com/ksc_assets/catalog/1428_PapersNAACPPart12SerC.pdf, p. 18.

16. Kate Dossett, *Bridging Race Divides: Black Nationalism, Feminism, and Integration, 1896–1935* (Gainesville: University Press of Florida, 2008), 2.

17. Brown, *History of the Order,* 188.

18. For a longer discussion of black women's participation in black nationalist movements in the 1920s see Dossett, *Bridging Race Divides,* esp. chap. 1, pp. 15–65.

19. For a discussion of the club women's movement, see Deborah Gray White, *Too Heavy a Load: Black Women in Defense of Themselves, 1894–1994* (New York: Norton, 1999). See also Paula Giddings, *When and Where I Enter: The Impact of Black Women on Race and Sex in America* (New York: Quill, 1984). For a discussion of black women and the church see Higginbotham, *Righteous Discontent.* See also Elsa Barkley Brown, "Womanist Consciousness."

20. Fannie Barrier Williams, "The Club Movement among Colored Women of America," in *Can I Get a Witness? Prophetic Religious Voices of African American Women: An Anthology,* ed. Marcia Y. Riggs (Maryknoll, NY: Orbis Books, 1997), 118.

21. Sometimes strict attempts at nonpartisanship and organizational individuality broke down. See Evelyn Brooks Higginbotham, "In Politics to Stay: Black Women Leaders and Party Politics in the 1920s," in *Unequal Sisters: A Multicultural Reader in U.S. Women's History,* ed. Vicki L. Ruiz and Ellen Carol Dubois (New York: Routledge, 2000), 299–300.

22. Brown, *History of the Order,* 174. The Dyer Anti-Lynching Bill was initially introduced by Senator Leonidas Dyer of Missouri in 1918. The bill enjoyed broad support from the NAACP and was the basis of the formation of a female-led NAACP group called the Anti-Lynching Crusaders, which organized in 1922, to lobby and raise money for the passage of this bill. Although the U.S. House of Representatives passed the bill in early 1922, it was killed through a filibuster in the U.S. Senate later that year.

23. Brown served as member and ward chairman of the Polk County Republican Committee and delegate to the Republican county and state conventions. She was

also appointed by the Republic National Committee as director of colored women in the 1924 presidential campaign. See Higginbotham, "In Politics to Stay," 299.

24. See letter to Mrs. S. Joe Brown from Robert Bagnall, director of branches, August 5, 1924, reel 10, Branch Records, Records of the NAACP.

25. Brown, *History of the Order,* 187.

26. Ibid., 174.

27. See White, *Too Heavy a Load,* chap. 1.

28. Summers, *Manliness,* 26.

29. Ibid., 27.

30. Ibid., 112.

31. Ibid., 113.

32. Ibid., 143.

33. Ibid.

34. Ibid., 144.

35. For the open letter penned by Harmony Grand Chapter, see Mary McFarland, "Grand Chapter of Missouri 1890," *The Appeal,* March 11, 1922. *The Appeal* was published in Minneapolis, not Missouri.

36. Summers, *Manliness,* 145.

37. Ibid.

38. Brown, *History of the Order,* 178, 183.

39. Ibid., 183.

40. Ibid., 174.

41. There is no agreement across differing Eastern Star manuals about what virtue or characteristic each woman represents. For an early version, see Robert A. Macoy, *Manual of the Order of Eastern Star* (1866; repr., Whitefish, MT: Kessinger Publishing, 2003).

42. Cheryl Townsend Gilkes, "The Virtues of Brotherhood and Sisterhood: African American Fraternal Organizations and Their Bibles," in *African Americans and the Bible: Sacred Texts and Social Textures,* ed. Vincent L. Wimbush (New York: Continuum, 2000), 399. See Judges, chapter 10, for a discussion of Jephtha's daughter, the books of Ruth and Esther for those characters, and 2 John for a discussion of Electa, or the Elect Lady. Some Bible scholars think Electa is an actual person, while others think that its English translation, "elect lady," is a metaphor for the church or a specific church that is the subject of 2 John. Martha was the sister of Lazarus and a friend of Jesus. She is discussed throughout the Gospels.

43. Gilkes, "Virtues of Brotherhood and Sisterhood," 399.

44. Ibid.

45. For more information on the kinds of leadership models used by various black fraternal groups, see Bayliss Camp and Orit Kent, "Proprietors, Helpmates, and Pilgrims in Black and White Fraternal Rituals," in *What a Mighty Power We Can Be: African American Fraternal Groups and the Struggle for Racial Equality,* by Theda Skocpol, Ariane Liazos, and Marshal Ganz (Princeton: Princeton University Press, 2006).

46. Higginbotham, *Righteous Discontent,* 128.

47. Ibid., 121.

48. Brown, *History of the Order,* 173.

49. Summers, *Manliness,* 132.

50. Patricia Hill Collins argues that in black feminist thought "knowledge for knowledge's sake is not enough—Black feminist thought must both be tied to Black women's lived experiences and aim to better those experiences in some fashion." See *Black Feminist Thought: Knowledge, Consciousness, and the Politics of Empowerment,* 2nd ed. (New York: Routledge, 2000), 31.

51. John M. Giggie, *After Redemption: Jim Crow and the Transformation of African American Religion in the Delta, 1875–1915* (Oxford: Oxford University Press, 2008), 73.

52. Ibid.

53. Ibid. See also the "Syllabus for Eastern Star Queen of the South and Amaranth Degrees," box 1, folder 10, Mamie Wade Avant Papers, Emory University, Atlanta.

54. Letter to Mrs. S. Joe Brown from the director of branches, August 17, 1926, Branch Records, Records of the NAACP.

7. The Prince Hall Masons and the African American Church

I thank the Louisville Institute and the Institute for Ecumenical and Cultural Research at St. John's University in Collegeville, Minnesota, for supporting the research and writing of this chapter.

1. "Bishop James W. Hood," *Masonic Quarterly* 1 (1919): 3.

2. Sandy Dwayne Martin, "Biblical Interpretation, Ecclesiology, and Black Southern Religious Leaders, 1860–1920: A Case Study of AMEZ Bishop James Walker Hood," in *"Ain't Gonna Lay My 'Ligion Down": African American Religion in the South,* ed. Alonzo Johnson and Paul Jerslid (Columbia: University of South Carolina Press, 1996), 111. I am indebted to Martin's fine biography for providing me with a great deal of information on Hood's life and career: *For God and Race: The Religious and Political Leadership of AMEZ Bishop James Walker Hood* (Columbia: University of South Carolina Press, 1999).

3. W. E. B. DuBois, *The Philadelphia Negro* (Philadelphia: University of Pennsylvania Press, 1899), 221–24.

4. Howard W. Odum, *Social and Mental Traits of the Negro: Research into the Conditions of the Negro in Southern Towns* (New York: Columbia University Press, 1910), 267. Booker T. Washington praised secret societies for teaching black businessmen how to create capital and thereby "greatly increase property in the hands of members of the race." *The Story of the Negro,* 2 vols. (New York: Doubleday, 1909), 2:169. By the 1930s, Carter Woodson found that two-thirds of all black physicians and lawyers were members of fraternal orders. *The Negro Professional Man and the Community with Special Emphasis on the Physician and the Lawyer* (Washington, D.C.: Association for the Study of Negro Life and History, 1934), chaps. 8 and 16. In 1967, John Hope Franklin asserted that the creation of independent fraternal organizations within the antebellum free black communities of the North was central to the struggle to achieve status in an evolving American society. *From Slavery to Freedom: A History of Negro Americans,* 3rd ed. (New York: Knopf, 1967), 165.

5. Frank Lincoln Mather, ed., *Who's Who of the Colored Race* (1915; repr., Detroit: Detroit Gale Research Co., 1976).

6. The most recent analysis of the economic influence of black fraternal orders is by David M. Fahey, *The Black Lodge in White America: "True Reformer Brown" and His Economic Strategy* (Dayton, OH: Wright State University Press, 1994). William A. Muraskin's *Middle-Class Blacks in a White Society* (Berkeley: University of California Press, 1975) emphasizes class. Other studies that to some degree include black fraternal orders and employ an analysis that weaves together economics, class, and politics include Earl Lewis, *In Their Own Interests: Race, Class, and Power in Twentieth-Century Norfolk, Virginia* (Berkeley: University of California Press, 1991); Joe William Trotter Jr., *Coal, Class, and Color: Blacks in Southern West Virginia, 1915–32* (Urbana: University of Illinois Press, 1990), 198–213; Peter J. Rachleff, *Black Labor in the South: Richmond, Virginia, 1865–90* (Philadelphia: Temple University Press, 1984; repr., Urbana: University of Illinois Press, 1989); David A. Gerber, *Black Ohio and the Color Line, 1860–1915* (Urbana: University of Illinois Press, 1976), 162; and the older yet still frequently cited study by Hylan Lewis, *Blackways of Kent* (Chapel Hill: University of North Carolina Press, 1955), 259–76.

7. The one exception is Nick Salvatore's recent study of Worcester's Amos Webber, *We All Got History: The Memory Books of Amos Webber* (New York: Times Books, 1996).

8. Steven C. Bullock, *Revolutionary Brotherhood: Freemasonry and the Transformation of the American Social Order, 1730–1840* (Chapel Hill: University of North Carolina Press, 1996), 321.

9. Joseph A. Walkes Jr., longtime editor of the Prince Hall research journal *Phylaxis,* frequently laments, in its pages, the absence of comprehensive state-by-state records. More than once in my efforts to gain access to a lodge, I was told that the lodge building and whatever records were there were not available to me because they were "secret." Nevertheless, a fairly large, though hardly comprehensive, public collection of Prince Hall materials can be found at the Iowa Masonic Library in Cedar Rapids, Iowa.

10. *Minutes of the Eleventh Session of the North Carolina Annual Conference of the African Methodist Episcopal Church in America* (Raleigh: John Nichols, 1875), 37–47.

11. Contemporary studies of African American Christianity's expansion in the South during the Civil War and Reconstruction include Daniel W. Stowell, *Rebuilding Zion: The Religious Reconstruction of the South, 1863–1877* (New York: Oxford University Press, 1998); Paul Harvey, *Redeeming the South: Religious Culture and Racial Identities among Southern Baptists, 1865–1925* (Chapel Hill: University of North Carolina Press, 1997); Reginald F. Hildebrand, *The Times Were Strange and Stirring: Methodist Preachers and the Crisis of Emancipation* (Durham, NC: Duke University Press, 1995); William E. Montgomery, *Under Their Own Vine and Fig Tree: The African-American Church in the South, 1865–1900* (Baton Rouge: Louisiana State University Press, 1993); Katherine L. Dvorak, *An African-American Exodus: The Segregation of Southern Churches* (Brooklyn, NY: Carlson Publishing Co., 1991); and portions of Forrest G. Wood, *The Arrogance of Faith: Christianity and Race in America from the Colonial Era to the Twentieth Century* (Boston: Northeastern University Press, 1990).

12. *Minutes of the Eleventh Session,* 23.

13. In an address to the North Carolina Grand Lodge in 1917, Hood stated that when he "was appointed by Bishop J. J. Clinton as Superintendent of Missions for the A.M.E. Zion Church, [he] also had an appointment by M. W. G. W. Titus, Grand

Master of Masons in New York, a[s] Superintendent of the Southern jurisdiction of the Grand Lodge of New York." *Proceedings of the Most Worshipful Grand Lodge,* Forty-Eighth Annual Communication (Nashville: A.M.E. Sunday School Print, 1917), 89 (hereafter cited as *Proceedings* [1917]). See also William Grimshaw, *Official History of Freemasonry among the Colored People of North America* (1903; repr., Freeport, NY: Books for Libraries, 1971), 258–59.

14. *Proceedings of the Most Worshipful Grand Lodge of Free and Accepted Ancient York Masons for the State of North Carolina* (Raleigh: Nichols and Gorman, 1872), 53–55 (hereafter cited as *Proceedings* [1872]); *Minutes of the Eleventh Session,* 37–47.

15. *Proceedings of the Most Worshipful Grand Lodge of Free and Accepted Ancient York Masons for the State of North Carolina at Its Fifth Annual Communication* (Raleigh: Nichols and Gorman, 1874), 5–9 (hereafter cited as *Proceedings* [1874]).

16. Ibid.; the bylaws can be found in *Proceedings* (1872), 14–21.

17. This statistical information was compiled from the following sources: AMEZ Church: *Minutes of the Eleventh Session; Minutes of the Twelfth Session of the North Carolina Annual Conference of the African Methodist Episcopal Zion Church* (Raleigh: John Nichols, 1875); *Minutes of the Thirteenth Session of the North Carolina Annual Conference of the African Methodist Episcopal Zion Church* (Raleigh: John Nichols, 1876), *Minutes of the Fourteenth Session of the North Carolina Annual Conference of the African Methodist Episcopal Zion Church* (Raleigh: John Nichols, 1877), and *Minutes of the Fifteenth Session of the North Carolina Annual Conference of the African Methodist Episcopal Zion Church* (Raleigh: John Nichols, 1878). Prince Hall Lodge: *Proceedings* (1872), *Proceedings* (1874); Joseph C. Hill, Right Worshipful Grand Secretary, comp., *Proceedings of the Most Worshipful Grand Lodge of Free and Accepted Ancient York Masons for the State of North Carolina, Sessions of December 1875, 1876, and 1877* (Wilmington: Hall, 1878) (hereafter cited as *Proceedings* [1878]); and *Proceedings of the Eleventh Annual Communication of the Most Worshipful Grand Lodge of Free and Accepted Ancient York Masons for the State of North Carolina* (Wilmington: Warrock, 1881) (hereafter cited as *Proceedings* [1881]).

18. Both the conference and the grand lodge founded societies along the routes of the new railroads that crisscrossed the state following the Civil War. Hood often pointed to the distance from railroad stations as a reason for a church or lodge's dormant state. In his 1874 report to the grand lodge, for example, he explained the slow growth of Rising Sun Lodge in Columbus County as due to the lodge's being situated "six or seven miles from the nearest railroad station." *Proceedings* (1874), 8. For an insightful discussion of the relationship between the expansion of southern railroads and the development of African American social institutions, see John Giggie, "God's Long Journey: African Americans, Religion, and History in the Mississippi Delta, 1875–1915" (PhD diss., Princeton University, 1997), 92–137.

19. *Minutes of the Eleventh Session; Proceedings* (1874).

20. *Proceedings* (1872), 54.

21. Albert J. Raboteau, *A Fire in the Bones: Reflections on African-American Religious History* (Boston: Beacon, 1995), 79–102. See also Gary B. Nash, *Forging Freedom: The Formation of Philadelphia's Black Community* (Cambridge, MA: Harvard University Press, 1988), 98–104. For a broader view, see William B. Gravely, "The Rise of African Churches in America (1786–1822): Re-Examining the Contexts," *Journal of Religious Thought* 41 (1984): 58–73.

22. Nash, *Forging Freedom,* 210.

23. James Oliver Horton, *Free People of Color: Inside the African American Community* (Washington, DC: Smithsonian Institution, 1993), 153.

24. Monroe N. Work, "Secret Societies as Factors in the Social and Economical Life of the Negro" in *Democracy in Earnest,* ed. James E. McCulloch (Washington, DC: Southern Sociological Congress, 1918), 343.

25. DuBois, *Philadelphia Negro,* 222.

26. James B. Browning, "The Beginnings of Insurance Enterprise among Negroes," *Journal of Negro History* 22 (1937): 421–29.

27. The African origins of these mutual benefit societies remain a field of specu-lation. Certainly in the South, some of these societies evolved from the "invisible" institutions and folk culture that slaves developed within their plantation communi-ties. Melville J. Herskovitz probably extrapolated from too little evidence when he held that they could be directly linked to African secret societies. Still, it is logical to assume that prior knowledge of African mutual aid systems would have been applied within the slave community. See Melville J. Herskovitz, *The Myth of the Negro Past* (New York: Harper and Brothers, 1941). Furthermore, structural similarities have been identified between the organization and rituals of the early mutual aid societ-ies and their African counterparts. See Deborah Gray White's study of the "female slave network," which contributed to the collective care of children, the sick, and the elderly, as suggestive of the African origins of this mutual aid system, *Ar'n't I a Woman: Female Slaves in the Plantation South* (New York: Norton, 1985), 119–41. Herbert Gutman believed that this web of social obligations reached back to family and gender responsibilities in Africa. *The Black Family in Slavery and Freedom, 1750–1925* (New York: Pantheon Books, 1976). Betty Kuyk suggests an even more direct link, noting the African birth of several founders of these American societies. "The African Derivation of Black Fraternal Orders in the United States," *Comparative Studies in Societies and History* 25 (1983): 559–94. And Susan Greenbaum argues that the earliest African American societies existed before the European organizations had much to offer in the way of a model. "A Comparison of African American and Euro-American Mutual Aid Societies in 19th Century America," *Journal of Ethnic Studies* 19 (1991): 111. Still, the traditional emphasis on secrecy and the need to hide organized behavior from their masters has left scant evidence of the existence of these societies among slaves. In contrast, evidence for the existence of northern societ-ies like the Free African Society of Philadelphia is much more visible. Jon Butler's review of recent work in African American religious history, "Africans' Religions in British America, 1650–1840," *Church History* 68 (1999): 127–28, summarizes what we know about the persistence of African religions in the United States.

28. Mary Ann Clawson, *Constructing Brotherhood: Class, Gender, and Fraternalism* (Princeton: Princeton University Press, 1989), 131–35.

29. Douglas Knoop and G. P. Jones, *A Short History of Freemasonry to 1730* (Manchester, UK: Manchester University Press, 1940), chap. 1.

30. As fully qualified craftsmen, free to enjoy the rights and privileges of the guild, masons were referred to as freemasons, much as other skilled tradesmen were sometimes called "free carpenters," for example, or men granted the rights of citizenship in a town were called "freemen." The several possible meanings of "free" include references to freestone, a building material found in Scotland, and

freedom from feudal serfdom. The term might also have referred to liberality (as in the seven liberal arts), though freemanship is the preferred meaning. See Dudley Wright, ed., *Gould's History of Freemasonry throughout the World,* 6 vols. (New York: Scribner's, 1936), 1:249–58; David Stevenson, *The Origins of Freemasonry: Scotland's Century, 1590–1710* (Cambridge: Cambridge University Press, 1988), 11, and Douglas Knoop and G. P. Jones, *The Genesis of Freemasonry* (London: Quatuor Coronati Lodge, 1978), 10–15. For changing meanings of the term in later Freemasonry, see Bernard E. Jones, "'Free' in 'Freemason' and the Idea of Freedom through Six Centuries," in *The Collected Prestonian Lectures, 1925–1960* (London: Lewis Masonic, 1983), 1:363–76.

31. Clawson, *Constructing Brotherhood,* 53–83.

32. Concerning migration to the Continent, Templarism, for example, originated as an aristocratic and anticapitalist version of Freemasonry in France, but it achieved its most thorough dominance in Germany, where it developed as part of a wider reaction against the rationalist values of the Enlightenment. See Klaus Epstein, *The Genesis of German Conservatism* (Princeton: Princeton University Press, 1966).

33. Bullock, *Revolutionary Brotherhood,* 85–162.

34. This term was coined by Ann Swidler to refer to a culture's "habits, skills, and styles from which people construct 'strategies of action.'" "Culture in Action: Symbols and Strategies," *American Sociological Review* 51 (1986): 273.

35. Nash, *Forging Freedom,* 217.

36. See William B. Gravely, "The Dialectic of Double-Consciousness in Black American Freedom Celebrations, 1808–1863," *Journal of Negro History* 67 (1982): 302–17.

37. Prince Hall, "A Charge, Delivered to the African Lodge, June 24, 1797," reprinted in *Early Negro Writings, 1760–1837,* ed. Dorothy Porter (Baltimore: Black Classic, 1995), 77.

38. Martin Delaney, *The Origins and Objects of Ancient Masonry, Its Introduction into the United States and Legitimacy among Colored Men* (Pittsburgh: W. S. Haven, 1853), 18; see also Prince Hall, "A Charge Delivered to the Brethren of the African Lodge on the 25th of June, 1792," reprinted in Porter, *Early Negro Writings,* 63–69.

39. *Proceedings* (1872), 27.

40. Grimshaw, *Official History,* 84–130.

41. James Walker Hood, *One Hundred Years of the African Methodist Episcopal Zion Church* (New York: AME Book Concern, 1895), 85–86; Martin, *For God and Race,* 22–58.

42. Hood, *One Hundred Years,* 2–26.

43. Ibid., 10.

44. Laurie Maffly-Kipp, "Mapping the World, Mapping the Race: The Negro Race History, 1874–1915," *Church History* 64 (1995): 610–26.

45. Hood, *One Hundred Years,* 27–55; Martin, *For God and Race,* 74, 134.

46. Grimshaw, *Official History,* 305; by 1909, 2,600 of 3,336 Prince Hall lodges came from the South. For example, there were 340 in Alabama but only 70 in Pennsylvania. W. H. Anderson, *Anderson's Masonic Directory* (Richmond, VA: W. H. Anderson, 1909). The order continued to grow in the twentieth century, with as many as 150,000 followers in the 1920s and 300,000 by the 1950s, before beginning to decline. See Muraskin, *Middle-Class Blacks,* 29. C. Eric Lincoln and Lawrence

Mamiya confirm this decline in *The Black Church in the African American Experience* (Durham, NC: Duke University Press, 1990), 152.

47. Moses Nathaniel Moore, "Orishatukeh Faduma and the New Theology," *Church History* 63 (1994): 64–66.

48. Throughout his career, Hood remained committed to the belief that the Bible was the pure and infallible word of God. His commentary on the book of Revelation, for example, reflects this literalist understanding. *The Plan of the Apocalypse* (York, PA: P. Anstadt & Sons, 1900). His sermon "Creation's First Born, Or the Earliest Gospel Symbol," in *The Negro in the Christian Pulpit* (Raleigh: Edwards, Broughton, 1884), 105–21, takes issue with Darwinian science. For examples of Hood's understanding of the nature of the Christian church in general and the mission of the black church in particular, see "The Polity of the A.M.E. Zion Church," *African Methodist Episcopal Zion Quarterly Review* 8 (1899): 1–9; "The Character and Power of the Christian Religion," *African Methodist Episcopal Zion Quarterly Review* 13 (1904): 11–19 and *Sketch of the Early History of the African Methodist Episcopal Church,* vol. 2 (New York: A.M.E. Book Concern, 1914), 66–69. Regarding Hood's position that Christianity is the unique pathway of salvation, see, for example, Hood, *Negro in the Christian Pulpit,* 105–21.

49. Henry Louis Gates, "The Trope of a New Negro and the Reconstruction of the Image of the Black," *Representations* 24 (1988): 155–99.

50. Maffly-Kipp, "Mapping the World," 617–19.

51. Hood, "The Negro Race," in *One Hundred Years,* 27–52.

52. Ibid., 53–55. For a discussion of similar race histories see Laurie Maffly-Kipp, *Setting Down the Sacred Past: African-American Race Histories* (Cambridge: Harvard University Press, 2010).

53. See, for example, Benjamin T. Tanner, *The Descent of the Negro* (Philadelphia: A.M.E. Publishing House, 1898). For an insightful discussion of the influence of Darwinian science on race and manhood, see Gail Bederman, *Manliness and Civilization: A Cultural History of Gender and Race in the United States, 1880–1917* (Chicago: University of Chicago Press, 1995).

54. Martin, "Biblical Interpretation," 134.

55. Rufus L. Perry, *The Cushite, or the Descendants of Ham* (New York: Literary Union, 1887). The *AME Church Review* in 1899 recognized this work as fourth in a list of the most important works by African Americans *(Narrative of the Life of Frederick Douglass was first).* See *AME Church Review* 16 (1899): 631.

56. *Star of Zion,* November 16, 1893, 2. James Melvin Washington believed not only that Perry was a Mason but that his history "shows signs of his Masonic influences." *Frustrated Fellowship: The Black Baptist Quest for Social Power* (Mercer, GA.: Mercer University Press, 1986), 75,131.

57. Delaney, *Origins and Objects of Ancient Freemasonry,* 16–19.

58. Hood, *Negro in the Christian Pulpit,* 107.

59. James Walker Hood, *Sketch of the Early History of the African Methodist Episcopal Zion Church* (published by the author, 1914), 60, 62.

60. *Proceedings* (1881), 10.

61. Ibid., 11.

62. Ibid., 12.

63. Ibid., 12–13.

64. Ibid., 12.

65. Ibid.

66. In 1903, the national total for members at each degree level was Entered Apprentice, 30,640; Fellow Craftsman, 20,482; Master Mason, 66,365; total, 117,487. Grimshaw, *Official History,* 305.

67. Harrison L. Harris, M.D., Grand Secretary of the Grand Lodge of Virginia, *Harris' Masonic Textbook: A Concise Historical Sketch of Masonry, and the Organization of Masonic Grand Lodges, and Especially of Masonry among Colored Men in America; Also, a Compilation of the Illustrations of Masonic Work, as Drawn from the Most Reliable Authorities on the Subject* (Petersburg, VA: Masonic Visitor Co., 1902), 134–93; Malcolm C. Duncan, *Duncan's Masonic Ritual and Monitor,* 3rd ed. (Philadelphia: Washington Publishing Co., 1880); Grimshaw, *Official History,* 318–28; Anthony Fels, "The Square and the Compass: San Francisco's Freemasons and American Religion, 1870–1900" (PhD diss., Stanford University, 1987), 145; and Mark C. Carnes, *Secret Ritual and Manhood in Victorian America* (New Haven, CT: Yale University Press, 1989), 29.

68. Reverend William Spencer Carpenter, Right Worshipful Past Grand Master Prince Hall Grand Lodge of Massachusetts, Rector Bridge Street A.M.E. Church, Brooklyn, N.Y., "Sermon Delivered to the Masons of the Second Masonic District, 16 May 1920," *Mason Quarterly Review* 1 (1920): 3.

69. Steven Bullock's study of the early years of the fraternity in America emphasizes Masonry's "multiplication of uses," which "involved Masonry in conflicting and even contradictory activities and ideas." *Revolutionary Brotherhood,* 2–3. Whereas Mary Ann Clawson's focus is on the social construction of class and gender, *Constructing Brotherhood,* 11, Mark Carnes sees Masonry providing young men with rites of passage away from the female-dominated home and to the masculine workplace, *Secret Ritual and Manhood,* ix, and an earlier work by Lynn Dumenil argues that the fraternity provided a "sacred asylum" in a rapidly changing society, *Freemasonry and American Culture, 1880–1939* (Princeton.: Princeton University Press, 1984), 32–42. All these scholars, to differing degrees, point out that the fraternity's religious message was ambiguous.

70. *Proceedings* (1872), 34; *Proceedings* (1878), 27–28.

71. *Constitutions of the Freemasons: Containing the History, Charges, Regulations, etc. of the Most Ancient and Right Worshipful Fraternity* (London, 1723; repr., Philadelphia, 1734). T. O. Haunch, "The Formation, *1717–1751,*" in *Grand Lodge, 1717–1967* (Oxford: United Grand Lodge of England, 1967), 80. The origins of eighteenth-century public displays in turn have been traced to later medieval towns, where large religious parades involving most of the townspeople brought together the many layers of the civic hierarchy. After the Reformation, the civic ceremonies that survived were oriented toward processions of the ruling oligarchy of town leaders to church or court with the townspeople participating only as onlookers. Peter Clark and Paul Slack, *English Towns in Transition, 1500–1700* (London: Oxford University Press 1976), 131–71, and E. P. Thompson, "Patrician Society, Plebeian Culture," *Journal of Social History* 7 (1973–74):, 389. For an overview, see Bullock, *Revolutionary Brotherhood,* 43, 52–56, 70, 78–79, 80–82.

72. Louis Armstrong as quoted in Lawrence W. Levine, *Black Culture and Black Consciousness: Afro-American Folk Thought from Slavery to Freedom* (New York: Oxford University Press, 1977), 268–69.

73. Harrison L. Harris, "True Masonry in Demand," *Masonic Visitor,* August 1887, 29.

74. *Proceedings of the Nineteenth Annual Communication of the Most Worshipful Grand Lodge* (Goldsboro, NC: Argus Publishing Co., 1889), 87.

75. See, for example, Don H. Doyle, "The Social Function of Voluntary Associations in a Nineteenth-Century Town," *Social Science History* 1 (1977): 338–43, and Rowland Berthoff, *An Unsettled People: Social Order and Disorder in American History* (New York: Harper and Row, 1971), 273–74.

76. Hood, *Negro in the Christian Pulpit,* 115.

77. Harrison L. Harris, "Masonry," *Masonic Visitor,* June–July 1887, 9.

78. *Proceedings* (1874), 7.

79. *Proceedings of the Seventeenth Annual Communication of the Most Worshipful Grand Lodge of Free and Accepted Ancient York Masons for the State of North Carolina* (Goldsboro: Messenger Steam Printing House, 1887),42–43.

80. *Proceedings* (1917), 90.

81. On "respectability," see Higginbotham, *Righteous Discontent,* 14–15, and Montgomery, *Under Their Own Vine and Fig Tree,* 36–37.

82. Harris, "Masonry," 9.

83. Charles Price Jones, as quoted in Otho B. Cobbins, ed., *History of the Church of Christ (Holiness) U.S.A., 1895–1965* (New York: Vantage, 1966), 18.

84. Martin, *For God and Race,* 17–18. For Hood's evangelical and Holiness views, see his *Negro in the Christian Pulpit,* esp. 33–48 and 247–59. On the emergence of the Holiness movement, see Montgomery, *Under Their Own Vine and Fig Tree,* 345–47.

85. For the Holiness attack on secret societies, see Giggie, *God's Long Journey,* 196–218.

86. Reverend Leonard of Olivet Baptist Church, as paraphrased in an article entitled "An Immense Congregation" in the *Indianapolis Freeman,* June 6, 1891.

87. H. T. Keating, "Secret Societies among the Negroes" *Christian Recorder,* April 12, 1883.

88. Ibid.

89. S. H. Coleman, "Freemasonry as a Secret Society Defended," AME *Church Review* 14 (1898): 327, 337.

90. G. L. Knox, as quoted in "An Immense Congregation."

91. See Carries, *Secret Ritual and Manhood,* 24–26, 74–76, and *The History of the National Christian Association* (Chicago: Ezra Cook and Co., 1875), 28–29. In contrast to the campaign against white Masonry, there is no evidence of an anti-Masonic campaign against Prince Hall Masons or of a decline in membership during the 1830s. To the contrary, the 1830s was a period of growth and prosperity for the order. As one Prince Hall historian put it, "perhaps" for the Prince Hall Mason "his subordinate and inconspicuous position permitted the storm [of anti-Masonry] to pass over his head." Harry E. Davis, *A History of Freemasonry among Negroes in America* (Cleveland: Scottish Rite, Northern Jurisdiction, 1946), 187–88.

92. Most white Masons regarded the lodge as their only religious institution. One study of late nineteenth-century San Francisco reported that an overwhelming majority of all Masons, more than two-thirds, did not belong to any religious institution. Fels, *Square and Compass,* 435. See also Carnes, *Secret Ritual and Manhood,* 77–79.

93. Salvatore, *We All Got History,* 262. See also James Oliver Horton, "Freedom's Yoke: Gender Conventions among Antebellum Free Blacks," *Feminist Studies* 12 (1986): 51–76.

94. Montgomery, *Under Their Own Vine and Fig Tree,* 114–15.

95. Salvatore, *We All Got History,* 66, 162, 207, 275.

96. Carnes, *Secret Ritual and Manhood,* 79.

97. *Proceedings* (1878), 29.

98. Late in life, Hood stated that "[t]here are three important organizations in this State in which I have taken special interest, namely: The A.M.E. Zion Church, the Masonic Fraternity, and the Eastern Star." *Proceedings* (1917), 89. In the 1920s the Prince Hall historian Harry A. Williamson remarked that *"[u]nlike the whites,* [his emphasis] Negroes do not appear to understand the great line of demarcation between the two [male and female orders]." "The Adoptive Rite Ritual," undated, Harry A. Williamson Collection on Negro Masonry, Schomburg Center for Research in Black Culture, New York Public Library, New York. Other black orders, like the True Reformers, incorporated women from the outset. See David M. Fahey, "Class, Gender and Race in Fraternal Ritualism: A Review Essay," *Old Northwest* 14 (1988): 161–69 and *Black Lodge in White America,* 7.

99. Sandy Dwayne Martin, "The Women's Ordination Controversy, the AMEZ Church, and Hood's Leadership," in *For God and Race,* 163–75.

100. Higginbotham, *Righteous Discontent.* See also Cheryl Townsend Gilkes, "The Politics of 'Silence': Dual-Sex Political Systems and Women's Traditions of Conflict in African-American Religion," in *African-American Christianity: Essays in History,* ed. Paul E. Johnson (Berkeley: University of California Press, 1994), 80–110.

101. *Carnes, Secret Ritual and Manhood,* 81–89.

102. For the Mormon appropriation of Masonry see John L. Brooke, *The Refiner's Fire: The Making of Mormon Cosmology* (Cambridge: Cambridge University Press, 1994). Steven Bullock explores the Masonic male private sphere in *Revolutionary Brotherhood,* 239–73. Beyond Christianity, Daniel Soyer has recently explored the relationship between fraternalism and American Judaism in "Entering the 'Tent of Abraham': Fraternal Ritual and American-Jewish Identity, 1880–1920," *Religion and American Culture* 9 (1999): 159–82.

8. "Arguing for Our Race"

1. Lewis Hayden, *Grand Lodge Jurisdictional Claim; or, War of Races: An Address before Prince Hall Grand Lodge of Free and Accepted Masons for the State of Massachusetts, at the Festival of Saint John the Baptist, June 24, 1868* (Boston: Edward S. Coombs, 1868), 45, Special Collections, Andover-Harvard Theological Library, Harvard Divinity School, Cambridge, Massachusetts. Quote in chapter epigraph is on page 68.

2. According to Alton G. Roundtree and Paul M. Bessel, the black Masonic tradition in the United States did not become commonly referred to as Prince Hall Freemasonry until the 1940s. Prior to the 1940s, they point out, black Masons, when referring to themselves or the fraternal tradition, typically used the modifiers Negro or Colored. Nonetheless, even though the historical scope of this chapter ranges from the 1860s to the 1940s, I have made the stylistic decision to use the term Prince Hall Freemasonry. See Roundtree and Bessel, *Out of the Shadows: The Emergence of*

Prince Hall Freemasonry in America (Over 225 Years of Endurance) (Camp Springs, MD.: KLR Publishing, 2006), 7, 32.

3. Harry A. Williamson, "Prince Hall Masonry: An Illustrated Lecture," n.d., 5, Masonic Writings, box 10, fol. 5, Harry A. Williamson Collection on Negro Masonry, Schomburg Center for Research in Black Culture, New York Public Library.

4. By "Masonic archive," I do not mean any individual Masonic library. Rather, I am referring to the aggregation of historical documents and artifacts—ranging across a host of temples, libraries, and personal collections—and the actual historical narratives that are rendered from these items.

5. Roundtree and Bessel point out that Masons attempt to keep some aspects of the order—including the rituals that confer degrees and open and close lodge meetings—secret but that there is no attempt to withhold knowledge of the fraternity's principles, membership, and overall objectives from the non-Masonic community. The historian Peter Hinks reminds us that Freemasonry is a "private" but not "conspiratorial" organization. Even the literary scholar Joanna Brooks— who, writing about black Freemasonry in the late eighteenth century, argues that "secrecy of the African Lodge was fundamental to the practice of self-possession and self-determination characteristic of the black counterpublic"—also concedes that the civic presence of black Masons "play[ed] the divide between a public Blackness and a secret African brotherhood." See Roundtree and Bessel, *Out of the Shadows,* 3; Peter Hinks, "John Marrant and the Meaning of Early Black Freemasonry," *William and Mary Quarterly,* 3rd ser., 64, no. 1 (January 2007): 110–11; Joanna Brooks, "The Early American Public Sphere and the Emergence of a Black Print Counterpublic," *William and Mary Quarterly,* 3rd ser., 62, no. 1 (January 2005): 85 (first quote); Brooks, "Prince Hall, Freemasonry, and Genealogy," *African American Review* 34, no. 2 (2000): 201 (second quotation).

6. My thinking on this has been influenced by John Ernest, who argues that historical writing is as much a "reflection, definition, and embodiment of lived perspectives" as it is an attempt to objectively render past events. See Ernest, *Liberation Historiography: African American Writers and the Challenge of History, 1794–1861* (Chapel Hill: University of North Carolina Press, 2004), quotation on 345n1.

7. For a good beginning discussion, however, see William A. Muraskin, *Middle-Class Blacks in a White Society: Prince Hall Freemasonry in America* (Berkeley: University of California Press, 1975), 193–218.

8. In other words, Prince Hall Freemasons' defenses of their own legitimacy as a fraternal order were intimately bound up in larger questions about equality and freedom for African Americans. For similar articulations of this idea, see Muraskin, *Middle-Class Blacks,* 193–94; Theda Skocpol, Ariane Liazos, and Marshal Ganz, *What a Mighty Power We Can Be: African American Fraternal Groups and the Struggle for Racial Equality* (Princeton, N.J.: Princeton University Press, 2006), 1–20; Corey D. B. Walker, *A Noble Fight: African American Freemasonry and the Struggle for Democracy in America* (Urbana: University of Illinois Press, 2008), 4 and passim; Stephen Kantrowitz, "'Intended for the Better Government of Man': The Political History of African American Freemasonry in the Era of Emancipation," *Journal of American History* 96 (March 2010): 1001–26. What I suggest in this chapter is that this linkage between fraternal legitimacy and the collective progress of the race was reflected in the very public way in which Prince Hall Freemasons addressed these controversies

over recognition. To Walker's and Kantrowitz's sharp analyses of the "tensions" between African American Masons' penchant to "critique the shortcomings of American political society while holding up the universals of Freemasonry" (Walker, *Noble Fight,* 84) and black Freemasonry's "avowed universalism versus its members' insistence that only certain special men were qualified to become Masons" (Kantrowitz, "Intended for the Better Government of Man," 1004), I would add a third paradoxical, or counterintuitive, dynamic: the persistent use of non-Masonic forums by a fraternity that, while not strictly a secret society, placed a premium on esoteric arcana. But rather than identify this as a tension, I argue that it was critical to Freemasons' attempts to position themselves as race men.

9. Harry E. Davis, *A History of Freemasonry among Negroes in America* (Philadelphia: United Supreme Council, Northern Jurisdiction, 1946), 45, 160–63; Loretta J. Williams, *Black Freemasonry and Middle-Class Realities* (Columbia: University of Missouri Press, 1980), 69; Hinks, "John Marrant," 107. As rare as this interaction was, it greatly exceeded that in the South, where black lodges were actively suppressed out of fears that they might serve as centers of antislavery activism. See Muraskin, *Middle-class Blacks,* 37.

10. The Illinois Grand Lodge implemented the policy in order to prevent the secession of a subordinate lodge in Jacksonville, which filed a formal complaint in 1845 that some Chicago lodges were receiving blacks as visitors and receiving petitions for admission from them as well. See "New Day—New Duty," *Pacific Appeal,* April 15, 1876, 1; Davis, *History of Freemasonry,* 175. On New York, see Williams, *Black Freemasonry,* 72.

11. Martin R. Delany, *The Origin and Objects of Ancient Freemasonry: Its Introduction into the United States, and Legitimacy among Colored Men. A Treatise Delivered before St. Cyprian Lodge, No. 13, June 24th, A.D. 1853–A.L. 5853* (1853), in *Martin R. Delany: A Documentary Reader,* ed. Robert S. Levine (Chapel Hill: University of North Carolina Press, 2003), 50–67.

12. Davis, *History of Freemasonry,* 45. As early as 1818, white Masons investigated the origins of Prince Hall Freemasonry and determined that it was illegitimate. Loretta Williams points out, however, that the (white) Massachusetts Grand Lodge took no legal action against black Masons. See *Black Freemasonry,* 72.

13. Davis, *History of Freemasonry,* 40–42; Williams, *Black Freemasonry,* 69–70. For contemporary counterarguments, see Hayden, *Grand Lodge Jurisdictional Claim;* "A Letter from Lewis Hayden, of Boston, Mass. to Hon. Judge Simms; of Savannah, Georgia," *Pacific Appeal,* October 10, 1874.

14. Hayden, *Grand Lodge Jurisdictional Claim,* 59.

15. Hayden quoted in "Masonic, Odd Fellow and Other Items from the Anglo-African," *Pacific Appeal,* August 23, 1862; Delany, *Origin and Objects of Ancient Freemasonry,* 57–58.

16. Lawrence W. Levine, *Black Culture and Black Consciousness: Afro-American Folk Thought from Slavery to Freedom* (New York: Oxford University Press, 1977), 30–55 (Higginson quote on p. 50); Mia Bay, *The White Image in the Black Mind: African-American Ideas about White People, 1830–1925* (New York: Oxford University Press, 2000), 26–36; Muraskin, *Middle-Class Blacks,* 197–98, 212–13; Brooks, "Early American Public Sphere," 84; Brooks, "Prince Hall, Freemasonry, and Genealogy."

17. Samuel W. Clark, "The Negro Mason in Equity," *Colored American Magazine,* September 1905, 527–30; George W. Crawford, *Prince Hall and His Followers: Being a Monograph on the Legitimacy of Negro Masonry* (1914; repr., New York: AMS Press, 1971), 78.

18. For examples of the attempted suppression of spirituals and ecstatic worship as a constitutive process of class formation among African Americans, see Levine, *Black Culture and Black Consciousness,* 155–69; Evelyn Brooks Higginbotham, *Righteous Discontent: The Women's Movement in the Black Baptist Church, 1880–1920* (Cambridge, MA.: Harvard University Press, 1993), 194–204; Victoria Wolcott, *Remaking Respectability: African American Women in Interwar Detroit* (Chapel Hill: University of North Carolina Press, 2001), 31–35.

19. "Masonic, Odd Fellow and Other Items" (original emphasis).

20. Hayden, *Grand Lodge Jurisdictional Claim,* 60 (original emphasis).

21. Progressive white Masons made similar rhetorical arguments against the "freeborn" qualification. John B. Felton, grand orator of the (white) Grand Lodge of California, gave a speech before black Masons in 1872, in which he argued the Emancipation Proclamation had the power of forever nullifying the freeborn prohibition. "Who will go back of that act, declaring our birth?" he asked. "Will it be any American citizen? But he knows that that immortal proclamation of freedom was but the declaration that you never had been slaves—that at your birth God made you free. It was a restoration and not a creation of your original right." See Masonic, *Pacific Appeal,* January 6, 1872; William H. Grimshaw, *Official History of Freemasonry among the Colored People in North America* (1903; repr., New York: Negro Universities Press, 1969), 217.

22. For an example of integrationist desire among African American Masons, see the letter from John F. Cook of the District of Columbia, to the editor in Masonic Correspondence, *Pacific Appeal,* March 2, 1872.

23. For an example of this argument, see "The Prince Hall Grand Lodge of Massachusetts," *Pacific Appeal,* June 5, 1875, 1.

24. Masonic Correspondence, *Pacific Appeal,* March 21, 1874, 1 (original emphasis).

25. Ibid. (original emphasis).

26. Masonic, *Pacific Appeal,* January 6, 1872.

27. Masonic Correspondence, *Pacific Appeal,* March 21, 1874.

28. "New Day—New Duty," *Pacific Appeal,* April 15, 1876, 1. For a general discussion of politics in the immediate postemancipation South, see Steven Hahn, *A Nation under Our Feet: Black Political Struggles in the Rural South from Slavery to the Great Migration* (Cambridge, MA: Harvard University Press, 2003). For recent histories of Prince Hall Freemasonry in the postemancipation period, see Kantrowitz, "'Intended for the Better Government of Man,'" esp. 1016–26; Walker, *A Noble Fight,* esp. 115–74; Leslie A. Schwalm, *Emancipation's Diaspora: Race and Reconstruction in the Upper Midwest* (Chapel Hill: University of North Carolina Press, 2009), 157–74.

29. "Masonry among Colored Men in Massachusetts," *Pacific Appeal,* May 25, 1872, 1.

30. On the National Grand Lodge experiment, see chapters 2 and 6 in this book. Also see Roundtree and Bessel, *Out of the Shadows,* 45–90.

31. Masonic, *Pacific Appeal,* August 3, 1878, 2.

32. Masonic, *Pacific Appeal,* November 16, 1872, 2.

33. For examples, see "Lodges of Colored Masons in Colorado, Enjoined by Court," *American Co-Mason,* November 1929; "Negroes Forbidden Use of Shrine Emblem," unidentified news article; "Negro Shriners Win Suit," *American Co-Mason* (ca. 1929), all in Clipping File, Williamson Collection.

34. W. Devoe Joiner, "Why Prince Hall Masonry?" in *The First Annual Report of the Research Committee of Lewis Hayden Lodge Number Sixty-Nine of the Most Worshipful Grand Lodge of the Most Ancient and Honorable Fraternity of Free and Accepted Masons [Prince Hall] of the State of New York, U.S.A,* comp. W. Devoe Joiner (n.p., 1928), Printed Material—New York, Williamson Collection. The 1895 speech by Washington, the black principal of Tuskegee Institute in Alabama, advocated deferring to racial segregation in exchange for the unfettered opportunity for African Americans to economically develop themselves. His speech is considered the classic expression of the accommodationist philosophy that was subscribed to by a significant segment of the black community in the early twentieth century.

35. S. R. S[cottron], "The Work of Brother Clark Considered," *Colored American Magazine,* November 1904, 696.

36. Harry A. Williamson, "Negroes and Freemasonry," typescript, February 1916, 165, Masonic Writings, box 10, fol. 4, Williamson Collection. For a discussion of the sexual content of segregationists' use of "social equality" rhetoric, see Kevin K. Gaines, *Uplifting the Race: Black Leadership, Politics, and Culture in the Twentieth Century* (Chapel Hill: University of North Carolina Press, 1996), 57–60.

37. Williamson to the editor, *American Tyler-Keystone,* copy, February 1, 1913, box 5, fol. 5, Williamson Collection.

38. Crawford, *Prince Hall and His Followers,* 85, 82.

39. Enclosure in Williamson to G. A. Kenderdine, copy, February 11, 1930, box 5, fol. 5, Williamson Collection.

40. Harry E. Davis to Williamson, December 6, 1935; Williamson to Davis, copy, December 11, 1935; Davis to Williamson, January 6, 1936, all in box 7, fol. 7, Williamson Collection. On the class dimension of Prince Hall Freemasons' efforts to root out bogus black Masonic lodges, see Martin Summers, *Manliness and Its Discontents: The Black Middle Class and the Transformation of Masculinity, 1900–1930* (Chapel Hill: University of North Carolina Press, 2004), 59–64.

41. This circumspect position toward recognition dated back to the immediate postemancipation period as well, with some African American Masons fearing that recognition would be on white Masons' terms rather than their own. See, for example, "Masonic Grand Lodge of Ohio," *Pacific Appeal,* October 21, 1876, 2; "Masonry in Ohio," *Pacific Appeal,* October 28, 1876, 2.

42. Williamson to editors of the *Trestle Board,* copy, February 7, 1928, box 4, fol. 7, Williamson Collection.

43. "At Home Negroes Do Not See Lodge Fellowship," unidentified editorial, Clipping File, Williamson Collection.

44. Moore, "A New Feature among Our Race Journals," *Colored American Magazine,* September 1904, 604–5.

45. Hazel Carby, *Reconstructing Womanhood: The Emergence of the Afro-American Woman Novelist* (New York: Oxford University Press, 1987), 123–27. Also see Tom Pendergast, *Creating the Modern Man: American Magazines and Consumer Culture, 1900–1950* (Columbia: University of Missouri Press, 2000), 69–85.

46. S. R. Scottron, "Introductory: Plan and Scope of Masonic Work," *Colored American Magazine,* October 1904, 644.

47. Masonic Department, *Colored American Magazine,* December 1904, 747.

48. Masonic Notes, *New York Age,* April 7, 1934.

49. Williamson to Davis, copy, April 28, 1934, box 7, fol. 7, Williamson Collection.

50. Harry A. Williamson, "A Chronological History of Prince Hall Masonry, 1784–1932," *New York Age,* December 8, 1934. Also see "A Contribution from Arthur A. Schomburg," *New York Age,* January 19, 1935, in which, among other things, Schomburg expressed hope that "Brother Williamson, the Prince Hall historian, will prepare his papers covering his years of service that will aid the coming university graduate to evaluate these institutions."

51. Scottron, "Work of Brother Clark Considered," 696.

52. For examples, see Clark, "Negro Mason in Equity"; *Proceedings of the One Hundredth Anniversary of the Granting of Warrant 459 to African Lodge as Boston, Mass., Monday, Sept. 29, 1884* (Boston: Franklin Press, 1885), 16–17; Grimshaw, *Official History of Freemasonry,* 67–83. In his biography of Prince Hall, Charles H. Wesley argued that Hall did not fight in the Revolutionary War. This inconvenient fact notwithstanding, the lore of the patriotic Prince Hall fighting for a country that would deny him the right to claim status as a Freemason reinforced the image of black Masons as selfless inheritors of the true Masonic spirit. See Wesley, *Prince Hall: Life and Legacy* (Washington, DC: United Supreme Council, Southern Jurisdiction, Prince Hall Affiliation, 1977), 42.

53. Williamson, "Chronological History," *New York Age,* August 4, 1934; "Chronological History," *New York Age,* September 1, 1934.

54. For examples, see Clark, "Negro Mason in Equity," *Colored American Magazine,* November 1904, 699, and March 1905, 168; "A New Lodge Instituted," *Colored American Magazine,* December 1904, 748; Williamson, "Chronological History," *New York Age,* August 4, 1934.

55. Masonic Department, *Colored American Magazine,* December 1904, 747.

56. Press release, box 10, fol. 5, Arthur Schomburg Papers, Schomburg Center; Jesse Hoffnung-Garskof, "The Migrations of Arturo Schomburg: On Being *Antillano,* Negro, and Puerto Rican in New York, 1891–1938," *Journal of American Ethnic History* 21 (November 2001): 3–49.

57. Williamson to Furniss, copy, December 2, 1927; Furniss to Williamson, December 16, 1927, both in Masonic Correspondence, "Indiana, 1922–40," Williamson Collection. On the cancellation, see Williamson to Furniss, July 18, 1933, box 7, fol. 57, Schomburg Papers.

58. Williamson to Schomburg, January 2, 1934, box 7, fol. 57, Schomburg Papers.

59. Williamson to Davis, copy, June 4, 1934. Also see Williamson to Davis, copy, April 26, 1943, where he expressed hope that the "collection will be accessible to all interested within a short period." Both in box 7, fol. 7, Williamson Collection.

60. "Contribution from Arthur A. Schomburg," *New York Age,* January 19, 1935.

61. Ernest, *Liberation Historiography,* 297.

62. Ibid., 17.

63. Masonic Correspondence, *Pacific Appeal,* March 21, 1874.

Contributors

Brittney C. Cooper is assistant professor of women's and gender studies and Africana studies at Rutgers University. Cooper is also cofounder of and blogger for the Crunk Feminist Collective. She is at work on her first book project, *Race Women: Gender and the Making of a Black Public Intellectual Tradition, 1892–Present.*

David Hackett is associate professor of religion at the University of Florida. He is the author of *The Rude Hand of Innovation: Religion and Social Order in Albany, New York 1652–1836* (Oxford University Press, 1991). The second edition of his reader, *Religion and American Culture,* was published by Routledge in 2003. His book *The Uses of Freemasonry in American Culture* is forthcoming from Princeton University Press.

Peter P. Hinks is the author of *To Awaken My Afflicted Brethren: David Walker and the Problem of Antebellum Slave Resistance* (Pennsylvania State University Press, 1997). Over the years he has worked extensively as a public historian and teacher. With John Blassingame and John McKivigan, he edited Frederick Douglass's three autobiographies, *Narrative of the Life of Frederick Douglass, My Bondage and My Freedom,* and *The Life and Times of Frederick Douglass* for Yale University Press. With John McKivigan, he edited *Encyclopedia of Antislavery and Abolition* (Greenwood Press, 2006).

Stephen Kantrowitz is professor of history at the University of Wisconsin-Madison. He is the author of *Ben Tillman and the Reconstruction of White Supremacy* (University of North Carolina Press, 2000), which won the Organization of American Historian's Ellis W. Hawley Prize, and *More Than Freedom: Fighting for Black Citizenship in a White Republic, 1829–1889* (Penguin Press, 2012).

Leslie A. Lewis is Past Most Worshipful Grand Master, Prince Hall Grand Lodge, F. & A.M., Jurisdiction of Massachusetts.

Chernoh M. Sesay Jr. is assistant professor of religious studies at DePaul University. His article about the ideological and religious foundations of African American Freemasonry will appear in a special edition of the journal FORECAAST (Forum for European Contributions in African American Studies), and he is currently writing a book that examines the origins of African American Freemasonry.

Martin Summers is associate professor of history and African and African diaspora studies at Boston College. His book *Manliness and Its Discontents: The Black Middle Class and the Transformation of Masculinity, 1900–1930* (University of North Carolina Press, 2004) won the 2005 American Historical Association–Pacific Coast Branch Book Award. His current research project is a social and cultural history of medicine that focuses on African American patients at St. Elizabeths Hospital, a federal mental institution in Washington, D.C.

Mark A. Tabbert, Director of Collections, George Washington Masonic National Memorial, is the author of *American Freemasons: Three Centuries of Building Communities* (New York University Press, 2006) and co-editor, with William D. Moore, of *Secret Societies in America: Foundational Studies of Fraternalism* (Cornerstone, 2011).

Corey D. B. Walker is associate professor and chair of the Department of Africana Studies at Brown University. Walker has served as an associate editor of the *Journal of the American Academy of Religion,* and he is the author of *A Noble Fight: African American Freemasonry and the Struggle for Democracy in America* (Illinois University Press, 2008). He recently completed a book-length manuscript titled *Between Transcendence and History: An Essay on Religion and the Future of Democracy in America.*

Julie Winch is professor of history at the University of Massachusetts–Boston. Her books include *Philadelphia's Black Elite: Activism, Accommodation, and the Struggle for Autonomy, 1787–1848* (Temple University Press, 1988); *A Gentleman of Color: The Life of James Forten* (Oxford University Press, 2002), which won the American Historical Association's Wesley-Logan Prize; and *The Clamorgans: One Family's History of Race in America* (Hill & Wang, 2011).

Index